Never See a Need

© Trustees of the Sisters of St Joseph 2016 All rights reserved.

Except as provided by the Copyright Act 1968, no part of this publication may be reproduced, stored in a retrieval system or transmitted in any form or by any means without the prior written permission of the publisher.

Series Editors: Josephite Editorial Committee
The Josephite Series offers contributions on various aspects of:
 Theology and spirituality
 Historical perspectives
 Cultures and life experiences, and Faith communities.

1. *In the Land of Larks and Heroes: Australian Reflections on St Mary Mackillop*, edited by Alan Cadwallader, 2011.
2. *St Joseph's Island: Julian Tenison Woods and the Tasmanian Sisters of St Joseph*, Josephine Margaret Brady RSJ, 2012.
3. *God's Good Time: The Journey of the Sisters of St Joseph of the Sacred Heart in Ministry with Australian Aboriginal and Torres Strait Islander Peoples*, Mary Cresp RSJ, 2013.

978-1-925486-32-2 Paperback
978-1-925486-33-9 Hardback
978-1-925486-34-6 epub
978-1-925486-35-3 Kindle
978-1-925486-36-0 pdf

National Library of Australia Cataloguing-in-Publication entry
Author: Foale, Marie Therese rsj
Title: Never See a Need: The Sisters of St Joseph in South Australia 1866-2010 Notes: Includes bibliographical references and index
Subjects: MacKillop, Mary, Saint 1842–1909.
Sisters of St. Joseph of the Sacred Heart--History.
Catholic Church--South Australia--History.

Dewey Number: 271.97609423

Except where stated, all the photographs are used with permission of the Trustees of the Sisters of St Joseph.

Previous publications:
Ain Karin: Twenty-five Years, 1984–2009 (2009)
Providence: 125 Years of Aged Care, 1868–1993 (1993)
The Josephite Story: The Sisters of St Joseph, their Foundation and Early History, 1866–1895 (1989)
The Josephites Go West: The Sisters of St Joseph in Western Australia, 1887–1920 (1995)
Think of the Ravens: The Sisters of St Joseph and Social Welfare (2001)
Foale, Marie T & Toohey, Denis, *In Joyful Hope: The Story of Siena College, 1971–2001* (2004)

Cover design by Sandy Leaitua
Layout by Astrid Sengkey
Text Minion Pro Size 10 &11

Published by:

An imprint of ATF Theology part of the ATF Press Publishing Group.
ATF (Australia) Ltd.
PO Box 504
Hindmarsh, SA 5007
ABN 90 116 359 963
www.atfpress.com
Making a lasting impact

Never See a Need

The Sisters of St Joseph in South Australia
1866–2010

Marie Therese Foale rsj

ATF Theology
Adelaide
2016

*This book is dedicated to
the many hundreds of
Sisters of St Joseph who have been part of
the South Australian story
and who have remained true
to the vision and spirit of their founders,
St Mary MacKillop
and
Julian Tenison Woods.*

Foreword

This book comes at an apt time as we celebrate the 150 years since the founding of the Sisters of St Joseph in 1866. It tells the story of the faithful living of hundreds of women who dedicated themselves to following in the footsteps of St Mary MacKillop and Fr Julian Woods from the beginning until the present day. Their contribution to the development of the Church and society in Australia and beyond cannot be underestimated. This history is a rich addition to the many historical works authored by Marie Foale rsj.

Inside these pages is the story of the founding of a new Religious Congregation—the Sisters of St Joseph of the Sacred Heart. It tells of its humble and heroic beginnings in the colony of South Australia. In the founding years from 1866–1871, many women, inspired by Mary MacKillop and Julian Woods' passion for God and God's mission, joined in the endeavour of pioneering new ways of living the Gospel in this land. It is the story of dedicated women living in scattered towns across South Australia, bringing life and hope to people as they lived among them in the towns and communities that shaped life in this part of the world. In many cases, these women were the living face of the Catholic Church as they brought faith, education and works of charity and social service to the isolated, the disadvantaged and the marginalised. Like the people whom they served, they went to places without regular access to the Mass and Sacraments.

This writing captures the courage of women who left the familiar to take the work of the Institute beyond South Australia. It is a story of endurance as women lived through the experience of the excommunication of their leader, betrayal by a bishop whom they looked upon as a friend and the loss of their first mother house at Kensington. It is also a story of hope, for these women held steadfastly to the dream that took roots in their hearts as they dedicated their lives to their 'good' God.

It tells an ongoing story of women 'listening to the whisperings of God in their own heart' (Mary MacKillop, 1868) as they opened and closed schools in changing circumstances, and established works of charity and outreach to those most in need in their time. Down through the decades they remained ever in tune with this movement of God as they established the motor missions, responded to the new needs of the post-war migrants, provided secondary schooling and brought life and culture to many a community through their musical talent and their prowess on the sporting field. It is a story of joys and sorrows embraced lovingly. It tells of women acting innovatively and choosing life in the inside-out and upside-down moments of life. Their practical, down-to-earth way of life and common sense approach to living as well as their sense of humour are told in these pages.

It is also a story of the Sisters of our time, who continue to embrace newly emerging possibilities: they stand alongside our Indigenous brothers and sisters in the movement towards reconciliation, become a voice for refugees, minister to the frail aged, and live in isolated situations. They are often the compassionate face of the Church, constantly looking for the new edge in the familiar and less familiar areas of mission, challenging the status quo in matters of justice, and assisting people to find the meaning of life in the spirituality of all that underpins our lives.

May you who read the story of these women who 'never see a need' without responding, be encouraged by their tenacity and wisdom, their love of life and capacity to find the light in the most trying situations. May their passionate hearts engage the passion within you so that you too are inspired to 'never see a need without doing something about it'.

Sr Monica Cavanagh
Congregational Leader
March 2016

Table of Contents

Dedication v
Foreword: Sr Monica Cavanagh rsj vii

Abbreviations xi
Introduction: Never See a Need 1

Part One
The Years of the Founders 13
1   The Foundation Years: 1866–1872   15
2   Establishing an Identity: 1872–1880   61
3   Identity Formalised: 1880–1895   99
4   New Hope—New Life: 1895–1909   153

Part Two
In The Tradition of The Founders 191
5   Mission in Focus—Catholic Education:1910–1929   193
6   Depression & War: 1930–1947   239
7   New Challenges—New Ministries: 1947–1968   277

Part Three
Return to The Charism of the Founders 327
8   Adaptation and Renewal: 1968–2010   329

Appendices   377–4

1. Josephite Foundations and Ministries in SA, 1866–2010   379
2. Recruits from the Sth East of SA & Western VIC 1866–1870   391
3. Number of Women who joined the Congregation and of Josephite
   Foundations, SA, 1867–1871   393
4. Sisters' Daily Timetable, 1866–1960s   397
5. Sisters' Daily Prayer Schedule, 1866–1960   399
6. Schools that remained open during Mary MacKillop's
   excommunication period, 1871–1872   401
7. Schools from which the Sisters withdrew, 1871–1872   403
8. Reasons for Mary MacKillop's Excommunication, 187   405
9. Irish Women who accompanied Mary MacKillop to Australia
   to join the Congregation, 1874–1875   411
10. Mary MacKillop's absences from and times at home in SA,
    1867–1909.   417
11. Closures of SA Convents, Schools & Institutions, 1880–1893   419
12. Convents, Schools & Institutions in SA, 1895   421
13. Mary MacKillop's Report on SA Visitation, 1899   423
14. Mary MacKillop re Languages & Select Schools, Sydney, 1901   431
15. Congregational, Provincial & Regional Leaders, 1867–2014   435
16. South Australian Provincials & Regional Leaders, 1870–2014   437
17. Josephite Monogram   439

Bibliography   441
Index   449

Maps
Adelaide Metropolitan Area   14
South Australia   328

Abbreviations

NOTE:
Unless otherwise indicated, archival material cited in this text is from the collection held by the Sisters of St Joseph in their archives at St Joseph's Convent, Mount Street, North Sydney, and/or St Joseph's Convent, Kensington, South Australia.

ACA	Adelaide Catholic Archdiocesan Archives
ADB	Australian Dictionary of Biography
ACD	Australasian Catholic Directory
AHC	All Hallows College, Dublin, Ireland
ASSJ	Archives of the Sisters of St Joseph, Kensington, SA, and/or North Sydney
CCD	Confraternity of Christian Doctrine
CCES	Catholic Church Endowment Society
CEC	Catholic Education Council
CEO	Catholic Education Office
CP	Congregation of the Passion/Passionist Fathers
CSC	Chaplet and Southern Cross
GRG	Government Record Group, State Records of South Australia
IBVM	Institute of the Blessed Virgin Mary/ Loreto Sisters
ICA	Archives of the Irish College, Rome
ITIM	Inter-Church Trade and Industry Mission
IH	Irish Harp
MATS	Metropolitan Adelaide Transport Study
MDA	Maitland Diocesan Archives, Maitland, NSW
MG	Mother General
MM	Mary MacKillop

MUP	Melbourne University Press
OP	Order of Preachers: Dominican sister or friar
OSA	Old Scholars Association
PEB	Public Examinations Board
PRO	Public Record Office
QC	Qualifying Certificate
RE	Religious Education
RI	Religious Instruction
rsm	Sister/Sisters of Mercy
rsj	Sister/Sisters of St Joseph
SA	South Australia
SACCS	South Australian Commission for Catholic Schools
SAGG	South Australian Government Gazette
SAGHS	South Australian Genealogy and Heraldry Society
SAPP	South Australian Parliamentary Papers
SC	Southern Cross
SCC	State Children's Council
SCCH	Southern Cross and Catholic Herald
SGS	Sister of the Good Samaritan/Good Samaritan Sisters
SJ	Society of Jesus/Jesuit Fathers
SOCG	Scritti Originale, Congregazione Generale, that is, letters from the Archives of the Sacred Congregation of the Propaganda, Rome
Sr	Sister
SRCO	An Archival Series in the Vatican Archives, which contains correspondence between the Vatican and bishops, clergy and lay people based in Oceania
VG	Vicar General
YCS	Young Catholic Students

Introduction
'Never See a Need'

Two remarkable people met at Penola in the Diocese of Adelaide, South Australia in the 1860s: colonial-born Mary MacKillop and Father Julian Edmund Tenison Woods, originally from London. On 19 March 1866, the feast of St Joseph, they founded (at Penola), the Congregation of the Sisters of St Joseph of the Sacred Heart.[1] Between its inauguration and the year 2010, when Mary was canonised a saint by the Catholic Church, many hundreds of women joined the Congregation. This book tells something of its foundation and of the many Sisters who lived and worked in South Australia between then and 2010.

The beginnings of the Congregation were small. Its founders aimed to meet specific pastoral needs. Penola, a small township almost 400 kilometres southeast of Adelaide, was part of a vast mission district, where Julian Woods was the only priest. Like most priests in rural Australia in the 1860s, he was regarded as a missionary.[2] His intention at the time was to do one thing only: to fulfil the mandate of the Bishop of Adelaide, Patrick Geoghegan, that all Catholic children

---

1. When Mary and Woods founded the Sisters of St Joseph the term used to describe it was 'Institute'. In modern times, the commonest term used in this context is 'Congregation', which describes a religious order whose members engage in teaching, nursing, or social welfare work outside their convents. Members of 'Religious Orders', properly so called, live cloistered lives and, as a rule, do not move outside their convents or monasteries. In the interests of consistency, the term 'Congregation' has been used throughout this work to describe the body of which the Sisters of St Joseph are members.
2. Prior to 1885, when the Australian bishops set up the parish structure that persists in Australia to the time of writing, (2014), priests were regarded as missionaries and had charge of missions or mission districts.

should have access to a sound education 'in accordance with the Faith and practices of [their] Holy Religion' [sic].³ The bishop had written:

> Wherever there is a Pastor and a Flock, we implore you to make a commencement of a Catholic School. Let each do what he can. Give from your scanty means . . . Exert yourselves for the work . . . Persevere . . . in united prayer for success, and the Father of Jesus Christ and his little ones will grant your supplication.⁴

The bishop's message weighed heavily upon Julian Woods and, after much prayer and many setbacks, he came up with the novel idea of establishing a new religious order of women whose way of life was suited to Australian conditions, and especially to those encountered in the Penola region.⁵

He dreamed that the members of his new Sisterhood would enable their pupils to 'learn as Roman Catholic children' in classrooms where they were 'constantly breathing the atmosphere of their religion'.⁶ To achieve this end he planned to recruit the daughters of local families, to send them in groups of two or three to isolated settlements where a priest seldom visited, and to house them in buildings similar to those occupied by the people of the area.⁷ In addition, he anticipated that these Sisters would be alert to the needs of members of the wider community and be ready to intervene where those needs were great.

For her part, Mary MacKillop, who was born in Melbourne in 1842, had desired since childhood to commit her life to the service

---

3. Osmund Thorpe, 'Geoghegan, Patrick Bonaventure (1805–1864)', (Canberra: *ADB*, National Centre of Biography, Australian National University, 1972). http://adb.anu.edu.au/biography/geoghegan-patrick-bonaventure-3602/text5589.
4. Patrick Geoghegan, *Pastoral Letter of Patrick Bonaventure, by Divine Grace and Favour of the Apostolic See, Bishop of Adelaide, to the Clergy and Laity of the Diocese, on the Education of Catholic Children* (Adelaide, 1860), 3 & 16. Patrick Bonaventure Geoghegan, of the Order of St Francis, (OFM), was bishop of Adelaide from 1859 until his death on 9 May 1864.
5. For further details regarding the background to the foundation of the Sisters of St Joseph, see Marie T Foale, *The Josephite Story* (Sydney: St Joseph's Generalate, 1989), chapters 1 & 2.
6. JET Woods, *Directory, and Order of Discipline* (Adelaide, ca. 1870), 84–86. Geoghegan, *Pastoral Letter* (1860), 8.
7. JET Woods, *Rules of the Institute of St Joseph for the Catholic Education of Poor Children*, approved by Bishop Sheil of Adelaide (Adelaide: 1868), article 1.

of God as a religious Sister by ministering to the poor, especially in isolated country districts or city slums. She was prepared to do what she could for people with no one to fight their battles. The story of her growing up in Victoria, her meeting with Julian Woods at Penola,[8] and her decision to accept his invitation to become one of the first members of his religious order is well documented.[9]

It is also well known that, following her move to Adelaide, numerous young women joined her as Sisters of St Joseph, and priests from many different mission areas invited them to take charge of their schools. Less well known are the stories of those individual women, the details of their struggles and their fidelity as they learned to be Sisters—with few guidelines to help them. This account of how they remained faithful to their commitment to their religious vows and how, over the years, they worked in wide ranging ministries among the people, makes great reading.

When the Congregation was founded, Catholics comprised between twelve and fifteen per cent of the white population of South Australia. While most were Irish immigrants and their Australian born children, there was also a significant sprinkling of English, Scottish and German Catholics among them. Few had received any formal education. Most were employed as labourers on farms and in factories, with limited prospects of improving their standard of living or their position in society. Many had large families. There were few priests and most mission areas comprised vast, thinly populated areas where Catholics lived in scattered settlements many miles apart. Most of the clergy welcomed Sisters who were willing to go to the outposts of their mission areas where, besides teaching the children in the schools, they instructed the adults in their Catholic faith.

---

8. Margaret Press RSJ, *Julian Tenison Woods: Father Founder* (Sydney: St Paul's Publications, 2004), and Mary MacKillop, *Julian Tenison Woods: A Life*, introduced and annotated by Margaret Press, RSJ (Melbourne: Harper Collins Victoria, 1997), are both well researched and readable biographies of Julian Woods.
9. Mary MacKillop [hereafter MM] to Bishop Sheil, 10 September 1871, in *Resource Material from the Archives of the Sisters of St Joseph*, Issue no. 4 (North Sydney: ASSJ, 1980), 46. She wrote: 'The way in which he described their wants [the neglected poor children of SA] so completely agreed with all my previous desires that when he asked me whether (provided he got the Bishop's consent to commence the Institute to meet these wants) I would remain and become one of his first children in the work, I joyfully consented.'

In May 1867, as Mary MacKillop and a companion prepared to leave Penola for Adelaide, Father Woods presented them with a copy of his newly drafted *Rules for the Institute of St Joseph*. In its opening paragraph he stated that their new Religious Congregation was being established for 'the pious education of children whose parents [were] in humble circumstances'.[10] In Article 13 he added that the Sisters were bound to:

> do all the good they [could] and never see an evil without trying how they [might] remedy it, and thus to take a most lively interest in every external work of charity in the gaols, poor houses, and hospitals, so as to leave nothing untried, no matter how difficult, provided it [might] advance the glory of God, the good of souls, and the prevention of sin in the world.

He went on:

> This is their mission, for though the Institute has its peculiar [particular] duties, yet the religious must do any good that they can, and make their charity all embracing.[11]

Mary MacKillop adopted those rules and her whole life was a testament to how seriously she took them. She impressed their importance upon all trainee Sisters of St Joseph, and those who have joined the Congregation since then have also endeavoured to live by them. They were strong women, who were prepared to live like and among the people of cities, suburbs or country towns.

In the late 1860s, the education of children from poorer suburban areas and country settlements was the first task to which they put their minds. Consequently, before many years had elapsed, Catholic people were taking it for granted that there would be Catholic schools managed by the Sisters of St Joseph in their local areas.

As the Sisters settled into life in Adelaide, they came to realise that there were many needy people whom they could not reach through the school system. True to Article 13 of the *Rules of the Institute,* they stepped out in faith, visiting people in their homes and establishing

---

10. Woods: *Rules of the Institute*, December 1868, Article 1.
11. Woods: *Rules of the Institute*, December 1868, Article 1

charitable institutions with a view to relieving suffering and bringing hope to those concerned.

On 16 June 1868, just one year after Mary MacKillop's arrival in Adelaide, Father Woods and the Sisters welcomed their first guest at St Joseph's House of Providence on West Terrace, Adelaide. Their intention was that this place be a home that offered shelter to unemployed, homeless, widowed, abused, or abandoned women, all the while giving special consideration to the destitute and the frail aged. Before the Sisters undertook this work they had set up a House of Refuge for prostitutes, unmarried mothers and women newly released from gaol, and had become fully responsible for the management of the local Catholic orphanage.[12]

This Josephite tradition of being on the alert for the needs of those around them was so ingrained into the Sisters' minds and hearts,[13] that they undertook the giving of religious instruction to Catholic children detained in Industrial Schools and Reformatories. Subsequently they and the Jesuit Fathers from Norwood became involved in the setting up of a Royal Commission into the administration of such institutions.[14] This, in turn, led to their long term participation in the care and reformation of Catholic detainees in such institutions.[15]

The growth of the new Congregation was remarkable. Records indicate that by the end of 1871 as many as 130 young women had volunteered to become Sisters of St Joseph. While most of these were from South Australia, there were also several from Victoria, including Mary MacKillop herself, and at least three from Queensland, and

---

12. See: Marie T Foale, *Providence: 125 Years of Aged Care, 1868–1993* (Sisters of St Joseph Aged Care Services, Adelaide, 1993); and *Think of the Ravens, The Sisters of St Joseph and Social Welfare* (Sisters of St Joseph of the Sacred Heart, Adelaide, 2001), for a fuller account of these institutions.
13. The term 'Josephite' may be used as a noun or as an adjective. For example: 'She is a Josephite', that is, a Sister of St Joseph; 'This is a Josephite school', that is, one operating in the spirit of the Sisters of St Joseph.
14. Jesuits are priests and brothers who belong to a Catholic Religious Order, the Society of Jesus. A number of Jesuit priests from Austria, Germany and Poland migrated to South Australia between 1848 and 1901. They settled at Sevenhill to the north of Adelaide and later took charge of the mission district of Norwood in the Adelaide metropolitan area. They contributed much to the life of the Catholic Church in South Australia and were always supportive of the Sisters of St Joseph
15. *SAPP, 1883–1884*, 'First Report of the Destitute Commission'; *SAPP, 1885*, no. 228, Appendix EE.

all proved their willingness to go wherever they were sent and do whatever they were called to do. What is even more remarkable than the increase in the membership of the Congregation is the way in which so many of its first members grasped the meaning of the religious life and persevered in it for their entire lives.

Most of these young women were members of Irish immigrant families and had been either born or raised in the colonies. Their parents had instilled the faith in them but, given their situations in the colonies, they had had only minimal contact with the Church. Most would have had few opportunities to attend Mass or receive the Sacraments. Very few would have heard of religious sisters and how they lived and worked in Ireland or Europe. Yet, when Father Woods or Sister Mary suggested that they might like to become Sisters, they came willingly. One might ask whether many, or even any of them would have dreamed of joining a religious order in other circumstances.

They were keen to do what was right, little realising that their leaders were still working out how to be Sisters of St Joseph and that they, too, had a part to play in finding the answer to that question. As they lived into the Josephite way of life, they encountered many hurdles. They made mistakes. From time to time, there were personal tensions and resentments among them. Some found the Josephite way of life too hard and left the group. All endured many painful experiences and suffered much.

Those who persevered as Sisters built their own traditions without the guidance of wise elders. Just over twenty years after the initial foundation at Penola, church officials in Rome decided that theirs was an authentic way of life, and gave them formal approval as a centrally governed Congregation of Pontifical Right. In other words, it was a Religious Congregation where all the members were governed by a general superior based in a central Mother House even when there were communities in a number of different dioceses.

Over the years, the Congregation has continued in the same spirit. Much has changed and today, 150 years after its foundation, there are fewer Sisters of St Joseph. Nevertheless, they still visit homes, hospitals, gaols, and detention centres and fight for the rights of the underprivileged. Few are engaged directly in the schools but they continue the work of education in other ways. Some are social workers or nurses or spiritual directors. These Sisters continue to go wherever they are called in the performance of their ministries and, when their services are no longer required, they move on. It is in this spirit that, since 1866, members of the Congregation have taught in at least 140 different schools and lived in at least 145 residences as they have ministered in widely separated parts of South Australia.

In some instances, the Sisters followed the people from one settlement to another. In others, they closed schools because of changes in local circumstances. Some small settlements had sprung up to cater for the families of the men building roads and railways. These people moved on as the railheads advanced across the countryside and the Sisters followed them. On other occasions, they handed over well-established schools to Sisters from other Religious Congregations so as to be free to go to the margins of settlement. In fact, in South Australia, and especially during the late nineteenth and early twentieth centuries, they were truly 'a people on the move'.[16]

At all times, they strove to meet the needs of as many disadvantaged children and adults as possible. Where necessary they accompanied parish priests on their visits to outstations for Sunday Mass and provided religious instruction for the local children. They also ran summer or vacation schools for the religious instruction of children with no access to Catholic schooling and prepared them for their first Sacraments. In the 1950s, they pioneered the Motor Mission movement founded by Archbishop Matthew Beovich of Adelaide.

The 1960s and 1970s were times of extraordinary change in both the Church and society, and the Sisters responded accordingly. During this era, governments began providing financial assistance to schools and charitable institutions so that they could reach and maintain the required standards of the day.

The years that followed the 'Second Vatican Council', also known as 'Vatican II', with its call for the renewal of religious life, were a time of great excitement and sometimes of great frustration as Sisters strove to rediscover the charism of their founders and interpret it for a different time.[17]

---

16. Marie T Foale, 'A People on the Move', in *Come Out Magazine* (Education Department of South Australia, 1980).
17. The Second Vatican Council, 1962–65 (also known as 'Vatican II') was a gathering of all the bishops of the entire Catholic Church at the Vatican in Rome, where

The years since Vatican II have been marked by continuous change. There are fewer Sisters, but they continue to live by the maxims laid down by their founders as they keep alert to the needs of the people of the twenty-first century. These women do not wear the habit designed by Mary and her first companions but they are no less Josephite than the brown clad women who walked Adelaide's streets and fanned out across the countryside between the 1860s and the 1970s.

Thanks to the development of modern technology, Sisters and others have gained easy access to the writings of Julian Woods, Mary MacKillop, and the wider group of founding Sisters. In more recent times, especially during the years leading up to Mary's beatification in 1995 and her canonisation in 2010, much has been written about her, and many of her own writings have been published.[18]

This book tells a tale of courage and resilience in the difficult circumstances of the foundation years and of a steady, somewhat quieter, but equally courageous perseverance in the years that followed.[19] Part I, which covers the years 1866–1909, is an account of the founding Sisters,[20] their works, their struggles and their determination to remain part of the centrally governed Congregation they had joined. Part II relates the events of the years between Mary's death in 1909 and Vatican II, during which time the Sisters worked to retain her spirit by living according to the traditions and practices established during the foundress's lifetime. Part III describes some of the events that occurred between 1970 and 2010, the year when Mary was declared a saint for the Universal Church.

The researching and writing of this book has been a great challenge and a great joy. For the period of Mary MacKillop's lifetime there was a plethora of material—the difficulty has been to decide what to

---

they discussed Church teachings and life in great detail. During this Council and at its end the Council Fathers proclaimed several major Constitutions and other documents which have had a profound effect on the lives of Catholics worldwide

18. Beatification is a step along the road towards the canonisation of a holy person by the Catholic Church. Mary was beatified on 19 January 1995 and canonised, or declared a saint, on 17 October 2010.
19. See Appendix One for a comprehensive listing of Josephite foundations and ministries in South Australia, 1866–2010.
20. In this work, the term 'founding Sisters' has been used to designate those women who joined the Congregation during the years 1866–1871, when they received instruction from both Mary MacKillop and Julian Woods.

include and what to omit. For many later years, the opposite has been the case. Fewer records were preserved, and the finding of relevant information was more difficult. One outcome of this problem has been that, while all South Australian foundations are named, some have been given more space than others. Much more could have been written, but limitations of time and space rendered that impossible.[21] What has become clear is that many local histories await the writing.

The reader may note some overlap in the information contained in Chapter Two and Chapter Three. Events, foundations and so on that occurred in the early 1880s are described in Chapter Two where they appeared to fit naturally, thus allowing Chapter Three to deal more fully with the significant events of the 1880s.

Unless otherwise indicated, the information in this history was sourced in the Archives of the Sisters of St Joseph in either Adelaide or Sydney.

This book could not have been written without the support and encouragement of many people: those who helped with research, those who read the text, those who enabled its writer to allocate many hours to this work. It is impossible to name all these people, and I apologise to anyone who has been omitted. Among those who stand out in my memory are Sisters Christine Rowan who commissioned the work ever so long ago and Marion Gambin who, while in South Australia, strongly encouraged one very easily side-tracked writer. Then came Srs Mary Reardon, Maryellen Thomas, Ann Leesue, Mary Ryan, Marie White, Margaret McKenna and many others who read all or part of various drafts and were consistent with their assistance.

What can be said about Mary and the late Barry Lemm, and their team of patient researchers, who spent many hours in front of microfilm readers in the State Library going through 'The Southern Cross' and noting/printing off any references to Josephite Sisters that they could find? Then there were my historian colleagues, David Hilliard and Robert Fitzsimons who so painstakingly cast their eyes

---

21. Much of the founding story, especially regarding the difficulties faced by Mary MacKillop, Julian Woods and the Church leaders of the time has already been dealt with in Marie T Foale, *The Josephite Story*. Hence, while some of this has been retold here, it could be helpful to read that volume in conjunction with Part I of this work. It relates the story of the institution itself. In this one, the emphasis is on its members, their lives and works.

over this work. Finally, there comes Sandy Leaitua who, with great skill and patience, has designed the book's lovely cover.

Like Tiny Tim from Dickens' 'A Christmas Carol', all this writer can say is 'God bless everyone'.

DORSETTA TERRACE, FLINDERS STREET, ADELAIDE

'Dorsetta Terrace, Flinders Street, Adelaide, south side, in March 1922. This building was erected by Emmanuel Solomon in the 1850s.' (Davies and Wooldridge, architects, March 24, 1922, no. 34257.)

The units set back from the street are where the Sisters stayed from October 1871–March 1872.

Where it all began. The stable school at Penola.

Bishop Patrick Geoghegan.
1859–1864

Part 1
The Years
Of The Founders

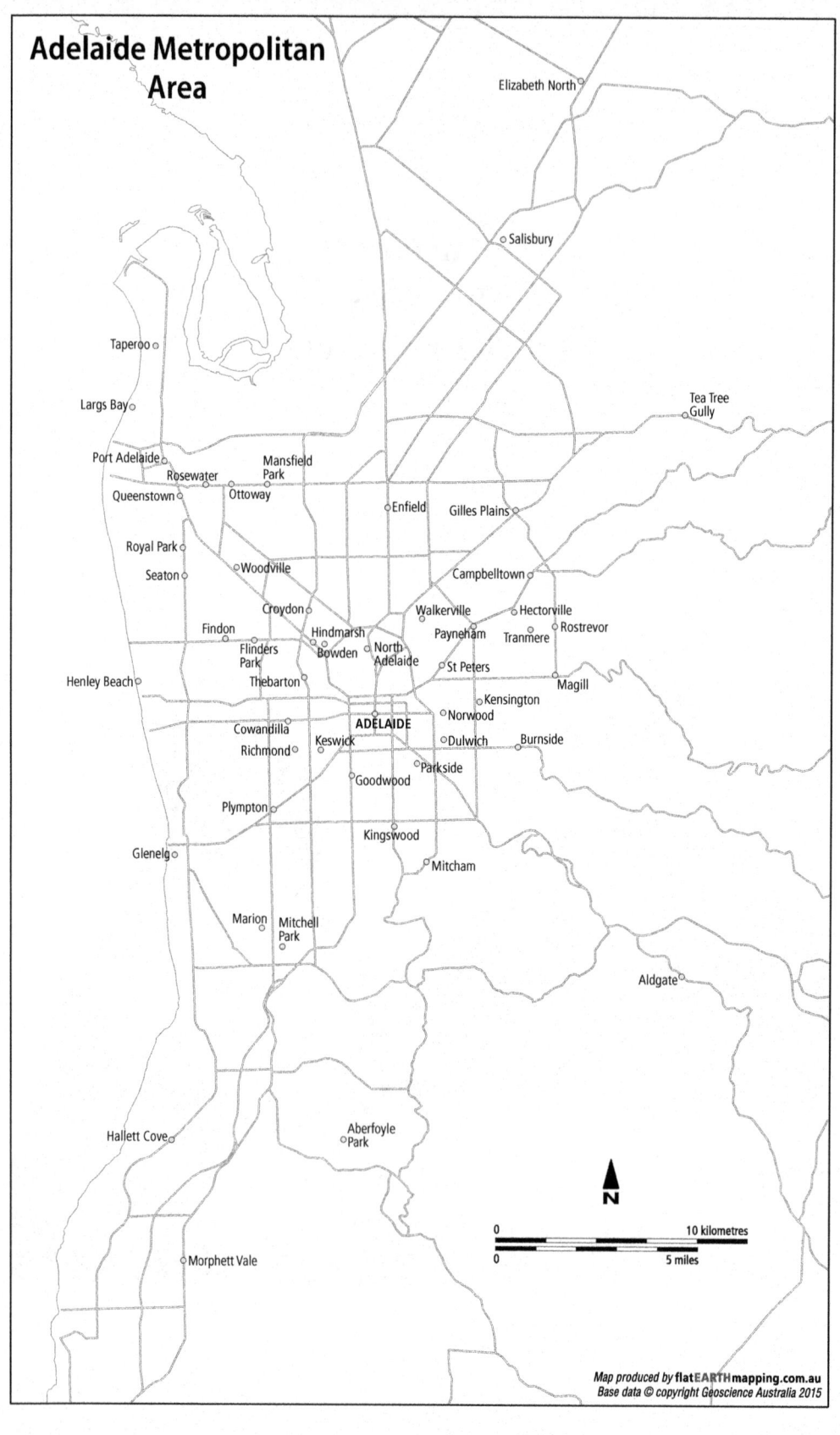

Chapter One
The Foundation Years: 1866–1872

Mary MacKillop first visited South Australia in 1860 when she went to Penola to be governess to her cousins, the Cameron children.[1] She remained there for almost two years and during that time, became acquainted with Father Julian Woods.[2] She heard his pleas for assistance in setting up Catholic schools in his mission area, as required by Bishop Geoghegan, and told him that, while she was willing to help him, her personal circumstances were such that she could not do so immediately. In fact, by late 1861 she had to leave Penola to help support her family at Portland in Victoria.

Before leaving Penola, she confided to Woods her desire to serve God as a member of a Religious Order. Subsequently, he became her spiritual guide, a position he held for the next several years. During that time, his dream of providing Catholic schools for the local children gradually evolved into the founding of the Sisters of St Joseph, a Religious Congregation of Sisters to manage these schools in different parts of his far-flung mission district.

At last, in January 1866, Mary was free to leave her family and return to Penola to take charge of Woods' school. Matters moved quickly for her after that and,

---

1. Alexander MacKillop's sister, Margaret, was married to Alexander Cameron, owner of Penola Station. They invited their niece, eighteen-year-old Mary, to be governess to their children, knowing that the wages they paid her would go to the support of her mother and family in Victoria.
2. Julian Edmund Tenison Woods (1832–1889) was an Englishman. Before migrating to Australia in 1854, he had tried his vocation with the Passionists in England and the Marist Fathers in France. He was ordained a diocesan priest in Adelaide in January 1857.

> when he asked [her] whether [she] would remain and become one of his first children in the flock, [she] joyfully consented.[3]

Consequently, on 19 March, the feast of St Joseph in that same year, she became the first Sister of St Joseph, and began wearing black as a symbol of her dedication. Under her leadership, the Penola School flourished and, thanks to Woods' enthusiasm for their new Religious Congregation, several local women accepted his invitation to join it. The first to come was Blanche Amsinck (Sister Francis Xavier) who arrived at some time in late 1866.[4] In April 1867 Rose Cunningham (Sister Rose) joined Mary at Penola.[4] Within a short time Woods sent her to assist Blanche in St Teresa's Catholic School at Mount Gambier leaving Mary to manage his school at Penola with the able assistance of her two younger sisters, Annie and Lexie MacKillop.

Others to become members of this little group were several women from Western Victoria: Mary Wright (Sister Clare) a young schoolteacher from Cape Bridgewater near Portland; her younger sister, Julia (Sister Gertrude); Grace Walsh (Sister, and later, Mother Bernard) and Anna Phillips (Sister Monica), all from the town of Portland itself. Others included Julia Fitzgerald (Sister Francis of the Five Wounds) from Mullagh Station, near Harrow, and Margaret Nolan (Sister Agatha) from Glenmire Station, near Casterton. Some time later, two very young girls, Jane Britt (Sister Jane Frances) from Penola, and Ellen Hudson (Sister Celestine) from Mount Gambier also volunteered to become Josephites.[5] Woods became spiritual director to all these women and helped them understand the meaning of Josephite Religious Life.[6]

---

3. MM to Sheil, from the steamer 'Kangaroo', 10 September 1871.
4. Rose Cunningham (Sr Rose) was born in County Westmeath, Ireland, on 24 June 1845. She migrated to Australia as a young woman, joined the Congregation on 3 May 1867, was professed on 24 May 1868, suffered a long and debilitating mental illness, and died in the Parkside Mental Hospital in South Australia on 2 October 1918. Little else is known of her.
5. See Appendix Two for further details regarding these women.
6. Spiritual direction is a way of leading a person to come closer to God. Father Woods filled the role of director for the first Sisters as they entered into the Josephite way of life or, as Mary herself put it, gave them 'certain rules for [their] spiritual guiding.' (MM to Monsignor Kirby, Irish College, Rome, Ascension Thursday, 22 May, 1873.)

What Woods did not know at the time was that, before long, the way he was dealing with the question of Catholic education in his mission region would be the proximate cause of a dramatic change to his own situation. Bishop Geoghegan died in May 1864 while on a visit to Ireland. His successor, Lawrence Bonaventure Sheil, OSF, Archdeacon of Ballarat, was consecrated Bishop of Adelaide in St Francis' Church, Melbourne, on 15 August 1866.[7] Sheil inherited a vast diocese comprising the entire colony of South Australia, which then extended from the Southern Ocean to Palmerston (Darwin) on the Timor Sea.[8] Woods attended Sheil's consecration in Melbourne and, while there, informed his new bishop of his ideas regarding education and his plans to bring them to fruition. What followed far exceeded his wildest hopes and dreams.

In fact, Sheil was so impressed with the young priest's enthusiasm that he gave tacit approval to the sisterhood, even though his ideas as to its organisation differed 'to some extent' from those held by Woods.[9] In addition, he appointed Woods to the newly-created position of Director General of Catholic Education and Inspector of Schools, and asked him to accompany him to Adelaide as his private secretary and personal chaplain. Woods could only rejoice at the position in which he so unexpectedly found himself. That the bishop should give his blessing to his new Religious Congregation had been as much as Woods had dared to hope for. The ways and means of realising his dream of providing Catholic schooling for all the Catholic children of the colony were now within his reach![10]

---

7. Bishop Sheil OSF was a member of the Order of St Francis, that is, a Franciscan priest. Ian J Bickerton, 'Sheil, Laurence Bonaventure (1815–1872)', *ADB* (National Centre of Biography, Australian National University, 1976) http://adb.anu.edu.au/biography/sheil-laurence-bonaventure-4568/text7497.
8. Australia became a nation on 1 January 1901, when six British colonies united to form the Commonwealth of Australia. Prior to this, it was a collection of six British colonies which were partly self-governing, but under the lawmaking power of the British Parliament. These colonies resembled six separate countries, each with its own government and laws, its own defence force and its own postage stamps. Each one collected tariffs on goods that crossed its borders. In this work, the term 'colony' is used when describing events which occurred before the year 1901. For further information see http://www.peo.gov.au/learning/closer-look/federation-cl.html
9. Woods to MM, 30 August 1866
10. Woods to MM from Melbourne, 30 August, 12 & 19 September 1866.

This appointment required that Woods move to Adelaide in January 1867 to undertake his new duties, one of which was that he travel throughout the length and breadth of the 'settled areas' of the colony to visit and assess existing schools.[11] He left Penola with high hopes for the future, only to find that it was not to be as bright as he had imagined. When he reached the city, eager to start work, he discovered that few of the clergy shared his passion for it. In fact, the Vicar General, Father John Smyth, feared that his enthusiasms were no more than 'fires of straw', and threw 'deluges of cold water' upon them, while many others of his colleagues openly ridiculed his ideas regarding the schools and the Institute of St Joseph.[12]

When he announced that the Sisters of St Joseph would form the backbone of his education system, they threw up their hands in horror. 'What', they asked, 'can you expect from colonial girls, without any knowledge of a religious life, and no one to train them?'[13] Woods was undeterred by such opposition. In fact, even though it was hard to bear, it seemed to augment rather than to quell the blaze of his enthusiasm. He regarded crosses (the term he used to describe any difficulties he encountered in the course of his ministry) as sure signs of divine approval, and hence as encouragement to press on with increased determination to succeed.

He soon discovered that most of the twenty-three Catholic schools in the diocese were functioning with untrained teachers, poor equipment and few facilities. He scarcely knew which way to turn, and decided that he needed Mary MacKillop's expert assistance. She was a skilful, Victorian trained teacher with a strong commitment to the ideals of a universal Catholic education where the religious and the secular were integrated into the curriculum and daily timetable. Therefore, she was well suited for the task at hand.[14] What more could he ask for?

---

11. 'Settled areas' was a term used until at least the mid-twentieth century to describe the limits of agricultural settlement in South Australia. They included Eyre Peninsula and most of the country south of a west-east line from Port Augusta to Renmark.
12. Woods to MM, 10 April 1867.
13. Woods to MM, 12 June 1867.
14. See Marie T Foale, *The Josephite Story*, Chapter 3 and Appendix 3 for further details re Mary's system of teaching.

In June 1867, when he invited Mary to join him, she and Sister Rose left their schools at Penola and Mount Gambier respectively, and travelled to Adelaide, where they arrived on Sunday 23 June. Their first convent was the small Grote Street house being rented by Miss Ellen McMullen, the head teacher of St Francis Xavier's Cathedral Hall School, which stood beside the cathedral in Wakefield Street, Adelaide. During the following week, the three women made a retreat under Woods' guidance and at its end, Mary and Rose donned their Josephite religious habits for the first time.[15] On the next day, 2 July 1867, they made their first public appearance, looking very nun-like in the black habits and veils they had made during the retreat.[16]

Sisters Mary and Rose began their Adelaide ministry as teachers in what had been Ellen McMullen's school beside the cathedral. Ellen, who had spent some time in the novitiate of the Sisters of Mercy in Melbourne and had left there voluntarily, felt drawn to join Mary and Rose as a Sister of St Joseph. She took part in their retreat and, when they donned their new religious habits, she dressed in a simple black dress and became known as 'Sister Josephine'. She, too, was a trained teacher and, with time, proved her worth in the classroom and as a leader among the Sisters.

After lessons finished on that first day, the three Sisters, two in their black habits and veils, and Sister Josephine in the black dress of a postulant, set out to lead the schoolchildren to their homes in the back streets of the city.[17] (This practice proved impractical and ceased within a few weeks, because the number of children was too great and they came from many different parts of the city).

---

15. 'Retreat' is a term used to describe a time when Sisters withdraw from their usual activities, and recharge their spiritual lives by spending six to eight days in quiet prayer and reflection. Usually they engage a priest, in this case Father Woods, to guide them through the retreat programme. Colloquially, 'making a retreat' is how participants describe this activity. Most Religious Sisters take time out for a retreat every year.
16. The first Josephite habits were black, but when Mary and the Sisters went to purchase more habit material they discovered that a particular dark brown fabric was much cheaper and so they opted for it instead.
17. A person at the beginning of her training to become a Sister wore a black dress and was known as a 'postulant', that is, someone asking to join the Congregation. A religious habit was the distinctive dress worn by all Religious Sisters until the 1970s.

In March 1891, as Mary MacKillop and the Sisters celebrated the silver jubilee of her decision to become the first Sister of St Joseph, she wrote:

> Little did either of us [a reference to Father Woods] then dream of what was to spring from so small a beginning.[18]

The same was certainly true of the people of Adelaide in the mid-winter of 1867. Little did they dream that they had become involved in the birth of a new Religious Congregation and a new, organised system of Catholic education, both of which would spread across the entire Australian continent and beyond, and would survive into the twenty-first century.

Penola marked the beginning. The Cathedral Hall School in Adelaide was a significant move forward, and the results that Mary and the trainee Sisters achieved there indicated that they knew how to teach and could manage a school well. According to the *South Australian Register*, the general public was impressed with the way they inculcated neatness and cleanliness in the children, so that even the poorest had 'a general look of tidiness and freshness about them that [was] very pleasing'. The people also noted that the new Sisters maintained good order and discipline in spite of the large numbers of children present, made singing an integral and enjoyable part of each day's work, and had an appealing system of rewards for good conduct and application.[19]

Within a matter of weeks, even the Sisters' sharpest critics, most notably Archdeacon Patrick Russell (the priest in charge of the Adelaide mission), were commending them for the quality of their work.[20] Parents showed their satisfaction by enrolling their children and ensuring that they attended school regularly.

Thus, sixty children arrived on the Sisters' first day at the Hall School. After six weeks, the number of children had more than

---

18. MM to the Sisters, 4 March 1891.
19. All details in this paragraph are from the leading article, 'Roman Catholic Education', *South Australian Register*, 7 March 1868.
20. Russell to Cardinal Alessandro Barnabo, 28 August 1867, SRCO (Rome) vol 8, ff. 907–908. Barnabo (1801–1874) was Prefect of the Roman Congregation Propaganda Fide, which arranged and supervised the Church's missionary works across the world.

doubled and, by the end of the year, it had passed the 200 mark. Several other factors contributed towards the parental satisfaction noted above. The most important of these were that Mary helped them clothe their children, did not demand fees from those who were unable to pay, and treated everyone equally, whether they paid or not.[21]

That public opinion was changing in their favour was probably the least of the Sisters' concerns during the latter half of 1867. They were so busy that they scarcely had time to worry about such matters. From 5 o'clock in the morning until 10 o'clock at night, their days were mapped out with set times for religious exercises and devotions, household chores, school duties, study and lesson preparation, as well as for the visitation of the sick and schoolchildren's families.[22]

Further, since all of them, including Mary herself, were beginners in the religious life, they had to devote a great deal of time and energy to learning how to think and behave as members of a Religious Congregation. This proved particularly difficult because they were adapting the religious life to suit colonial conditions, something not always understood by immigrant priests, bishops or lay people. In addition, they had no established traditions and customs to fall back upon in cases of doubt, and no elders 'to distil for them the matured wisdom of the past'.[23]

When Mary MacKillop arrived in Adelaide in June 1867, Woods informed her that she was to be headmistress of the Cathedral Hall School and that all new recruits were to spend some time working with her as pupil teachers. He considered it important that they not go out to other schools until they had mastered the principles and practice of teaching. In reality, this did not happen because, as the membership of the Congregation increased at a rate that neither he

---

21. *South Australian Advertiser*, 15 August 1867, Report of meeting of the Catholic Education Council; *SCCH*, 20 September 1870, 9, 'An Appeal'; 20 January 1868, 64.
22. Woods, *Rules*, article 5, 'Of Employments', Article 6: 'Of the daily Duties', Article 8: 'Of the Meals'; Woods, *Directory and Order of Discipline of the Sisters of St Joseph of the Sacred Heart* (Adelaide, ca. 1870), passim; Woods, *A Book of Instructions for the Sisters of St Joseph of the Sacred Heart* (Adelaide, 1870), passim.
23. Douglas Pike, 'A Society without Grandparents', in *Melbourne Studies in Education, 1957-1958*, edited by EL French (Melbourne: Melbourne University Press, 1958), 57.

nor Mary had anticipated, Woods found himself under pressure from his fellow clergy to provide Sisters for their schools.

The continuous demands for help, and his anxiety to fill all requests as quickly as possible, gave rise to some serious problems for the Congregation. That its members were still struggling to understand the meaning of the religious life they had embraced, to master the art of teaching, and to ensure that their pupils attained the required standards seemed not to worry him at all. In fact, so great was his enthusiasm that he was unable to see that his haste had serious potential for disaster.

For their part, these young Josephite novices began with great enthusiasm, confident in the guidance of their charismatic Father Director.[24] As their numbers increased, they willingly undertook new works. In fact, by the end of 1867 (just six months after Mary's arrival in Adelaide), she and nine other trainee Sisters had charge of three schools: the Cathedral Hall and Bowden in the Adelaide metropolitan area and Yankalilla, seventy-two kilometres away at the southern end of the Mount Lofty Ranges. In addition, two of these Sisters were assisting with the supervision of a Refuge or halfway house for women recently released from gaol or in need of protection.

Expansion began in late August 1867. There were five Sisters and so Woods agreed that they should undertake the management of the Catholic school at inner suburban Bowden. He chose Sisters Josephine McMullen and Clare Wright to replace the lay teacher who had been working there in far from ideal conditions.[25] Neither Clare nor Josephine had been Josephites for more than a few weeks.

Woods was keen to have Sisters at Bowden because, as he reported in *The Southern Cross and Catholic Herald* of October 1867:

> This is the poorest district in the colony and is inhabited by Catholics to a large extent. No poor quarter of any colonial city could vie with it in poverty and its usual accompaniments. The Sisters of St Joseph have a school in a room literally worse than a stable. The inconveniences and squalid misery

---

24. A novice is a person who is going through a period of probation before pronouncing her vows as a member of a Religious Congregation. The term novitiate is used to describe the probationary period and also the place where it occurs.
25. *SCCH*, 20 March 1869, 290; *IH*, 6 April 1872, 4.

of the place where ninety children are congregated could hardly be believed.

He followed this statement with what proved to be a successful appeal for £300 to build a new church-school in the area.[26] This building was ready for occupation by the beginning of the 1868 school year.

Josephine and Clare resided in community with Mary MacKillop and the other Sisters in their little cottage convent in Grote Street, and travelled to and from Bowden each day by train or (when weather permitted) on foot. The Bowden Sisters' journey became a little shorter when, in early 1868, a much larger house on a Church owned block at the western end of Franklin Street became available and all the Adelaide Sisters moved in there.

The first to move away from that initial community and set up a new one (at Yankalilla) were Sisters Clare Wright (a novice) and Francis Fitzgerald (a postulant). Having arrived in Adelaide on 4 October, Francis scarcely had time to find her feet in Adelaide before Woods sent her and Clare to this distant foundation. In so doing, he had to find a replacement for Clare at Bowden. Thus began his practice of moving Sisters like pieces of a jigsaw puzzle every time he accepted a new foundation, an arrangement that did not augur well for the success of his education system.

Even so, despite some initial difficulties, what happened at Yankalilla was the beginning of a remarkable experiment in female religious life. Two Sisters, with only a few weeks' experience of convent living, were based in a small, isolated settlement where there was no resident priest. They were without daily Mass which was considered at the time to be an absolute necessity for religious Sisters. In those days before the invention of the telephone, they had only limited means of communication with the Sisters in Adelaide. They had with them, however, copies of their daily timetable, their Josephite 'Rule of Life', and their school timetable and curriculum.[27]

---

26. A church-school was a building, which served as a church on weekends and as one or more classrooms during the week. It usually fell upon the Sisters and their pupils to rearrange the furniture for Mass at the end of classes on Fridays and then make it ready for school on Monday mornings.
27. See Appendices Four A and Four B for details of the Sisters' daily timetable and prayer schedule.

They sent Woods and Mary regular written reports regarding their management of the school and their community living. Thus, in January 1868, Sister Francis Fitzgerald reported to Mary that they had attended Sunday Mass at St Peter's Church, Normanville, approximately eight kilometres away (there has never been a Catholic church in Yankalilla), and had visited a sick woman.

She went on to say that the local school board was raising funds for a new schoolroom, that she was doing well with her study, that there were thirty children in the school, and that the little ones were not very advanced. In fact, she claimed that she was so busy that, by the time she came home from the school and prepared dinner, it was already 6.30 in the evening. She added another reason for her lateness: she no longer had the domestic help to which she was accustomed. She had to tidy the classroom and make the fire in the house herself![28]

For Francis, the youngest daughter of a wealthy Irish family, and sister to the owner of a prosperous station property in Western Victoria, the need to do her own tidying up and to set her own fire came as a shock. Nevertheless, she persevered as a Sister and, along with those who joined the Congregation at this time, laid a firm foundation for its future. Even at this early stage, she and her companions had taken to heart that line of their Rule, which read:

> [The Sisters are bound] to do all the good they can and never to see an evil without trying how they may remedy it.[29]

The success of the Yankalilla foundation proved that the founders' aim to reach all Catholic children in the colony was a realistic one. They were confident that they could go ahead and establish houses in other country areas, regardless of their distance from the larger towns where there were resident priests. For their part, the clergy watched developments with growing interest. Those who were satisfied that these new Sisters could teach, and that they cost less than lay teachers to maintain, asked Woods for Josephite communities. Consequently, in January 1868, three Sisters went to the copper mining town of Kapunda (some eighty kilometres to the north of Adelaide), where enrolments soon exceeded one hundred.

---

28. Sr Francis Fitzgerald to MM, 2 January 1868.
29. Woods, *Rules of the Institute*, December 1868, Article 13.

Next came Gawler, forty kilometres from the city, where they made a foundation in April. In early May, two Sisters went to Penola and another two took up residence in the St Vincent de Paul's Orphanage in Adelaide. In June, the village of Macclesfield in the Adelaide Hills welcomed two Sisters. In July, three others moved to Port Adelaide to manage the school there. Willunga (in the Southern Vales) and suburban Queenstown (which was close to Port Adelaide) followed soon afterwards. All communities except those in Adelaide, Port Adelaide/Queenstown, Gawler and Kapunda comprised two Sisters only. Such expansion was possible only because there was a constant stream of new recruits presenting themselves at the convent door.

When Sisters moved away from their city Mother House, Mary insisted that they write to her regularly, reporting on their community living and prayer life, their teaching, and their visitation of the sick and needy outside of school hours. For her part, she was always ready to help them prepare their lessons in Arithmetic and English Grammar. Sister Aloysius O'Leary wrote from Macclesfield:

> Dear Sister, I cannot think of anything to write about, except if you would be so kind as to send a parsing lesson. I would be so thankful.[30]

The provision of suitable schoolbooks for the use of the Sisters and the children had exercised Woods' mind ever since he had become Inspector of Catholic Schools. In fact, as early as September 1867, he had invested between £300 and £400 of his own money for the purchase of the 'cheapest and most serviceable books for both secular and religious instruction' that he could obtain.[31] These included texts from the Catholic Council of Education in London.

Less than twelve months later, he was discussing the possibility of his writing and having printed cheaply a geography text and a grammar for the use of the teachers. By September 1868, the geography was on sale at the Catholic Book Depot and the grammar was almost ready for printing. He had published a Catechism before the end of 1869.[32]

---

30. Sr Aloysius O'Leary to MM, 2 November 1868.
31. Woods, 'Report of Meeting of the Central Council of Catholic Education', *SCCH*, 20 September 1867.
32. Woods, *SCCH*, 20 May, 12 July and 29 September 1868 & 20 June 1869.

The situation regarding the schools changed so rapidly that, by early 1868, Mary found it necessary to abandon the classroom teaching she loved, and travel to the schools and convents to assist the Sisters with their work and to instruct them in the religious life. Surviving evidence suggests that, thanks to Mary's tuition and the texts that Woods imported or produced himself, most of the founding Sisters could hold their own in front of classes of children at the level for which they had been trained.

These women knew that the primary aim of the Congregation was the education of poor children. Its members also lived by their maxim that they should do all the good they could. Therefore, they did everything within their power to improve the quality of life of the disadvantaged residents of the city of Adelaide and beyond. Thus, in 1867, besides running their schools they took responsibility for the Refuge, as already mentioned, and made regular visits to the homes of the children attending their schools. They also visited the Adelaide Gaol, the Adelaide Hospital, the Adelaide Destitute Asylum, and similar institutions in country areas.[33]

But that was not all. In June 1868, just twelve months after Mary's arrival in the city, they undertook the management of two more charitable institutions. The first was the St Vincent de Paul's Orphanage where some sixty children were housed. The second was a House of Providence, which was large enough to house at least ten disadvantaged people at any one time and in which the Sisters accommodated needy women of all ages, especially the frail aged.

Mary and Woods showed good judgment when they appointed to the Providence one of their most recently arrived postulants, Susan Etheridge (Sister Elizabeth). At eighteen years of age, colonial born Susan was barely literate. It seems, however, that this young woman had a natural gift for understanding and caring for frail aged women. She became the first Josephite aged care nurse and faithfully served the elderly residents at the Providence for the next forty years.[34]

---

33. See Marie T Foale, *Think of the Ravens* (Adelaide: Sisters of St Joseph, 2001), for further details regarding the Josephites' social welfare work between 1867 and 1980.
34. Sr Elizabeth Etheridge was born at Port Adelaide on 15 April 1850. She joined the Josephites on 24 May 1868, made her religious profession on 24 June 1869, and spent the rest of her active life ministering at the Providence. She died at Kensington on 9 March 1912, aged sixty-two years.

By late December 1868, the Congregation had forty-eight members, only eight of whom had made their religious profession. The remainder were either novices or postulants. None had more than eighteen months' experience of the religious life and only a handful had prior training or experience as teachers.[35] These were exciting times indeed and, for their part, the new Sisters willingly followed Woods' instructions, adhered to their daily timetable with its balance of work and prayer, and fulfilled the duties allotted to them to the best of their abilities. Most Catholic parents were delighted that their children could attend a Catholic school, and enrolments in every school increased with time.

Trouble was brewing in some quarters, however, for in his haste and enthusiasm for the work, Woods admitted a number of women who were unsuited to the religious life. In fact, seventeen of those who joined the Congregation during 1868 had left it by 1880. The first of those to move out was nineteen-year-old Priscilla Giles, whose convent career lasted for six months and who caused quite a stir in Adelaide circles when she alleged that her family had needed to rescue her from it by force. It seems that in September 1868 Miss Giles, a recent convert to catholicism, left home to become a Sister without her parents' blessing. Her time as a Josephite was uneventful, but the Adelaide secular press made the most of her 'escape' from the convent, much to the embarrassment of the local Catholics, and especially of the bishop and clergy.

The various conflicting accounts of this so called 'Convent Case' that appeared in local papers make it impossible to reconstruct accurately the events surrounding it.[36] Priscilla herself appears to have had so little knowledge of convents, religious orders, or Catholic schools, that her most serious allegations against them concerned their supposed mistreatment of non-Catholic children attending a school run by the Dominican Sisters in Franklin Street.[37]

---

35. See Appendix Three, which shows how the new foundations followed hard upon the heels of the arrival of new recruits in the convent.
36. Woods' account of events, as reported in the *Register*, and the *SCCH*, 20 April 1869, 301–302, differs significantly from Giles'. Further accounts confuse the issue even more. See 'The Adelaide Convent Case', *South Australian Register*, 23 March 1869; also the leading article, *Register*, 27 March 1869, and 'Open Column', *Register*, 9 & 13 April 1869.
37. Helen Northey OP, *Living the Truth: The Dominican Sisters in South Australia*,

Beyond the Sisters' alleged refusal to allow her free access to her family, she made no other accusations against them. This is remarkable, given the nature of the case and the fact that the local papers were on the alert for any scandal involving Catholics. The inspection of convents, with a view to rescuing helpless young women locked up there against their will, became an issue for a time, but, after several weeks, the affair faded from public memory.[38]

Woods himself could have avoided this unfortunate incident by using greater care when inviting potential members into the Congregation.

On the whole, while this event upset the bishop and some of the clergy it did not interfere with the general running of Josephite affairs and, in particular, with Mary's efforts to ensure that all Sisters could manage their duties in the schools. In fact, as soon as she was free of her obligations at the Cathedral Hall School, she began what was to become for her a lifelong practice, namely, that of going with Sisters to new foundations wherever and whenever possible, and staying with them until they had settled into their new homes and routines. Her first such journey was to Kapunda,[39] and over succeeding months she accompanied newly appointed communities to Clare, Macclesfield,[40] Willunga and Penola.[41]

1868–1968 (Adelaide: Holy Cross Congregation of Dominican Sisters, 1999), recounts the story of the arrival of the Dominican Sisters in December 1868 and their settlement in a convent and school adjacent to the Josephite convent on Franklin Street. Their fee-paying students came from the better off Catholic families in Adelaide. The school referred to above opened in February 1869.

38. Priscilla Giles (Sr Nicholas) was born on 24 March 1849 to Edward Giles and Elizabeth Anna Hole of Noarlunga, SA, Adelaide Registry Office, book 2, no. 127. She was baptised a Catholic by Woods on 3 January 1868, Adelaide Baptismal Register H, Register of Converts. *Register*, 20, 22, 23, 24, 25, 26, 27 & 30 March 1869, and 1, 3, 5, 8, 9, 10 & 15 April, Open Column; 27 March, leading article, 'The Convent Detention Case', 23 April, leading article, 'The Late Convent Case'. *The Advertiser* carried similar material but was less generous with editorial space. The *Northern Argus*, 26 March 1869, devoted a short article to it, while *Pasquin*, 3 April 1869, 109 and *Adelaide Punch*, 25 March 1869, 81, refused to take the affair seriously. Punch announced that he had just heard that the editor of the *Register* had been forcibly detained in a convent at North Adelaide. *Punch*, 88. Woods to MM, 2 & 20 April 1869.
39. Sr Clare Wright to MM, 15 February 1868.
40. Sr Monica Phillips to MM, 9 June 1868.
41. Sr Mechtilde Woods, 'History', 6, mentions that MM had accompanied the Sisters

In late April 1868, she travelled to Penola with Sisters Teresa McDonald and Agnes Smith. As usual, she stayed for a while. Then, at some point on her homeward journey by overland coach, the horses bolted. The driver and his passengers had a good shaking, but, to everyone's relief, all escaped unhurt.[42]

Thirty-four new Sisters arrived during 1869, thus making possible the foundation of convents and schools in the copper mining towns of Wallaroo and Kadina, some 160 kilometres northwest of Adelaide, St Johns near Kapunda, Mount Barker in the Adelaide Hills and Clare in the Mid-North, as well as in suburban North Adelaide, Thebarton, Glenelg, Marion and Le Fevre Peninsula (near Port Adelaide). Among the new arrivals were several who were to play significant roles in the life of the developing Congregation. These included Sisters Laurence O'Brien (a future Mother General), Mechtilde Woods (Julian Woods' niece), Andrea and Calasanctius Howley (whose names will appear frequently throughout this history), Casimir Meskill (a future general councillor and Novice Mistress), and Raymond Smyth (future leader of the New Zealand foundation and Provincial there for many years).

During this year, the Sisters also took charge of what was known as the Poor School adjacent to their Mother House, and a small institution called the 'Solitude of Mary'. Woods established the Solitude as a secluded home for any women from the Refuge who expressed a desire to 'make reparation for their former misdemeanours'. In 1869, these women, acting under Woods' guidance, formed a religious society (not a religious congregation) known as 'Magdalens of the Compassionate Heart of Mary'. They promised to follow a rule of life whereby they lived almost as religious Sisters: in community, sharing all that they possessed in common and giving strict obedience to one of their number, who was known as the 'Mother Magdalen'. The house they occupied was called the 'Solitude of Mary' and there, under the supervision of the

---

to Macclesfield and Willunga. On page 11, she notes that MM also went to Clare when that convent and school opened in July 1869. Woods to MM, 28 April 1868, indicates that she had accompanied Teresa and Agnes to Penola for the same reason.

42. Sr Teresa McDonald to MM, 13 May 1868.

Sisters, they received and cared for sick and frail aged women who could afford to pay for their keep.

Few records of the Solitude have survived, but it appears that there were four Magdalens and possibly several more. At different times, they occupied houses at Glenelg, St Johns, or Queen Street, Norwood, this last being distinct from the Refuge, which was in Queen Street from 1872 until 1901. Over a period of nine years the Magdalens cared for at least five needy women and possibly many more. The Solitude closed in 1877 and those in residence transferred to the Providence. Almost nothing is known of its effectiveness as a reforming agency or of its usefulness as a nursing home.[43]

During 1870, another thirty women joined the Congregation, bringing its total membership to 111. This increase in numbers enabled Woods to respond to requests for Sisters to open eleven more convents and schools, mainly in the city and the Lower North region of the colony. The country foundations were at Burra, Moonta, Greenock, Marrabel, Tarlee and Rhynie in the north, and in suburban Glen Osmond, Mitcham, Hectorville, Morphett Vale and Lower North Adelaide.[44]

Late 1869, too, the Congregation made its first foundation outside South Australia. Bishop Sheil's enthusiasm for this new religious congregation in his diocese made such an impression on Bishop James Quinn of Brisbane that he asked Sheil if he could have some of these Sisters to do similar work in the poorer areas of Brisbane and the widely scattered settlements along the Queensland coast. Sheil agreed at once and decided that Mary MacKillop herself should lead this little group. Soon afterwards, he set out from Adelaide on a lengthy journey to Europe and Ireland, leaving his Vicar General, Father John Smyth, in charge at home. He was away from his diocese from December 1869 until February 1871.

---

43. Letters having reference to the Sisters of St Joseph, 1876–1878, 50-61, ASSJ, Kensington. MM to Woods, 29 November 1869 & 9 October 1875; Woods to MM, 28 November 1869.
44. The Tarlee foundation was sometimes known as Gilbert and was located in or near the present township of Tarlee, some seventy-four kilometres north of Adelaide. Navan was a few kilometres further to the north and there is no evidence to suggest that the Sisters were there after the time of Mary's excommunication in September 1871.

At the same time, Mary set out with a group of four Sisters to make a Josephite foundation in Queensland. Before her departure Woods appointed Sister Teresa McDonald as Provincial, that is, as Mary's deputy, in South Australia.[45] Everyone expected that Mary would be home within a short time, but she did not reappear until April 1871.

The Sisters chosen for Brisbane were Clare Wright (aged almost twenty-six years), Augustine Keogh (aged twenty-four), Francis de Sales Sullivan (aged twenty), and a twenty-three year old novice, Teresa Maginess. Mary herself was not yet twenty-eight. She and Clare became the first Sisters to make their final profession as Josephites, which they did on the eve of their departure for Brisbane.

Another group comprising one professed Sister, namely Helena Hartney, (aged twenty years), and three novices, Mary Francis Bartolsmeier, (aged twenty-three), Francesca O'Brien (aged eighteen) and sixteen year old Vincent Smith, went to Brisbane from Adelaide in January 1871, and soon after their arrival, three new recruits joined their little group as postulants. By September 1871, the eleven Josephites in Queensland were managing four schools, three in Brisbane and one in the coastal port of Maryborough (some 255 kilometres to the north).[46] In South Australia, 112 Sisters were managing thirty-seven schools and four charitable institutions.

While Mary was in Queensland she maintained a prolific correspondence with Woods and the Sisters at home in Adelaide. As time passed, she received reports indicating that all was not well among the Sisters there. It seems likely that Woods was suffering from what is known today as 'burnout', for he was making unwise decisions regarding the training and deployment of young Sisters and at times behaving erratically. His refusal to take Mary's advice or allow her to return home troubled her and gave her cause for serious concern about what was happening among the Adelaide Sisters.

---

45. Sr Teresa (Margaret McDonald) was born in Inverness Shire, Scotland, in 1838. She was professed on Christmas Day 1868, and died at Bathurst on 13 January 1876. Mary's journey to Queensland proved to be the first of the many times when she was absent from South Australia on Congregational business. See Appendix Nine for details of the different times when she was away from and was present in South Australia.
46. For a full explanation of developments in Queensland, see Margaret McKenna, *With Grateful Hearts! Mary MacKillop and the Sisters of St Joseph in Queensland, 1870–1970* (North Sydney: The Trustees of the Sisters of St Joseph, 2009).

Some of her correspondents complained that a fractious spirit had developed in the Mother House community. In August 1870, Sister Teresa McDonald wrote that one Sister, whom she did not name, was 'eating egg (sic) and having butter and milk while the other Sisters were having dripping and no milk'.[47] Soon afterwards Sister Aloysius O'Leary informed Mary that she could not bear to go to the Mother House because 'everything seem[ed] so cold and cheerless'.[48]

Why was this? First, there was tension between Teresa and the Sisters on the one hand and Woods on the other, because he had taken over the roles of General Superior and Provincial, as defined in the *Rules of the Institute of St Joseph*. At the same time he had reached a point where he believed that he held these offices by divine appointment and defended his conduct on the ground that he was 'the exponent of the will of God, their superior ... and the priest appointed to direct them and therefore, that he could not be mistaken in his dealings with them.'[49]

Consequently he regulated their affairs without due reference to Sister Teresa. Instead, he sent her to reside at the Refuge, which was near the church on the corner of Maitland Street and St Michael's Road in the village of Mitcham, and at some distance from the city.[50] While there she was little more than a figurehead, for the real power lay in the hands of twenty-four year old Sister Ignatius (Mary Jane O'Brien),[51] the Little Sister, or local superior of the Mother House and one of Woods' particular favourites.[52]

---

47. Sr Teresa McDonald to MM, 28 August 1870.
48. Sr Aloysius O'Leary to MM, from Gawler, 28 August 1870.
49. Woods to MM, 14 August 1870.
50. Woods to MM, 12 July, 14 August and 27 September 1870. MM to Woods, 3 December 1871. Teresa to MM, 11 July 1870.
51. Mary Jane O'Brien (Sr Ignatius) was born in Sydney in July 1846 and came to Adelaide with her family in 1848. She joined the Congregation in February 1868, was professed in March 1969, and left it in July 1872. For an account of her subsequent career, see Cunneen, Chris, 'Abbott, Gertrude, 1846-1934', *ADB*, vol 7. (National Centre of Biography, Australian National University, 1979.) http://adb.anu.edu.au/biography/abbott-gertrude-4960/text8227.
52. 'Little Sister' was the term that Woods and Mary used to denote the superior or leader of a Josephite community. Mary MacKillop wrote that the Little Sister 'should so govern as to show that she considers herself the loving servant of all', *Rules for the General Guidance of the Sisters of St Joseph of the Sacred Heart* (Sydney, 1883), 22.

The Sisters were annoyed and confused. Many of them disliked and mistrusted Ignatius and did not know where to turn. Teresa was involved in the management of the Refuge and so could give them only limited attention. She did not know where she stood in her role as Provincial or her dealings with Ignatius. This Sister's close friendship with Woods did not help matters, and before long, the relationship between herself and Teresa was strained indeed.[53]

On the one side was Teresa, the gentle Scotswoman with her two feet planted firmly on the ground and, like Mary, of a practical turn of mind. On the other was colonial born Ignatius, who leaned towards the extraordinary and the unusual in her living out of her vocation to the religious life. She claimed that she was the recipient of remarkable spiritual and mystical favours from God and quickly attracted Woods' attention to herself.[54] He was more than delighted to think that she and several others, especially the seventeen year old Mistress of Novices, Sister Angela (Catherine Carroll), were so favoured by God, and felt certain that these Sisters were well on the way to high sanctity.[55]

When Ignatius, Angela, or any of their little coterie of 'visionaries', as they came to be called, confided to him messages allegedly emanating from the Blessed Virgin or some other heavenly source, or details of horrifying visitations from evil spirits, he applied the only tests he knew. In his view, these Sisters were interested in nothing but holiness—many saints in the past

---

53. Sr Teresa to MM, 12 June & 18 August 1870. Sr Josephine McMullen to MM, 25 June, 5 August & 29 November 1870. Sr Rose Cunningham to MM, 2 August 1870. Sr Maria Healy to MM, 28 August 1870. Sr Bernard Walsh to MM, 18 August & 24 November 1870. Woods to MM, 23 August 1870. Sr Francis Xavier Amsinck to MM, 15 August 1870.
54. Sr Teresa to MM, 13 February & 28 August 1870. MM to Woods, February 1871. Sr Teresa, evidence to Apostolic Commission, 3 June 1872. Woods to MM, 5 October 1868, 20 January 1869, 2 April 1869, 7 November 1869, 12 & 28 March 1870.
55. Catherine Carroll (Sr Angela) was born in Ireland in the September of 1850 or 1853. (Marriage certificate, SAGHS, gives 1853) came to SA with her family, and lived with them at Kapunda until she joined the Congregation in July 1868. She was professed in August 1869, left the Congregation in 1872, married Thomas Donohue at Kapunda in July 1877, had two sons and died at the Providence in December 1924.

had had similar experiences. He was convinced, therefore, that their experiences were genuine and worthy of credence.

It did not occur to him that such an apparent desire for holiness could be deceptive and superficial or be suspect in its attention seeking qualities. Instead, he was so delighted that such marvels were taking place in their midst that he failed to notice just how far these Sisters' behaviour was disrupting the harmony of their community life, disturbing their neighbourhood, and contravening the Rules of the Institute that they professed to follow.

Woods treated the two principal visionaries, Sisters Ignatius O'Brien and Angela Carroll, with the greatest deference, respect, trust and sympathy, and gave them responsible posts in the hope that they would lead the rest of the community along the path to high holiness. He also granted them certain privileges, and thus unwittingly placed them in a difficult position when, as beginning religious, they should have been treated with firmness and trained to self-discipline as they learned to live according to their Rule of Life.

As a result, these young Sisters found themselves at the centre of an admiring crowd and were subject to the adulation and envy that such a position can entail. Unsure of themselves in their recently acquired status as Sisters, they were unable or unwilling to face the consequences of an honest acknowledgment of the deception they were perpetrating. They and their credulous director seem to have been caught in a vicious circle of their own making and, in order to keep up appearances, they resorted to subterfuge and deceit.

They advanced from visions of saints or demons, which were necessarily highly personal and private experiences, to allegedly preternatural or supernatural happenings, which could be observed by, and sometimes affected, other members of the community and even outsiders as well. Over time, some of their behaviours became bizarre. Thus, they set the house on fire and threw oil, logs of wood, or other objects at each other, apparently without any thought of possible outcomes. At night, they rang bells, turned on taps, and generally disturbed the neighbourhood. They created supposedly supernatural fragrances by eating oranges or splashing scent around unobserved and used various means to create self-inflicted stigmata.[56]

---

56. Woods to MM, 16 January, 12 & 28 March, 11 & 19 April, 20 May 1870.

Several of them left the convent by stealth and later reported that they had been spirited away by the devil. Others opened Mary's letters to Woods over mugs of hot water and then impressed him with their supposedly infused knowledge of her affairs in distant Queensland. Some sent anonymous letters to Woods, the Vicar General and members of the Franklin Street community. The hapless Dominican Sisters, whose convent was close by and who were the butt of a number of the behaviours detailed above, became so afraid at night that they called on the priests living at the Bishop's House in nearby West Terrace for protection.[57]

Some of these clergy realised what was happening and became critical of the Sisters and their Father Director. Woods, for his part, could not be persuaded that these unusual occurrences had any but a supernatural source, and came to believe that he, too, was the favoured recipient of many remarkable gifts from God. As already noted, adverse criticism had the opposite from the desired effect upon him. He saw it as part of the opposition the saints endured and, hence, as something to be borne but not taken seriously. On the other hand, when any of the Sisters raised the issue of adverse opposition with him, he told them that they were being tempted by the evil one and must work to overcome such temptations.

When Sister Teresa expressed her misgivings about the allegedly spiritual experiences that the visionaries laid claim to, she was banished from the Mother House. Mary, who was still in distant Brisbane, was uneasy and longed for the day when she could return home. Woods consistently assured her that she had no cause for alarm, even as he related the latest marvels in detail. He made it clear that he did not want her at home, claiming that it was not God's Will that she return yet. Knowing her unquestioning obedience to the Will of God he left it at that, and many critical months elapsed before she reached Adelaide once more.[58]

---

57. Woods to MM, 28 March & 27 September 1870. James McLaughlin, Port Adelaide, to Cardinal Barnabo, 25 September 1873. Sr Helena's confession, Sr Angela's confession, ca 1875, ASSJ. Russell to Barnabo, 22 October 1870. Confessions made and signed by Srs Helena, Paula and Angela, ASSJ. Woods to MM, 28 March & 27 September 1870.
58. MM to Woods, 6 April & 6 August 1870 & 10 April 1871. Woods to MM, 11 & 22 April & August 1870.

In the meantime, Woods himself was going through a trying period where overwork and lack of sufficient food and rest were taking their toll. As pastor of Penola, with space for quiet reflection, reading and study, he was able to refresh himself physically and spiritually during the course of his labours. In Adelaide, where he had sole responsibility for a large and expanding Catholic Education System and a community of more than 100 young Sisters, as well as a full load of parochial duties and the task of editing a monthly journal, his health began to fail. His friends urged him to act prudently, but he retorted that God was his only guide and that he neither could nor would follow their advice. Hence, he continued on his way towards a physical and mental breakdown. He came close to both on several occasions during 1870 and 1871 and, in the circumstances, it is remarkable that he did not break.

Josephite affairs gradually built up to an unhappy climax. The visionaries vied with each other in their attention seeking activities, while Woods steered dangerously close to the edge of reality. It is difficult to gauge why young women from lower middle or working class backgrounds and belonging to a Congregation devoted to active works outside the cloister, should have shown such predilection for the extraordinary. Perhaps they saw in it an escape from the very ordinariness of their lot, or as an opportunity to rise above their station and achieve notoriety of a kind otherwise beyond their reach.

Or, perhaps, they were victims of Woods' interpretation of the religious life (as he understood it from his own limited experiences of life in men's religious orders before he migrated to Australia in 1853), and were trying to practise spiritual asceticism before they had acquired a solid background in theology and the teachings of the spiritual masters.[59] It seems to have been a case of infants in the religious life suffering the unhappy consequences of being given the food of mature adults before they were ready for it. Besides Sisters Ignatius and Angela, others who claimed to be having visions and other mystical experiences were Sisters Helena (Mary Anne Myles),

---

59. Mary MacKillop, *Julian Tenison Woods: A Life* (North Sydney: Trustees of the Sisters of St Joseph, 1997), 5, note 3.

Sebastian (Mary Bridget Fitzgerald),[60] Paula (Elizabeth Green),[61] and Julian (Jane Brown).[62] Very little is known of any of these women except Ignatius (Mary Jane O'Brien) who came from a well-respected Catholic family in the Salisbury area, some twenty kilometres to the north of Adelaide.

Mary Jane was the eldest of the eight children of Irish schoolteacher, Thomas O'Brien and his wife, Rebecca (née Matthews). Thomas ran a small, mediocre school at Dry Creek, a short distance from Salisbury, and it appears that the family had known poverty. The O'Briens seem to have enjoyed a stable family life, however, and Mary Jane grew up an intelligent and literate young woman. Existing evidence suggests the possibility that, had she enjoyed the same opportunities and undergone the same long training in the spiritual life as Mary had received before she became a Josephite, she too might have emerged as one of its leaders.

Sister Angela (Catherine Carroll) was very different from Ignatius and, it seems, was one whom a discerning director would have discouraged from becoming a religious. She was born in Ireland and came to Australia with her parents and family at an early age. Her father worked as a labourer in the Kapunda district, she had at least one brother and two sisters, and she was fourteen when she joined the Josephites. It seems that, from childhood, young Kate, as she was known, was subject to a condition which rendered her liable to go into 'nervous trances'.

The evidence suggests that Angela was rather simple, open to suggestion, and likely to take to heart and act upon anything presented

---

60. Mary Bridget Fitzgerald (Sr Sebastian) was born in Ireland on 25 August 1851. Nothing is known of how, when or with whom she came to Australia. She joined the Congregation in about April 1869, was professed in August 1870, and left it in early 1872. Nothing further is known of her.
61. Elizabeth Green (Sr Paula) was born in Ireland in May 1847 and nothing is known of her family or her coming to Australia. She joined the Josephites in October 1868, was professed in January 1870, and became a close friend of Sr Angela Carroll and a key member of the visionary group. She left the Congregation in 1872.
62. Jane Brown (Sr Julian) daughter of Jonathan Brown and Mary Holt, was born at Liverpool, England, in June 1854. The family migrated to South Australia between the time of her birth and that of her sister, Esther, who was baptised at Gawler on 24 August 1856. Jane joined the Josephites in June 1869, shortly after her fifteenth birthday, was professed in November 1870 and left the Congregation in 1872.

to her by an important role model, such as her Father Director. Her artlessness and apparent sincerity quickly won Woods' heart and he read her trances as spiritual ecstasies and, hence, as manifestations of great holiness and sure signs that she was a chosen soul requiring special treatment. Such treatment suited her well and she made sure that her days were marked by all kinds of remarkable happenings![63]

Under the leadership of these two chosen ones, the Sisters in the Adelaide community were very unhappy. Some of them complained to Mary of the strange occurrences that were disrupting their lives, and the harsh treatment Sister Ignatius was meting out to them whilst frequently mitigating the 'Rules of the Institute' in her own favour.[64]

In fact, as long as she remained at the helm, these rules were flouted frequently and community life was disturbed by the visionaries' strange conduct.

Woods was certain that the troubles upsetting the peace of the Franklin Street convent emanated from the evil one, who was out to destroy the good work so recently begun by the Sisters of St Joseph. Hence, when Sister Francis Xavier was in the throes of one of her 'silent temptations', and when others believed or said extraordinary things about each other, or made life unbearable for the most recently arrived postulants, he maintained that these Sisters were being tempted by the devil. He refused to call them to order or to take steps to prevent a recurrence of such unacceptable behaviour. Neither then nor later could he accept the possibility that his two special favourites, Ignatius and Angela, might have been deceiving him and been the proximate causes of much of the trouble.[65] In fact,

---

63. Sr Angela to MM, 13 March & 23 April 1872; to Woods, 29 April 1872. Tappeiner to his General, 14. Woods to MM, 18 March, 12 May, 2 June 1870 and 29 April 1872.
64. Sr Maria Healy to MM, 28 August 1870. Sr Teresa McDonald to MM, 12 June & 28 August 1870. Sr Josephine McMullen to MM, 25 June & 25 August 1870.
65. Woods to MM, 1 & 12 August, 27 September & 11 October 1870. On 27 September, he complained to her that some who had witnessed the disturbances at the convent had thought them all 'human'. Sr Ignatius to MM, 5 October 1870. Tappeiner to his General, 13–15.

he complained to Mary that some of those who had witnessed the disturbances at the convent thought them to be of human origin![66]

Matters reached crisis point at Easter 1870, soon after Vicar General, Father John Smyth called one Father Patrick Keating to Adelaide to face several charges regarding alleged misconduct towards children attending the Josephite school at Kapunda. On the Tuesday of Holy Week, someone rifled the tabernacle in the Franklin Street convent chapel. The Sisters were shocked and hurriedly called Woods, who was most upset. At first, he suspected Keating, who would have made a convenient scapegoat, but was forced to abandon that idea when he ascertained that this priest could not possibly have been in the area at the time.

Next, Woods decided that the whole thing was nothing short of miraculous and that God had withdrawn from them in horror at the outrage that had so recently occurred at Kapunda. He never doubted the allegedly miraculous origin of three drops of blood found on the altar cloth on the following day or of the several fires, which allegedly broke out spontaneously in the convent at about the same time and did minor damage before being extinguished. The Vicar General and clergy were much nearer to the truth when, in their alarm and annoyance, they asserted that it was the Sisters themselves who had perpetrated these supposedly mysterious crimes.[67]

Vicar General Smyth felt that he should report the whole affair to Church officials in Rome, even though he was afraid that such action could result in the suppression of the Congregation. He did not do so, however, for he became ill as a result of the stress of dealing with the accusations that Woods brought against Keating on behalf of the Kapunda Sisters. In this instance, he found the evidence so compelling that he ordered Keating to leave the diocese and return to his Irish homeland at once. Keating's friend, Father Charles Horan, was furious at both Smyth and Woods for this turn of events and declared openly that he would destroy the latter through the Sisters of St Joseph. Smyth's sudden death on 30 June 1870

---

66. Woods to MM, 1 & 12 August, 27 September & 11 October 1870. Sr Ignatius to MM, 5 October 1870. Tappeiner to his General, pp. 13-15.
67. Woods to MM, 19 April 1870.

was doubtless hastened by the persecution that Keating's friends subjected him to after he banished that priest from South Australia.[68]

After Smyth's death, Woods felt that he stood alone among a group of priests who were hostile to him and what he was trying to achieve. He longed for a strong hand to guide the local Church and prevent the many 'disturbing things' that were occurring around him. Just what those things were he did not confide to Mary, for he did not discuss diocesan business with her. He lamented:

> But now he is gone I may say that I stand absolutely alone... There is, besides this, a very strong feeling against me amongst some of the clergy... Worst of all is, a number of the clergy are determined to have the government grant back and so much are they prepared for the consequences of this, that some of the best and most influential of the clergy are openly contending that the religious teaching in the schools is not necessary; that the Sunday school would be enough, especially that the clergy have no right to be burdened with the anxieties they have to endure in providing for schools when on a mere point of no moment, the government aid would be given.[69]

Given the above, it could have been assumed that the newly founded Congregation of the Sisters of St Joseph was about to disappear from the South Australian scene.

Not all was doom and gloom however, for, as Sisters living away from the city informed Mary, they were happy in their country communities. Thus, Sister Joseph Mary Fitzgerald wrote from Kapunda:

---

68. Woods to MM, 20 May 1870. Sr Mary Joseph Dwyer to MM, 4 July & 3 September 1870.
69. Woods to MM, 20 May 1870. The government grant to which Woods refers was, in fact, not a grant. It was the wages paid to teachers in the secular state schools in South Australia. In 1851, the South Australian Government had legislated that it would support only those schools that provided 'good secular instruction, based on the Christian religion' but avoided 'all theological and controversial differences on discipline and doctrine'. The legislation forbade the use of any form of denominational catechism and only those teachers who abided by the regulations under the Act were licensed to teach and to receive payment from the Government Board of Education. *South Australian Statutes*, No. 20 of 1851.

> I am very happy, thanks to God, and like Kapunda very much, for everything seems to breathe peace and the love of God. The school is so nice and the children so good.[70]

From Rhynie in the Jesuit mission area, Sister Anne McMullen reported that the local priests were very kind to the Sisters, that they could not have daily Mass as the nearest church was five or six miles away, and that the farmers drove them to Sunday Mass.[71] Thus, while some city based Sisters were troubled by the turn of events there, others were so busy laying the foundations of the Congregation in their schools and local communities that they were unaware of the forces gathering against them.

Back in Adelaide, some priests had been complaining about these inexperienced Josephite Sisters for some time. In May 1870, when their anger at Keating's dismissal was at boiling point, Sister Ignatius reported to Mary that several of them were working to have the Congregation 'put down'.[72] Some were dissatisfied with the standard of the Sisters' work and the frequency with which Woods moved them from one school or community to another. Others complained because they had no control over the Sisters' activities in their mission areas and that finding enough money to support them was placing an unbearable burden on the people.[73]

As the months passed, priestly dissatisfaction grew. It had reached a new level of intensity by the August of that year when Ignatius wrote:

> They are remodelling all our schools and trying to do away with religion teachers. It is the Vicar's [Archdeacon Russell's] desire to put secular teachers in all the schools on Sunday, and place them entirely under the direction of secular teachers. This is not all. They are trying to undo and change

---

70. Sr Joseph Mary Fitzgerald to MM, 28 November 1868.
71. Sr Anne McMullen to MM from Rhynie, 14 December 1870. Anne was the eldest daughter of Sr Josephine McMullen's brother, Michael and his wife, Mary Anne, née O'Sullivan. She was born in Ireland on 7 March 1851, migrated to Australia with her family in 1855, joined the Josephites in December 1868, was professed on 19 March 1870 and died of consumption on 11 January 1874 aged twenty-two years and ten months.
72. Sr Ignatius O'Brien to MM, 2 May 1870.
73. See Appendix Seven for a detailed explanation of the reasons for their dissatisfaction.

our system of teaching completely. They are also trying to prevent any young person from entering the Institute as they say in a few years we will be smashed and no trace of it left in this colony.[74] (sic)

When Bishop Sheil returned home in February 1871, several of the priests concerned presented him with a list of their complaints about Woods and the Josephites. At first, he ignored them but weakened as Horan and his supporters from among the clergy pressured him to remove Woods from his positions as Director of Catholic Education and the Sisters' Spiritual Guide. They succeeded. In early August 1871, Sheil sent him away from the colony for a protracted period and, once he was gone, listened to those who were insisting that the Sisters should change the *Rules of the Institute* to suit their ideas of how religious sisters should live and be managed. Matters came to a head in September 1871, when the Josephites were in charge of forty schools, fourteen in the metropolitan area and twenty-six in the country. There had been two more country schools but, on her way home from Queensland in the previous April, Mary had called in to Penola and Mount Barker to see the Sisters, only to find that their circumstances were such as to warrant their immediate removal from those places.

She took them from Penola because Woods' successor, Father Michael O'Connor, complained that they were incapable of managing the boys and had decided to get a schoolmaster in their place. At Mount Barker, the Sisters were virtually starving because their priest, Father Timothy Murphy, refused to support them on the grounds that they were incompetent and disobedient. According to the *Irish Harp*:

> Father Murphy would not allow the Sisters to beg, he would not collect for them in the Church, they got so few school fees that they had not enough to support them, and for some days they actually lived upon raw vegetables. They sat in the dark because they had no candles and they were put to the most distressing expedients to keep their few garments in respectable repair.[75]

---

74. Sr Ignatius O'Brien to MM, 1 August 1870.
75. *IH*, 28 October 1868, 8.

When Mary reached Adelaide in late April 1871, she was keen to resume her role as foundress and leader— but that was not to be. Instead, Woods ordered her to remain at Port Adelaide and keep away from the Mother House. Then, three weeks later, he insisted that she set off with Sisters Angelica Greene (a professed sister, aged twenty-one years) and Angela Crugan (a twenty-three-year-old novice) to establish a new foundation at Port Augusta.[76] This settlement, which was some 300 kilometres north of Adelaide, was accessible only by sea and was one of the poorest and most spiritually deprived outposts in the colony. As yet, there was no Catholic church in the area. One of the Jesuit Fathers from Sevenhill visited there quarterly and celebrated Mass in a private house.

Mary stayed with the two Sisters for about a fortnight. She helped them settle in and advised them on how best to organise their school, given that fifty or so children were attending it by day, and quite a crowd of illiterate young adults (including men) was coming in the evenings. She noted that the local committee had taken a suitable house for them, its only drawback being that it became flooded whenever it rained.[77] Fortunately for those pioneer Sisters, rain was a rare event in Port Augusta!

By the end of May, Mary was free to return to Adelaide and, at last, she could begin visiting the Congregation's twenty-one remaining convents and schools in country districts, catching up with the Sisters (some of whom she was meeting for the first time), and examining the schools. These included two recent foundations in the Jesuit mission district of Sevenhill.[78] Since new foundations were made only at the invitation of the clergy, they signify Jesuit

---

76. Catherine Greene (Sr Angelica), daughter of Francis Greene and Mary, née McMahon, was born in County Clare, Ireland, in March 1850, joined the Congregation in October 1868, made her first profession in January 1870, and died at St Joseph's Convent, Kensington, in April 1917. Mary Crugan (Sr Angela) was a native of County Clare, Ireland, where she was born in June 1847. She joined the Congregation in January 1871, received the habit in April 1871 and left the Congregation in January 1872.

77. *CSC*, 12 May 1871, 218 records that they had left for Port Augusta on the *SS Lubra* on 9 May. MM to Woods from Port Augusta, 22 May 1871.

78. *IH*, 5 June 1871; Father Anton Strele SJ, 'Historia Domus', 16, noted the arrival of Sisters at Hoyleton with a view to opening a school there (Jesuit Archives, Melbourne). *CSC*, 29 July 1871, 250, reported on the opening of Auburn in late July.

confidence in the Josephites at a time when their approval ratings were low in some other parts of the colony. In fact, five of the seven convents and schools opened during 1871 were in Jesuit territory at the time of their establishment. Those at Rhynie, Hoyleton, Port Augusta, and Auburn were in the Sevenhill Mission District while the one at Magill was in the Norwood area.

In each of the places she visited, Mary examined the schools thoroughly and, while she found much that pleased her, she discovered that some of the clergy had good grounds for complaint. A case in point is that of Sister Ursula (Anne Ross) of Kadina, who was unsure whether to continue as a member of the Congregation, and who had upset the local priest at times. Mary was at Kadina in June and again in August, when illness forced her to stay longer than she had intended. While there, she had many opportunities to observe Ursula and help her to reach a decision about her future.[79]

By the end of August, Mary had spent time in all the convents and schools to the north of Adelaide but had not yet visited those in the metropolitan area or to the south of the city. It is likely that she intended to see them later in the year but that did not happen. During the month of September 1871, the Congregation faced a major crisis and its extinction was a distinct possibility.

Bishop Sheil, who had always appeared to be fully supportive of the Sisters and their work, succumbed to pressure from Horan and his clique to enforce their proposed changes to the Sisters' rule. As already mentioned, in early August he sent Woods to New South Wales to arrange with Bishop Matthew Quinn of Bathurst for the establishment of one or more Josephite foundations in his vast diocese.[80] This task completed, he became involved in a busy round of missions and retreats and there was no question of his immediate return to Adelaide.[81] In fact, it appears that Sheil asked Archbishop Polding of Sydney to keep Woods in his diocese for as

---

79. MM to Woods from Wallaroo, 30 August 1871.
80. Quinn had visited Adelaide in the previous June to check whether the Josephites would be suitable for his diocese. He had been so impressed with their schools that he had asked Sheil for Sisters for Wentworth and Bourke on the River Darling in western New South Wales.
81. In this context, a mission was a series of sermons and religious activities held in a particular area with a view to reinforcing the faith of believers and bringing back to the church any careless or lapsed members of the community.

long as possible.[82] It also appears that once Woods was gone, Sheil expected the Sisters to be more accepting of his proposed changes! What he did not realise was that he was underestimating the courage, strength and commitment of Mary MacKillop and the other 'colonial women' with whom he was dealing.[83]

Matters came to a head during mid-September when Mary made it clear to the bishop that she could not in conscience remain a member of the Congregation if he changed the rule according to which she had made her vows.[84] Sheil was furious at her and took the dramatic steps of excommunicating (cutting off or banishing) her from the Church and attempting to disband the Congregation.[85]

Mary's excommunication caused major disruptions in the life of the Catholic Church in Adelaide, and, in particular, to the successful Catholic Education System that Sheil and Woods had put in place. But the Education System did not fail! More than half the priests with Josephite schools in their mission districts considered Mary's sentence of excommunication to be invalid, and encouraged the Sisters to remain where they were and carry on with their teaching or charitable works. The remainder dispensed the Sisters in their areas from their religious vows and evicted them from their schools.

Overall, fifty-one Sisters were forced (or sought permission) to lay aside their religious habits, while sixty continued wearing theirs and working in their various ministries. Seventeen schools closed while twenty-one remained open.[86] The Orphanage, Refuge and Providence struggled for survival but managed to continue operating until the crisis passed. The troubles in Adelaide did not impinge upon the status of the Sisters across the border in Queensland.

---

82. At the time, neither Woods nor anyone else realised that he would never minister in Adelaide again. He returned briefly in mid-1872 but, when he was informed that he could no longer be the Sisters' director, he left for good.
83. Marie T Foale, *The Josephite Story*, 88
84. MM to Sheil from the steamer 'Kangaroo', 10 September 1871.
85. An excommunicated person is one who is cut off from the active life of the Church, cannot enter a church while living, and may not be buried in consecrated ground. Anyone who associates with an excommunicated person risks being excommunicated.
86. See Appendices Five & Six for details regarding the locations of these schools and the clergy in charge.

While some clergy scrambled to find suitable lay teachers to replace the Sisters, school closures sent many children back to the streets or to their homes with few prospects of attending school in the near future. Sheil soon realised the effect of his recent actions on the Catholic schools in the diocese as a whole and that he had no way of paying off the outstanding debt of £2,000 owing on the Franklin Street convent. In mid-November, therefore, he offered the convent and its associated school to the Dominican Sisters with the proviso that they pay off the debt and enrol the Josephites' former pupils.

The Catholic community of Adelaide was thrown into chaos. Those who remained loyal to the Sisters supported them as far as they could while a Protestant lady ensured that Mary had a roof over her head. Both the Catholic and the secular press made the affair public and, in so doing, halted the destruction of the Congregation. Several Catholic laymen, including James Woods (father of young Sister Mechtilde and brother of Father Julian) took the unprecedented step of writing to Church authorities in Rome on the Sisters' behalf.

These men described recent events in Adelaide and begged the Roman authorities to inquire into diocesan affairs. Their letter alerted the most senior officials of the Church Universal to Adelaide's troubles and proved a catalyst for action. Almost at once, they set up an Ecclesiastical Commission to look into what was happening in Adelaide and take steps to restore order there. Thus, it was the Catholic laity who brought this work of destruction to a halt and set in motion the processes, which ultimately led to the official restoration of the Congregation.[87]

Generally, there was much confusion among the Catholic community and this in turn led to the development of ill feeling among the various parties. Mary herself refused to criticise the bishop or any of the priests concerned, and strongly discouraged the Sisters from indulging in such criticism. While some of the Sisters who were expelled from the convent returned to their families,

---

87. Adelaide Catholic laymen to Cardinal Barnabo, 5 December 1871, SOCG 1873, vol 1000, ff. 1332-1347. JD Woods, CJ Fox, JA Allison, W de Normanville, DA Barker, and J Plunkett, all of whom were leading members of the Adelaide Catholic community, signed this letter. JD Woods was Julian's older brother. Ellen, his sixteen-year-old daughter, had taken her vows as Sr Mechtilde on 24 September 1870.

Mary did what she could to keep the rest together and encouraged them to continue living as a religious community in so far as that was possible. Thanks to her long-time friend, Emanuel Solomon, a respected leader of the local Jewish community, she had access to suitable accommodation for the homeless Sisters in one of his houses in Dorsetta Terrace, Flinders Street, Adelaide. Mary described their position as follows:

> There are now a great number of Sisters out of the Habit, living in community together in a house which I think I before told you, was kindly lent to us by a Jew. They are supported by sewing and by the kindness of the people.[88]

The income from these sources was insufficient for the support of these penniless women who had lost what little revenue they had been receiving from the schools. Mary, therefore, encouraged some of the older members of the community to find positions where they could earn a wage. Among these was Sister Monica Phillips (aged thirty-six years) who sent £5 from her earnings to help pay a bill. Sisters Ita Moriarty (aged thirty-seven), Philippa Callaghan (aged thirty-four), and Gonzaga Lynch (aged twenty-eight) together provided most of the money required to support the novitiate which Mary maintained at Dorsetta Terrace throughout this difficult time. As she put it: 'It is truly wonderful how God keeps this place up. What we cannot buy we do without.'[89]

Sisters Laurence O'Brien[90] and Raymond Smyth,[91] both of whom were seventeen years old at the time, and, as already noted, were to

---

88. MM to her mother, 22 November 1871; to Woods, 19 December 1871. See Eric Richards, 'Solomon, Emanuel', *ADB*, vol 6. (National Centre of Biography, Australian National University, 1976).
http://adb.anu.edu.au/biography/solomon-emanuel-4623/text7613
89. MM to Woods, 14 February 1872.
90. Sr Laurence (Veronica) O'Brien, was born in Ireland, 23 December 1853, migrated with her parents, 1855, joined the Josephites, 15 February 1869, was professed, 2 July 1870, served in Queensland, 1872–1879, was Superior General, 1918–1931, and died at Kensington, 24 August 1945, aged ninety years.
91. Sr Raymond (Mary) Smyth was born at Kapunda, 28 December 1853. She joined the Josephites on 23 December 1869, was professed on 19 March 1871, led the first Josephite foundation to New Zealand in 1883, was Provincial leader there, 1889–1896 and 1901–1917, and died in Auckland, 4 May 1917, aged sixty-four

hold important leadership roles in the Congregation in later life, were taken home by their mothers. These two young women refused to stay away from the community, however, and so, somewhat reluctantly, Mrs O'Brien and Mrs Smyth returned them to Mary's care. In January 1872, when she responded to an urgent appeal from Woods that she send more Sisters to Brisbane, she decided that Sisters Laurence, Bonaventure Mahony (aged thirty-one), Agnes Smith (aged twenty) and Gertrude Wright (aged twenty-two) should be the ones to go. When these young women left Adelaide, they were dressed in lay clothes, but were confident that they would be able to resume the wearing of their habits when they reached their destination because Bishop Quinn had not disbanded his Sisters.[92]

Although still under the shadow of her excommunication, Mary kept Woods, who made no attempt to return home, up to date regarding events in Adelaide. On 5 February 1872, she informed him that all the Sisters were doing well and that the novices had made a retreat under the guidance of Father Hinteroecker SJ. She added that nineteen-year old Casimir Meskill had left her parents' home to be with the community and was now living in the Auburn convent with Sister Bridget Cremen, who still wore her habit.[93]

About ten days later, Mary reported that Sister Gertrude Hayman was sadly persecuted at her home and would, she thought, have to run away.[94] The difficulty for Gertrude was that the Catholic community was divided over the issues surrounding Mary's excommunication, and that some members of her family, especially her father, supported the clergy who were working against Woods and the Sisters of St Joseph.

Mary treated Gertrude with great gentleness and understanding and allowed her to take her time in deciding whether to resume her religious habit or not. Eventually she did so, and went on to do good work in South Australian schools and later on in New South Wales and Victoria. She was leader of the first Josephite community to go to Victoria in December 1889 and spent many years ministering to the

---

years.
92. Woods to MM, 14 November and 19 December 1871.
93. MM to Woods, 5 February 1872.
94. MM to Woods, 14 February 1872.

underprivileged of that state before moving to New South Wales, where she died in 1929.

During this uncertain time some Sisters, who wondered where they stood in relation to the Church, were comforted by the fact that several members of the clergy were supporting them openly. These priests allowed those who had been forced to take off their habits to join the fully functioning communities in their mission districts. Mary showed her appreciation for the backing of these men when she told her mother:

> Some of the priests are already openly suffering in the cause of the Congregation. May God bless them. They have proved themselves sincere and fearless friends.[95]

The Jesuits from Norwood and Sevenhill were outstanding in the way they assisted the Sisters. In particular, Father Joseph Tappeiner SJ of Norwood did everything to ensure that any Josephites in his district were well cared for.[96] In December 1871 Mary reported to Woods that:

> Three of the Sisters are going to stay at Magill to make one less at the convent. Sisters Calasanctius and Christina are with Sister M Joseph at Hectorville, and Sisters M Aloysius, Francesca Mary and Mary Francis at Magill. Poor Father Tappeiner has gone out today in the rain to see to their comforts. He is so watchful and kind.[97]

With time, Sheil, whose health was failing rapidly, regretted his hasty actions. Then, on 22 February 1872, five months after the event, he lifted Mary's sentence of excommunication and restored her to her position as leader of the young Congregation. He died several days later, on 1 March 1872. Subsequently, Dublin born Father Christopher Augustine Reynolds (1834–1893), formerly parish priest of Gawler, became administrator of the diocese. (Reynolds, who had migrated

---

95. MM to her mother, 22 November 1871.
96. Father Joseph Tappeiner SJ was born in Austria in 1820. He was ordained priest in 1846, migrated to South Australia in 1853, and served at Sevenhill in the Mid-North until 1869 when he became the first parish priest of Norwood. He remained there until his death in February 1882.
97. MM to Woods, between 19 & 23 December 1871. Magill and Hectorville were suburban settlements in the Jesuits' Norwood mission district.

to Australia as a young adult, was ordained to the priesthood in Adelaide in 1860.)[98] Soon after Reynolds' appointment to his new role, the Sisters, many of whom had suffered greatly during this uncertain time, began asking about the possibility of their being restored to their habits sooner rather than later. Thus, Sister Francis Xavier Amsinck wrote to Mary, possibly speaking for others besides herself:

> In case we are to resume our habits, will you try and find me a veil, for mine was taken from my habit, a rather dark one? Also please make enquiries about my poor Crucifix... It would be nice if we could resume our habits on St Joseph's day in St Ignatius' Church.[99]

Reynolds, who was aware of the Sisters' suffering, wasted no time in fulfilling Francis Xavier's wish. He arranged with Father Tappeiner to reinvest in their religious habits those Sisters who wished it on 19 March 1872, their patronal feast day. They held this ceremony in St Ignatius Church. Mary reported to Father Woods, who was still in New South Wales, on this and a subsequent similar event, held in the same place. She wrote:

> On our glorious Patron's night, 11 of us [professed Sisters] received back our Habits and openly renewed our vows in St Ignatius' Church—and yesterday, feast of our loved Mother's Dolours, 17 more at 11 o'clock. Of these latter, three renewed their vows, four novices resumed their habits, four postulants received theirs, and six novices were professed. The ceremony, between the sermon by Father Hinteroecker and the other parts by Father Tappeiner, was long, there being so many repetitions it took three hours... Father Tappeiner had to act for you by desire of Father Reynolds.[100]

All told, thirty-seven of the fifty-one Sisters who were dismissed from the Congregation resumed their habits then or during the next

---

98. Ian J Bickerton, 'Reynolds, Christopher Augustine (1834–1893)', *ADB*, (National Centre of Biography, Australian National University, 1976). http://adb.anu.edu.au/biography/reynolds-christopher-augustine-4470/text7293
99. Francis Xavier Amsinck to MM from Morphett Vale, early March 1872.
100. MM to Woods, 23 March 1872.

few weeks, while fourteen of these women decided that Josephite Religious Life was not for them and moved elsewhere.

During Woods' absence from the colony, Mary assumed her rightful position as leader of the Congregation. Even so, she kept him informed of all that was happening, including her decisions regarding the Sisters' appointments and the management of their affairs. Whenever she saw the need to act decisively in ways that might not please him, however, she did so even though she knew that her actions might upset him.[101]

Woods appeared to be in no hurry to return to Adelaide, even travelling as far as Brisbane to visit the little community there. While in that city he learnt that the Josephites would be welcome in many parts of Queensland and pleaded with Mary for reinforcements from Adelaide. For her part, she begged him to be less hasty in sending Sisters out on mission before they had spent some time in formation and had had some training as teachers. She wrote:

> No house in Adelaide has had the opportunities, the uninterrupted calm of the Brisbane community. But can we not try to have something more settled now, try to be less hurried in our movements and less frequent in our changes?[102]

It was 1875 before she sent any more Adelaide Sisters to Queensland!

While Mary was busy organising the novitiate, deciding the Sisters' appointments and so on, forces continued to work against her and the Congregation. In particular, Father Charles Horan, the architect of the whole fiasco, was furious because Sheil passed over him and appointed Reynolds, who was eight years his senior, as administrator of the diocese. He did his utmost to turn members of the Adelaide Catholic community against Woods and the Sisters, especially by publishing his panegyric for Bishop Sheil. The greater part of this sermon, which he delivered at the one month anniversary (month's mind) of Sheil's death, was nothing more than a malicious attack on Woods, Reynolds, and the Sisters of St Joseph.[103]

---

101. MM to Woods, 22 January 1872.
102. MM to Woods, 2 April 1872.
103. Charles Horan, *Funeral Oration on the Right Rev Dr Sheil OSF* (Adelaide: Advertiser Press, 1872), *passim*.

Soon afterwards, the editor of the *Protestant Advocate*, a paper noted for its anti-Catholic bias and rhetoric, published two letters, and a lengthy article aimed at destroying the wider community's trust in them. Much of the information contained in these writings was drawn from Horan's sermon. The letter writer, James McLaughlin, headmaster of a Catholic boys' school at Port Adelaide and a Catholic himself, accused the Sisters of being 'drunkards, thieves, blasphemers, prostitutes and murderesses' and denounced Reynolds as 'an ignorant, blind tyrant' who participated in the Sisters' alleged crimes by offering them his protection. As for Woods, McLaughlin declared that he was no more than a dreamer who went about with his head in the clouds.[104]

Whatever the result McLaughlin or the paper may have hoped for, it did not eventuate. Reynolds and James Woods, whose daughter Ellen (Sister Mechtilde) was one of the maligned Sisters, initiated proceedings for libel against the paper's editor, James Lewis. Mary was called to give evidence at the subsequent criminal proceedings, which were heard in the Supreme Court on 5 and 6 June 1872. The case was decided in favour of the prosecution because the defendant could not substantiate the charges he had laid against the Sisters. He was gaoled for six months and fined £50. The jury recommended mercy on the grounds that, when the paper went to print, Lewis had believed in the truth of the statements in question because they came from a Catholic source.[105]

---

104. *Protestant Advocate*, Adelaide, 6 & 13 April 1872. James McLaughlin was headmaster of the Port Adelaide Grammar School, St Vincent St, Port Adelaide. *SCCH*, 20 April 1868, Report of CEC lists McLaughlin as affiliated with the Catholic system. The Eighteenth Annual Report of the Central Board of Education lists him among teachers licensed by the state. *SAGG*, 14 April 1870. The reasons behind his transfer from the Catholic to the state system have not been found. *SAPP*, 1875, no. 26, lists McLaughlin as having a 'Second Class A' teachers' certificate from the South Australian Education Department. He seems to have been very sensitive to any imputations against his character and, in *IH*, 4, 11 & 18 November 1871, threatened to take action for libel against anyone who might suggest that he was responsible for the correspondence (concerning the Sisters of St Joseph and the bishop) that was then appearing in the *IH* and the Adelaide dailies. MM to Sr Andrea Howley, 26 April 1872, wrote that 'Mr McLaughlin of the Port' was the author of the letters against the Sisters and Reynolds.
105. *IH*, 8 June 1872, 3 (an account of court case copied from the *Advertiser*).

For his part, Lewis came to rue the fact that he had accepted the material without checking its veracity or having the writer append his name, even though he knew that person's identity. It seems that his reasons were mercenary rather than vicious for, as the counsel for the prosecution, Samuel Way QC, put it in his summing up of the case:

> The object of publishing the letters was to make the paper go. He [Lewis] knew that a publication of such a character would secure for his paper the widest possible circulation amongst those people who were ready to believe any slander uttered in respect to persons not connected with the Church to which they belonged, and amongst those whose prurient inclinations led them to like reading nasty, indelicate garbage. There could be little question that the view with which the libel was inserted was to sell the paper and to increase its circulation.[106]

The outcome indicates that Lewis had seriously miscalculated Protestant interest in a local Catholic quarrel. At the initial police court hearing, he agreed to give up the name of the writer, to pay costs and to make a public apology to the parties concerned, but then changed his mind and allowed the case to proceed to the Supreme Court.

According to the editor of the *Irish Harp*, Lewis

> backed out of it, apparently because he thought a great demonstration would be made on his behalf, that he would become a great Protestant martyr, and would make a good thing out of the subscriptions which would be collected for him.[107]

If this were so, the result was disappointing. A single contributor to the *Register* bewailed the fact that no one had come forward to express sympathy for a man who, that writer believed, had received an unduly harsh punishment. The Reverend Henry Hussey, a Baptist

---

106. JJ Bray, 'Way, Sir Samuel James (1836–1916)', *ADB*, (National Centre of Biography, Australian National University, 1990) http://adb.anu.edu.au/biography/way-sir-samuel-james-9014/text15875.
107. Leading article, *IH*, 8 June 1872.

minister and a regular contributor to the *Protestant Advocate*, was disappointed at the general Protestant reaction, although he did notice that the paper's circulation increased marginally for a time. Whatever the aims of those initiating this affair, it passed off rather quietly and, if anything, increased public sympathy for the Sisters and their friends.[108]

While this court case was in process, Bishops Matthew Quinn of Bathurst and Daniel Murphy of Hobart arrived in Adelaide with full authority from Rome to set up an Episcopal Commission to look into the troubled situation there. As already mentioned, the move for this event originated with the letter that the laity sent in the previous December. It arrived in Rome at some time in January, and, as Bishop Sheil lay dying, the wheels of Roman power were set in motion and its intervention in Adelaide affairs was not far off.

On 29 February 1872, the day before Sheil's death, Cardinal Barnabo wrote to five members of the Australian hierarchy concerning these affairs. In his letter, he announced the appointment of Bishop Daniel Murphy of Hobart as official visitor, and explained that his role was to check the facts, refer his findings to Church authorities in Rome, and take any immediate measures he considered necessary in order to restore peace and order.[109] Archbishop Polding invited Bishop Matthew Quinn of Bathurst to accompany Murphy to Adelaide.

The two bishops arrived on the day the Commission was scheduled to begin, and over succeeding days invited all parties concerned to give their evidence about the state of the diocese and, in particular, about the events surrounding Mary's excommunication. Witnesses included Mary herself, Sisters Teresa McDonald, Ignatius O'Brien, Paula Green and Monica Phillips, Fathers Woods, Horan and several other priests and also a representative of the lay letter writers.

At the end of their investigation, the bishops declared that they had found Mary to be innocent of any wrongdoing and gave their

---

108. Reynolds to Barnabo, 23 May 1872, f. 1323. Report of Hearings in the Supreme Court, *Register*, 26 April & 1 May 1872, 2 and 6 & 7 June 1872, 2. *IH*, 8 June 1872.
109. Propaganda Archives, Letters, 1872, I, vol. 367: Barnabo to Sheil, ff. 279-280; to Murphy of Hobart, ff 280-282; to J Quinn of Brisbane, ff. 282-283; to JA Gould of Melbourne, ff 283-284; to JB Polding of Sydney, ff 284-285.

blessing to the Congregation and its work. They decided, however, that Woods, who had returned to Adelaide to appear before the Commission, lacked the qualities required of a spiritual director for Sisters and was to cease acting in this role forthwith. He was heartbroken and, despite the fact that Reynolds offered him a post in the diocese, he left Adelaide to begin a missionary and scientific career in the eastern colonies. He never returned to South Australia.[110]

Woods went away, seemingly determined to circumvent the Commissioners' ruling that he refrain from having any dealings with the Josephites. In particular, the very thought of leaving the guidance of his special protégées, the so-called visionaries, to someone other than himself proved too much. He hastily arranged for four of them, under the leadership of Mary Jane O'Brien, the former Sister Ignatius, to sever all association with the Congregation and move to Camden near Sydney in New South Wales. His idea was that they should live a quasi-contemplative religious life as they supported themselves by whatever work might become available to them, especially needlework or other handcrafts.[111]

With Woods gone, it fell to Mary to oversee the restoration and expansion of the Congregation into the future. The loss of their Father Director came as a blow to many of the Sisters. They had known and trusted him ever since their entry into the community and could scarcely imagine being without his encouraging presence. For some this was too hard and they left the Congregation. Others, like Mary, accepted the Commissioners' decision as being God's Will for them and carried on with their lives under the guidance of Father Tappeiner, whom the Commissioners appointed to replace Woods as their spiritual director.

As the drama and the tragedy of the events described above were played out, certain Sisters stood out as being women with significant initiative or leadership skills. Sister Teresa McDonald was one who made an impression during that difficult time when Mary was in Queensland and Woods was deferring to his favourites. Woods

---

110. Final Report of the Apostolic Commissioners, Daniel Murphy (Bishop of Hobart-town) and Matthew Quinn (Bishop of Bathurst), 10 July 1872. ACA.
111. Woods to MM, 20 May, 15 August, 15 September, 3 October 1872 and 24 June 1875.

himself had appointed her Provincial during Mary's absence and, therefore, he should have ensured that she was living at the Mother House. Instead, he sent her to Mitcham and she was unable to influence happenings at the Mother House. While at Mitcham, however, she used her leadership skills within a much smaller sphere of activity. In particular, she demonstrated her natural empathy and strength of character when dealing with mentally ill Rose Cunningham who was committed to a mental asylum in July 1871.

Others who deserve mention are Sisters Calasanctius and Andrea Howley, Monica Phillips, Bernard Walsh, Francis Xavier Amsinck, Gertrude Hayman, Michael and Hyacinth Quinlan and Raymond Smyth. All were to play significant roles in the future development of the Congregation.

For its part, the Congregation was six years old and had survived a crisis of epic proportions. The Sisters' enforced inactivity over the previous several months had enabled them to reflect more deeply on the meaning of Josephite religious life in the light of the instructions they had received from Mary and Woods and their recent experiences. The Congregation was gradually taking shape as one well suited to conditions in Australia and New Zealand. Consequently, those who now gathered around Mary were stronger and more mature women who looked towards the future with hope.[112]

In fact, these ninety-two women were the founding Josephites, the only ones to have enjoyed instructions from both Julian Woods and Mary MacKillop during their time of formation. They had come with enthusiasm for the cause, had gone willingly wherever they were sent and had often worked in difficult circumstances. As their surviving letters indicate, they carried on in what Woods described as "the spirit of what I consider the Institute was intended to be."[113]

Some had already left Adelaide to minister in Queensland and New South Wales. Many more would follow them there or make new foundations in other colonies. The only major Josephite foundations that did not have one or more of these founding Sisters among

---

112. For a more detailed analysis of the events mentioned above see: Marie T Foale, *The Josephite Story*, Chapters 5 and 6
113. Woods to MM, 13 June 1875. See *Mary MacKillop and her Early Companions: A Collection of Letters from 1866 to 1870*, edited by Sheila McCreanor (North Sydney: Trustees of the Sisters of St Joseph, 2013).

them were at Goulburn and Lochinvar in New South Wales. During the course of their lives, some of the founding Sisters ministered in more than one Australian colony/state while several crossed the Tasman to work among the people of New Zealand. Fifty-two lie buried in South Australia, thirty in New South Wales, five in Victoria, one in the Maryborough General Cemetery in Queensland, and two in New Zealand. Teresa McDonald is in the Josephite cemetery at Perthville, near Bathurst, NSW while Hyacinth Quinlan's grave is in Hobart, Tasmania.

Future Mother General, Sr Baptista Molloy, as a very young Sister

Srs Hilda & Mechtilde McNamara

Sister Hyacinth Scanlan whose mother donated a large sum of money towards the cost of the 1905 building at Kensington

Sr Leonard Schmidt

Sr Bernardine Ledwith who spent her whole life at the Refuge.

Sr Elizabeth Etheridge, the first Josephite Aged Care Nurse.

Sr Aloysius O'Leary.

The Franklin St Chapel
where Mary MacKillop's excommunication took place.

> **MARY MACKILLOP**
> (1842 — 1909)
> MARY RECEIVED SHELTER AND SUPPORT HERE
> FROM MEMBERS OF THE SOCIETY OF JESUS.
> SHE AND TEN SISTERS WERE READMITTED TO
> THE HABIT OF THE INSTITUTE IN THIS CHURCH
> ON MARCH 17TH 1872.
> MARY LIVED IN THE PARISH FROM 1871 TO 1883.

Bishop Lawrence Sheil,
1866–1872

St Ignatius Church, Norwood.
Plaque acknowledging that this was where the
Sisters were reinvested in their habits in 1872.
(NOTE: Date should be 19th.)

St Francis Xavier's Cathedral and Hall, site of Mary's first Adelaide school.

Chapter Two
Establishing An Identity: 1872–1883

The Episcopal Commissioners left Adelaide on 2 July 1872. In his sermon in St Francis Xavier's Cathedral on the previous Sunday, Bishop Quinn declared that he and Bishop Murphy had the utmost confidence in the Sisters of St Joseph. He confirmed the Commission's finding that the Sisters were innocent of all charges brought against them before or during the Commission and ratified Mary MacKillop's position as leader of the Congregation. In conclusion, he urged the people to prove their loyalty to the Church by obeying Father Reynolds for as long as he was administrator of the diocese.[1]

It appears that, while he was in South Australia, Quinn neither heard nor saw anything that gave him cause to withdraw his request for Sisters of St Joseph for his diocese. This is borne out by the fact that, prior to his departure from Adelaide, he finalised arrangements for three Sisters to make a foundation there as soon as possible.

With Woods gone, Mary took full responsibility for the appointment of Sisters to the different convents and schools and for the choice of those to make the Bathurst foundation. To place every Sister in a position that matched her abilities was a challenging task, and one that became more difficult when Father Reynolds, acting in his role as administrator of the diocese, asked for Sisters for the schools at Hamley Bridge and Stockport, two outstations of the Gawler mission area. She also needed to consider the welfare of all her Sisters, those who had carried on virtually

---

1. For a fuller treatment of this period of Josephite history, see Marie T Foale, *The Josephite Story*, Chapter 6.

undisturbed throughout the recent upheaval and those who had suffered great hardship during this time.

Mary's correspondence with Woods during the weeks prior to the Commission shows that she agonised over these appointments, giving special consideration to each Sister's willingness and ability to form community with the others appointed to the same 'destination'.[2] Mary did not include in her final list the three charitable institutions, with their specially trained staff who seldom moved elsewhere, or the names of the professed Sisters and novices who were residing with her in the house at Norwood.

What follows is her first destination list, copied from an original in her own handwriting. (Where possible, family names have been added as a means of better identifying the Sisters concerned).

APPOINTMENTS, JUNE 1872[3]

Port Augusta	Srs Angelica [Greene], Sylvester,[4] and I do not yet know the third. [Sic]
Robe	Srs Michael [Quinlan] and Veronica [Champion]
Yankalilla	As you left it [reference to Woods]
Willunga	Srs M Josephine [Mahony] and Lucy [Crowley]
Morphett Vale	Srs F Xavier [Amsinck], Helena [Myles], Modesta [Noonan]
Marion	Srs Hyacinth [Quinlan] and Joseph [Lonergan]
The Peninsula [Kadina, Moonta and Wallaroo]	Srs Joseph [Hearney or O'Brien], Gertrude Mary [Bertheau], Agatha [Nolan], Dorothea [Ryan] and Germaine [Scanlon]

---

2. MM to Woods, collected letters, April – June 1872, with particular reference to that of 13 April 1872. 'Destination' or 'Destie' is a term used by Josephites to indicate the place and/or ministry to which they have been appointed.
3. Handwritten copy dated 18 June 1872. The author has added Sisters' family names in order the better to identify them. These did not appear in the original text in MM's hand.
4. This Sister's name does not appear in the Register and hence, she must have either changed her name or else left the Congregation before she 'received the habit', that is, became a novice and was entitled to wear the Josephite religious habit.

Clare	Srs Josephine [McMullen], Ambrose [Hughes], Raymond [Smyth], Barbara [Otto?], Alphonsus [Drislane]
Burra	Srs John Baptist [Fitzgerald], Vincent de Paul [Smith], Mechtilde [McNamara]
Auburn	Srs Bridget [Cremen] and Casimir [Meskill]
Rhynie	Srs Alexis [Sheedy] and Margaret [O'Loghlen]
Tarlee	Srs Anne [McMullen] and Ludwina [Ford]
Stockport	Srs Maria [Healy], Magdalen [O'Brien], F Borgia [McNally]
Hamley Bridge	Srs Collette [Conway] and Stanislaus [Lyddy]
Gawler	Srs Aloysius [O'Leary], Anselm [Smith], M Felix [O'Rourck], Eulalie [McDermott]
Kapunda	Srs Bernard [Walsh], Augustine [Brady], Clare [Brown, possibly at St Johns],[5] Srs Joseph Mary [Fitzgerald] and Aloysius [Lenihan] a postulant, Marianna [Wall], Raphael [McKeown]
Marrabel	Srs M Raphael[6] and Mary Anne [Byrne] Hectorville Srs M Joseph [Dwyer], Matilda [Rogers], Scholastica [possibly a postulant]
Magill	Srs M Aloysius [?], Francesca [Holland] and M. Magdalen [O'Keeffe]
Greenock	Srs Gertrude [Hayman] and Catherine [Ruine]—but these last only for a time. [Sic]

As it happened, when Mary came to make her final decision regarding the Bathurst foundation, she had to change some of the appointments she had made. Her eventual choice was for Hyacinth Quinlan from Marion and Mary Joseph Dwyer from Hectorville (both of whom were twenty-two years old), to go with thirty-two year old Teresa McDonald, the leader of the little group. Mary allowed Ada Braham (Mary Joseph), also aged twenty-two, to accompany these Sisters

---

5. Sr Clare Brown is recorded as having joined in August 1872. It is possible that she was the person listed here.
6. This Sister may have been a postulant or a novice who left the Congregation before profession. Her family name has not been recorded.

when they left Adelaide on 4 July 1872.[7] On Tuesday, 16 July, after having travelled for almost two weeks, they reached their destination, 'The Vale'. (Later on, this small settlement near Bathurst became known as 'Perthville'.) The Sisters settled in quickly and opened their school on Monday, 22 July.[8]

By the end of June 1872, most of the South Australian Sisters were at work in their ministries of teaching or caring for the underprivileged. Once again, they were in a position where they were able to follow the daily timetable Woods had drawn up for them in 1867. They rose at 5 am, gathered in their tiny oratories or chapels at 5.25 am for morning prayers and meditation. Then followed further vocal prayers, housework and morning Mass wherever there was a priest at hand, and all this before they set out for their day's work in the schools or institutions. All told, their sixteen or seventeen-hour days were punctuated by at least four hours of community prayer and meditation. The Mass and most of their common vocal prayers, such as the Lord's Prayer and the Hail Mary, were spoken in Latin.[9]

These Sisters lived in rented or church-owned houses on location, but, as a centrally governed group, they had a problem. They needed to come together from time to time for retreats, rest, recreation or study and none of the houses they occupied was large enough to accommodate them all. Nor was any one of these buildings in a sufficiently central location to be their Mother House. The diocesan owned convent in Franklin Street had served this purpose until September 1871 but as already mentioned, was now home to the Dominican Sisters.

Fathers Tappeiner and Reynolds, the priests now responsible for the welfare of the Congregation, were aware of the Sisters' predicament. Therefore, when a well-established property in suburban Kensington became available for rental they were quick

---

7. Ada Braham, also known as Mary Joseph, (1849–1877) was with Mary MacKillop in Queensland, where she tested MM's patience to its limits. On her return to Adelaide in 1871, MM appointed her to Sr Teresa's community, as Teresa possessed the patience necessary to deal with this difficult young lady. For her part, Ada loved and respected Teresa and went willingly to Bathurst with her.
8. See Marie Crowley, *Women of the Vale: Perthville Josephites, 1872–1972* (Melbourne: Spectrum Publications, 2002).
9. See Appendices Four A & Four B for details of the Sisters' daily timetable and their daily prayer schedule.

to make an offer. This extensive triangular block of land, comprising four large town blocks and surrounded by roads on all three sides, had the added advantage of being within walking distance of St Ignatius Church, Norwood. A large, eight-roomed house stood at its centre and there was a small cottage at its northern end. Father Reynolds rented this place in the name of the Catholic Church, and Mary and her Sisters moved in on 29 August 1872.

As soon as possible after this move, Mary responded to the Jesuit Fathers' request for Sisters to set up a school in the cottage on the convent grounds, and to replace the lay teacher in the Catholic school on Beulah Road, Norwood. The arrival of fourteen new postulants during 1872 helped Mary in this instance, and in her response to the priests seeking Sisters for the small country towns of Virginia and Mintaro. The newcomers also filled some of the gaps left by the Bathurst Sisters and the fourteen who had severed their affiliation with the Congregation during the previous twelve months.

The cottage school in the convent grounds could not accommodate all the local Catholic children of school-going age. Therefore, on Christmas Eve 1872, Father Tappeiner signed a five-year lease on a building in Bridge Street, Kensington (a few minutes' walk from the convent), and this became the Norwood parish school. When the lease on this property expired in 1877, Tappeiner purchased it and it served its purpose from then until 1916.[10]

The move to Kensington was a good one as the Sisters now had the security of a long-term lease on the property. Given its size and convenient location, it had potential to become the Congregation's administrative centre. Because by now there were Sisters working in three widely separated dioceses, it was important that they decide whether the Kensington convent should be Mother House for South Australia.

The bishops of Bathurst and Brisbane strongly opposed the idea of central government, that is, government by a general superior with oversight of Sisters located in more than one diocese. These men were determined to control the activities of any Sisters based in their dioceses because, judging from their experience in their Irish

---

10. Hilary Raimondo, 'Opening of St Joseph's Memorial School, [Norwood]' unpublished ms 1992.

homeland, they believed that Congregations of women religious functioned much better this way.

What the Sisters needed was some certainty as to the way in which the Congregation would be governed into the future. Both Reynolds and Tappeiner could foresee the possibility that those bishops who disagreed with the 'Rules of the Institute of St Joseph' might, like Sheil, try to enforce their ideas and, if they failed, do as Sheil had done—evict the Sisters concerned from their convents.

With a view to preserving the central government so strongly espoused by Julian Woods and Mary MacKillop, Fathers Tappeiner and Reynolds sent Mary to Rome to present the 'Rules for the Institute of St Joseph' to the pope with a view to having him give them his stamp of approval. They were confident that she would succeed in two important areas. Firstly, she would obtain security and protection from any future threat of eviction and secondly, she would ensure that all future leaders of the Congregation would know where they stood when dealing with the Church hierarchy.

Mary found it impossible to see Woods before she left Australia because he was doing missionary work in outback Queensland and could not be contacted. He was deeply hurt when he received a bundle of her letters several weeks after her departure, and no one could convince him that she was acting in good faith when she set out for Rome without his blessing.

Mary began her epic journey on 28 March 1873. Six months later, in November 1873, news of Father Reynolds' appointment as fourth bishop of Adelaide reached that city. Shortly afterwards, Archbishop Polding arrived from Sydney to preside at the new bishop's episcopal consecration. At this point, it seems that Reynolds moved into a role in which he was never comfortable. His extensive correspondence with authorities in Rome and Ireland and complaints made against him by some of his clergy indicate that he lacked a number of the qualities of a good leader.[11]

---

11. Reynolds to Kirby, 20 May 1873, ICA K206; 18 June 1873, ICA K240; 6 November 1873, ICA K412; he lamented the sad state of the diocese and his difficulties regarding money and his clergy. Reynolds to Patrick Moran, Bishop of Ossory, Ireland, 20 April & 13 July 1876, were in the same vein, ACA. So too were those to Dr William Fortune, President of All Hallows College, Dublin (1866-1891), 30 January 1875, AHC AD 18; and to Bishop James Murray of Maitland, 26 January 1875, MDA A-4-2. Diocesan priests: James Maher to Daniel Fitzgibbon,

As for Mary, she was absent from Australia for almost two years.[12] Finally, her task completed, and accompanied by fifteen young Irish women who had volunteered to become Josephites,[13] she arrived back in Adelaide in early January 1875. In her luggage, she carried documentation confirming that the Congregation had received interim Papal approval, and the newly drafted *Constitutions of the Sisters of St Joseph of the Most Sacred Heart of Jesus*.

During Mary's absence, the Sisters had carried on as before. Knowing that she would be gone for some time, and having no absolute guarantee that she would return safely, Mary had placed 'in charge' three of her most trusted Sisters, Monica Phillips, Calasanctius Howley and Francis Xavier Amsinck. She gave Sister Bernard Walsh, who was stationed at Kapunda, responsibility for the welfare of Sisters based to the north of Adelaide. These four women took their tasks seriously indeed, and led the South Australian communities wisely and well. They kept Mary informed about current events, and where necessary, took such decisions as the situation required.

Monica, who was Mistress of Novices, admitted nine new postulants into the community and presented eight or nine for their first profession.[14] She, together with Sisters Calasanctius and Francis Xavier accepted seven new foundations in the country: Georgetown, Farrell Flat, Polish Hill River and Lower Wakefield in the Jesuits' Sevenhill mission district, Port Lincoln and Blinman in the Port Augusta mission region, and Head Station in the Kapunda area. In late April 1874 Monica, writing to Mary from Kapunda, described some of these events:

> Dear Sister Calasanctius does her duty well though she thinks she is *no good*. I suppose you will be surprised to see that I am in Kapunda and away from my novices, but I have only come for a week or two to remain during Sister Bernard's absence.

---

23 February 1874, SRCO vol 10, ff 684–685. Michael O'Connor to Fitzgibbon, 22 March 1874, SRCO vol 10, ff 686–687. Fitzgibbon enclosed these two letters with one of his own to Kirby, 13 July 1874, ff 681–682, in which he complained bitterly of Reynolds' behaviour towards his clergy.

12. For details of MM's journey see her various biographies.
13. See Appendix Eight for further information re these young Irish women.
14. The exact number of Sisters who made their religious profession is unknown.

> She is going to establish a new mission on the Blinman [sic], a place up the North where the Bishop wishes to send Sisters. Sister Bridget [Cremen] and Sister Clare [Brown] are to go. It will be a long and fatiguing journey. The Bishop is here at present, he came to give Confirmation. It took place yesterday when there were about a hundred and eighty persons confirmed. His Lordship was busy hearing Confessions all Saturday and was much pleased at the numbers who approached the Sacraments. He celebrated Mass today at the Head Station about seven miles from here and will return to Adelaide on Wednesday. There are two Sisters at the Head Station, Srs Ambrose [Hughes] and Marcella [Dwyer] and they have a nice little school.[15]

The Blinman foundation was delayed by about three weeks. Then, on 21 May, Reynolds wrote informing Mary that the Sisters were 'about leaving for Blinman'.[16]

Four months later Sister Monica told of a new foundation to be made at Port Lincoln which, at that time, was only accessible from Adelaide by sea, and commented on conditions at Blinman:

> The Bishop took two Sisters to Port Lincoln on last Tuesday, Feast of the Nativity of our Blessed Mother. I hope she will obtain for them a safe passage. The Sisters who went were Srs Mary Anne [Byrne] and M Evangelista [Weir], the latter is in better health now than she used to be. Sr M Stanislaus [Lyddy] is getting on well at Hill River. Poor Sr Bridget has a wild mission in the Blinman but I hope the people will get more civilised after a time.[17]

It is impossible to discover whether the residents of Blinman became more civilised or not, for it appears that Sisters Bridget and Clare left there before the end of 1874 and did not return because, as Father Tappeiner explained to Mary:

> The Blinman mine is now standing still, people going away, so it is doubtful what will become of the school there. So far as

---

15. Sr Monica Phillips to MM, 20 April 1874.
16. Reynolds to MM, 21 May 1874.
17. Sr Monica Phillips to MM, 10 September 1874.

this they maintain their ground. Father Nevin sends them potatoes and other things as I told him he must keep them in good condition.[18]

When Mary and her youthful companions arrived home on 4 January 1875, the Blinman Sisters, and many more, had much to tell her of their doings during her absence. For their part, they would have been happy to hear of her overseas travels. She had little time for rest and storytelling, however, for according to the instructions she brought back from Rome, the Congregation was to hold its first General Chapter on St Joseph's feast day, 19 March, that is, in less than three months' time.[19] Mary explained these arrangements to the Sisters:

> You must all distinctly understand that this Chapter is called under authority, Cardinal Franchi knowing already the very day upon which the Sisters are to meet.[20] The object of it is not only to elect Superiors for the next six years, but also to have laid before it in due form the decisions of the Propaganda with regard to our Rule. In this Chapter also, all vexed and tiresome questions are to be discussed by the Sisters, subject to the approval of the Sacred Congregation.[21]

This Chapter took place according to these instructions. After much discussion and explanation of the changes to the Rule, the Chapter Sisters accepted their new Constitutions unanimously, thus confirming their commitment to central government and to the new ruling regarding the ownership of property, which read:

---

18. Fr Tappeiner in *Southern Cross & Catholic Herald*, 4 December 1874, 5.
19. In this context, a General Chapter is a gathering of the members of a Religious Congregation for the purpose of electing their leaders and making important decisions regarding the life of the Congregation. The Chapter can change the Constitutions, but Roman authorities must approve these changes before they can come into force.
20. Cardinal Alessandro Franchi (1819–1878) was born in Rome in 1819, ordained a priest in 1842 and became a cardinal in 1874. He served in the Vatican for most of his priestly life and became Papal Secretary of State in 1874, the year Mary MacKillop visited Rome.
21. MM to the Sisters, 16 January 1875.

> Besides the special property of each house, the Congregation itself may possess money, land and income.[22]

One of the Chapter Sisters' most important duties was to decide who would be their Mother General or leader for the next six years. For most the choice was easy: they elected Mary to this position with the title of 'Mother Mary of the Cross', chose Sisters Calasanctius Howley, Francis Xavier Amsinck, Francis of the Five Wounds Fitzgerald and Bernard Walsh as her councillors or advisers, and decided that for the future the Kensington convent should be their Mother House. Other Chapter decisions included one specifying that the novices were to wear white veils and were not to be appointed to communities outside the Mother House. At the conclusion of the Chapter, all Sisters present renewed their vows according to the new Constitutions.

Woods was deeply hurt by the fact that, in his view, the community accepted the Roman decision regarding the ownership of property too easily. He could not understand how the Romans could have found that the strict Franciscan poverty he advocated so strongly was unsuitable for a religious congregation of women such as the Josephites. As had been her wont in the past, Mary sent him a full account of all that had transpired at the Chapter. He was so upset at the outcome regarding poverty that it was several weeks before he could bring himself to respond to Mary's letter. He then wrote:

> It has been almost a deathblow to me to see the poverty and simplicity of the Congregation of St Joseph destroyed without my being able to say a word in its defence. I can never get used to that and it makes me sick with sorrow whenever I think of it ... No one understands the spirit of what I consider the Institute was intended to be, who does not think that the essential point of all. (Sic) Unity without poverty and simplicity is a poor privilege.[23]

For the Sisters themselves, that decision regarding property gave them a sense of security that they had lacked in the past. In fact,

---

22. *Constitutions of the Sisters of St Joseph of the Most Sacred Heart of Jesus* (Adelaide, 1875), 23.
23. Woods to MM, 13 June 1875.

Mother Mary of the Cross, (the Mother General), could now purchase the Kensington property in the name of the Congregation. Just two weeks after the closure of the Chapter, on 5 April 1875, she finalised the deal by paying the previous owner the sum of £1,000.[24]

That she was able to do so was indeed remarkable because she did not have £1000. What she did have was a very good friend who *gave* her the necessary money. As she told her mother, this 'Protestant lady friend', Mrs Joanna Barr Smith, and her husband, Robert,[25] were well known by name to Fathers Reynolds and Tappeiner for 'their generosity and liberality'. They moved in 'the highest society' in Adelaide and 'Mrs RB Smith [was] an elegant and accomplished Scotch lady, a woman of very superior mind'. Just why she was 'so singularly attach[ed]' to Mary was something that the latter could not understand.[26]

Both Robert and Joanna Barr Smith, or Mr and Mrs Barr Smith, as Mary always called them, proved generous friends who supported her and her Josephite charitable works in and around Adelaide over many years. In this instance, they paid for the property but were unable to finance the erection of the much needed new building which Mary authorised soon afterwards.

In order to do this, Mary employed architect, Michael McMullen, Sister Josephine's brother, to draw up the plans for a large functional structure of three storeys to be attached to the existing house. It was to be built of Glen Osmond stone and McMullen engaged a builder named Mr Enhill who agreed to an estimated price of 'somewhat under £2,000'. Mary found most of this money by mortgaging the property for £1,650 at seven per cent for four years. She relied on the support of other benefactors and the hard work of the

---

24. SA Lands Titles Office, Volume 331, fol 21. Transfer from Elizabeth Maine, proprietor, to Mary MacKillop of Norwood, spinster, in consideration of the sum of 1,000 pounds. Transaction appears in Registration Book 168, fol 126, tr 55649, 5 April 1875. Entered in Register, 23 September 1875. No attempt has been made to convert any sums of money cited into 21st century values because to the constantly changing value of the Australian dollar. One source has suggested that the £1000 of 1875 would have been worth $300,000 dollars in 2014.
25. See: Dirk Van Dissel, 'Barr Smith, Robert (1824–1915)', *ADB* (National Centre of Biography, Australian National University, 1976), http://adb.anu.edu.au/biography/barr-smith-robert-63/text7591.
26. MM to her mother, 21 January 1873.

Sisters to raise both the balance owing and the interest on this mortgage. At this point Mary and the Congregation unwittingly entered into a cycle of debt that was to have serious repercussions in coming decades.

Bishop Reynolds laid the foundation stone of the new building on 5 September 1875.[27] Mary, who stayed at home during the construction phase of the new building, complained bitterly about the workers' slowness and how it appeared that no one except herself was urging them on. She was particularly frustrated by the builder who seemed to be in no hurry to complete his task. As she put it:

> Both masons and carpenters tell us that Mr Enhill is much to blame. He has already received more than 75 per cent of his money. Fancy the opening to be in less than a fortnight and no painting done yet. It really is too bad.[28]

Nevertheless, she looked forward to the day when it would be ready for occupation because it would be 'nice and comfortable' for the Sisters. She enjoyed the view from the top dormitory, from where she could see 'all Kensington and for many miles around'.[29]

On Friday 5 May 1876, the following notice appeared in *The South Australian Tablet*, the Catholic newspaper of the time:

> The new Convent of the Sisters of St Joseph at Kensington will be solemnly blessed and opened on Sunday next, the 7th instant, by His Lordship the Bishop of Adelaide. Pontifical High Mass will be celebrated in the Convent Chapel at 11 o'clock and the choir of the Cathedral will be present and render Weber's Mass in G. The Very Reverend Father Cahill SJ will preach on the occasion. Admission will be by ticket only, which can be procured from any of the clergy, at the Catholic Book Depot, or at the office of this paper.[30]

This opening was a special occasion indeed, and one that was long remembered by the Sisters

---

27. *Irish Harp*, 10 September 1875.
28. MM to Sr Josephine McMullen, 4 April 1876.
29. MM to Sr Josephine McMullen, 24 April 1876.
30. *South Australian Tablet*, 5 May 1876

Thus, one decision from the 1875 Chapter was acted upon successfully with a minimum of fuss. The maintaining of central government was a different matter. The bishops of Brisbane and Bathurst both refused to accept the Chapter decision and demanded that Sisters stationed in their respective dioceses come under their jurisdiction. Consequently, and after much pain and heartache, Mary withdrew from those bishops' dioceses any Sisters who wished to retain their affiliation with the Adelaide Mother House. Her negotiations with them were long and difficult and, as a result, she was obliged to be absent from South Australia for lengthy periods during the latter half of the 1870s. This was unfortunate as at this time the Adelaide Sisters were grieving the loss of Woods and would have benefitted greatly from her continued presence among them.[31]

Despite the Commission's order that Woods cease directing the Sisters, he kept in contact with some of them until the late 1870s. In January 1874, he moved to Tasmania from where he sent at least fifteen prospective postulants to the mainland to join the Congregation in either Adelaide or Brisbane. Since most of these young women were from very poor families he provided their outfits and passage money from his own earnings and, as a consequence, he retained a strong claim on their loyalty. After Mary's return from Europe with the new Constitutions, he sent any interested young women to Bathurst instead.

Most of the Sisters whom Woods had encouraged to enter the Congregation were devoted to him and inclined to follow his suggestions implicitly, without realising how their behaviour might effect the Congregation as a whole. In Queensland where the bishop was strongly opposed to the Sisters' being affiliated with the Adelaide Mother House, Woods did his best to have them break with Mary and Adelaide. She was annoyed and tried to prevent his affecting them by controlling any correspondence between them. Some Sisters resented Mary's actions and took steps to circumvent her ruling re their letters.[32]

---

31. See Appendix Nine for details re MM's times away from SA before 1883.
32. MM to Sr Bonaventure Mahony, 13 December 1878; to Sr Josephine McMullen, 19 February, 1879; to Dr Grant, Rector of Scotch College, Rome and a former friend of her father's, 28 December 1877 & 6 September 1878; to Woods, 12 September 1879; to Mons Kirby, Rector of the Irish College, Rome, 21 April 1875,

Matters came to a head in Adelaide in July 1877, when Mary discovered that Sister Francesca O'Brien[33] (who had charge of the Solitude of Mary) and two of the Magdalens resident there had been corresponding with Woods without her knowledge or consent.[34] The Magdalens were not Sisters of St Joseph and hence did not owe Mary the same obedience as vowed members of the Congregation. Furthermore, the Sisters' role in their regard was a supervisory one, and was to continue for only as long as they needed guidance. They were irritated at the restrictions Mary placed upon them and decided to abandon their penitential life rather than submit. Francesca also refused to comply with Mary's instructions and chose, instead, to leave the Congregation without waiting to obtain a dispensation from her vows, as required by Church Law. Subsequently, the Solitude closed permanently.[35]

Mary could not understand Woods' behaviour and after this incident, the rift between them widened. Their prolific correspondence ceased and the last of Mary's letters to him makes painful reading indeed. Shortly after Francesca's departure, she wrote of him that:

> Had it not been that some of his letters were intercepted, several who are now good and happy religious would have been led away in the vain hope of joining one or other of the several Orders he has in contemplation. It is so painful that he should be like this; he is so holy and so amiable in every way...

ACA. Sr Bonaventure Mahony to MM, 20 January & 6 October 1879.

33. Sr Francesca O'Brien (1852–1938), was a younger sister to Sr Ignatius O'Brien. She joined the Congregation in 1870, was professed in 1872, and left in July 1877.
34. The Solitude, as it was known, was a small institution founded by Woods for former inmates of the Refuge who had decided to do penance for the 'wicked ways' of their past lives and to live a semi-religious life in community.
35. MM to Sr Josephine McMullen, 31 July & 22 September 1877; to Sr Josephine Carolan, 7 August 1877; to Archbishop Vaughan, 18 August 1877; to Dr Grant and Cardinal Franchi, Rome, 28 December 1877; 'Some Observations relating to the Solitude of Mary', typescript, ASSJ, 3–7. *South Australian Tablet*, 5 May 1876, 2.
George O'Neill, *Life of the Rev JET Woods* (Sydney: Pellegrini, 1928), 287, mentions a letter from the Magdalens to Bishop Reynolds informing him that they would prefer quitting their habits to being refused the right of free and unsupervised correspondence with their Father Director.

> I feel disappointed in him, and sometimes fear that unless he is more guarded he will do more harm than good.[36]

The late 1870s proved a difficult time for Woods, Mary and the Sisters as they continued to work out for themselves the meaning of Josephite religious life. A number were torn between two loyalties—to their founder and former Father Director on the one hand, and to the Congregation under Mary MacKillop's leadership on the other. For some the tension was too great. Between 1875 and 1880, at least nine of the Sisters whom Woods had trained before 1872 left the Congregation. Francesca O'Brien's case has been discussed already.

The others who left at this stage were Veronica Martin, Stanislaus Lyddy, Catherine O'Brien, Dorothea Ryan, Ambrose Hughes, Margaret Mary Fox, Gertrude Wright, Faith Daniels and Helena Myles.[37]

Some of these Sisters' close associates remained in the convent, only to cause further dissension later on because they had not yet fully resolved their dilemma. Others persevered in their loyalty to Mary and the Roman Constitution even as, like her, they continued to mourn the loss of their former guide and mentor. Sister Bonaventure Mahony echoed the feelings of this group in her response to a Sister who, it seems, was criticising Woods' behaviour towards Mary:

> As you have mentioned SM Gertrude's displeasure at your mention of FD's [Woods'] conduct towards our dear Mother [Mary MacKillop], I would venture to say she feels it but too keenly herself, as I do, to bear to have it mentioned, and the desire to hide our much loved Father Founder has made her, and me too, a bit pugnacious. Now, dear Sister, I do not doubt for an instant the sincerity of your feelings towards our poor F, [sic] but do not make his shortcomings the subject of a letter to any Sister unless obedience commands. My own natural feelings would be to knock down anyone that would speak harshly of my Father [Mr Mahony] and I believe nearly all F Founder's early children love him with as strong an affection.[38]

---

36. MM to Dr Grant, Rome, 28 December 1877, ACA.
37. Register of the Sisters, entries for 1866–1880.
38. Sr Bonaventure Mahony to Sr Josephine Carolan, 24 August 1879.

During this time of unrest, there was constant movement among the Sisters because the membership of the Congregation, and the number and locations of their schools were in a continual state of flux. The community welcomed the fifteen Irish women who arrived with Mary in January 1875, only to bid a sad farewell to one of them, Rose Kane, who died on 26 March, just a few weeks after her arrival in Adelaide.[39]

They rejoiced on 18 April 1875 when eleven of the Irish postulants received their habits, thus becoming the first ever Josephite novices to wear white veils and undertake their novitiate training in their newly designated Mother House under the guidance of Sisters Clare Wright and Monica Phillips.[40] The Sisters also rejoiced when the two Irish postulants who had decided to wait a while before entering the novitiate did so. Fourteen of the Irish women who came to Australia with Mary can be accounted for today, but it seems that one, whose name is unknown, left the group soon after they reached Adelaide. Eleven of those who entered the novitiate made their first profession in due course and accepted appointments to different convents and schools throughout the colony of South Australia and beyond.

The overall membership of the Congregation reached 200 at the end of 1875. Even so, and in spite of the profession of the Irish Sisters and the arrival of fourteen Sisters from Bathurst in early 1876, Mary still struggled to meet requests for foundations in newly settled areas of the colony. During the early 1870s, the government surveyed large tracts of land to the north and east of Port Pirie and in the mallee scrublands of the northern Adelaide Plains and Yorke Peninsula into farming blocks of up to 320 acres in area. It made these blocks available for settlement and, according to the terms of the Waste Lands Amendment Act (more often known as the Strangways Act) of 1869, a purchaser could buy a property on credit, on condition that he resided there until he paid it off. Consequently, many former labourers became landowners and there was a new wave of settlement, especially in the Mid-North region of South Australia.[41]

---

39. We know nothing of this Sister beyond that she came from Ireland with Mary and died at Kensington on 26 March. The cause of her death is not recorded.
40. MM to the South Australian Sisters, 27 April 1875.
41. RM Gibbs, *Under the Burning Sun: A History of Colonial South Australia, 1836-1900* (Mitcham: Southern Heritage, 2013), 250-256. Charles Fenner, 'A Geographical Inquiry into the Growth, Distribution and Movement of Population in South Australia, 1836-1927', in *Transactions of the Royal Society of*

The ensuing movement of people from districts close to Adelaide, including the Southern Vales (where the Josephites had foundations at Morphett Vale, Willunga and Yankalilla), the Adelaide Hills, the Kapunda region, and the northern Adelaide Plains had serious repercussions for the Catholic Church and the Sisters. Some church congregations became so small that their churches and schools closed. This was the reason for the Sisters' departure from Hoyleton and Rhynie in the Jesuits' area to the south of Sevenhill. At Undalya and Saddleworth church attendances were reduced to a mere handful and before long, priests and Sisters from these locations also moved north.[42]

The Jesuit Fathers, who had lived at Sevenhill since 1849 and whose mission area included most of the newly surveyed lands, lost no time in following the settlers. As they went, they built churches and schools in many of the new towns that were springing up. In fact, during the year 1875 alone, they completed the construction of their mission church at Sevenhill, opened six churches further to the north, and laid the foundation stones for two more.[43]

Father JE Pallhuber SJ, who had moved to Georgetown and had charge of an area to the north of Clare, appears to have been keenest of all when it came to establishing Catholic schools and staffing them with Josephites. To his mind, they were ideal for local needs because they were willing to go wherever they were asked and to live in any available accommodation, no matter how poor or inconvenient.

On 14 March 1876, Tappeiner wrote to Sister Josephine McMullen, who, by this time, was Provincial of Queensland: 'Father Pallhuber wants to open nine new schools'.[44] Such was this priest's enthusiasm that he approached Mary with a request for Sisters

---

South Australia, vol 53 (1929): 130. According to the census returns, 1866-1901, between 14.39 and 15.44 per cent of the colonists in this region was Catholic.

42. Fr Anton Strele SJ, 'Historia Domus: A History of the Jesuit Foundation in South Australia' (1876), 16. ACA.
43. Annual Letters, College of St Aloysius, Sevenhill, 1877-1882, 34, and Strele, 'Historia Domus', 22, mention new church buildings at Laura, Narridy, Port Pirie, Jamestown, Caltowie, and Yackamoorundie (now Gulnare), and foundation stones at Appila-Yarrowie and Redhill. Archives of the Society of Jesus, Melbourne.
44. Fr Tappeiner to Sr Josephine McMullen, 14 March 1876.

to manage his nine schools as soon as possible. She could not comply immediately but he did not give up. On Sunday, 14 January 1877, he informed her that:

> Everything is ready in Laura and Caltowie–Jamestown and Yarrowie are getting ready. In Laura we have to rent a cottage until we build one for them. If we can get Sisters for Laura it would be well to open school there tomorrow week. I would like to know either Thursday or Friday, to get the house ready for them. For Caltowie, His Lordship promised them for after Christmas. He saw our two rooms and approved of them until we build a cottage. Everything is ready; they will have it very convenient there with the three rooms. We would like to open school about tomorrow fortnight. The number of the children may not be very great; two Sisters would be sufficient for the teaching at first.[45]

Mary was able to supply the Sisters for Laura and Caltowie as requested and, before the year was out, sent others to Gulnare and Yarrowie.

Between 1869 and 1881 inclusive, Pallhuber and his Jesuit confreres at Sevenhill established at least twenty-two Josephite convents and schools in districts under their care. The first was at Clare, which opened in 1869. Burra, Marrabel and Rhynie followed in 1870, Port Augusta, Hoyleton, Auburn and Undalya in 1871, Mintaro in 1872, and Georgetown, Armagh, Farrell Flat/Hanson and Polish Hill River in 1873. Then came Manoora in 1875, Laura, Appila-Yarrowie, Caltowie, Mintaro Station, and Yackamoorundie (Gulnare South, now Yacka) in 1877, Sevenhill in 1879, Jamestown in 1880 and Whyte Yarcowie in 1881.[46] At the time, Mary regretted that she could not provide Sisters for Port Pirie.[47]

One may well ask why these men were in such a hurry. The answer, it seems, is that the South Australian Education Act of 1875 had made school attendance compulsory for all children aged between seven and thirteen years, and that the Catholic clergy and their people

---

45. A Sister of St Joseph, *Life and Letters of Mother Mary of the Cross* (Westmead, NSW, 1916), 251 & 268–269, citing Fr Pallhuber to MM, 1876 & 14 January 1877.
46. See Appendix One for further details of these foundations.
47. MM to Sr Bernard Walsh, 18 June 1882.

were keen to keep one step ahead of the government in dealing with the expected influx of children.[48] All were determined to maintain any advantage they already had, such as having Catholic schools in places where, as yet, there were no government schools.

Their aim was to prevent Catholic children from attending state schools because most state schoolteachers were not Catholics. Hence, they planned to get in before the government realised that the number of school aged children in an area warranted its building a school there. Pallhuber used this reasoning to pressurise Mary into action in January 1877, when he wrote:

> In four townships, government schools are nearly finished. We may lose our children if we do not try to have our schools opened before theirs.[49]

Another of the priests who was busy keeping one step ahead of the government was Bernard Nevin, a diocesan priest who took up his appointment to the Port Augusta mission area in early 1874. In February 1881, Nevin wrote to the Vicar General in Adelaide, Father Frederick Byrne, that his only chance of keeping the children from the state schools was to commence building his own at once and so 'have the start of them'.[50]

Nevin's mission district, which opened for closer settlement somewhat later than the Jesuits' area, extended from Pekina in the Mid-North to the Northern Territory border. Most of the land beyond Port Augusta was sparsely settled, with 'a small population, exceedingly poor and widely scattered over a vast extent of country' and included the small villages of Appila-Yarrowie, Tarcowie, Mannanarie, Yongala, Pekina, Melrose, Port Augusta, Blinman, Beltana, Sliding Rock, Wallerberoina and Hookina.

When he arrived in 1874, Nevin found a Josephite community at Port Augusta. Over time, he provided consistent support for their school and did what he could to improve their working conditions. He built churches at Melrose, Willochra [Hammond], Port Augusta,

---

48. 'An Act to amend the Law relating to Public Education', *South Australian Statutes*, Act No. 11 of 1875.
49. Fr Pallhuber to MM, January 1877.
50. Fr Nevin to Fr Byrne, 15 June 1880 and 21 February 1881. W Czernezkyj, *Pekina: Century and Beyond* (Adelaide, 1974), 27.

Pekina, Yatina, Orroroo and Carrieton, and invited the Josephites to establish schools in Blinman, Saltia, Pekina, Orroroo and Willochra.[51]

As already mentioned, the most distant and isolated of these was the northern Flinders Ranges village of Blinman where the Sisters stayed for less than twelve months. By the 1880s, thanks to the efforts of the Jesuits and Father Nevin, most Catholic children in the 'settled areas' had access to Catholic schools run by either Josephites or dedicated lay teachers. In some districts the Catholic school was the only one for many years. The Sisters were the first to have a school in the small town of Pekina and, until the time of writing (2014), there has not been a state school there. In 1894, the *Southern Cross* reported:

> The only school here is the one conducted by the Sisters of St. Joseph, and there are 70 children on the roll with an average attendance of about 50. As well as the ordinary education, music, singing, drawing, painting in oils, &c., [sic] are taught, and with very good results. Recently a choir was formed by the Sisters, consisting entirely of schoolchildren, and the way they play and sing the Mass and Benediction is highly creditable to both teachers and children, especially when it is remembered that the majority of the little ones are under twelve years of age.[52]

The settlers in the northern districts endured many hardships as they cleared their land, planted their crops, and waited for the harvest. During the 1870s, they experienced a succession of good years with bountiful crops but, as the 70s merged into the 80s, there were several successive years of severe drought. Many farmers were forced to abandon their holdings and those who stayed had little to show for their efforts. The Sisters were aware of their situations and made as few demands on them as possible. As already mentioned, where their housing was an issue, they accepted whatever was available, whether it was free standing or attached to a church or schoolroom.

---

51. Fr Nevin, 'Northern Areas Record Book', 2-3, Nevin to Bishop Reynolds, n.d. but *circa* 1874, and Fr F Byrne, 2 May 1879, 15 June 1880, 30 August 1880, 21 February 1881; ACA.
52. *SC* 22 May 1894.

Thus, at Farrell Flat, a settlement near Burra, the future Bishop Reynolds

> found a good school for grownup children who would have to go to the Protestant schools and the younger portion to be left in ignorance were it not for the good Sisters of St Joseph. This locality [was] poor, only newly settled, so a wretched mud hut, exposed to wind and weather, [was] the school-room by day and the convent by night. No secular teachercould be paid, nor would one live, as the Sisters, who beg for their support.[53]

In 1876, the people of Marion near Adelaide raised funds to build a convent for their Sisters, who had lived in the sacristy of the church for the previous seven years.[54] At Whyte Yarcowie likewise, the Sisters made their home in the church vestry.[55] At Georgetown, as Sister Dorothea Ryan put it:

> We are living in the church. We have the gallery divided into two parts which serve as our dormitory and community room. It is indeed quite snug. We have no cooking to do as yet because we have no fireplace.[56]

In all, the Josephites opened or reopened thirty-seven schools and nearly as many convents between 1872 and 1883. Among those reopened were Penola (1875), Glenelg (1876),[57] Bowden and Port Adelaide (1877), and North Adelaide (1878).[58] They also returned to

---

53. Bp Reynolds to Mons Kirby, 20 May 1873.
54. *South Australian Tablet*, 23 June 1876, 7. The Sisters first went to Marion in 1869.
55. Sr Magdalen Foley to MM from Whyte Yarcowie, 9 January 1881.
56. Sr Dorothea Ryan to Sr Editha Flanagan, 5 May 1873. Dorothea (Catherine Ryan) was born in London in April 1854, migrated to South Australia before 1868 when she joined the Josephites, was professed in December 1870, and left the Congregation during 1877.
57. According to MM's letters and various lists of schools and convents, the Sisters left Glenelg in September 1871 and returned in 1876. There is little information about this foundation from then until the 1890s.
58. Kensington Convent Account Book, 1875–1880, October 1877, indicates that the Sisters had returned to Bowden recently and were living at Kensington. Soon after the North Adelaide convent reopened the Bowden Sisters moved there. MM to Sr Josephine McMullen, 7 August 1877: 'We have opened the Port at last and have a large school there. The N. Adelaide new school was opened yesterday.'

the city of Adelaide, where they took charge of a school in Pirie Street in 1875, and another one in Russell Street in 1877. The total number of schools under their charge increased by only thirteen, however, because at the same time they left a number of places where the schools were no longer viable.

Taken overall, the length and permanency of the Sisters' stay in any locality depended upon the stability of the Catholic population and its ability to support them and their school.

Such was not the cause of their departure from Russell Street, however. They left that school in late 1880 and stayed away until the end of 1882 because Mary handed it over to the Sisters of Mercy. These Sisters arrived in Adelaide during 1880 to find that there was neither convent nor school ready for them. True to that tenet of Woods' *Rules of the Institute of St Joseph* of 1867, that the Sisters must 'give place and preference to the religious of every other Order, and their highest ambition must be to remain unknown and poor,'[59] Mary also offered the newcomers the Providence in Gouger Street, where the Josephite Sisters' main responsibility was the care and support of unemployed servant girls. (This did not mean that they had abandoned their ministry of care for elderly women, several of whom were in residence at this time.) The Mercy Sisters accepted Mary's offer. Sister Elizabeth Etheridge found a suitable house for rent in Flinders Street and, when the changeover occurred, she and the older women moved there. Mary described the situation thus:

> Besides my own Congregation duties, the coming of the Sisters of Mercy gave me a great deal of extra work, for we had 24 of them with us for nearly a week. We gave them up our Russell Street School and Servants' Home, which latter they will convert into a House of Mercy. They are nice Sisters and very grateful to us for helping them. At first I offered them the Port schools which I thought would give them better support, but they dreaded teaching boys, and as the place would not support a Master also, I thought it best in the interests of *charity*, and our common cause in religion, to offer them Russell Street. There is room and work enough for all, and I can now help some poorer country places.[60]

---

59. Woods, *Rules of the Institute of St Joseph*, Article 1.
60. MM to Srs Josephine and Bonaventure, 18 May 1880. Emphasis Mary's. Anne

The Sisters of Mercy purchased a property in Angas Street, Adelaide in 1882 and subsequently opened a school and erected a House of Mercy to accommodate the unemployed women in their care. The Josephites returned to the Russell Street School in 1883, and in that same year Sister Elizabeth obtained a lease on a building at the west end of Franklin Street and the Providence made its home there for the next twenty-two years.

In 1877 Mary wrote that the schools were 'increasing greatly in attendance, particularly in Pirie Street, where they [had] a new room built for the advanced children, and [had left] the present one for the infants'.[61] Existing schools were thriving but she could not fill all requests for foundations. In August 1876 she wrote from Penola that:

> Sisters are required now at Mt Gambier, Naracoorte, Millicent and Murat Bay in this district, so, if we could but supply them, this would be one of our finest Provinces. Here and at Robe, our dear ones are real missionaries, helping the priest in earnest to save souls.

Demands elsewhere were so great that this province did not come into being. Instead of making more foundations in the South East, the Sisters left Robe at the end of 1879 because of low school enrolments. This little seaport was a neglected outpost of the Penola mission and the priest rarely visited. Just before the Sisters' departure, Sister Gaetano O'Brien informed Mary that it was seven months since they last saw a priest, noting that this was a long time for the poor people to be left without the Sacraments, and that the Catholics were very glad to have the Sisters with them.[62] Nevertheless, Mary considered it better that they not remain in this lonely spot. The local Catholics, in the person of Annie Bond, begged her to send them back:

> I hope you have not forgotten your promise to send us Sisters as they are so much wanted. I have been anxiously looking for a letter saying they were coming as the little ones here will all be lost if you do not take pity on us.[63]

McLay, *Women on the Move: Mercy's Triple Spiral: A History of the Adelaide Sisters of Mercy* (Adelaide: Sisters of Mercy, 1996).
61. MM to Sr Josephine McMullen, 26 January 1877.
62. Sr Gaetano O'Brien to MM, 19 December 1878 & 15 September 1879.
63. Annie Bond to MM, 31 December 1880.

The Sisters did not return to Robe because they were needed elsewhere, especially to augment the numbers in New South Wales. Sadly, the little ones about whom Annie was concerned were forced to attend the local state school.

There were many reasons why Sisters left foundations. They moved away from Polish Hill River in 1877 because the priest in charge, Father Leon Rogalski SJ, would not allow them to do their work in peace. She wrote:

> We are removing the Sisters from Hill River to the Saltia, near Port Augusta. F. Rogalski was so hard to please that I at last advised him to get a Master, for our Sisters could not do more than they had done, and we wanted them very much for another place ... Father Nevin has been waiting so patiently for the Sisters for the Saltia. They were promised at Easter but we could not send them.[64]

They found a welcome in Saltia, a teamsters' settlement at the entrance to the Pichi Richi Pass through the Flinders Ranges between Port Augusta and Quorn. Nevin had a house ready for them when they arrived some time after 25 April 1877.[65] Little is known of their school beyond that it was small and that, with the completion of the railway between Port Augusta and Quorn in 1879, bullock teams became redundant and Saltia was abandoned. Where the Saltia Sisters went has not been recorded, but there is no doubt that they found a place in one or other of the forty-three schools for which the Congregation was responsible at the time.[66]

Another short-term foundation of the 1870s was at Lower Wakefield on the southernmost boundary of the Jesuits' Sevenhill mission and twenty-four kilometres east of Balaklava. The Sisters, who were there for the years 1873–1875, lived in a small cottage across a creek from the church. They left when most of the Catholic

---

64. MM to Sr Josephine McMullen, 11 June 1877.
65. Fr Nevin, 'Northern Areas Record Book', entry for 1877, 5, indicates that Nevin purchased allotment five at Saltia for £200 for the Sisters of St Joseph. ACA.
66. MM to Sr Josephine McMullen, 11 July 1877. Nevin, 'Northern Areas Record Book', 5. Reg G Mayes, *Pictorial History of Port Augusta* (Adelaide, 1974), 27–29.

families in the area moved north to take up land freed for use by the Strangways Act.[67]

The Catholic population in the Kapunda district also declined because of the migration of farmers to the north. When the Sisters went to Kapunda in 1868, there were more than a hundred children in their school. The number of children in the area was so great that they also made foundations at nearby St Johns in 1869, at Greenock in 1870 and Bagot's Gap in 1871. In 1870, Sister Josephine McMullen described Greenock thus:

> [It] is a nice little convent, only two rooms, but they teach in the church which is only across a paddock. It was originally a Protestant place of worship and Fr Byrne bought it when he was at Kapunda. The school is not very large but there are a number of bad Catholics[68]

For a short time between 1875 and 1880, the Sisters had two more schools in the Kapunda area. The first was at Baker's Flat, near the Kapunda Mines. It operated only during 1876 and 1877, by which time the copper was running out and families were moving away. (The mines closed altogether in 1879). The second was at Bagot's Head Station or Koonunga, several miles to the southeast of St Johns, on the road between Kapunda and Truro. Sisters were there from 1874 until 1879 when again, numbers declined and the school was no longer viable. Sisters Marcella Dwyer and Ambrose Hughes were there in 1874 when they had 'a nice little school'.[69] The Sisters left Greenock in about 1875, St Johns in 1879, and Bagot's Gap in 1883.

Freeling, to the southwest of Kapunda, was also a short-term foundation. The *South Australian Tablet* of March 1877 reported that:

> St Scholastica's new mission school has been opened in Freeling by the Sisters of St Joseph. Fr J Maher is in charge of Kapunda Parish of which Freeling is a part.[70]

---

67. Sr Callista Neagle, 'Notes on foundations', ASSJ, Adelaide.
68. Sr Josephine McMullen to MM, 29 December 1870.
69. Sr Monica Phillips to MM, 20 April 1874. Sr Ambrose, (Jane) Hughes was born in Adelaide in October 1850, joined the Josephites in January 1869, was professed on 6 January 1871, and left the Congregation during 1877.
70. *South Australian Tablet*, 29 March 1877, 5.

It was closed by August 1878 because of a misunderstanding between the Sisters and Father Maher. It appears that he was upset because they took the train when going to Mass. He believed that they should have travelled in 'carts' with any of the locals who offered them a ride. As Sister Andrea Howley put it:

> I said the Bishop forbid [sic] the Sisters going in carts if there could be public conveyances got. Oh well, he said, but I am sure that cannot be done. You will always have to go more or less with people in carts.[71]

As early as 1872, Father William Kennedy of Kadina was asking for Sisters for Port Wakefield even though he was sure that the people there could not support two of them. Mary promised him Sister Alexis Sheedy for a time with the proviso that a second Sister would go there as soon as the place could support her.[72] There is no evidence to suggest that Alexis actually went to Port Wakefield but in 1879, Sister Matilda Rogers wrote to Mary from Kadina that Father Kennedy was speaking about getting Sisters for Port Wakefield.[73]

Matilda went on to say that there were thirty-four Catholic children in the area and that they also expected a number of non-Catholics to enrol at the school. Two Sisters went to Port Wakefield in 1880 but their stay was shortlived, for they had closed the school and left the town by the end of 1881. The reason for their departure is unknown because, according to the *Catholic Monthly*,

> It [was] universally acknowledged by all denominations, that the Sisters [were] the best residents and teachers to be had, by their good example and works.[74]

Josephite Sisters were in Warooka, a small township on southern Yorke Peninsula, in 1881 and 1882. This farming town, established in 1875, was one of the first settlements on the peninsula and most of the early settlers were Irish Catholics. Until St Brigid's Church opened in 1877, the priest celebrated Mass in one or other of their homes

---

71. Sr Andrea Howley to MM, 10 August 1878.
72. MM to Woods, 19 February 1872.
73. Sr Matilda Rogers to MM, 2 February 1879.
74. *Catholic Monthly*, 11 February 1881.

whenever he visited the district. In September 1880, he announced that the Sisters of St Joseph were prepared to come to Warooka in the following year if a guarantee for their support was forthcoming. Mr J Cusack offered them his house and made it comfortable for them. Its main disadvantage was that it was about 2.4 kilometres from the town. As it happened, times were tough. Persistent droughts and falling prices meant that the people had no income. They could not support the school or the Sisters, who withdrew at the end of 1882 after having been there for only two years. In the following year, thirty-two of their former pupils enrolled at the local state school.[75]

Two Josephite Sisters arrived in Orroroo in August 1880. One of them, Sister Mary Borgia Fay, reported to Mary MacKillop on their first day at the school that:

> Today is very wet, a very good thing for our tank which is almost empty, but not so good for the opening of our school. We only have four pupils this morning.[76]

Two weeks later numbers had increased to seventeen. Of these children, only four had reached Third Class level. All the rest were in Primer (the infant class). The convent was not yet blessed, but the Sisters were hoping that the priest would see to that at some time during the following week. Sister Borgia wrote that:

> There is a little galvanised iron room attached to the back of the house. The roof wants repairing as a couple of the sheets [of iron] were blown off last week, so I think we might get it done up and a stove fixed in it. It would then do nicely for a kitchen and we could keep our community room neat.[77]

Mary MacKillop bought this convent for £200 on 27 October 1880, seemingly because the local people could not afford a house for the Sisters.[78] The school was very small, most likely because of the exodus caused by drought, and the Josephites withdrew from

---

75. Sr Callista Neagle, 'Notes on foundations', ASSJ, Adelaide. Register of enrolments, Warooka Primary School, PRO, GRG 18/222/1, vol 1. *Catholic Record*, 22 October 1880, 10 and 13 May 1881, 10.
76. Sr Borgia Fay to MM, 6 September 1880.
77. Sr Borgia Fay to MM. 22 September 1880.
78. South Australian Land Titles, 1880, vol 302, folio 136.

Orroroo after just one or two years. When the Sisters left, they rented out the property until 1912 when they sold it for £125.[79]

Willochra was a small settlement on the 'wash' of Coonatto Creek, at some distance to the north of Orroroo. The local St Dominic's Church and convent were in the corner of Mr JB Cormack's paddock, on the road between Wilmington and Hammond. The Sisters arrived in early 1881 and, thanks to the continuing drought, had left by late 1883.

According to the *Catholic Record*, the people had built 'a neat little convent adjacent to the Church', which was 'on the most central site available' and a priest came to celebrate Mass bi-monthly.[80]

Two years later, Sister Winifred Hogan went north to meet with Father Nevin, who was now Dean of the North, regarding matters relating to the former convent at Willochra.[81] She reported to Mary:

> I have been to Port Augusta and seen Dean Nevin. I had a letter from Sister Monica [Phillips] to him, so that I did not have much difficulty as he understood by the letter the business I came on. That was to call to Willochra at my return to take our Convent things. He was most kind and nice as I always found him and bought some of the things for which I was very glad, to save us the trouble of bringing them to Town. We left on Easter Saturday and were at two Masses on Easter Sunday in Carrieton Church. We arrived at the Port [Augusta] on Tuesday. We saw the Dean on Wednesday.[82]

The Josephite school at Port Elliot, near Victor Harbor on the southern Fleurieu Peninsula, opened in 1880 but closed before the end of 1884. Initially, thirty-eight children enrolled but their number gradually decreased. Attendances were particularly poor during peak periods of activity on local farms.[83] By January 1884 Sister Rodriguez O'Brien reported that their numbers were so low that she hardly thought it would be open very long. In fact, the Sisters withdrew at the end of that year because 'there were so few Catholic children there'.[84]

---

79. South Australian Land Titles, transfer number 567720.
80. *Catholic Monthly*, 13 May 1881, 10.
81. 'Dean' was a title given to the senior priest of a particular ecclesiastical region.
82. Sr Winifred Hogan to MM, April 1885.
83. Sr Peter Gough to MM, 28 August and 23 September 1880.
84. Sr Martina Rogers to Sr Monica Phillips, 24 May 1884, Sr Rodriguez O'Brien to

The last of this group of foundations was at Strathalbyn on the eastern slopes of the Mount Lofty Ranges, about ten kilometres from Macclesfield. It seems that the Sisters went there in 1882 and left in 1889 or 1890. They taught in St Barnabas' Catholic Church in Rowe Street and lived in a little cottage nearby.[85] Historically, the proportion of Catholics in this area has been low when compared with other parts of South Australia. However, it was quite large during the 1880s when the enrolment at the Josephite school ranged between fifty and seventy pupils. Enrolments were good and so it seems that the Sisters left for reasons other than lack of support or fewness of students. The following excerpt from a letter sent to Mary in 1884 indicates that the Sisters were well loved, and that she had visited there at least once:

> About this time last year you were with us in Strathalbyn. The people send very nice kind messages to me. Some have been down to see me. The train is to run tomorrow to Strathalbyn and they sent messages to say they were all coming down. I was amused. There is to be a very grand Show there too, so I am afraid my visitors will be a few poor people so good and kind. After Penola I think I liked Strathalbyn.[86]

Mary MacKillop worked hard to support the South Australian Sisters throughout the 1870s, even though she was often called to Bathurst or Brisbane where the bishops were intent on forming the Sisters into diocesan Congregations under their immediate control. In spite of the pressure she was under, she maintained a regular correspondence with the Sisters at home and visited them whenever possible. The longest continuous period during which she was at home in South Australia was from late 1876 until the end of March 1878.

She visited Port Lincoln in January 1877 and was in and around Adelaide until September, when she spent time at Marion, Morphett Vale and Willunga. In October and November she visited all the convents in the Mid-North, from Gawler in the south to Laura and Appila-Yarrowie in the north. That done, she was in

---

MM, January 1884 and 22 February 1885.
85. This church became St Barnabas' Hall after the erection of the Church of the Good Shepherd early in the twentieth century. At the time of writing (2014) it is a private residence.
86. Sr Agnes Smith to MM, 14 Sept 1884.

Adelaide until 8 March 1878, when she received some terrible news. Nineteen-year-old Sister Laurentia Honner had suffered serious burns in a fire in the Port Augusta church and was in imminent danger of death.[87] Her companion, Sister Immaculata Punyer, was also badly burned. Mary set out on the long journey north at once and reached Laurentia's bedside before the young woman died.

Mary stayed in Port Augusta for about a week after Laurentia's funeral in order to comfort and console Immaculata. Years later, this Sister remembered that:

> Mother remained until after Sister's funeral and was kindness itself to me. I was hard to manage being only semi-conscious ... Mother spent a lot of her time with me during the week she stayed—praying for me and consoling me.[88]

By the end of March, Mary was on her way to Queensland again. Although neither she nor the Sisters knew it, she would never again spend such a long, uninterrupted period in South Australia. This time, she was away from Adelaide for the latter half of 1878, all of 1879 and until the end of March 1880. By then, she had helped the former Queensland Sisters settle into their new homes in the New South Wales dioceses of Sydney and Armidale and in so doing, had laid the foundation for another chapter in Josephite history.[89]

Most but not all Josephite Sisters in Adelaide were schoolteachers. A number ministered in their three charitable institutions, the Refuge, the Providence and the Orphanage. Several, including Sister Mechtilde Woods, who was totally blind, gave religious instruction to Catholic children detained in state-run industrial schools and reformatories in and around Adelaide. These Sisters informed the Jesuit priests about what appeared to be discrimination on religious

---

87. Sr Laurentia (Mary) Honner, daughter of Richard and Mary Honner, was born at sea between June & September 1858. She joined the Congregation on 25 December 1874, was professed in July 1877 and died on 11 March 1878, aged nineteen years.
88. Sr Stanislaus (Elizabeth) Punyer, of Penshurst, NSW, 20 November 1925, in *Memories of Mary by Those Who Knew Her* (Mulgrave, Victoria: John Garratt Publishing, 2010). The Sr Immaculata of Port Augusta became Sr Stanislaus at some time during the late 1800s. It seems that MM enforced this change but it has been impossible to discover her reasons for doing so.
89. Barry Evans, 'Mary MacKillop's Journeys', ASSJ, North Sydney, 2010.

grounds against some of the young people in these institutions and, in particular, about allegations that authorities had forced some children to change their religious affiliation.

They and the Jesuits lobbied the government regarding these issues and were largely responsible for the collection of 8,000 signatures on a so-called *Roman Catholic Petition*. In this document the signatories asked the government to inquire into the level of care being given to children who had been through the court system and to ensure that any form of proselytism was banned in the institutions under scrutiny. Their political representatives presented this petition to the South Australian Parliament in October 1882.

The response was almost immediate. In May 1883, the government set up a Royal Commission chaired by Chief Justice, Sir Samuel Way, to inquire into the Destitute Act and its administration as well as the matters raised in the petition. The Commission, which published its final report in October 1885, insisted that the government make a number of significant reforms. One of the most important was its requirement that young people in care be housed in decent quarters. In particular, this ruling applied to the situation of the boys confined in the *FitzJames*, a hulk lying off the coast at Largs Bay. Their living and working conditions left very much to be desired.[90]

As regards the catalyst for this inquiry, the issue of religious persecution, the Commissioners discovered little to substantiate any charge of proselytism. They declared that, according to available evidence, no more than eight children had changed their religion between 1869 and 1883: there were sixty-four Catholic children in detention in 1883 alone.[91] The Commission recommended that the government fund denominational reformatory schools, a decision that was to have repercussions for the Josephites in years to come.[92]

The Sisters' regular prison visitation had one unexpected outcome. In early 1883, Adelaide Catholics were shocked to learn that thieves had stolen a gold ciborium full of sacred hosts from the tabernacle

---

90. A hulk is the empty hull of a ship that has been wrecked or is too old to be sailed.
91. *South Australian Parliamentary Papers*, 1885, no. 228: 'Final Report of Destitute Commission'; Sr Mechtilde Woods, 'Record of Religious Instruction at Magill, 1882–1889'.
92. See Marie T Foale, *Think of the Ravens* (Sisters of St Joseph, 2000), for further details.

in the Dominican Convent, Franklin Street. The thieves emptied it somewhere in the Adelaide Parklands, and made off with the ciborium itself. Everyone despaired of finding those sacred hosts, but:

> Through the good offices of the Sisters of St Joseph visiting the Adelaide Gaol, one of the thieves, a Catholic, revealed the spot in the Parklands where the Sacred Species had been hidden.[93]

Given the number of foundations that the Josephites had made in South Australia by 1883, it is evident that they were being extended to their limits. The Sisters who came to Adelaide from Bathurst in 1876 had long since been absorbed into their workforce. Their numbers were almost static because few young women were joining the Congregation and several of the founding Sisters had recently left it.[94]

A further drain upon their resources was the continuing need to supply professed Sisters to the Queensland Province to replace the postulants who had travelled to Adelaide for their novitiate year since the 1875 Chapter. When word of the impending exodus from Queensland filtered through, therefore, priests and Sisters must have looked forward to improved levels of staffing in their existing schools and institutions and to the possibility of being able to respond freely to requests for new foundations.

The Congregation had reached its limits in the area of finance. Mary made frequent journeys to Queensland and/or Bathurst during the late 1870s. Sisters moved from place to place both within and beyond the borders of the colony. In some South Australian districts Mary purchased dwellings for Josephite communities because the people could not afford to do so.[95] All of the above cost money and, when that amount was added to the interest on the mortgages and the loans that Mary had taken out, (by November 1879 the community had a bank overdraft of £3,000) the Congregation

---

93. *Catholic Monthly,* April 1883, 41.
94. The Founding Sisters were those women who joined the Congregation during its earliest years, that is, between 1867 and 1872.
95. These included Port Adelaide, Kapunda, Orroroo, Kadina, and Kensington. Thanks to the generosity of Joanna and Robert Barr Smith, the Mitcham property cost the Sisters a token five shillings. Mary mortgaged it for its market value soon afterwards.

was in a precarious financial position. Their slide into debt had begun in 1876 when Mary mortgaged the Kensington property to pay for the new building there! How could they bring it to an end?

In 1879, Bishop Reynolds set off to pay his first and only *ad limina* visit to Rome and was away until June 1881.[96] He left the administration of the diocese to his Vicar General, Father Frederick Byrne, who lost no time in reporting to him on the state of the Josephites' finances. Byrne was particularly concerned because their debt exceeded the value of their property and the diocese, which was also heavily in debt, could not afford to stand security for the Congregation.[97]

Initially, Reynolds brushed off this news, saying he was sure that the Sisters' indebtedness was a passing phase and they would soon be in the clear again. He granted that they could have practised greater economy in some areas of their lives but was unwilling to lay all the blame for the debt at their door. He believed it had arisen because some of their schools and institutions had not supported them as they should have, and hence, that they had needed to draw too freely on the limited funds available at the Mother House.

He was sure that once Mary finalised the Congregation's affairs in Queensland and settled permanently in Adelaide again, matters would right themselves and all would be well.[98] It is easy to conclude that Reynolds expected the Queensland Sisters to move to Adelaide, and hence, that all schools and institutions in his diocese would be fully staffed. It also seems that he expected to become superior of the Congregation in fact, if not in name, that is, that it would become a diocesan Congregation like the one Bishop Matthew Quinn had set up in his diocese.

For her part, Mary felt that the vicar general did not understand the Congregation fully and that she could not trust him on financial matters as much as she wished.[99] She also had a real concern that Sister Clare Wright was spending too much time talking to Byrne and

---

96. An *ad limina* visit is one where, at set times, local bishops go to Rome to report to the Pope on the condition of their dioceses, to receive his advice and to pray at the tomb of St Peter. During the nineteenth century, Australian bishops went about once every ten years. Bishop Reynolds went only once during his twenty-year episcopate.
97. Fr Byrne to Reynolds, 3 November 1879.
98. Bp Reynolds to Fr Byrne, 14 January 1880.
99. Documents held in the ACA indicate that Byrne lacked good business skills.

that, thanks to her gossip, the Sisters were in a 'perfect panic' over their financial position. The cause for such panic was that either Byrne or Archdeacon Russell (a priest who never liked the 'working class' Josephites) were saying publicly that the Congregation was £13,000 in debt. (By this time, it was, in fact, about £10,000). Much to her horror, 'even seculars had it as a topic of conversation'.[100]

While Mary worried over this situation, it seems that she had not grasped its full import. Sadly, neither she nor Reynolds had a real understanding of financial matters and there was no one at hand to advise them regarding the basics of good bookkeeping or the risks entailed by entering into debt. She attempted to explain her financial situation to Reynolds thus:

> The actual overdraft when I sent for the book [a simple cash book] last week was £2,700 odd, since which we have lodged nearly £200 more. When we take into consideration the little help we have been able to get from our schools in the last two years and how we have had to assist country convents, the new building here and all, it does not, after all, seem so great a sum.
>
> I am so grieved for the extra anxiety to which you have been put. If I could, I would send you a telegram to make your mind easy, but as I can't do this, must hope that our good God will tell you not to fear. Considering that this house has to train all the Sisters for the Congregation and to maintain the invalids, the debt in proportion is very little.
>
> Of course I feel the responsibility of it very much, but am not afraid. I think of all the schools that would have to be closed and the poor children that would be deserted if some such responsibility would not be endured, and know well that there are ways and means of clearing the debt in time. Meanwhile, please God, now that I am home, I can help it more. Do not be uneasy.[101]

'Bethany' was the name the Sisters gave to the new building that Mary referred to above. This sixty by twenty-four foot (approximately 24 by 11.5 metre) zinc, wood and iron structure, was completed in 1881. It stood beside the original eight-roomed house, and served

---

100. MM to Reynolds, who was overseas at the time, 2 April 1880
101. MM to Reynolds, 2 April 1880.

the community for many years. It soon proved its worth, for it replaced the large tents the Sisters put up each summer when they came in from the country for retreat. At the time of its completion Mary MacKillop wrote: 'It is very nice and will be a great comfort.'[102]

When Reynolds returned from overseas he still hoped that at least some of the Queensland Sisters would come to South Australia to augment the staffs in his schools and charitable institutions. But they did not come! In 1880, the Government of New South Wales passed a 'Public Instruction Act' which introduced several significant changes to public education in that colony.[103] The most important, from a Catholic point of view, were the withdrawal of State Aid from denominational schools as from the beginning of 1883, and the introduction of compulsory education.

This meant that, as of 1883, the NSW bishops would have to maintain their Catholic schools on a vastly reduced budget. All but Bishop Matthew Quinn of Bathurst, whose diocesan Josephites were firmly established, were unprepared for this exigency and looked about anxiously for religious Sisters and Brothers to staff their schools. From their point of view, the Josephite withdrawal from Queensland could not have occurred at a better time.[104]

The Josephite entry into the Sydney Archdiocese was perhaps the single most important event in the Congregation since the restoration of the Sisters to their habits eight years earlier, and it was to have far-reaching effects on the Congregation's future development. It seems that ever since she passed through Sydney in December 1869, Mary had regarded that city as a possible centre for Sisters based in the eastern colonies. It was more central than Adelaide, the Church was more firmly established and financially secure than in South Australia, and a number of its priests, especially the Marist Fathers, supported the concept of central government. In addition, the incumbent Archbishop of Sydney (the English Benedictine,

---

102. MM to Sr Bernard Walsh, 19 December 1881.
103. Public Instruction Act, NSW, 1880. http://www.governmentschools.det.nsw.edu.au/story/instruction_act.shtm
104. Ronald Fogarty, *Catholic Education in Australia, 1806-1950*, 2 volumes (Melbourne: Melbourne University Press, 1959), vol 1, 238-39, 250-55; vol 2, 288.

Roger Vaughan),[105] supported this important aspect of the Josephite Constitution. Their future prospects seemed bright indeed.

That, however, was not the case for the Sisters in South Australia. Although unaware of it at the time, they were heading inexorably towards one of the most difficult periods in their short history, to a point where they had to decide once and for all, whether they wanted to belong to a centralised Congregation or a diocesan one. The Bathurst and Queensland Sisters had already made that decision, with most of them packing up, moving out, and cutting family ties in order to retain their affiliation with Mary MacKillop and the Adelaide Mother House. How would the South Australian Sisters respond to that same challenge?

Sr Francis Xavier (Blanche) Amsinck, about 1868.

Sr Francis of the Five Wounds (Julia) Fitzgerald, about 1868.

---

105. For further information re Archbishop Vaughan see: AE Cahill, 'Vaughan, Roger William Bede (1834–1883)', *ADB*, (National Centre of Biography, Australian National University, 1976).http://adb.anu.edu.au/biography/vaughan-roger-william-bede-4773/text7941.

Sisters outside the new Kensington chapel, about 1876.
The chimneys to the eight-roomed house are visible behind the bushes to the left of the chapel.

Novices & postulants at the side of the new chapel, possibly as early as 1876.

Bishop Christopher Augustine Reynolds.
1873–1893

Sr Laurentia Honner who died from burns at Port Augusta in 1878.

Georgetown Church where the Sisters slept in the gallery during the 1870s.

Chapter Three
Identity Formalised, 1880–1895

In marked contrast with the movement and turmoil of the previous decade, the 1880s dawned with the promise of peace and consolidation. The Congregation was fourteen years old and had 200 members. Most were based in South Australia. The balance, that is, those who had served in Queensland during the previous decade were in the process of settling into the Sydney and Armidale dioceses in New South Wales. On the whole, these Josephite women understood what it meant to be religious Sisters and more particularly, to be members of an indigenous Australian religious congregation at a time when both immigrant and colonial born Australians looked to countries half way across the world for inspiration and support.

Most of these Sisters were very young. Only eighteen (less than one tenth of them) had turned forty and none was yet fifty years old. Their oldest member, Sister Kevin (Catherine Kiernan) of Adelaide, was forty-eight, while the youngest was fifteen-year-old postulant, Sister Leonard Schmidt, who came to Adelaide from Queensland with Mary in March 1880. The foundress herself was just thirty-eight and had been a Josephite for fourteen years. A large proportion of the Sisters had not yet made their final profession.[1] They were well on the way but, at this point, the Congregation was still essentially 'a society without grandparents'.[2] Its members were still finding their way. The living and writing of their own story was proving difficult indeed and they still had many a hurdle to cross before they would be able to give a true account of its growth and development.

---

1. Register of the Sisters, ASSJ, Adelaide
2. Douglas Pike, 'A Society without Grandparents', 57.

In the year 1880, the South Australian Sisters had charge of forty-two Catholic primary schools and were managing three charitable institutions. Some who had joined the Congregation before September 1871 continued to grieve Father Woods' departure. At least nine from that vintage had left the Congregation during the previous two or three years but the arrival of an equivalent number of new postulants had offset their loss.[3] Priests and people in many parts of South Australia were asking for foundations. Mary was unable to respond positively to a number of these requests because she did not have enough Sisters to go round. Most Sisters were looking forward to her return from Queensland and New South Wales, where she had been since April 1879, and were hoping that in future she would be free to spend more time with them.[4]

Little did they know that clouds were gathering in an unexpected quarter and that before long their loyalty to the Congregation and its foundress was to be tested once again. Bishop Reynolds, their long-time friend and supporter, was about to change his position regarding central government for the Congregation and would try to force it to fit into the diocesan government mould espoused by Bishop Quinn of Bathurst. The reasons for Reynolds' change of heart appear to have been that he suffered from chronic ill health, did not enjoy being bishop of Adelaide, and was unable to control the rising tide of debt in his diocese.

The circumstances of his life were such that he received only limited theological education, and hence, was uncomfortable in the presence of priests or bishops who had completed lengthy seminary studies. Some of his clergy, especially the young, energetic and able, gave him scant respect and he was ill at ease when dealing with them. They charged him with having attained his position by dishonourable means and claimed that he treated them harshly and unjustly. Several of them left the diocese soon after he became bishop and, from the safety of distance, wrote a damning indictment of his administration to Roman Authorities.[5]

---

3. See Marie T Foale, *The Josephite Story*, chapter 7, especially page 141 in order to gain a better understanding of the reasons for the departure of those Sisters.
4. MM to Reynolds in Rome, 2 April 1880.
5. Frs J Nowlan OSA, JJ O'Sullivan, M Henderson OFM Cap, C Horan OSF, JJ Roche, R Cleary, PJ Byrne & M Kennedy to Cardinal Barnabo, nd but by internal evidence, April 1872, SRCO vol 9, ff. 1355–1356. Frs M Kennedy, M O'Connor,

The ever-loyal Mary MacKillop, who was aware of his weaknesses and of some of the difficulties he faced as bishop, expressed her opinion of him at least twice. In 1876 she wrote that he was good and holy 'but not clever enough for some he has to deal with'.[6] Three years later she described him as being a 'good, holy, hardworking bishop, but not what many would call a clever man'.[7]

One positive in Reynolds' diocese was the presence there of the Josephites, a unique group of religious women who were providing good basic education for most of its Catholic children, even those living in distant country areas. It seems that his relationship with these women soured when the Sisters leaving Queensland accepted Archbishop Vaughan's invitation to move into the larger, and in his eyes, more important Sydney Archdiocese, instead of coming to Adelaide as the Bathurst Sisters had done.

Mary, who considered it her duty to keep him informed of important matters concerning the community, told him of her delight at the way the Sisters were made welcome in New South Wales and kept him up to date regarding developments there. Initially he agreed to her taking several Adelaide Sisters to Sydney to help staff the schools there. Yet, his insecurity was so great that he read her positive messages regarding New South Wales as implying that the priests of the Sydney and Armidale dioceses were more friendly towards and more supportive of the Josephites than the South Australian clergy. He also became fearful that Sydney might supersede Adelaide as the administrative centre of the Congregation and therefore, that his diocese would be disadvantaged in some way.[8]

On an even more serious note, his diocesan debt was rising at an uncontrolled rate and he had just become aware of the enormity of the Josephite debt. In his perplexed state, he was easily influenced by two or three discontented Sisters who went to him with tales and complaints alleging that Mary and some of the other Sisters were mismanaging their limited funds. Another factor affecting his behaviour was that, even though he supported the idea of central

---

C Van der Heyden, JJ Roche, R Cleary & possibly JJ O'Connor, from Beechworth, Victoria, to Cardinal Franchi, 15 September 1877, SRCO vol 11, ff 263–276.
6. MM to Monsignor Kirby, 12 July 1876.
7. MM to Dr Campbell, Scots College, Rome, 22 March 1879.
8. MM to Archbishop Vaughan, 8 August 1881.

government for the Congregation, it seems that he did not fully understand its implications. Therefore, he saw himself as the South Australian Sisters' ecclesiastical superior, with complete control over the Congregation, its houses and its membership.

Throughout his episcopate Reynolds maintained constant contact with Monsignor Tobias Kirby in Rome (the Monsignor Kirby who helped Mary when she was there some ten years earlier). During the intervening years Kirby had become Roman agent for the Irish born bishops in Australia. In this role, it seems that he heard from the Quinn brothers and Bishop James Murray of Maitland about what they believed were Mary MacKillop's strange ideas regarding the governance of religious congregations in the colonies and her determination to cling to those ideas.[9] Furthermore, it appears that Reynolds had written to him of his fear that Sydney would supersede Adelaide as the centre of the Congregation. Hence, on 18 July 1884 and seemingly in response to a query from Reynolds, Kirby wrote that the Josephite Constitutions had 'not an atom of Papal or Propaganda authority', and were only 'a verbal recommendation of some officials in Propaganda'.[10]

The content of this letter helps explain Reynolds' behaviour towards the Sisters between 1884, when it came into his hands, and 1888, when the Congregation received papal approval. For their part, Kirby and his correspondents seem to have forgotten what Reynolds wrote when he appealed for funds for the Sisters in 1876:

> The position of the Sisters and the occurrences that had so much disturbed the members of the Catholic Church in the colony had been brought prominently under the notice of the Holy See, and after they had been carefully inquired into in the colony and in Rome, *the Institution was taken under Papal protection and established under Papal charter.*[11]

---

9. Monsignor Kirby was Roman agent for the bishops, that is, he was the one to whom they wrote when requiring information, support, etc, from Roman authorities.
10. Mons. Kirby to Reynolds, 18 July 1884. Emphasis that of the author.
11. *The Institution of the Sisters of St Joseph of the Most Sacred Heart of Jesus in Australia* (Adelaide: Advertiser Office, 1876). Emphasis is that of the author. On page 2 is a note reading: 'I beg to recommend the works under the care of the Sisters of St Joseph to the charitable consideration of the public. C.A. Reynolds, Bishop of Adelaide, 16 July 1876.'

Reynolds attached to this document the letter that Mary MacKillop had received from Cardinal Franchi in 1874. It stated clearly that the Sisters were to submit their new constitutions, with their articles on central government, to their diocesan bishop to obtain his consent before they put them into practice and that, after some years' trial, they were to return them to the Holy See for definitive approval.[12]

In 1880 Mary found herself in a difficult position. On the one hand, she was unwilling to move Sisters in ways that might disadvantage the Adelaide diocese. Yet, on the other, she was being pressured to supply communities for New Zealand and Western Australia as well as for New South Wales. After one persuasive request for Sisters to go to the South Island of New Zealand, she explained to Archbishop Redwood of Wellington that:

> There are many calls upon us in this diocese alone. The Bishop knows that we cannot spare Sisters from here without loss to some of his own schools, but he generously overlooks that and tells us to do what we consider best for our Congregation and the general good of the Sisters. Demands for more Sisters keep coming in from Sydney, Armidale and West Australia. We cannot meet all, but are trying to do our best in each case.[13]

The demands in Adelaide were great indeed. During the year 1880, when the Sisters already had charge of forty-three schools, they made foundations at Sevenhill, Port Elliot, Ororoo and Jamestown. In 1881, they opened schools at Port Wakefield, Warooka, Whyte Yarcowie and Willochra and in 1882, two Sisters went to Stathalbyn.[14] Some of the Sisters required for these eight foundations, most of which were short-lived, came from five long established foundations, namely those at Moonta, Robe, Stockport, Undalya and Willunga, all of which closed in 1880. The reasons for these closures are unclear but it seems likely that the Sisters moved away because persistent drought and low commodity prices were forcing people to abandon their properties and move to the city.

---

12. *The Institution of the Sisters of St Joseph.* 12.
13. MM to Archbishop Redwood, Wellington, NZ, 2 January 1882.
14. See Chapter 2 for further information regarding some of these foundations.

Given the above, it comes as no surprise that Mary refused many appeals for help from Sydney. Thus, when Sister Bernard Walsh, who was now Provincial in the Sydney archdiocese, persisted in asking for reinforcements, she wrote:

> You are trying to do too much in opening so many schools, and will, I fear, have me placed in an awkward position I know, dear, that it is hard for you to be unable to meet so many demands, but do you forget that I had to meet the same here and refuse. The bishop asked for Sisters last week for a new foundation and I had to say no, that it was impossible. Port Pirie is becoming very important again. I have had to refuse . . . There is no use trying to do too much . . . If we only had the subjects[15] you ought to know how gladly I would see them at work. So far, Dr Reynolds is truly friendly to us . . . but we must not try him too far . . . My own dear Sister, don't think I would not help you if I could.[16]

The help Mary gave the dioceses of Sydney and Armidale during the years 1880–1883 was limited by the number of Sisters available and the demands of priests and people at home in South Australia. Even so, several of the best school Sisters were among those she transferred to New South Wales and, although their exact number is unknown, it was probably fewer than ten. Among them were Sisters Bernard Walsh, Bridget Cremen (the daughter of two experienced Adelaide school teachers), La Merci Mahoney (formerly of Bathurst), and Victor Lane (a young Queenslander who had just completed her novitiate training).[17]

Another was Sister Veronica Champion, whom Woods had sent from Sydney to join the Congregation in Adelaide during its low time in October 1871 and whom Mary appointed to Picton, New South Wales in 1880.[18]

---

15. In this context, the term 'subjects', implies new members of the Congregation.
16. MM to Sr Bernard Walsh, 18 June 1882.
17. 'Murphy Journal', vol 1, 119 (Condon edition-MS), ACA. Bridget's parents were Irish immigrants, David and Anne Cremen, who had moved from Sydney to Adelaide in 1847 at Bishop Murphy's invitation to take charge of a Catholic school there.
18. Sr Veronica Champion, who joined the Congregation in 1871 and made her profession in 1873, spent most of her time in South Australia at Robe or Penola.

These Sisters' departure upset those priests whose schools were affected by their going. Mary, who could see the bigger picture, was frustrated at their seeming unwillingness to help the overall cause, while it appears that she failed to realise that they might have good grounds for complaint. Her response to Sister Bonaventure Mahony's appeal for help gives an indication of her feelings on this matter:[19]

> You ask me to send some more Sisters—*I cannot*. I cannot meet the wants here and already there is great dissatisfaction amongst the priests who have accused me of sending Sisters to NSW who were required here. I grieve to say that I can scarcely keep my temper with some of them; they are so selfish, so unlike the generous ones you meet in New South Wales. If the Archbishop mentions the matter again, please tell him that I cannot send any more at present at any rate.[20]

Even as she dealt with these problems, Mary also had to cope with unrest among some of the South Australian Sisters. Several who had been longing for her return became frustrated when her chronic ill health prevented their seeing her whenever they wished. Soon there were rumours that she was overdosing on the brandy the doctor had ordered for her when she was ill, and hence that she was unavailable because she had a hangover. Bishop Reynolds, who was overseas for more than two years between April 1879 and June 1881, was unaware of this turn of events. During his absence Sister Clare Wright and some of her friends carried rumours about Mary's alleged drinking habits to the vicar general and his friend, Archdeacon Patrick Russell. As already noted, neither had much love or respect for the working class Sisters of St Joseph and both knew of the Congregation's financial position. Hence, they concluded easily that the Sisters were overspending in order to satisfy Mary's habit.

    She was in Penola when MM called her to Sydney to be Little Sister at Picton in the Southern Highlands of NSW. Sr Veronica to MM from Penola, 22 & 31 January and 2 & 9 February 1877 and 16 September 1878. Sr Josephine Carolan to MM from Sydney, 25 September and 2 November 1880.

19. Sr Bonaventure Mahony, who joined the Congregation in S.A. in December 1868, was stationed in Queensland from 1872 until she moved to New South Wales in 1880.
20. MM to Sr Bonaventure, 10 June 1880.

As it happened, Clare's association with the clergy at the Bishop's House had serious repercussions for both herself and Mary. One day in early 1881, Father Thomas Lee, the assistant priest in the Mount Barker/Macclesfield parish, overheard Byrne and Russell discussing the Josephites' finances and planning to have Mary arrested for some outstanding debts. When he realised that they were serious, the young priest hurried to the Kensington convent to warn her of her danger, only to discover that she had left earlier that day to visit the Sisters at Macclesfield, some forty kilometres away. He hurried there, explained the situation to her, and accompanied her by carriage as far as the South East. From there she continued on her way to Sydney, via Melbourne, by overland coach or coastal steamer.

Mary was away for six weeks. On her return in late March 1881, she was shocked to find that Clare had left the convent without a dispensation from her vows. The reasons for her departure are unclear but it seems that she moved out because she felt responsible for Mary's flight and was unable to face her former friend on her return. Mary herself thought so. She was devastated at this turn of events and explained to Archbishop Vaughan that:

> She (Clare) had from time to time given us trouble and caused anxiety, but I never expected so sad an end. If I may believe half that is said, pride and ambition were at the bottom of it all.
>
> Sister Mary Clare was her name in religion, and she is well known to our Sisters in Sydney. Many things that were a mystery to me before have now come to light, and I believe that it was her dread of an investigation that caused her to leave before I returned.
>
> Amongst the Sisters she has been secretly advancing Father Woods' views, whilst to me she always expressed the greatest disapprobation of them.[21]

That was in early April 1881. In June, Bishop Reynolds arrived home from his visit to Rome tired and dispirited, to find that the financial situation of his diocese was worse than he had anticipated. However, he did not let this prevent his presiding at the Congregation's second General Chapter where he showed some support for the Sisters' move

---

21. MM to Archbishop Vaughan, 5 April 1881.

into New South Wales. It soon became clear, however, that his support was limited for he strongly opposed any suggestion that they should establish a novitiate in Sydney, and complained bitterly when he discovered that Archbishop Vaughan had gained permission from Rome to do so at the appropriate time.[22]

Over the following twelve months or so, matters appear to have run relatively smoothly for Mary and her community, although, unknown to her, several disaffected Sisters continued carrying to Reynolds tales accusing Mary of financial mismanagement and, in particular, of wasting money on alcohol. As time passed, he became more and more certain of three things: the diocese was deeply in debt; the Sisters' debt far exceeded the value of their property; if they foreclosed, the Church would have to stand security for the Congregation and it could not afford to do so.[23] In short, as bishop he was ultimately responsible for the Josephite debt. He could not afford to allow it to become bankrupt—and he did not know where to turn.[24]

What Reynolds seems not to have realised was that the Sisters had incurred much of their debt in the interests of the people of his diocese. Mary had borrowed money to purchase houses in areas where the local Catholics could not provide accommodation for the Sisters. She had used borrowed money to pay Sisters' fares to impoverished areas and for their living expenses whilst in those

---

22. Sr Josephine Carolan to Dr Campbell, 3 April 1884. MM to Sr Mechtilde Woods, 10 December 1883.
23. Bishop James Murray of Maitland to Cardinal Moran, 'Report of Inquiry into Financial Affairs of the Archdiocese of Adelaide, 10 April 1888', ACA. As the 1880s progressed Cardinal Moran arranged for Bishop Murray to conduct an investigation into Adelaide's financial affairs. The only financial records that he could find from this period were simple cashbooks and books containing the results of various collections.
24. Reynolds to Moran, 16 November 1884; Josephite Account Books, 1875–1883, ASSJ. As already noted, MM mortgaged the Kensington property in 1876. She purchased the Port Adelaide land on 18 October 1882 (tr 151030) for £650. Mitcham was virtually a gift from Robert Barr Smith who transferred it to Mary MacKillop (tr 144897) on 18 May 1882 for the nominal sum of five shillings. She purchased the Kapunda property, which came in three lots (tr 116707 & 116708, 29 September 1880 and tr 114164, 27 July 1880) for a total of £238 pounds and 10 shillings. The Ororoo house (tr 117802, 24 August 1880) cost £200.

places. Besides this, she had needed to finance her many journeys to Queensland and Bathurst, and the fares of Sisters travelling Adelaide and those two places.[25]

As Reynolds worried over the seemingly impossible situation in which he found himself, his uncertain health deteriorated and he turned on Mary and the Josephites. He brought matters to a head on 4 July 1883 when he announced that, in accordance with instructions he had received while in Rome, he was holding an Apostolic Visitation of the community.[26] During its course, so he said, he intended examining all financial matters, checking all convent buildings, and interviewing each Sister separately. Mary, who was aware of her Sisters' weaknesses and faults as well as their strengths, organised for there to be Exposition of the Blessed Sacrament in the convent chapel on 8 July 'to draw God's blessing on the Visitation'. She hoped that 'from this Visitation more unity and charity [might] reign among [the Sisters]'.[27]

On the morning of 10 July 1883, Reynolds arrived at the convent accompanied by four priests—Archdeacon Patrick Russell (who had replaced Frederick Byrne as Vicar General), Fathers Michael O'Sullivan (the Bishop's personal secretary), Anton Herberg SJ, of Norwood and William Kennedy of North Adelaide (formerly of Kadina). He celebrated Mass for the community, breakfasted in the convent, addressed the assembled Sisters in the oratory, and did a tour of the convent grounds. Finally, he interviewed Sisters Monica Phillips and Gertrude Hayman, to each of whom he administered an allegedly prescribed oath to tell 'The truth, the whole truth, and nothing but the truth, and [to keep] inviolable secrecy *until death* of all that [was] said in the room'.[28]

On the following day, the four priests returned without the bishop and met with Sisters Aloysius O'Leary, Joseph Lonergan, Andrea Howley and Borgia Fay.[29] All members of the community were shocked and surprised at this turn of events, but, following

---

25. MM to Reynolds, 2 April 1880.
26. Eventually, Reynolds had to admit that he had received no such instructions.
27. MM to the Sisters, July 1883.
28. MM to Dr Campbell, 30 March 1884.
29. MM's report of these events, as given in *Resource Material from the Archives of the Sisters of St Joseph of the Sacred Heart,* Issue 5 (January 1881).

Mary's instructions, they answered as truthfully as possible. For Sister Joseph, being bound by oath for life proved too hard. She gradually slipped into an unreal world and before long had to be hospitalised at the Parkside Mental Asylum where she died on 30 December 1886, aged forty-six years. As Sister Leonard Schmidt recalled some years later:

> Sister M Joseph who gave evidence was living with me later at Port Augusta and, as a result of the strain of the investigation, became unhinged in mind.[30]

Sister Joseph's dying caused Mary great grief indeed. She wrote:

> The news of Sister Joseph's death, even before I heard any of the particulars, gave me a great shock and made me cry more bitterly than the death of any Sister had ever done.[31]

Over the next six weeks or so, most of the Sisters were examined and all felt the weight of the oath upon them. Mary arranged for exposition of the Blessed Sacrament again on 1 August. On that day, at the bishop's orders, she wrote to Bernard Walsh in Sydney asking that she send back to Adelaide Sisters La Merci Mahony and Collette Carolan to attend the visitation.[32] She wrote:

> This Visitation is a long and trying business, but will bring good results, I am sure.
>
> Today the Bishop sent me a formal demand *in obedience to the Holy See*, to summon at once Sisters La Merci and Collette here to attend it . . . I am at my wits end to know how you can arrange for their schools, but beg that you will try to get

---

30. Sr Leonard Schmidt (1864–1951), 30 April 1950. See also Adelaide Asylum: alphabetical list of patients, 1846–1901, SAA GRG 34/90, 196 of 86.
31. MM to Sr Andrea Howley, 26 January 1887
32. Tasmanian born Sr La Merci Mahony (1860–1910), joined the Congregation at Perthville in 1874, travelled to Adelaide with other Bathurst Sisters in January 1876, did her novitiate training there, and remained in SA until Mary called her to Sydney in the early 1880s. Sr Colette Carolan (1844–1906) joined the Congregation in Queensland in 1870, was professed there in 1872, and continued there until the Sisters' exodus in 1880. It seems that Mary had appointed her to South Australia for a time and that she had moved to Sydney in about 1882.

> someone (even a secular for the time being) to take them . . . Between one thing and another, I am nearly crushed . . . Let us pray for one another and put all our hope and trust in our good God.[33]

Mary met with the bishop and his team of investigators on 3 August. When they had seen all the Sisters they wished to interview, but not, so it seems, those in communities located within the Jesuit mission areas to the north of Adelaide, Reynolds informed her that

> though made in the strictest form, the results of the Visitation proved that, though many little things would have to be improved, there were no grave evils or scandals to correct, and that he had been able to send a most consoling report to Rome . . . and that later he would give [her] a written statement of the decisions arrived at by the Commission.[34]

It soon became apparent that the bishop was far from satisfied. He gave no reasons for his next action: on 9 October 1883, he presented Mary with a 'Memo of Directives', to be implemented at once. It included an order that she remove Sisters Raymond Smyth and Bernardine Ledwith from the Refuge, even though, to her mind, both were well suited for the work there. Reynolds also commanded that the reception of visitors at the convent and the making of visits by the Sisters be strictly limited, that, for reasons unspecified, Sister Angelina Kent (a Bathurst Sister) was to leave the Congregation at once, and that one Sister only was to have charge of the Congregation's business affairs.[35] On the same day he ordered Mary to include Sister Calasanctius Howley in the small group of Sisters who were about to set out for Temuka on the South Island of New Zealand.[36]

---

33. MM to Sr Bernard Walsh, 1 August 1883.
34. MM to Dr Campbell, 7 December 1883.
35. Sr Angelina Kent, who was born in Bathurst in 1855, travelled to Adelaide as a novice in 1876, was professed there in 1876, and worked in various South Australian schools until she was dismissed on Reynolds' orders in late 1883.
36. On 24 July 1879, Fr Tappeiner responded as follows to MM's request for advice regarding the wisdom of appointing Sr Calasanctius to replace Sr Josephine McMullen as Provincial in Queensland. His words help to explain the conflict between this Sister and the bishop and also some of the difficulties she encountered when Provincial of Port Augusta during the 1890s.

Calasanctius was thirty-five. She had served faithfully as Mary's Assistant General for the past ten years and was noted for her outspoken loyalty, and now she was banished to New Zealand as community leader at Temuka. Her companions were Sisters Immaculata Punyer, who was twenty-four years old (and who, at nineteen, had survived the Port Augusta fire that cost Laurentia Honner her life), and twenty-nine year old Raymond Smyth, who had been unceremoniously removed from the Refuge a few days earlier. These Sisters left Adelaide with heavy hearts and reached Temuka on 31 October 1883, deeply concerned for those they left behind.[37] Within six months, Mary sent Sisters Mary Joseph Dwyer and Anselm Smith from Adelaide to give them extra support and to enable Sister Calasanctius to return home. Reynolds, who was annoyed when he heard of this second contingent, demanded that all future transfers of Sisters to New Zealand be made from Sydney where the Congregation was about to establish a novitiate.[38]

Back in Adelaide, matters were coming to a head. Soon after the Sisters' departure for New Zealand, Fathers Francis O'Neill and Michael O'Sullivan delivered to Reynolds the financial statement they had drawn up from the convent books. Their findings confirmed his worst fears regarding the Josephite debt which equalled £10,000, or more than half the sum owed by the whole of the diocese of Adelaide.[39] If true, this was very serious but its size should not have surprised him. Over previous months he had had access to the Sisters' books and in late September had attempted to rationalise their

---

'I also spoke to Sister Calasanctius about your intentions with regard to herself. She seemed to be ready for everything. But I suppose she has written herself. With regard to her fitness for the position of Provincial of Queensland, I can say nothing that you do not know yourself. She has good qualities, such as good judgment, firmness, ability for business, etc. but also some drawbacks, rather rough manners, not always sufficiently delicate, a little inclined to party spirit, sulky and distant when displeased, and frequent indispositions, such as violent headaches, which is also a considerable obstacle in a Superior. These things you will have to weigh carefully before you come to your final decision. I hope some of the points mentioned she will be able to correct if well advised and warned.' (sic)

37. Sr Calasanctius to MM from Temuka, New Zealand, 3 November 1883.
38. Marie T Foale: *The Josephite Story*, 181.
39. TF O'Neill & M O'Sullivan, Financial Statement, 23 October 1883, ACA. *Catholic Monthly*, December 1883, 172: 'Diocesan Debt', noted that the total sum owing by the diocese was £19,252 & 5 shillings. The Josephites owed approximately £10,000.

position by replacing several of their smaller mortgages with a new one for £5,000 at 7½ per cent for five years.[40]

It is difficult to reconstruct the exact sequence of events during October and November 1883 but it appears that shortly after Reynolds received the financial statement referred to above, he sent Dean Kennedy to interview Mary, with a view to having her tender her resignation. She refused. Reynolds then ordered her to leave for Sydney at once and to stay away at his good pleasure because, according to him, she no longer had any jurisdiction in his diocese. He demanded that she go quietly, telling the Sisters that she was leaving for health reasons and also for 'the assumed fact of some duties' calling her there.[41]

Mary reacted characteristically to this turn of events. She maintained her undying loyalty to the office of bishop and insisted that the Sisters do the same. Then, on 17 November 1883, she left Adelaide for good after informing the Sisters of her imminent departure and of the likelihood that she would be away for some time:

> My letter this time will give you great surprise but not greater than I feel myself at the news I have to give you. Circumstances call me to Sydney. Sr Bernard says that, if I go for one week, they will be satisfied, but I have reason to think that I shall be longer than that away. In any case you will soon know more than I am at liberty to mention now.
>
> Meanwhile I leave you in God's keeping and, as Sr Calasanctius had to go away, Sr Monica took her place as Assistant. Knowing the love and veneration in which you hold Sr Monica, I am glad that it is so. As Sr Collette (sic) has also to come with me for the *present*, Sr Mary de Sales will be Little Sister. Later this may be changed.[42]

None of the Sisters other than her four Councillors was aware of the true state of affairs. The following, from the youthful Sister Leonard Schmidt, gives clear evidence of this:

---

40. MM, Account of Visitation, 14–17. On 16–17, she had copied a letter from Reynolds, 26 September 1883, telling her of this new mortgage and of how, as additional security, he had affixed the official diocesan seal.
41. Reynolds to MM, 13 November 1883.
42. MM to the Sisters, 17 November 1883.

> I was never so stunned in my life as when I heard of your departure from us so near Xmas. Indeed, I am sure, dear Mother, that if we had Sr Bernard over here, we would put her head in a bag for coaxing you to leave us like orphans. Tell her that I am shocked at an ancient religious like her to be so selfish.[43]

All became disturbed and confused when their superior general did not return to Adelaide for Christmas. Her desk was cleared and the place felt so empty without her. The atmosphere in the house was very different from what it was two years previously, at the Christmas of 1881. On that Christmas Day, they were happy together and they remembered well Mary's surprise and joy when they presented her with a new desk. At the time she wrote:

> On Xmas Day (sic), our Sisters gave me a great surprise in a most affectionate address, accompanied with one of those desks or writing tables I had always so much wished for. They also gave me a typograph (writing press) with the aid of which I can easily copy much that I could not otherwise do.[44]

The Sisters also remembered how she spent some days at the new Mitcham convent, built on the land that the ever-generous Robert Barr Smith sold to the Congregation in 1881 for five shillings. This large block adjoined the Mitcham General Cemetery and so Mary and her council had decided to allocate part of it for use as a Sisters' cemetery. Barr Smith had also arranged for the erection of a convent on the lower half of the block, so that Sisters ministering in the district could have a permanent home. In the April of 1882 Mary had written:

> I am writing this at Mitcham where I have had to come for a few days' quiet. The convent is very pretty, but the oratory is not quite finished, so Mass has not been said in it. It is so nice

---

43. Sr Leonard Schmidt to MM, from Bagot's Gap, 22 November 1883. At the time Leonard, who was originally from Queensland, was just nineteen years old and had been professed for about eighteen months.
44. MM to Sr Bernard Walsh, 2 January 1882. This desk is among the archival artifacts held at St Joseph's, Kensington.

to have a Sister buried here as every day she gets so many prayers.[45]

Now, in December 1883, everyone was labouring under that dreadful oath of secrecy and felt insecure. Sister Monica did her best but she was not Mary and could not tell them any more of Mary's movements than they already knew. They agonised as they wondered what was going on and whom they could trust.

In fact, the crisis the Sisters in South Australia now faced was even more serious than the one they had weathered in 1871. In neither instance was the Congregation in danger of annihilation for there were Josephite houses in other dioceses. Nevertheless, it could have disappeared from South Australia in either 1871 or between 1883 and 1886. A notable difference between the two crises was that during the later one, the Sisters' relatives and friends were unaware of what was happening and of the effect it was having on them. Sister Gertrude Hayman, who had joined the Congregation in 1867 and had weathered that first storm, wrote to Mary:

> I often think of the time of your excommunication. We had you then and then our Sisters were one, but now it's changed.[46]

Sister Eustelle Woods, youngest daughter of Julian Woods' brother, James, was concerned at what might happen if her father became aware of the situation. She knew how quickly he sprang to the defence of his brother Julian and her older sister, Mechtilde, back in 1871–1872, and was particularly concerned that he might say or do something against the bishop.[47]

Hence, there was no intervention by the laity. The Sisters stood alone with no one to mount their defence, but they were better

---

45. MM to the Sisters, 14 April 1882. Prior to this, the Sisters' convent was adjacent to the little church-school at the intersection of Maitland Street and St Michael's Road, Mitcham. After the opening of the new convent, the school Sisters walked approximately two kilometres down the hill to the school each day. The deceased Sister to whom she referred was Sr Louis Molloy, originally from Queensland, who died at Kensington on 26 December 1881 aged twenty-two years.
46. Sr Gertrude Hayman to MM, 2 February 1885.
47. Sr Eustelle Woods to MM, 17 May 1885. Eustelle, who was Sr Mechtilde's younger sister, joined the Congregation in June 1879 when she was nineteen years of age.

prepared than they were in 1871. Over the years, their understanding of their rights and obligations as members of a religious congregation and their level of literacy had increased to such a degree that some were able to write to the head of the Sacred Congregation of the Propaganda and other Roman officials stating their case and questioning the legality of Reynolds' actions. Sister Josephine Carolan, formerly of Queensland, wrote from Sydney asking whether the Holy See had given Bishop Reynolds any special authority or power over the Congregation or could be called its protector. She concluded:

> We are very hurt to find that Dr Reynolds has power to set aside the superior in whom we have every confidence and to appoint another in her place without legal reason.[48]

They were sure enough of their position to know that, according to their Constitutions, Mary was their lawful superior and had the right to appoint a Sister to lead the local community during her absence. Hence, they were well satisfied when Mary made Sister Monica Phillips her Assistant General, and gave Monica's place on the Council to Sister Mechtilde Woods. Reynolds, who was unaware that Mary had made these appointments, confirmed Monica as interim leader and accepted her suggestion that Sister Mary de Sales Tobin, the Sister whom Mary and the council had named for the post, become the leader of the Kensington community.

Subsequently, the bishop appointed several Sisters to key positions without reference to Monica but, thanks to her astuteness and the loyalty of the Sisters most closely associated with her, the Sisters in South Australia continued to be led by women who were true to their foundress and the Constitutions. As far as possible, they ruled as she would have wished and kept her informed about what was happening. It was largely due to Monica, a quietly spoken, gentle but strong Irishwoman, who held the Sisters' confidence and was unafraid of the bishop, that the Josephites in South Australia remained members of the centrally governed Congregation.[49]

As 1883 merged into 1884 the Adelaide Sisters waited and prayed for Mary's return. But she did not come. They did not realise that

---
48. Sr Josephine Carolan to Dr Campbell, December 1883, from Sydney.
49. Sr Monica Phillips to MM, 12 December 1883.

she could not do so because of the manner of her dismissal. They were pleased to receive her Christmas circular where she explained many things and encouraged them to persevere in the lives they had chosen:

> Though unable to be with you in person this Christmas, I can be so in spirit, and with all my heart I now wish you, one and all, a most holy and happy Christmas. We have had much sorrow and are still suffering its effects, but sorrow or trial lovingly submitted to do not prevent our being happy— it rather purifies our happiness, and in so doing draws our hearts nearer to God. That such may be the case with all of us, my dear Sisters, I earnestly pray. I think that we can all honestly admit that we wanted some external cross to make us amongst ourselves what true Sisters of St Joseph and humble spouses of a suffering and most charitable God should be.[50]

Even so, as the Sisters continued in their various ministries, they grieved Mary's loss. In the following March, Sister Aloysius O'Leary wrote from Mitcham:

> Why don't you write? I have not heard a word about you since Xmas. (Sic) I wrote two letters to you, but you did not answer either. Do please answer this. If you only knew how very anxious I was about you I'm sure dear Mother you would write and let me know how you are getting on.[51]

Sister Gonzaga Lynch asked:

> My dear Mother, why did you go away from us as you did?[52]

While Sister Angelica Greene wrote:

> If only you saw the woebegone faces you would see the affection and undying love of the majority of us for you.[53]

---

50. MM to the Sisters, 17 December 1883.
51. Sr Aloysius O'Leary to MM, Mitcham, 28 March 1884.
52. Sr Gonzaga Lynch to MM, 19 January 1884.
53. Sr Angelica Greene to MM, 11 January 1884.

For the time, Mary was limited to advising her South Australian Sisters to 'go on quietly', trusting in God and the patronage of St Joseph. Then there was one small sign of improvement. In March 1884, news came from Rome that the Holy See had not given Bishop Reynolds any special powers over the Congregation and that he had no right to depose the superior general from her office.[54] The Sisters now felt free to write to Rome and explain their situation. Their letters bore fruit for, in October 1884, Archbishop Moran (who had succeeded Vaughan as Archbishop of Sydney in May 1884 and had arrived there in the September of that year) wrote to Mary:

> I have just received a rescript from the Sacred Congregation of the Propaganda to the effect that His Holiness has been pleased to absolve the Sisters of St Joseph of the Sacred Heart from the oath taken at the late visitation in Adelaide to maintain silence regarding the whole interrogatory.
>
> I hasten to make known to you this benign decision of His Holiness, and I pray you to communicate it without delay to the Sisters whom it may concern.[55]

Reynolds was furious when he learned of this rescript, and was even angrier when he discovered that Rome had appointed the Archbishop of Sydney to look into and report on Josephite affairs in Adelaide. At last, he began to see that the Sisters were deeply upset and that his chances of breaking their loyalty to Mary were slim indeed. Therefore, he set out to test their feelings on this matter at the conclusion of their annual retreat on 6 January 1885, the Feast of the Epiphany. He went to Kensington and asked the professed Sisters to remain in the chapel after Mass for he wished to address them or, as Gertrude Hayman put it, to 'dress them down'.[56]

He declared that the Roman dispensation was invalid and therefore, that they were still bound by the oath of secrecy. He accused Sister

---

54. MM to the Sisters, 24 March 1884.
55. Archbishop Moran to MM, 20 October 1884. Moran (1884–1911), Roman-trained, the Archbishop of Sydney was a nephew of Cardinal Cullen of Dublin and had close connections with Bishops James and Matthew Quinn and James Murray. Moran was raised to the cardinalate in July 1885. See AE Cahill, 'Moran, Patrick Francis (1830–1911)', *ADB* (Canberra: Australian National University, 1986). http://adb.anu.edu.au/biography/moran-patrick-francis-7648/text13375.
56. Sr Gertrude Hayman to MM, January 1885.

Monica of allowing disorder to reign in the convent, alleged that Sister Calasanctius was a serious troublemaker, and declared that he would expel from the Congregation any Sister who broke the Rule. In fact, so he said, he believed that the Congregation was on its way to suppression and that, if the Sisters continued their current behaviour, he could put the whole community under interdict and remove the Blessed Sacrament from the convent. Following such an event, no priest would be able to say Mass there, and the members of the community would be deprived of access to the Sacraments of the Church while living and be denied Christian burial in the case of death. During his address Reynolds spoke in 'a very exasperated manner' and caused 'a large number of the Sisters who were trying to be good to become disheartened and dejected'.[57]

Within days Mary received a sheaf of letters from South Australia, all carrying reports of this event and statements of loyalty to her and the Constitutions. It was becoming patently clear that Reynolds' aim was to separate them from their Mother General and some Sisters were so upset that they begged Mary to move the Mother House to Sydney. As she read their letters, she realised that they were 'being tried beyond their strength in Adelaide' and had 'suffered wonders in silence'.[58] Therefore she concluded that she was in duty bound to permit any of them to leave Adelaide if they requested permission to do so. For many, this move on Mary's part proved a lifesaver.

The first to leave were Sisters Gonzaga Lynch and Tasmanian born Austin O'Meara. Austin came to Adelaide from Queensland where she had joined the Congregation in 1874. She did not settle well in South Australia and had been pleading with Mary for some time to take her to Sydney. Gonzaga, who entered in Adelaide in 1870, had no great desire to leave South Australia but, when the time came, agreed to go with Austin as her companion. Both were stationed at Penola in 1884–1885 and earlier that year, Austin, who disliked the place intensely, had stated firmly to Mary: 'I will not stay here longer than Easter', before asking:

> Could you not let me go to NSW? I look at the coach passing every day and think how I should like to step into it. I have a

---

57. Sr Monica Phillips to Cardinal Simeoni, 29 January 1885.
58. MM to Archbishop Moran, 21 January 1885.

> great mind to do so, only I fear you might be blamed for the training the MG (Sic) gave her Sisters. I am reckless as to what would be done to myself.[59]

As her anxiety increased, she worked out how to fund her trip without arousing any suspicions on the part of the parish priest or the people. She wrote:

> We have no money to pay our fare but I asked our good friend Mr Darwent to get up a concert for our benefit on 17th ... Of course the net proceeds of the concert will be our private property. I do not consider I am obliged to give any account of it but I will put it down in the book and then we shall be able to go to town if we are ordered to do so ... Now dear Mother, do write soon ... I want to tell the priest we are going to town in time to have the Blessed Sacrament removed ... Of course going to town is all I shall say. It will be perfect truth as I hope to go to Sydney town.[60]

Sister Austin's plans gradually fell into place. The concert was a success, raising more than £12. She gave their non-resident parish priest the impression that they were going to Adelaide for retreat at Easter and waited until the last moment before informing Sister Monica of their impending departure.[61] Then, on Easter Tuesday, 7 April, she wrote from Melbourne to notify Mary that she and Gonzaga were about to board the steamer *Cheviot* for Sydney.[62] Austin's going upset Monica, who was unsure how Reynolds or Cardinal Moran would react when they discovered what she had done. She wrote to Mary:

> I only yesterday received the intimation from S M Austin that she would be out of the diocese when her letter would reach me. I trust her step will bring no trouble on you with the Archbishop as His Grace said we were to do nothing to annoy

---

59. Sr Austin O'Meara to MM, 1 January 1885. In the above context, 'entered' means 'joined' the Congregation.
60. Sr Austin O'Meara to MM, 9 March 1885.
61. Sr Austin O'Meara to MM, 9 & 19 March 1885.
62. Sr Austin O'Meara to MM, 7 April 1885.

the Bishop of Adelaide and I suppose this will exasperate him very much.[63]

The Penola people, who knew nothing of the Sisters' difficulties or heartaches, were shocked to find them gone and the school closed without prior notice. Little did they know that they were the first of the many to lose their Sisters during that and subsequent years!

In her responses to all the Sisters, Mary reminded them that, regardless of what occurred, they must remain loyal and obey the bishop, 'no matter how harshly or unjustly he [might] act, as long as he [did] that to individuals only'. She added:

> Should he demand separation, the true Sisters will then stand by their lawfully elected superiors, and Rome will stand by them.[64]

She wrote that at the beginning of Lent 1885. On Easter Tuesday Reynolds put the Sisters' loyalty to their Mother General and their centrally governed Congregation to the test once more. He went to the convent and demanded to see all the professed Sisters in the chapel where he proceeded to 'dress them down' again. This time he prefaced his remarks with the following patently untrue statement:

> I, as Bishop of Adelaide, received letters from Rome during Passion Week, and it has been decided that the Congregation of St Joseph is to be divided into diocesan communities, and the Bishop in each case is to be the superior in his own Diocese. Mother Mary's authority here has ceased and she will never under any circumstances whatever, return to this diocese.[65]

Later on in his lecture he declared:

> Mother General has nothing to do with you till you hear from Rome and I forbade you before to have any communication with her. I'm your Bishop and your Superior and I have a right to know everything.[66]

---

63. Sr Monica Phillips to MM, 5 April 1885.
64. MM to the Sisters, 20 February 1885.
65. Sr Scholastica Byrne to Cardinal Simeoni. 11 April 1885.
66. Sr Patricia Campbell to MM, 10 April 1885.

He concluded by saying that Sister Monica, whom he believed he had appointed to the role of Mother Vicar in January, no longer had his confidence and that he intended to depose her and make his own arrangements for Sisters under his jurisdiction. Next, he demanded that they decide, there and then, whether to remain under his rule or leave, adding:

> You will not be received in the archdiocese, [that is, Sydney] believe me; and the Archbishop is not hoodwinked. And I am very doubtful if you will be received by other bishops.[67]

When he stopped for breath, one of the Sisters stood up and asked respectfully for a longer time to consider such an important decision. He reluctantly agreed and indicated that he would return the next day to receive each Sister's answer individually. All were in shock but Sister Monica kept her head and immediately sent a telegram to Mary, asking whether the bishop's claim about Archbishop Moran was true or not. Much to their relief, Moran indicated that he would receive any Sisters coming from South Australia.

When Reynolds returned next day, most Sisters asked for more time and indicated clearly that they would remain faithful to their Constitutions especially regarding central government. As soon as he realised that many of them were prepared to leave the colony he tried another approach. He announced that he was deposing Sister Monica and appointing in her place Sister Michael Quinlan, a good, reliable Sister but one lacking the self-confidence she needed to manage this role. He forbade Michael to give any departing Sisters passage money to Sydney. She replied that they would go regardless.[68]

Soon after these events, all but three of the Sisters in the colony put their signatures to a petition begging their Cardinal Protector in Rome, Cardinal Simeoni, to ensure that they be allowed to continue as members of the centrally governed Congregation as founded by Mary MacKillop and Father Woods. Sister Monica explained the situation to the cardinal:

---

67. Sr Patricia Campbell to MM, 10 April 1885.
68. Sr Monica Phillips to Cardinal Simeoni, 10 April 1885. They travelled by coastal steamer as the railway line between Adelaide and Melbourne was not completed until 1887.

> I wrote about four weeks since [April 10th] relative to some troubles of our Congregation, and informed Your Eminence of the steps our Bishop, Dr Reynolds had taken in order to induce us to separate from our lawful Superior, Mother Mary of the Cross. I also explained to Your Eminence that the Sisters of St Joseph here in S. Australia are entirely opposed to such a change being made in their form of government.
>
> The Sisters of St Joseph in this Colony and also those of NSW and New Zealand all wish to adhere to the central form of government, which has been laid down for us in the Constitutions we received from Rome, that is, the entire Congregation is governed by one Superior General who is subject to the Cardinal Protector and to Rome and not subject in her government to the Bishop of the Diocese. The Sisters in South Australia have already sent a petition to Your Eminence entreating you to use your influence to obtain for us the favour of being allowed to continue under the said form of government, and to prevent us from being subjected against our will to the Diocesan form of government, in which the Bishop would be in each case the absolute Superior and not subject to Rome. All the Sisters in this Diocese, with the exception of three, have signed their names to this petition. [There are a hundred and thirty-three names to it.][69]

The fact that three Sisters did not sign this petition is significant, as it indicates that several were dissatisfied and unhappy with Mary and the way the Congregation was developing. There is also evidence to suggest that some did not like (or even perhaps, resented) Sister Monica in her role as leader in South Australia. It is now impossible to discover the identities of these Sisters or their reasons for deciding against signing the petition. That they were seen to be troublemakers is evident from the occasional comments other Sisters made in their letters to Mary. One writer stated that she did not know whom to trust.[70]

One of the alleged troublemakers sent an anonymous letter, after signing it 'A Sister of St Joseph', to Archbishop Moran in November 1884. She claimed that those who, like her, were going to refuse to

---

69. Sr Monica to Simeoni, 6 May 1885.
70. Sr Gertrude Hayman to MM, 2 February 1885.

sign the petition referred to above were likely to be made suffer for their refusal. As she put it:

> Some of us were unfortunate enough as to have had to reveal under the solemnity of an oath facts which were injurious to Mother General's character for temperance and her observance of poverty.[71]

Such difficulties and any infighting within the Josephite community were of no concern to the bishop or his Vicar General. What did worry them was the number of Sisters who were serious about leaving the diocese. In his anger, Reynolds seems to have lost sight of the implications of his attempt to take over as their superior and, in particular, of the reality that, if they all left, most of the Catholic schools and all the Catholic charitable institutions in South Australia would be without staff and would close. Therefore, in what seems to have been a last ditch attempt to frighten the Sisters into staying in the colony, Russell, acting on Reynolds' behalf, appealed to Moran to withdraw his offer to accept them in Sydney. He claimed that he was doing so because he was afraid of the scandal that would ensue when the schools closed.[72] The following sharp rebuke was all the reward he received for his trouble:

> I would be unfaithful to the duty imposed on me by the Holy See were I to prejudice its decision by refusing to receive them ... my duty to the Holy See requires me, in dealing with any Sisters that may come to Sydney, to completely ignore any new regulations that his Lordship may have made.[73]

Mary responded to Sister Monica's account of events by assuring her that the bishop had 'no authority' for what he had done and was sure to be censured. As the year drew to a close, she became concerned at the possible outcome of the First Plenary Council of the Catholic Bishops of Australia and New Zealand that was scheduled for November 1885. She wrote:

---

71. A Sister of St Joseph to Archbishop Moran, 12 November 1884, St Mary's Cathedral Archives, Sydney.
72. Archdeacon Russell to Bishop Murray of Maitland, 15 April 1885, MDA.
73. Cardinal Moran to Russell, 20 April 1885. ACA (copy is in Russell's hand).

> The Irish Bishops will do their utmost at the Synod to have our Congregation made *Diocesan*, but will fail if the Sisters hold out as they have done and are doing. Rome is very jealous of its authority, and the manner in which it has been set aside in Adelaide will not help the Bishop's cause.
>
> The great thing for our Sisters is to keep as quiet as possible, and for the sake of religion to keep on the schools if they can. Advise them to suffer anything short of *consenting to separation* rather than have to leave the place without Sisters. Of course, those who are really in danger or whom the Bishop particularly dislikes had better leave as quietly as they can. If they would only have courage and not be afraid of his threat of *expulsion*, I would tell them wait on. Rome will not *force* anything upon them . . . Let them try to be patient.
>
> The A.S.N. [Australian Steam Navigation] Company's agent is now instructed to give passages to any Sisters who want to come. There is no limit as we feared; should any trouble arise, you might be in a fix what to do [Sic].[74]

For some it was too difficult and they went to Sydney. For his part, Moran appears to have been pleased that so many Sisters were coming into his diocese for he was in desperate need of Religious to manage his Catholic schools and this was an opportunity for him to obtain the services of a significant number of experienced teachers, without effort or cost to himself or the diocese.

The Sisters themselves were heartbroken at what was happening. Sister Alphonsus Drislane wrote:

> Of course you know that there is nothing here but crosses and troubles. Every Sister seems downhearted.[75]

Sister Eustelle Woods would have liked to have gone to Sydney with so many of her companions, but was confident that if they 'all kept quiet and minded their schools' the trouble would soon blow over.[76] She stayed and continued working in the schools until her premature death on 28 February 1898, aged thirty-seven years.

---

74. MM to Sr Monica Phillips, 21 April 1885. Emphases are Mary's.
75. Sr Alphonsus Drislane to MM, 1 May 1885.
76. Sr Eustelle Woods to MM, 17 May 1885.

Soon after Easter, Reynolds announced that he would profess only those novices who agreed to separation from their superior general, insisting that he alone was their superior. Consequently, the six young women then in the novitiate accepted Mary's offer to them to move to Sydney. At the time, there were three postulants in the colony and they too moved away. For the first time in its short history, Adelaide was without any novices or postulants.[77]

And so the exodus began. Among the first to leave from Adelaide itself were Sisters Francis Xavier Amsinck and Agnes Smith, who arrived in Sydney on about 21 April. They were followed by Sister Gertrude Hayman and the novices and postulants who set sail on 27 April. On the following day Monica wrote to Mary:

> I sent you a telegram yesterday about Sr Gertrude, novices and postulants having sailed. The steamer went out at four in the afternoon. The house is so lonely without the poor young Sisters, not a white veil about. It seems so strange, but I am glad they are gone to where they will have some peace. We are kept in continual agitation and excitement here, as His Lordship has gone so far there is no knowing what his next step will be.[78]

Mary replied:

> As things have turned out, you do right in sending over the novices and the Sisters you have named... The Archbishop is very cautious and won't commit himself to anything, but he seems very pleased so many Sisters are coming over.[79]

Over the next twelve months or so, more Sisters moved to New South Wales but most stayed in South Australia because of their concern for the children and the residents in their charitable institutions. As Sister Annette Henschke from the Refuge put it:

---

77. MM to Father Bianchi, Rome, 17 April 1885. The novices were Srs Anne Joseph Waters, James Feehan, Clare O'Donnell, Finbar Foley, Walburgh Bannock and Imelda Gleeson, while the postulants were Srs Columba O'Brien, Romaeus Sheehan and Sylvester Higgins.
78. Sr Monica Phillips to MM, 28 April 1885.
79. MM to Sr Monica Phillips, 30 April 1885.

> It would be a great pity if all have to go, and what will become of all the poor children?[80]

In July, Sister Baptista Long let Mary know that:

> The poor Bishop got a great fright when he found the Sisters took him at his [word] by leaving when they did not intend to acknowledge him as their Superior. Now he says he did not mean it in that way.[81]

Sister Monica was keen to keep the schools open for in October she wrote:

> Certainly I do not grudge any Sister or any teacher to NSW but I know dear Mother that your wish was that we should keep on the schools in SA as long as we could honourably do so for the sake of the children. And really since our last troubles in April the children seem to have increased in attendance.[82]

Keeping all the schools open soon became impossible. Overall, during the period from 1883 until 1892, seventeen Josephite schools and associated convents closed. Of these, the first three to go (Port Wakefield, Willochra and Port Elliot) were abandoned because of unsustainably low enrolments. The next two, Penola and Gulnare, closed in 1885 when the resident Sisters left for Sydney.[83] The Sisters left Virginia, Laura, Georgetown, Port Lincoln and Auburn in 1887, Appila, Maitland, Mintaro and Strathalbyn in 1889, Tarlee in 1890, Whyte Yarcowie in 1891 and Manoora in 1892. Falling enrolments because of persistent drought may have been a factor in some closures. On the other hand, several schools, including Port Lincoln, Laura and Strathalbyn, had healthy numbers and the lack of Sisters to staff them appears to have been the reason for their closure.[84]

Mary seems to have had a particular interest in the Georgetown school and was upset when she heard of its having closed. This was

---

80. Sr Annette Henschke to MM, 3 May 1885.
81. Sr Baptista Long to MM, 29 July 1885.
82. Sr Monica Phillips to MM, 23 October 1885.
83. Srs Regina Magee and Amelian Dempsey to MM, 14 April and 10 May 1885.
84. See Appendix Ten for details of these closures.

in spite of the fact that in early 1886 Sister Patricia Campbell, one of the Irish postulants who travelled to Adelaide with Mary in 1875, wrote from Georgetown that:

> We have a very small attendance here. So many people have left. Fr Reschauer [SJ, the parish priest] thinks it will not be worth keeping open.[85]

Despite Patricia's comments, when Mary heard this news she asked Sister Andrea Howley:

> Can you tell me why Georgetown was closed and *who* closed it? Did Sr Calasanctius wish it done? Poor Mother Bernard seems much annoyed about it.[86]

Several months later, Sister Gertrude Mary Dewe (a former Benedictine nun who travelled to Adelaide with Reynolds in 1881 to join the Josephites and moved from Georgetown to Jamestown early in 1887), explained the situation as follows:

> I am sure you were surprised to hear of Georgetown being closed but Fr Reschauer seemed to think it was the best thing to be done as the people gave him so much trouble.[87]

On the other hand, Reynolds maintained that the Sisters left Georgetown so that Mother Bernard could accept a new foundation in Western Australia.[88] As it happened, the four Sisters who went to the West that year, namely Ursula Tynan, Mechtilde McNamara, Irene Ryan and Camilla Doran, were drawn from communities other than Georgetown.[89] Soon after their departure Sister Monica reported to Mother Bernard as follows:

---

85. Sr Patricia Campbell to MM, 29 February 1886.
86. MM to Sr Andrea Howley, 26 January 1887. Mother Bernard Walsh had been Superior General since November 1885 and so was the one responsible for authorising the opening or closing of Josephite foundations.
87. Sr Gertrude Mary Dewe to MM from Jamestown, 4 April 1887.
88. Bishop Reynolds to Mons Kirby, ca 1888.
89. Sr Monica to Mother Bernard Walsh, 14 October 1887. For further details of this foundation, see Marie T Foale, *The Josephites Go West* (Perth: Notre Dame University, 1995).

> Now I must tell you how Archbishop Reynolds has acted. As I told you before when Dr Gibney [the Bishop of Perth] spoke to him about getting the Sisters, His Grace tried to put the matter off saying it was time enough when Rome had settled our affairs &c. (Sic). All the preparations were made and when on Wednesday (the day before they sailed) he came out to the Convent and said that as Archbishop of the diocese he protested against the Sisters leaving it. I said the Sisters had got orders from their Mother General and were bound to obey her, that Dr Gibney had been promised the Sisters, and that Adelaide would not be inconvenienced. He said he had written to you protesting against the Srs going and that we ought to await your answer. He said a great deal more about waiting till Rome would decide &c &c— and went away. (Sic)[90]

The four Sisters went to the West in November 1887 as planned. It is difficult to establish exactly how many other Sisters left South Australia during the 1880s but the evidence suggests that at least sixty-five were lost to the colony between September 1882 and the General Chapter of 1889. What is clear is that, in December 1889, there were 107 Sisters resident in South Australia. At Chapter time, 146 Sisters (just over half the Congregation's total membership of 288) were stationed in New South Wales, while there were six in Western Australia, four about to go to Victoria from Sydney, and twenty-five in New Zealand. During this period, nine South Australian Sisters died and eleven left the Congregation. These losses were partly offset by the arrival of fourteen new recruits, but at least fifty-nine (including the six in Western Australia) had taken up ministries elsewhere. It appears that at least fifty-three of these women had transferred to New South Wales.

During this troubled time the South Australian Sisters made only three new foundations and undertook only one new ministry. Firstly, they returned to the working class suburb of Thebarton, a place they had left at the time of Mary's excommunication in 1871. In 1883, newly arrived parish priest, Father John Healy, made it known that he was anxious to have the Sisters there because he was

---

90. Foale, *The Josephites Go West*.

keen to provide elementary schooling for the children and night classes for illiterate adults in a Catholic setting.

He began by erecting a new church, under the patronage of Our Lady of the Angels—generally known as Queen of Angels Church which opened in September 1883. Then, in 1885, he arranged for the erection of a convent and a school for the Sisters of St Joseph.[91] These buildings were ready in the September of that year and Sisters Scholastica Byrne, Alacoque Smith and Vincent Smith (who were not related to each other) moved in and opened the school.[92]

At Macclesfield, where there had been a Josephite community since 1868, the Sisters undertook a new ministry in addition to their work in the schools. In 1890 they accepted a government appointment as official visitors to local homes where state children, that is, children who were wards of the state, were being boarded out. They held this position until 1898.[93]

Bishop John O'Reily, the first bishop of the newly formed diocese of Port Augusta, arrived there in 1888 and was responsible for the Sisters' accepting two new foundations in his region.[94] Before doing so, however, he visited a number of Josephite schools elsewhere in order to check them out for himself. Only then did he invite them to Quorn in 1889 and Gladstone in 1890.

Sister Calasanctius recorded the Quorn opening in a signed statement in her scrapbook where she wrote:

> In January 1889 two Sisters of St Joseph opened a school in the Church of the Immaculate Conception, Quorn. During that month about 15 children attended the school which has steadily increased in numbers from that time. The number at present [July 1892] is 81: 50 are Catholics, 31 non-Catholics. A rented cottage was used as a Convent till Dec. 1890 when the Sisters came to live in their pretty Cottage Convent adjoining the Church, built at a cost of £430.[95]

---

91. *Catholic Monthly*, September 1883 & June 1885.
92. No records of school enrolments at Thebarton could be found.
93. State Children's Council, Annual Reports, 1888–1899.
94. John O'Reily (1846–1915), a native of Kilkenny, Ireland, was educated at All Hallows College, Dublin, where he was ordained in 1869; he ministered in Western Australia from that year until his appointment as Bishop of Port Augusta in 1887.
95. Sr Gertrude Mary Dewe to MM, 12 October 1890; *Australasian Catholic Directory*, 1890 & 1891.

During the following year two Sisters became established in Gladstone where there was a 'good attendance at school'.[96] Shortly after the General Chapter of December 1889, O'Reily informed Mary of his doings. He wrote:

> While in Adelaide I made a point of seeing all your establishments and schools as far as I could. Everywhere, I need scarcely say, I was gratified by the extent and value of the work being done . . . It is important that she [Sister Calasanctius] is appointed Provincial . . . She is always welcome in the Diocese of Port Augusta and its Bishop will do all he can to facilitate her work within the limits of the territory under his jurisdiction.[97]

In 1891, the Sisters withdrew from Whyte Yarcowie because of small enrolments. Lack of personnel made it impossible for them to return to any of the places they had vacated during the previous decade. In fact, when O'Reily arrived in the diocese, he found only six Josephite convents and schools: at Port Augusta, Pekina, Jamestown, Caltowie, Burra and Whyte Yarcowie. There were also seven former convents scattered across the countryside at Laura, Appila, Saltia, Gulnare, Willochra, Georgetown, and Ororoo. In his first annual financial report for the diocese, he commented that:

> In the Willochra account the sum total of liabilities includes a debit balance still remaining due on a cottage built as a convent. This cottage is, I regret to say, but one out of seven in the Diocese which, bought or built as residences for the Sisters, were no longer in use at the date of my arrival in the Diocese for their original purposes. The shifting of the population leaving the Sisters without pupils, the schools had to be closed and the communities removed to other scenes of labour.[98]

---

96. Sr Gertrude Mary Dewe to MM, 12 October 1890; Australasian Catholic Directory (1890 & 1891).
97. A Sister of St Joseph, *Life of Mother Mary, Foundress of the Sisterhood of St Joseph of the Sacred Heart* (Sydney: Westmead, 1916), 375-copy of O'Reily's letter.
98. Rev John O'Reily, *Report on the Liabilities of the Diocese of Port Augusta* (Port Augusta, 1890), 16. The convents in question were at Willochra, Ororoo, Laura, Georgetown, Gulnare, Appila-Yarrowie, and Saltia.

Nearer to Adelaide, two new buildings were making the Sisters' work easier. The first was a new parish school building at Kapunda. In March 1885 Sister Felix O'Rourck wrote to Mary that:

> We will be very grand here by and by. Dr Byrne is building a grand school for us. He says it will be ready for us in about June. He will furnish it with every convenience for teaching.[99]

In hindsight it seems that Byrne may have been preparing for the arrival in his parish of a community of Dominican Sisters from Adelaide. He wanted them to open a select school for the local girls and also to manage his parish primary school. This changeover did not happen quickly, however, for it was 1893 before these Sisters were ready and the Josephites could move out.

The second new building in the archdiocese was a convent for the Sisters teaching at the Brompton/Bowden School. They had reopened their school in the industrial suburb of Bowden in 1877 but, because they were unable to find suitable accommodation in that district, they lived with the North Adelaide community in Walter Street, North Adelaide and walked across the parklands to their school each day. Then, in 1887 and thanks to the initiative of the local people, they took possession of a house on the corner of Chief Street and Port Road, Brompton. It was within a few minutes' walking distance from their school!

The changes described above were made in different areas by concerned individuals and parish communities but did little to alleviate the pain the Sisters suffered during this period. In particular, Cardinal Moran's announcement in November 1885 that he had appointed Sister Bernard Walsh to replace Mother Mary as their Mother General came as a severe blow to them. It seems that Moran asked Roman authorities to review Mary's position as Superior General in the light of the accusations Bishop Reynolds was making against her. He claimed that he did so because Mary had been leader of the Congregation since Sheil approved it in 1868, and therefore, that her re-election as Mother General in 1881 was invalid.

It is possible that he planned this action with a view to having Mary out of office before the First Plenary Council of the Australasian

---

99. Sr Felix O'Rourck to MM, March 1885.

Catholic Bishops that was to take place in Sydney later that year. It seems too that he and most of his fellow bishops expected the Council to rule that the Sisters of St Joseph should be divided into separate diocesan Congregations, each under the immediate control of their local bishop.

The news of Moran's intervention and its outcome surprised everyone, including Mary herself. For her part, she saw it as a sign that the Holy See was indeed caring for the Congregation and ensuring that everything was in due order. She wrote to Sister Monica:

> At last we have news from Rome and thank God we are protected there. The Constitutions are upheld, Mother House also, but my last election is declared *invalid* on the plea of an interval having been necessary before a fresh election such as was made. The Cardinal was deputed to make this known to me, and to *appoint a temporary* Sup. Genl. (sic) until there could be a fresh election at a General Chapter.
>
> Now, dearest Sister, this is *good news*. There is no fault found with *us* and the Cardinal is most kind. He is quite satisfied that this [New South Wales] should be a Province until Rome decides otherwise, and in this sets an example to other Bishops. Oh Sister, I hope you feel as I do about all this.[100]

Mary was equally positive in her remarks to the Sisters when she announced Mother Bernard's appointment. Even so, for some this was almost too much, while others were more concerned about Mary than about their own sorrow. Sister Thecla Harding, who had spent all her life, both before and since her entry into the Congregation in 1868, caring for the orphans wrote:

> I need not say the grief it caused me when I heard you were going to leave us orphans. I am sure you know how much we all loved you and what it will cost us to lose you as our Mother. But, still if it be for the greater honour and glory of God we must be resigned.
>
> Now dearest Mother I need not say have courage . . . Again dear Mother courage in this time of trial.

---

100. MM to Sr Monica Phillips, 12 November 1885.

And then, as a PS she added:

> I cannot help weeping and sobbing.
>
> Hoping to hear from you soon & (sic) trusting you will use the well-known term Mother.[101]

While the Sisters in Adelaide were coming to terms with this news, the bishops of Australia and New Zealand were meeting in Sydney. The gathering decided that the large and unwieldy dioceses in some colonies should be subdivided. Of significance to this history is the fact that the sparsely settled northern regions of South Australia were separated from Adelaide and designated the diocese of Port Augusta with its centre in that town. This enabled the creation of an Ecclesiastical Province in South Australia, Adelaide became an archdiocese, and Reynolds became the first Archbishop of Adelaide. He accepted this change and Cardinal Moran formally inducted him into his new position in September 1887. As already noted, John O'Reily, a priest of the diocese of Perth, became the first bishop of Port Augusta and took up residence there in 1888.

The status of women religious in Australia (and, in particular, of the Sisters of St Joseph) was high on the Plenary Council's agenda, and the bishops present decided by a majority of fourteen votes to three that in any diocese where Josephites were stationed they should be constituted as a diocesan Congregation. As soon as the South Australian Sisters heard of this decision, some of them, under the leadership of Sister Patricia Campbell of Georgetown, appealed to Rome to have it overturned.

As had been the case in 1884, Roman officials decided in the Sisters' favour. Therefore, when they received the decrees from the Plenary Council for ratification and approval, they rescinded the one relating to the government of the Congregation. They noted that they did so because the bishops gave no reasons for their decision and also because they had no authority to interfere in matters concerning a Congregation under pontifical protection.[102]

---

101. Sr Thecla Harding to MM, undated letter, but almost certainly from this period and probably from 1885.
102. 'Acts of the Sacred Congregation of the Propaganda', Rome, 1887, vol 257, 111–113, Report with Summary and note of the Archive concerning the *Acts and*

Immediately upon receipt of this news from Rome, Cardinal Moran asked authorities there to decide, once and for all, on the canonical position of the Congregation. Propaganda responded with a formal decree erecting it into a Regular Congregation of Pontifical Right with its Mother House in Sydney. According to the terms of this decree, any bishop wishing that the communities in his diocese should remain distinct from the centrally governed Congregation was to constitute them as a diocesan Congregation. The decree further stated that the current acting Mother General, Sister Bernard Walsh, was to remain in office for the next ten years.[103]

This decree, dated 25 July 1888, reached Sydney in early December, by which time there were Josephite houses in the dioceses of Adelaide, Armidale, Auckland, Wellington, Perth, Port Augusta and Sydney. Bishop O'Reily immediately indicated his willingness to allow his Sisters to retain their affiliation with their Mother House. Reynolds refused to do so.

On the one hand, he did not want his Sisters to be part of a centrally governed Congregation with its Mother House in Sydney. On the other, as already noted, he was afraid that, if he insisted on their becoming a diocesan Congregation, they would all move to New South Wales and that, as a consequence, most of the Catholic primary schools in his diocese would be without teachers, and he would be left responsible for the Sisters' debts, which amounted to £9,000.

The Sisters assured Reynolds that they would willingly meet their financial obligations if they were allowed to remain united to the Mother House in Sydney. Moran reminded him sharply that the Holy See would regard it as a 'slight upon the authoritative decree relating to the Sisters' if he persisted in his refusal to accept its decision.[104] Six trying months elapsed before he was ready to

---

Decrees of the Plenary Synod of Australasia, issued March 1887, Copy in ASSJ, North Sydney. A decree of the plenary synod that did gain approval was the one that authorised bishops to divide their dioceses into parishes with clear boundaries.

103. Moran to Propaganda, June 1888, SRCO vol 16, f 29. Decree of Approval, issued at Rome, 25 July 1888, received in Sydney, 8 December 1888.
104. Moran to Reynolds, 4 February and 6 March 1889.

announce, albeit grudgingly, that the Sisters of St Joseph in his archdiocese might remain united to their Mother House.[105]

He showed his displeasure at having been forced to come to this decision by removing the Sisters from the charge of the St Vincent de Paul's Orphanage, which was now in suburban Goodwood. On 17 December 1889, without prior warning, he notified the Sister in charge, Sister Maria Skudder, that he had decided to entrust the orphans to the Sisters of Mercy as from 1 January 1890. He stated that he was making this change:

> In the interests of religion and the wellbeing of the most helpless of my flock . . . I have long felt there is no hope of any permanent good to be expected in the management of the Orphanage whilst the Sisters of St Joseph are as they are. For the last 18 months I have been set at defiance, no sense of honour or honesty amongst a party who were forced upon that institution.[106]

It has been impossible to identify Sister Maria's assistants at the orphanage or what Reynolds considered as being dishonest or dishonourable behaviour, or which Sisters, if any, might have been guilty as charged.

As already noted, during the period under review, the Sisters were weighed down by the burden of their debt. As soon as Reynolds agreed to their retaining their affiliation with the Mother House, they assumed full responsibility for it. Acting on his advice, in early 1889 they took out two large mortgages at a medium rate of interest in place of several smaller ones at higher rates: one for £6,000 at seven per cent with the South Australian Mortgage Company and one for £4,000 at five per cent with the Catholic Church Endowment Society (CCES). Their annual interest bill came to £620, a large sum indeed, given the poor economic climate

---

105. Moran to O'Reily, 29 July 1889, ACA. Reynolds to M Bernard Walsh, 31 January & 12 February 1889; to Moran, 2 March 1889, ACA. M Bernard Walsh to Reynolds, 5 February 1889. Bishop John O'Reily, Port Augusta to Sr Monica Phillips, 4 August 1889, Resource 9, 110.
106. M Bernard Walsh to Reynolds, 21 December 1889, ACA. Reynolds to M Bernard Walsh, 17 December 1889; to Sr Maria Skudder, 27 December 1889, ACA.

of the time and the community's limited income.[107] Fundraising became the order of the day as the Sisters scrimped and saved in order to pay off their debts.

Their problem was so great that the General Chapter of December 1889 authorised Mother Bernard Walsh to sell the Kensington property, in spite of the fact that it was the Congregation's first official Mother House. At the time this appeared to be the only way for the Sisters to raise enough money to meet their interest bills and, eventually, to pay off the principal.[108] They needed desperate action to solve a desperate problem. While the proceeds from such a sale might have paid off their debt, a serious side effect would have been the end of the Josephite presence in the Archdiocese of Adelaide.

After the Chapter, Mother Bernard sent Sister Veronica Champion, who possessed some skills in financial management, to Adelaide to arrange for the Kensington sale and to investigate ways of resolving this problem. Veronica consulted various experts in the field and reported to Mary:

> I went to Mr McDonald today ... He was very nice and felt sorry for the Sisters. He thinks that Kensington is the best to sell, to pay the first mortgage, £6000 he thinks. Mitcham and Port Adelaide should not be sold until last of all. Mitcham particularly on account of the Cemetery as few would like to take it from the Sisters. He also thinks it a bad time to sell and does not envy me having to deal with the Archbishop. After leaving Mr McDonald I went to the Secretary of the Mortgage Company. He says that the Archbishop's consent will have to be asked as it is usual in business to do so.
>
> Before going to Hawkes, I went to Mr Glynn's office and found out the value of Kensington as the Company would not tell. I was very glad I had done so as I was able

---

107. Patrick McMahon Glynn, memo. (nd, but by internal evidence, 1888), listed five mortgages, for a total value of £8,020 and a bank overdraft for £1,600, making a total of £9,620, ACA. Glynn, lawyer for the RSJ, was M Bernard Walsh's nephew. Report of Third General Chapter, December 1889. See: Gerald O'Collins, 'Glynn, Patrick McMahon (Paddy) (1855–1931)', *ADB* (National Centre of Biography, Australian National University, 1983). http://adb.anu.edu.au/biography/glynn-patrick-mcmahon-paddy-6405/text10949.
108. Report of Third General Chapter, December 1889.

to tell Mr Hawkes that Kensington ought to be able to meet their claim. He says that our position is an awkward one as the Company can sue the Trustees if the property does not bring in the money and that we should be prepared.[109]

A few days later, she informed Mother Bernard that Mr Hawkes had advised her to engage a good land agent and have the property cut up and sold for building sites.[110] Reynolds refused to agree to this sale! As Veronica put it:

> I have tried my very best to see the Archbishop so there is no use trying any longer. It is evident to everyone that he will not give his consent to sell.[111]

Consequently, and in spite of Veronica's best efforts, the sale did not go ahead, and the Sisters of St Joseph in the Adelaide Archdiocese retained their home at Kensington and remained in South Australia.

Other important Chapter decisions that impinged on the Sisters' lives were that the Adelaide and Port Augusta dioceses should be constituted as separate provinces of the Congregation and that Sisters should be allowed to teach music where necessary. The Chapter Sisters elected Sister Monica Phillips as Provincial of the Adelaide Province and Sister Calasanctius Howley as Provincial of the Port Augusta Province.

The Adelaide Sisters found it hard to accept that Kensington was no longer their Mother House or that Adelaide was now a Province of equal status with Port Augusta, Armidale in New South Wales and Temuka in New Zealand. It seems that some had complained about the proposed sale of Kensington and also, perhaps, other Chapter decisions for, in December 1890, and not long after Veronica's return to Sydney, Mary rebuked them for having

> used their tongues too freely, judged their Superiors where they should not, murmured and criticised ... thought they knew better than their Superiors, that they could have things

---

109. Sr Veronica Champion to MM, 14 August 1890.
110. Sr Veronica Champion to M Bernard, 21 August 1890.
111. Sr Veronica Champion to M Bernard, 3 September 1890.

> done better than their Superiors . . . misjudged [them] or sought to take other opinions against [them].

Mary also needed to remind them that:

> By all accounts some of you seem to have strange ideas about the relations between Port Augusta and Adelaide . . . Kensington is no longer Mother House—it is simply a Provincial house, as also are Port Augusta, Armidale, and Temuka. None of these Provincial houses depends directly upon each other, but upon the Mother House and Mother General. No one Provincial is Superior of another, nor has any one Provincial control over the Sisters outside her own Province. Yet all are Sisters with their respective Superiors *under one head*. This does not separate Armidale or Temuka from Sydney nor from each other. Neither does it separate Port Augusta from Kensington.[112]

This was a hard lesson for them to learn and, for many, it was years before they were at peace with this new arrangement.

Julian and Mary forbade the teaching of individual music lessons to paying pupils in the earliest days of the Congregation. They took this step because their foundation was for the education of children from disadvantaged circumstances and such children would be unable to afford musical instruments. Neither of the founders would allow anything to interfere with their determination to be true to their decision that:

> The poor [were] the Sisters' charge; and hundreds of poor [could not] be neglected or injured for the sake of two or three whose positions in life entitle[d] them to things unbecoming their humbler companions.[113]

Mary claimed that the Sisters themselves

---

112. MM to the South Australian Sisters, 5 December 1890.
113. MM, 'Necessity for the Institute' (London, August 1873), in *Resource Material from the Archives of the Sisters of St Joseph of the Sacred Heart*, Issue no. 3 (January 1980).

> for their own sakes as *poor religious*, [should] have nothing to do with instrumental music. They [should] make a sacrifice of any taste, and strive to forget any knowledge they may have got, upon entering the Congregation, and they [should] do so for motives upon which it [was] not necessary to enter.[114]

She also decried the actions of 'foolish parents' who encouraged their daughters to take music lessons and commented on how she had noticed that:

> hardworking mothers toiled without mercy to themselves, and allowed their children to grow up without any idea of the true duties of their state. And how often, these daughters learned to despise and be ashamed of the poor hardworking mother who had brought them up so idly. And how often, too, these daughters had learned to despise and be ashamed of the poor hardworking mother who had brought them up in such ignorance of their duty towards God and herself.[115]

By 1889 many people's circumstances had changed for the better and, particularly in the larger, more well-established New South Wales parishes where the Josephites now had charge of schools, parents were asking for music lessons. Therefore, the Chapter decreed that:

> Music may be taught by the Sisters where necessary or advisable,
>
> and
>
> That no Sister be permitted to teach music unless examined by one appointed by Mother General and her council.[116]

Another reason for this major change was the Sisters' financial situation. Hence, it was not long before qualified South Australian Sisters were giving individual music lessons in both city and country convents. The money they raised by this means, or 'music money' as

---

114. *Resource Material*, January 1980.
115. MM to Woods, 23 April 1869.
116. Report of Third General Chapter, December 1889.

it was called, went to Kensington where it was used to help liquidate their debt and support the novitiate.

Mother Bernard paid very few visits to South Australia after her appointment, but she was there from late March until July 1886, when she met many of the Sisters and visited city and country convents. An unnamed Sister, writing to Sister Ignatius McCarthy (who was anxious to please the bishop and was in South Africa on a round-the-world fundraising mission, which she undertook for him without prior discussion with Mothers Bernard or Mary MacKillop) wrote:

> The day after you left, [Date unspecified] Mother Bernard went to the country and visited nearly all the Convents in SA. She returned here on 16th June and remained until 5th July when she left for Sydney accompanied by Sister M. Imelda [O'Brien]. She went overland, visiting Strathalbyn and Penola on the way.[117]

At this time, some Sisters wrote to Mary expressing how they longed for her return, while one stated that:

> Dear Sr Bernard is with us. She is so nice, the dear old thing, but still we want your own dear self to complete our happiness.[118]

They could never see Mother Bernard in the same light as Mary. She was a 'dear old thing' who visited them on rare occasions while Mary was their true leader and mother. Little did they then know that, thanks to Bishop Reynolds, Mary could not come back, even if she wished to. They did know, however, that they would have to wait for at least ten years before she could become Mother General again.

In 1891 some Sisters had a brief glimpse of Mary, who went to South Australia on Mother Bernard's behalf to settle some difficulties between the Sisters in the Port Augusta diocese and their Provincial.[119]

---

117. Unnamed Sister to Sr Ignatius McCarthy, 13 September 1886. Ignatius travelled round the world on a fundraising mission for Bishop Reynolds. There is no evidence as to the amount of money she raised. After her return, she settled into life in Adelaide again and remained there until her death in January 1914.
118. Sr Winifred Amos to MM, 24 April 1886.
119. Paul Gardiner SJ, *Mary MacKillop: An Extraordinary Australian* (Sydney: EJ Dwyer, 1993), 419–421.

Mary, who was there for the duration of a retreat, interviewed all the Sisters present and made several new appointments, some of which were received with bad grace. Thus, while most Sisters went off happily to their places of ministry, Sister Marianna Wall showed how upset she was at being unable to return to Burra and Sister Andrea Howley, whom Mary had decided should move from Pekina to Jamestown, was unhappy because she would be unable to call into her former home on her way to her new destination. Mary also decided that Sisters Angelica Greene and Francis Borgia McNally should leave the diocese altogether and join the Adelaide province under Sister Monica's leadership. She was taken aback by their negative reaction when informed of her decision.[120]

While on her way to and from Port Augusta, Mary needed to travel through the Adelaide Archdiocese. Hence, she was able to visit several convents quietly, making sure not to anger Reynolds by appearing publicly in or near the city. In her report to Mother Bernard she wrote:

> I was obliged to remain in Kensington from Tuesday until Friday ... I had been so well all the time and had managed to see all the convents in the North [the Port Augusta diocese] besides calling at Clare, remaining a night at Seven Hill (sic), a few hours at Gawler—(I saw the Hamley [Bridge] Sisters at the Station), [spent] a night at the Port and then on to Kensington on Tuesday.[121]

Mary left Adelaide once more, and the Sisters carried on with their work in the schools and charitable institutions. The 1880s were a hard time for them as they struggled to find their way without their foundress and their many companions who had moved to Sydney or been appointed to ministries in far-off places such as Western Australia or New Zealand.

They no longer had charge of the orphanage but the Providence and the Refuge were still very much a part of their ministry. Ever

---

120. MM to M Bernard, from the Providence in Melbourne, 2 November 1891.
121. MM to M Bernard, 2 November 1891. 'The North' or 'The Northern Diocese' are terms used by locals when referring to the Port Augusta diocese. The houses MM named in her letter were all in the Adelaide archdiocese.

since 1872, the Refuge, which was now under the charge of Sister Annette Henschke, had occupied two buildings adjacent to St Ignatius' Church in Queen Street, Norwood, and was well established there. It had the advantage of close proximity to the Kensington convent, which meant that Sisters from there could help out if needed.

On the other hand, the Providence had had a somewhat chequered existence over the years since its foundation. Because it had no fixed income, the Sisters could not afford to purchase the buildings they occupied; their premises were too small or the rent was too high; and they had moved themselves and their elderly and disabled residents at least six times between 1868 and 1883 when they settled at the western end of Franklin Street. They remained there until 1905 when the Providence found a larger and more permanent home on nearby West Terrace. As previously noted, Sister Elizabeth Etheridge, who was the first Sister of St Joseph to care for frail aged people, had charge of the Providence throughout most of this period.[122]

In 1867, Father Woods and Archdeacon Russell established a Catholic newspaper, the *Southern Cross and Catholic Herald*. This was published monthly and remained in circulation for less than five years. Following its demise, several other short-lived Catholic newspapers appeared and disappeared at intervals. Then, in July 1889, Archbishop Reynolds re-established the *Southern Cross* as a weekly. It was well received and proved a useful vehicle for keeping Catholics informed of church affairs, and of advertising and reporting on events run by church members, especially Religious Sisters and Brothers.

Thus, the first issue of this paper, which appeared on 5 July 1889, carried a notice advising the public of 'a grand Juvenile Concert', to be given by 'the pupils of St Joseph's School, Kensington' on 11 September. It also reported on a 'Grand Vocal, Instrumental and Dramatic Entertainment' performed on the previous day by the pupils attending St Joseph's School, Port Adelaide. According to the issue of 13 September 1889, both concerts were well attended,

---

122. For further details of these and other institutions managed by the Josephites during that era, see: Marie T Foale, *Think of the Ravens: The Sisters of St Joseph in Social Welfare* (Adelaide, Sisters of St Joseph, 2001).

the children were a credit to the Sisters, and the Port Adelaide event raised £40 towards for the support of their Sisters.

During October 1889 it informed its readers of the death of Father Woods in Sydney on the 7th of that month. Although this news was expected, given his long and debilitating illness over the past two or three years, the Sisters and his many relatives and friends in Adelaide grieved his passing deeply. Mary lost no time in writing to his niece, Sister Mechtilde Woods, and also to Sister Monica who, while remaining faithful to Mary and the Roman Constitutions, had maintained her friendship with him:

> I was about a quarter of an hour late to see him die and had no idea he was dying when I started out to see him. Of course, he had been, so to say, dying so often and got better. I saw him about a fortnight before, and then he said, 'It looks like the end but it's not.' It was so painful to see him and be of no use that, after that, I used to send and enquire but did not care to go too often myself. They told me he used to like a few strawberries. I tried now and then to send him [some].

She enclosed flowers from his coffin for them and also for Mrs Catherine Woods (his sister-in-law and Sister Mechtilde's mother), and for Nettie and Agnes Woods (his brother, Terry's two daughters). Her aim over coming days, she said, was to write to all the 'old Sisters' individually as soon as possible and she urged her readers to 'imitate his virtues of charity and gentleness' and under no consideration to forget him in their prayers.[123]

At the end of the month, Mary wrote to all the Sisters, and especially to those who had known Woods:

> Let us hope that the gentle spirit of our Father Founder may plead for us before the throne of God in Heaven. Whilst we, his children from whom he was separated on earth, must in duty bound pray for his departed soul, we may surely hope that even from Purgatory he will do much to help us with God. He died very happily, full of resignation and charity and leaving his blessing to all who wore the Habit. I had not seen him for some days before his death and just got to his room about a quarter of an hour after it. He had been received

---

123. MM to Srs Mechtilde Woods and Monica Phillips, 10 October 1889.

back into the Passionist Order some time before his death and this was a matter of deep thankfulness to me, as I knew how ardently he had desired this favour in earlier days. I ask you, my dearest Sisters one and all—those who knew him personally and those who have only heard of him— to remember that he dearly loved the Institute and that he wished to see the Sisters humble and full of charity towards each other. We must try to honour his memory by imitating his virtues.[124]

In December 1889, while the Sister delegates to the third Josephite General Chapter in Sydney were on their way to New South Wales, the Sisters in Clare were preparing for their annual school concert and display of children's work. Then, early in the New Year, the *Southern Cross* informed its readers that all present were impressed by the standard of the children's work and that 'the singing and acting of the children were capital, and reflected credit upon their tutors'.[125]

The paper also reported that, even though Mid-North farmers were struggling to survive droughts and low wheat prices, the Pekina people had made some substantial improvements to the convent, and put a galvanised iron fence around the convent block. As already noted, the Pekina Sisters were offering their seventy students tuition in music, drawing, painting in oils and singing, as well as the ordinary subjects laid down in the school curriculum and all who heard them were delighted with the children's singing in the church.[126]

At Thebarton in 1894, the Honourable JV O'Loghlin, MLC, a well-known Catholic politician, opened a cake fair with words of praise for the parish priest and 'the good Sisters' who assisted him in the areas of education, temperance and charity.[127] It noted that these Sisters had donated fancy goods for sale, while pupils from the Josephite schools in the city had taken part in the nightly entertainment offered to patrons.[128] This fair was the forerunner of

---

124. MM to the Sisters, 28 October 1889.
125. *SC*, 3 January 1890, 8.
126. *SC*, 25 May 1894.
127. Peter Travers, 'O'Loghlin, James Vincent (1852–1925)', *ADB* (National Centre of Biography, Australian National University, 1988). http://adb.anu.edu.au/biography/ologhlin-james-vincent-7905/text13747,
128. *SC*, 27 July 1894, 7.

the many that took place over subsequent years. As usual, the Sisters were in the background, training the children for their parts in the proceedings, providing goods for sale and assisting with the catering.

Records of such events are few and far between but it is easy to imagine similar activities taking place in other Josephite schools throughout this period of history and, as a consequence, of small but useful sums of money being handed to the Sisters at their conclusion. As already noted, fundraising was of the utmost importance as the South Australian Sisters had been left to carry the burden of their debt without help from the Mother House in Sydney. In fact, Mother Bernard Walsh deemed it inopportune to commit the Mother House to finding £100 annually towards it. She did this even though many Sisters in Sydney and other provinces of the Congregation, including herself, had begun their religious lives in South Australia and had been provided with all their needs while there.[129]

The loss of Mother Mary, the Mother House and so many of their religious Sisters to Sydney in particular, and the knowledge that they were on their own regarding the debt gave rise to an anti-Sydney feeling among some of the Sisters. A letter to Mary in 1894 from Sister Calasanctius (who seems to have been having a bad day) gives a glimpse of how she and some of her peers were feeling. She wrote:

> I got a telegram from Norwood yesterday that Mother General has arrived there [Adelaide]. I shall be glad indeed to see her. How will they be in Sydney—ruled by an ex-widow and an ex Sr of Mercy? I can't say I envy them there as I see nothing to admire in these ex-Nuns whatever.[130]

The Sisters to whom she was referring were Veronica Champion and Josephine McMullen. Veronica was a young widow grieving the loss of her husband and her baby daughter when she responded to Father Woods' invitation to become a Josephite. Josephine, as already noted, had spent some months as a novice with the Sisters of Mercy in Melbourne before returning to Adelaide and taking charge of the St

---

129. Archbishop O'Reily to MM, 13 August 1895, O'Reily letter books, vol 2, 64-65, ACA.
130. Sr Calasanctius Howley to MM, 25 February 1894, Port Augusta.

Francis Xavier's Cathedral Hall School, where she became the first Adelaide resident to join the Congregation.[131]

Archbishop Reynolds died on 12 June 1893, aged fifty-nine years.[132] Despite all that the Sisters had suffered at his hands, it seems that it was because of him that they gained Roman approval for their central government as soon as they did. It appears that with Reynolds' demise the Congregation's period of youth and early maturity came to an end. Its members were now secure in the knowledge that never again could a bishop interfere with their Constitutions or force them to abandon their existing structures.

The statistics for the time paint an interesting picture. In September 1882 the 172 Sisters in the colony were managing forty-six schools and three charitable institutions. Between then and 1893 they closed eight convents and schools in what was then the new Port Augusta diocese, and withdrew from twenty convents and schools and one charitable institution in the Adelaide archdiocese. They still managed the Refuge and the Providence but the Orphanage had passed into other hands.[133] In January 1895, when John O'Reily

---

131. Sisters of Mercy Archives, Nicholson Street, Fitzroy, Victoria. Marie T Foale, *The Josephite Story*, Chapter 3. 'Reports of Josephite General Chapters, 1875-1899', ASSJ, North Sydney. Veronica Champion, born Sarah Tobin, was the widow. She married Thomas Champion at St Mary's Cathedral, Sydney, in 1863. Both were natives of Ireland. They lived at Bungendore in NSW where Sarah gave birth to a baby girl who died as an infant. Her husband died of tuberculosis, aged twenty-nine years; both he and the baby are buried at Bungendore. Sarah met Woods in Sydney in 1871 and, at his invitation, went to Adelaide with two others to join Mary and the Josephites, even though, technically, they were suppressed. She took the name of 'Sister Veronica' and served in South Australia before returning to New South Wales in 1880.

    The other was Sr Josephine McMullen, who migrated to Adelaide with her brother Michael and his family in the late 1850s. She worked as a teacher in a Catholic school at Marybank (Hectorville) until she joined the Sisters of Mercy in Melbourne in 1863. She left them voluntarily while she was still a novice, and joined the Josephites in July 1867. She served in South Australia until Mary appointed her Provincial of Queensland from 1875 until 1879 when she returned to South Australia. She moved to Sydney during 1885. In 1896 she became Provincial of the Armidale province and was a member of the General Council from 1899 until her death in 1904.

132. Ian J Bickerton, 'Reynolds, Christopher Augustine (1834-1893)', *ADB*, National Centre of Biography, Australian National University, 1976. http://adb.anu.edu.au/biography/reynolds-christopher-augustine-4470/text7293.

133. See Appendices Ten & Eleven for details of these major changes.

left Port Augusta to become Archbishop of Adelaide, he left behind twenty-three Sisters in seven convents with their attached schools. In the archdiocese he found 102 Sisters working in eighteen schools and two charitable institutions. Hence, in South Australia there were 125 Sisters living in twenty-four convents, teaching in twenty-five schools and managing the Orphanage and the Refuge. In short, the number of Sisters had fallen by one third and the number of schools by almost half.

Former Vicar General, Father Frederick Byrne, became administrator of the Adelaide Archdiocese after Reynolds' death and continued in this role until O'Reily's formal installation as Archbishop in January 1895. Byrne reported to him that the Josephites had houses only in the city and the larger country towns and were neglecting the smaller and more isolated settlements for whose benefit they were founded.[134] There was some truth in what he said. During the previous thirty years the Sisters had taught in approximately eighty-five different localities throughout the colony and subsequently they had withdrawn from sixty, mostly in smaller country places. The reasons for their withdrawal were many and varied and often outside their control. Nevertheless, their constant movement had given Reynolds cause to complain to Monsignor Kirby in Rome that they were restless and unwilling to remain in any one place for long, while Byrne had gained the impression that they were 'fond of rambling about'.[135]

Whether they were settled in one place or 'rambling about', as Byrne put it, these Sisters were so busy that it is likely that few if any of them were aware of important changes, such as the introduction of women's suffrage, that were taking place in the wider South Australian community. What these Sisters did have was first-hand experience of the effects of the constant droughts that ravaged the land and the depressed state of the economy, the high level of unemployment and the consequent hardship and poverty being endured by many of the people among whom they ministered.

---

134. Fr F Byrne, Report of his administration of the diocese from 12 June 1893–15 March 1895, O'Reily letter Books, vol 1, 10–12, ACA.
135. F Byrne, 'Report on the State of the Diocese' (18 March 1895), 9, O'Reily letter books, vol 1, ACA; Reynolds to Kirby, 22 October 1887, ICA K530.

KENSINGTON COMMUNITY, LATE 1905

Back Row: Sisters Attracta Murray, Reginald O'Loughlin, John Baptist Fitzgerald, Gabriel Gillman-Jones, Daphne Knowles, Aiden Cooney, Ethelreda Clark, Carolus Büring.
Third Row: Sisters Gonzaga Casey, Andrina Clarke, Sebastian Lee, Cornelia O'Loughlin, Madeleine Carroll, Adrian Riggs, Lourdes Riggs, Georgina Sheridan, Felix O'Rourck.
Second Row (Seated): Sisters Julianna O'Brien, Beatrice Blackwell, Regis Butler, Scholastica Byrne, Monica Phillips, Victor Lane (Provincial), Baptista Long, Ignatius McCarthy, Mida McMahon
Front Row: Sisters Beatrice Fitzpatrick, Benedetta Murphy, Romuald O'Donoghue, Dorothea Hennessy, Magdalen O'Reilly, Dolorosa Tucker, Daria Bell.
Note: Sisters Beatrice Fitzpatrick & Dorothea Hennesssy both left the Congregation at a later date

Joanna Barr Smith, ca 1908
(State Library of South Australia, B 59767.)

Robert Barr Smith, ca 1908
(State Library of South Australia, B 59765.)

Sr Baptista Long

Sr Raymond Smyth, First Provincial of New Zealand

Sr Patricia Campbell, strong advocate of central government

Sr Monica Phillips, Assistant General, 1883–1889; Provincial, 1889–1899 Novice Mistress, 1899–1910

Sr Michael Quinlan, sister to Hyacinth

Sisters and children outside St Barnabas Church, Strathalbyn, 1880s.

Students outside the Caltowie church and convent in about 1905, the year when the Sisters returned there.

School children in front of the new Georgetown convent, about 1910.

Confirmation at Macclesfield, about 1878. Note the convent in background.

Chapter Four
New Hope—New Life: 1895–1909

The year 1895 began with the installation of John O'Reily as Archbishop of Adelaide and James Maher, former parish priest of Pekina, as Bishop of Port Augusta. All Catholics in the archdiocese welcomed O'Reily warmly because of his reputation as a strong, just, and kindly man with a good business head and the ability to free the diocese of its crippling debts. Among those who greeted him was Sister Annette Henschke who wrote:

> It is with delight and pleasure that we congratulate you on your appointment . . . I need not say what great consolation it will be to our dear Mother Mary to know that she is once more free to come back again to Adelaide where she has suffered so much.[1]

For his part, O'Reily proved himself a man of action. Within weeks of his installation he was investigating both diocesan and Josephite finances and taking steps to deal with them. On 13 August, just seven months after his arrival, he wrote to Mary MacKillop with suggestions as to how the Sisters might manage their debt, which then stood at almost £7,000. He hoped that Mother Bernard and her council would allocate £100 to South Australia annually for the next five years, but this assistance was not forthcoming. Hence, as he took pains to inform Mary, he asked the Josephites' creditors to lower their interest rates to a more sustainable level.

---

1. Sr Annette Henschke to O'Reily, 6 February 1895. Other letters that have survived are M Bernard Walsh to O'Reily, 5 February 1895; and Sr Gertrude Mary Dewe to O'Reily, 14 January 1895. O'Reily papers, ACA.

Quite remarkably, he succeeded in this strategy and almost at once the Sisters began to experience a lightening of the millstone that had hung around their necks for the twenty years that had passed since Mary mortgaged the Kensington property in 1876. Through O'Reily's organising skill and hard work and the Sisters' own efforts, by 1910 they owed only £443.[2] This reduction occurred despite the fact that, during this same period of time, they had built a new convent at Kensington, a new Refuge at Fullarton, new convent and school buildings at several other places in the archdiocese. They had also acquired a new Catholic Orphanage at Largs Bay.[3]

When O'Reily arrived in Adelaide, Sister Monica Phillips was Provincial of the Adelaide Province while Sister Calasanctius Howley held the same role in Port Augusta. Relations and movement between the two provinces relaxed after Archbishop Reynolds' death and it was only a matter of time before they could become one. In fact, they did so during the Josephite General Chapter of 1896, when the Sisters present ruled that Adelaide and Port Augusta were to be united as the Province of South Australia and decided that Sister Monica Phillips should be Provincial of this new entity.[4]

Mother Bernard's term of office did not expire until 1898 and so there was no election for Mother General. The voting for her councillors went ahead, however, and the Chapter Sisters re-elected Mary as first councillor and assistant to the Mother General. The other councillors were Sisters Veronica Champion, Collette Carolan and Patrick Barry, all of whom were resident in New South Wales at this time.

The Sisters suffered greatly during the latter half of Reynolds' episcopate. As already noted, one third of those resident in South Australia in 1880 left the colony to avoid being forced to become members of a diocesan Congregation. The overall climate was such that only fourteen young women, at least two of whom were from another colony, joined the Adelaide Josephites between 1885 and

---

2. O'Reily to Sr Victor Lane, Provincial: 'The Story of a Debt', *SC*, 2 September 1910, 681.
3. O'Reily to MM, 13 August 1895, O'Reily Letter books, vol 2, letter 29. See also Marie T Foale, *The Josephite Story*, 185-186 for further details re the liquidation of the debt.
4. Report of the Fourth General Chapter of the Sisters of St Joseph, Sydney, 1896.

1893.[5] Because the tension in Adelaide was so palpable, Sister Monica sent most of these women to Sydney for their novitiate training.

Under O'Reily matters improved markedly. During the latter half of the 1890s, fifty-seven young women joined the community in Adelaide.[6] They more than replaced the twenty lost through death during the same period and boosted the numbers available to staff the schools and institutions. Things were looking up but, even so, Sister Monica still found it difficult to staff all the Josephite schools in the colony.

When the 1896 Chapter ruled that novices were not to work as teachers in local schools as they had done in the past, and she needed to provide Sisters for two new foundations, she complained to Mother Bernard:[7]

> We will be short of Sisters at Christmas, having to open Petersburg (Peterborough) and the Reformatory.[8]

Moves for the establishment of these foundations had been afoot for some years and it was important that they be made without delay. The first to come up for consideration was the reformatory, which was to be located in the old church-school and convent at St Johns, near Kapunda. The report of the Royal Commission into the Destitute Act 1881–1885 recommended that delinquent children should be placed in institutions run by the religious denomination to which they belonged, that the government should support these children, and that each institution should be open for government inspection.

In the late 1880s, the South Australian Government accepted Reynolds' offer to place its female Catholic inmates under the care

---

5. Srs Gabriel and Aelred Gillman-Jones both came from Western Australia to enter, the one in 1885 and the other in 1888. Register of the Sisters, Adelaide, entries 330 & 364.
6. Register of the Sisters, Kensington, SA.
7. Report of Fourth General Chapter, 1896.
8. Sr Monica Phillips to M Bernard Walsh, 2 November 1896. Initially, the town of Peterborough was named Petersburg, after the landowner, Peter Doecke, who sold land to create the town. It was one of the sixty-nine places in South Australia renamed in 1917 because of anti-German sentiments during World War I. In any references to this town for the period 1897–1917, its original name will be used. See Geoffrey Manning, *Place Names of South Australia* (Modbury, South Australia: Gould Books, 2006).

of Sisters trained specifically for this work.[9] At that point, however, nothing happened because the archbishop's health was declining and the diocese was virtually bankrupt.[10] By 1895, the government was tired of waiting and took the initiative. It passed an Act empowering the State Children's Council to proclaim private reformatory schools and to pay a subsidy for each inmate on condition that only children belonging to the denomination setting up the reformatory were accepted into it.[11]

O'Reily responded to this Act as soon as practicable by seeking permission to take charge of all the Catholic girls currently in the State Reformatory. The government approved his offer and agreed to pay ten shillings a week for each girl, provided that the new institution was located as far from the city as possible. Hence, it readily accepted the archbishop's offer of the abandoned church and priest's house (also former Josephite convent and school) at St Johns, some five kilometres to the southeast of Kapunda. It seems that some Sisters were unhappy at the idea of bringing girls who had been through the courts into this idyllic setting. Thus, for example, in October 1896, Andrea Howley, who was stationed at the Refuge, wrote to Mary (possibly on behalf of others besides herself):

> Dr Byrne was here during the week. He told S Annette it was not settled yet about the St Johns affair. I hope they will go somewhere else. He said the Archbishop and the government men were to go to St Johns before anything was done.[12]

Matters were finalised soon after the archbishop's meeting with the government officials. Within a few months, he had the new institution gazetted as an Industrial School under the State Children's

---

9. *South Australian Parliamentary Papers* (SAPP): 1885, no. 228; Report of the 1881– 1885 Commission. Appendix P; 1885, par 177; Appendix XXX, par 121 & 186.
10. SCC Report, Adelaide, 1889. *SAPP* 1896, no. 95. State Children's Act, 1895.
11. John O'Reily, *Reports on the Liabilities of the Archdiocese of Adelaide* (annual), 1896– 1911; State Children's Act, 1895.
12. Sr Andrea Howley to MM, 12 October 1896. Fr F Byrne was Vicar General and Administrator during the latter part of Reynolds' time as Archbishop. His parish of Kapunda included the St Johns area. It seems that he assumed the title of Doctor while he was Vicar General (He did not have a Doctorate in Theology.)

Act of 1895 and had arranged with Mother Bernard and Sister Monica for the appointment of four Sisters to go there during 1897.[13]

The second new foundation in 1897 was at Petersburg in the Port Augusta diocese. Local parish priest, Father John Norton, had been asking for Sisters to take charge of his already functioning Catholic school since the late 1880s, when he had purchased a block of land for a convent. By 1896 it was ready and Sister Monica was prepared to appoint a community to go there in the following January.

The Petersburg and St Johns foundations took place while Mary MacKillop was in South Australia on her first official visit since her banishment in November 1883. She arrived in Adelaide on 21 July 1896 and was there almost continuously until 6 October 1897. Her journey to Adelaide began almost immediately after the General Chapter of 1896 when, at Mother Bernard's request, she set out from Sydney to visit the seven communities in the Armidale Province. She was back at North Sydney in June and, on 2 July she left for Victoria where she spent a short time at each of the six foundations in that colony.

Finally, on 20 July she caught the Melbourne Express for Adelaide.[14] What a change this was from the journeys by coastal steamer that she and the Sisters had endured for so many years! On the following morning Sister Monica and the South Australians welcomed her home with joy.[15] One can imagine the reminiscing and the grieving together that would have taken place over the following days and weeks as founding members of the Congregation met with their foundress for the first time in many years.

Within a week of her arrival she was on the road, beginning a gruelling round of visitation of all the convents, schools, and institutions in the colony. First of all, she spent time at each of the city convents, beginning with Kensington itself. She was in Gawler on 27 July and back in the city two days later. Then, during August she visited Hectorville, Thebarton, Brompton, Lower North Adelaide, Mitcham, the Providence and the Russell Street and Pirie Street

---

13. John O'Reily to SCC, September 1896; SCC to O'Reily, 12 January 1897; *SA Government Gazette* 3 June and 10 June 1897.
14. The trains between the colonies of NSW, Victoria and SA had made travel so much easier by this time. The Sydney to Melbourne line opened in 1883 and the Melbourne to Adelaide one in 1887.
15. Research by Barry Evans (2012).

schools in the city, and was back in Kensington by the end of the month. While there she informed the Sisters that she was impressed with the spirit among those she had met so far. As she wrote to an unnamed Sister:

> It is so nice to be here once more amongst so many true and faithful Sisters. All are so happy and united—no contentions, strife or jealousies here, thank God, and this is as it should be.[16]

She reported that there were nine novices and ten postulants, 'all very nice and promising ones', in the novitiate. With this injection of youth and enthusiasm among the older, well-seasoned members of the community the future looked promising indeed.

Of grave concern to Mary was her discovery that, with Mother Bernard's permission, Sisters in some metropolitan convents had set up small, select secondary schools for those who could pay. It is difficult to identify these schools except for the one at Glenelg. Two years later, in 1899, Mary listed them as being at the Kensington Convent School (the one on the convent grounds), Brompton in the western suburbs, North Adelaide and the Mitcham Convent Boarding School with its twelve boarders.[17] To her mind, select schools cut right across the Josephite ideal of service to the poor without discrimination. Hence she made no secret of her determination to get rid of them and of her feelings when they failed. She wrote to one Sister: 'The Select Schools have proved a dead failure. Thank God.'[18]

Before the year was out the issue came up again and this time she was even more forthright in her condemnation of it:

> The 'Select [exclusive or elite] Schools' have been a complete failure, and no longer exist as such. Glenelg Convent School will most likely be given up altogether. The Archdeacon [Russell] has just proposed this and we are delighted. It was the only 'Select School' we had any trouble about breaking up. I tell the Sisters and priests that God could not bless those schools and that they could not have the protecting care of St

---

16. MM to an unnamed Sister, from Kensington, 28 August 1896.
17. SC, 4 May 1900, p. 286.
18. MM to a Sister, 28 August 1896.

Joseph, as they were completely opposed to the spirit of his Congregation and the wishes of the founders.

Fancy Mrs Barr Smith saying to me, 'Some way, Mother Mary, the Sisters do not seem to have the spirit of humble simplicity that so appealed to the worldly mind in the early days,' and she was, in a measure, right, but all true Sisters must try to regain that spirit if they have lost it. (Thank God very few have.) And then God will do wonders through the poorest of them.[19]

At the time of Mary's visit, forty-four primary school children and thirty-four secondary students were enrolled at Glenelg. When Archdeacon Russell, who was now parish priest of Glenelg, was on the Catholic Education Board under Father Woods in the late 1860s, he complained that the Josephites concentrated on the poor and disadvantaged to the detriment of the better off. Judging by Mary's comment above, it appears that he was not at all pleased at having to close the select section of his school and was more than willing to invite the Dominican Sisters from Cabra Convent, Cumberland Park, to replace the Josephites. As it happened, it was 1904 before that community was ready to make a foundation at Glenelg. In the meantime, and with the interests of the poor children at heart, Mary allowed the Sisters to continue as before, but without the secondary classes, for as long as they were needed. Finally, at the end of 1903, they were free to leave this area.

While at Kensington during 1896, Mary went to Mitcham, to visit her long-time friend Joanna Barr Smith, at her home, 'Torrens Park'. Then, after some further time in the metropolitan area, she set out for the North, that is, the convents between Gawler, just forty kilometres from Adelaide and Quorn, at the limits of the settled areas of the colony. As she visited each Josephite house, she found that most of the Sisters were working steadily in their appointed places. Since there had been no new foundations since 1891 and no withdrawals since the Sisters' departure from Kapunda at the end of 1893, it appears that they were entering into a period of stability and consolidation. She had few complaints, although she confessed

---

19. MM to Sr Raymond Smyth, New Zealand, 9 December 1896. See Appendix Thirteen for a further insight into Mary's feelings re secondary teaching, and especially Select Schools.

that she dreaded going to Jamestown, Caltowie and Gladstone.[20] She did not say why she felt like this and, during the course of her visitation, spent some time at each of these places.

At the end of 1896, however, the Sisters left Caltowie for good. No explanation for this move has been found among Josephite records but it seems likely that Mary herself advised it. There is no doubt that Sister Monica would have been glad to have the three Sisters from there to help staff the new foundations planned for 1897.[21] A lay teacher managed the Caltowie School for the next eight years. Then, in 1905, three Sisters under the leadership of Sister Laurence O'Brien returned to this little town.

It seems that, regardless of any ill feelings the local people might have had because of the Sisters' withdrawal in 1896, they were happy to have them back and to provide them with new accommodation in the form of a solid, six room convent in Killarney Drive at Caltowie.[22] Father Norton from Petersburg, who was also vicar general of the Port Augusta diocese, blessed and opened it on 24 May 1904.[23] Besides running a day school, the Caltowie Sisters cared for a small number of primary school aged weekly boarders who came in from the more distant farms in the district.

While in the North, Mary renewed her acquaintance with the Sisters of the Good Samaritan at Port Pirie. On many occasions, these Sisters had made her and any other Sisters travelling between Adelaide and Brisbane most welcome in their Sydney convents.[24] Their community

---

20. MM to Sr Annette Henschke, 24 September 1896. For Mary's description of her visitation to the North, see *Mary MacKillop in Challenging Times 1883—1899: A Collection of Letters,* edited by Sheila McCreanor (North Sydney: Sisters of St Joseph, 2006), 313–17.
21. ACA, 1896, Report for Port Augusta diocese.
22. SC, 17 November 1905, 736.
23. Bishop Maher died at Pekina on 20 December 1905 and Father Norton was consecrated third bishop of the diocese in December 1906. He did not move to his cathedral town of Port Augusta but remained in Peterborough for the rest of his life.
24. Archbishop Polding founded the Good Samaritans (The Institute of the Sisters of the Good Samaritan of the Order of St Benedict) in Sydney in 1857, and in 1861, they opened their first school (in Sussex Street, Sydney). For an account of the relationship between Mary MacKillop and the Good Samaritans, see Margaret Walsh, *Opening the Door to a Saint* (Sydney: Good Samaritan Sisters, November 2010).

leader was Mother Magdalen Adamson who was their Mother General when the Good Samaritan Sisters made a foundation in Port Pirie in 1890, and had accompanied them there. Her term of office expired in 1894 and subsequently she moved to Port Pirie as community leader. Her stay there was short, however, for in August 1896 she suffered a stroke and became seriously ill. She longed to return to Sydney and two Sisters came from there to help her make the long journey home.

Mary, who was visiting the Gladstone convent and school when she learned of Mother Magdalen's illness, hurried to visit her. When the Sisters told her how they planned to take Mother Magdalen home, Mary contacted Sisters Monica and Annette asking them to ensure that Mother Magdalen was made comfortable during her stopover in Adelaide. She explained these plans to Annette:

> Sister Monica will tell you that I invited the poor invalid Mother to stay at the Providence the night she is in Adelaide, and that I want our invalid chair to be taken into town for her. Will you see Mrs McDonald for me and ask her to let the chair be left at her house until it will be wanted? We all owe a debt of gratitude to Mother Magdalen for kindness to us when we had no convent in Sydney. More than once, she and some of her nuns gave up their cells and beds to us in our travels and this when our Sisters came to them unexpectedly and at dead of night. The poor old nun cried with joy when she saw me. The M.G. is over from Sydney to take her home, and is accompanied by Sr Angela— the Vicar General of Sydney's sister (sic) [the sister of the Vicar General of Sydney]—a great friend of mine. In their sorrow and distress what could I do but tell them to consider any house of ours as their own.[25]

Thanks in part to Mary's kindness, Mother Magdalen survived the long train journey and was cared for by her Sydney Sisters until her death several months later.[26] In the meantime, Mary completed her

---

25. MM to Sr Annette Henschke, 22 October 1896. Sr Sonia Wagner, SGS, Port Pirie, 15 March 2013.
26. In 1905, and indeed, until well after World War II, the fastest and most comfortable way of travelling between Port Pirie and Sydney, was by train—a day train to Adelaide from Port Pirie and then two night trains, the first between Adelaide and Melbourne and the second between Melbourne and Sydney. This was a vast

visitation of the North by early December and returned to Kensington where she was as busy as ever. Besides meeting with the Sisters in the local community and organising various business and other gatherings, she accepted their invitations to attend end of year school celebrations. Thus, she wrote:

> I am too busy for a letter—Kensington Display this afternoon, North Adelaide tonight, Russell Street, Pirie Street and Beulah Road tomorrow, and I am expected to be at each.[27]

And again:

> I cannot help not writing. I am always so busy, visiting and examining schools, at Displays, and one thing or another.[28]

The Sisters from all the country convents in both the Adelaide and Port Augusta Dioceses arrived at Kensington on or before 17 December and enjoyed their first general meeting with their mother foundress since Christmas 1882. One might ask whether, while she was in the house, they gave her the use of the desk they gave her back then! [At the time of writing that desk was at the Kensington convent.]

They all made a Retreat together, and at its conclusion everyone departed for their places of ministry, with the exception of the members of the new Petersburg community: Sisters Benizi Casey, M. Joseph (possibly Sweeney), Clothilde Roughan and Aloysius Joseph Thomas, who waited in Adelaide until Mary was ready to travel with them. (She had gone to Melbourne for a few days, and only returned on Friday, 15 January.) Next morning she felt ill but did not let this prevent her being up early enough to catch the 6.30 am train for Petersburg. When they reached their destination later that day the new arrivals discovered that, according to Mary:

> Father [Norton] is very kind to us and had such a nice convent for us. The house is new—six large rooms and well furnished.

---

improvement on the coastal steamers that Mary and the Sisters used to patronise in earlier years.
27. MM to an unnamed Sister, 15 December 1896.
28. MM to Sr Ethelburga Job, 15 December 1896.

> It is a detached house, not one minute's walk from the church and two minutes from the school.[29]

They opened school in the following week with ninety-three children and the promise of more to come. According to her custom of settling Sisters into their new convents and schools, Mary stayed at Petersburg for at least a week and during that time made sure that she met and got to know the school children.[30]

Next came the setting up and opening of the girls' reformatory at St Johns in early May. This time, Mary accompanied Sisters Helena Hartney, Cyril Welsh, Mary Xavier O'Leary, and an unnamed postulant to the new foundation. (Later that year Sister Genevieve Bird replaced the postulant.)[31]

Mary herself has described their adventures after their arrival at St Johns:

> We took possession of our almost empty house yesterday, brought out a loaf of bread, some butter, polony [fritz],[32] fruit, soap, mustard of course, candles, tea, etc. but had no cups, mugs, or anything else to drink out of or wash in, or boil water, so, after a time we walked over to Rodgers' where we got something to eat and drink. Then Mrs Rodgers had the horse put in the buggy and drove us back, bringing some cups, kettle, etc. etc. and sheets, also her daughter Mary to stay with us. We slept comfortably in the old sanctuary, Mary in the part outside the partition. There are seven beds, and the rest to come on Monday.[33]

And again two weeks later:

> We live about four miles out from Kapunda. The old church of Saint Johns and the presbytery are being done up for us at the Archbishop's expense, and he also pays for our chaplain who

---

29. MM to an unnamed Sister, 22 January 1897.
30. MM to an unnamed Sister, 22 January 1897.
31. MM to Mrs Wantstill, 6 June 1897.
32. What South Australians call 'fritz' is a lunch meat usually made from pork and traditionally enclosed in an orange skin. It is known as 'devon' or 'luncheon meat' in the eastern Australian states and 'polony' in Western Australia. See also: http://www.samemory.sa.gov.au/site/page.cfm?u=383
33. MM to Sr Monica Phillips, 2 May 1897.

> comes out from Kapunda for daily Mass. This is the place which has so long had the name of being haunted, but we have seen no ghosts, though there are plenty of graves near us; the cemetery is quite close, and a nice one, too.[34]

Mary stayed at St Johns on and off until the end of June, by which time she was satisfied that the Sisters understood how the Archbishop and the SA State Government expected them to carry out this 'great undertaking' for the benefit of 'young girl prisoners'.[35] The first contingent of girls arrived at the beginning of June and she was there with the Sisters to welcome them.[36]

These foundations were made in the late 1890s, some years after the Sisters began taking individual music lessons, as allowed by the 1889 General Chapter. Mary herself encouraged younger Sisters with some musical training to try to improve themselves in that area, so as to be ready to undertake this work when required.[37] She also brought in her own sister, Annie MacKillop, who was an experienced music teacher, to help out. During 1897 Annie lived with the North Adelaide community and the Sisters enjoyed her company very much. Sister Borgia Fay wrote to Mary:

> We are quite at home with your dear little sister and she is so truly nice and amiable that she almost makes us believe she is quite at home with us. She commenced the music lessons on Monday at 8 a.m. so we did not give her much spare time, poor little thing. We are pleased and grateful to have her here and are already forming great plans for preparing pupils for this year's musical exams.[38]

While Annie MacKillop was occupied with her music pupils at North Adelaide, Mary continued her busy round of visitation of convents, especially St Johns, until 6 October when she left for New Zealand.

---

34. MM to Sr Gertrude Mary Dewe, 17 May 1897.
35. MM to Sr Gertrude Mary Dewe, 17 May 1897.
36. MM to Mrs Wantstill, 6 June 1897. For further details re the foundation and history of the reformatory, refer to Marie T Foale, *Think of the Ravens* (Adelaide, 2001).
37. MM to Sr Francis de Sales Mahony, 27 January 1897. This Sister was an experienced music teacher.
38. Sr Borgia Fay to MM from North Adelaide, 27 January 1897.

Fundraising continued to be important as, under Archbishop O'Reily's guidance, the Sisters gradually reduced their debt. They were doing so well that, by late September 1897, one week before Mary's departure from South Australia, he decided that the diocese and the Sisters could risk committing capital to an expensive new project. With that in mind, he invited Mary to meet him at suburban Fullarton, so that together they could inspect a property that he hoped would be suitable for a new and larger Refuge to replace the overcrowded institution at Norwood. As Mary wrote:

> I have to go out now to meet His Grace at Fullarton. No words can express all he has done for us and how he really loves the Sisters and their work.[39]

Soon after their meeting, O'Reily purchased a disused jam factory in Wattle Street, Fullarton, and authorised the erection of a new convent and an accommodation block large enough to house at least ninety adults and forty young children. There was also a separate lying in home for those women who wished to deliver their babies at the Refuge, and a kindergarten and play room suitable for small children up to the age of three.[40] That done, he arranged for the factory building to be converted into a modern, well-equipped laundry that could service the laundry needs of even more clients than the Sisters had dealt with at Norwood. The building work was completed by October 1901 and, as soon as possible, Sisters and residents moved there from Norwood. Sisters Annette Henschke, Bernardine Ledwith, and the other members of the Refuge community were now able to offer a better service to the unmarried mothers, their children, and those members of the public who patronised the laundry.

While this building project was under way, the Congregation underwent a major change in its leadership. On 3 August 1898, Mother Bernard Walsh died suddenly at Lithgow in New South Wales. Less than a year earlier, on 8 December 1897, she had received a communication from Cardinal Moran stating that:

---

39. MM to Sr Augustine Brady, 30 September 1897.
40. In the nineteenth century, a lying in home was a place where women could have their babies.

> Authorities in Rome [have] come to the decision that, as your General Chapter was so lately held, it [would] not be expedient to summon another Chapter so soon as next year for the election of the Mother General... It [has become] my pleasing duty, therefore ... to confirm you in your present office as Mother Superior General... till the celebration of the General Chapter as prescribed by your rule in 1902.[41]

This news came as a shock to Mary and the Sisters. All had been looking forward to the day when they could re-elect her as their leader after having been denied that right at their two most recent General Chapters. As was her custom, Mary accepted Rome's decision as being God's Will for the Congregation, encouraged her Sisters to do the same, and wrote to Sister Annette Henschke:

> Do not grieve too much over the news from Rome... Have patience and go on quietly with your work. It is God's work and you are doing it *for Him*.
> Personally I am not disappointed or pained, but I am sorry for the disappointment of my dear good Sisters, and oh, I am so sorry for Mother Bernard herself.[42]

Several weeks later she had cause to write as follows to Sisters who were unhappy about Mother Bernard's reappointment:

> With regard to the news you heard last Christmas, we must all, my dear Sisters, take that as a message from God, making known to us *His Holy Will*. Any murmurings or expressions of disapproval now would be unworthy of St Joseph's children and really pain the Heart of our Divine Spouse. Think of all this. Be patient and work generously in the service of our Divine Lord, keeping as near *Him* under the Cross as you can, and then what can you, or any of us, be but happy? Courage, dear Sisters, one and all—try and make Mother General's cross as light as you can. Remember it is a heavy one, but each Sister

---

41. Sheila McCreanor, *Mary MacKillop in Challenging Times*, 339. This communication was a rescript from the Roman authorities, that is, a response to a request from a writer. This suggests that Cardinal Moran worked to keep Mary out of office for as long as possible.
42. MM to Sr Annette Henschke, 30 December 1897.

can make it lighter by the manner in which she discharges the duties assigned to her.[43]

Just five months later, while Mary was visiting the Josephites in New Zealand, she received news of Mother Bernard's sudden death. Although in deep shock, she set out for Sydney at once because, as assistant to the Mother General, she needed to step up into that position at once.[44] Her most immediate duty was to organise a General Chapter for the election of Mother Bernard's successor. This event took place in January 1899 and, as everyone expected, Mary became their Mother General once again.

At the conclusion of the Chapter, she and her council asked a number of Sisters to undertake new ministries and, as she put it, she 'had to pain some re the Adelaide appointments'.[45] In particular, she was referring to the fact that she had relieved sixty-five year old Sister Monica Phillips of her role as Provincial. Monica had held the reins of governance since Mary's departure from South Australia in 1883, and most Sisters so loved and respected her that they could scarcely imagine life without her at the helm. Monica was not lost to South Australia, however, for Mary asked her to take charge of the Adelaide novitiate. Her long experience and her personality made her eminently suited for the role of Mistress of Novices, which she took up following her return to Adelaide.

Next, Mary appointed Sister Bonaventure Mahony as Provincial of South Australia in Monica's place. Bonaventure, who joined the Congregation in Adelaide in December 1868, was a member of the small group of Sisters who went to Queensland in January 1872. During the Josephite 'exodus' in 1880 she moved from there to New South Wales where, after a short time in the city, she was stationed at Lithgow. Her stay there was brief, for within a few weeks Mary asked her to lead a community to Inverell in the Armidale diocese, where she served for a number of years.[46] At this time Mary wrote of her as follows:

---

43. MM, Circular to the Sisters, 3 March 1898.
44. MM, Diary entry for 4 August 1898.
45. MM to her brother, Donald MacKillop SJ, 16 January 1899.
46. MM to the Sisters, 17 & 24 March 1881; to Vaughan, 8 August 1881.

> A better and truer Sister and one more fitted for a Provincial's place, if her health permitted, we have not got in the Institute . . . She will communicate with the Bishop or priests on anything necessary and can always tell the Provincial [in Sydney] anything she thinks the latter or myself should know.[47]

In short, Mary made Bonaventure acting Provincial of the two houses then in the Armidale region. (By 1890 there were ten and Armidale was a fully constituted province covering the dioceses of Armidale and Lismore.)[48] Mary had already showed her high regard for Bonaventure when, in 1885, she included her name in the list of those whom she recommended to Archbishop Moran as her possible successor.[49] Moran selected Sister Bernard, and Bonaventure remained in New South Wales until her election as Provincial of New Zealand at the General Chapter of 1896. After less than three years in that role, she accepted her appointment to Adelaide and so returned to South Australia after an absence of twenty-seven years.

Other changes that affected the South Australian Sisters were that Sister Patricia Campbell (who accompanied Mary from Ireland as a postulant in 1875 and proved her loyalty during the troubles of the 1880s) was now one of Mary's councillors. This meant that she was lost to South Australia, where she had served since her arrival, and had to move to Sydney where she became Mistress of Novices. Sister Alban L'Estrange, another of the fifteen from Ireland, became Little Sister (leader) of the Kensington community.[50] Sister Casimir Meskill, who had been Mistress of Novices at Kensington for the past twelve years, became Provincial of Armidale.

Sister Laurence O'Brien, who was in charge of the Russell Street School, became Little Sister [leader] at the Providence in Franklin Street, while Sister Elizabeth Etheridge continued to manage all

---

47. MM to Sr Casimir Meskill, 12 August 1881.
48. The Armidale diocese, which was established in 1869, covered the North Coast and New England regions of northern NSW. In 1887 it was divided into two and the coastal section became the diocese of Lismore.
49. MM to Sr Annette Henschke, 16 November 1885.
50. Just how long Sr Alban filled this role is unclear, as, according to the *Australian Catholic Directory* of the era, the incumbent provincial was also the superior of the Kensington community.

matters pertaining to the Providence itself. Mary was aware that the South Australian Sisters held Patricia and Casimir in high regard and found it hard to see them move elsewhere. As she put it, some of the moves she made were 'a great disappointment to a few of the Adelaide Sisters present, [at the Chapter]', but was pleased to note that 'they soon made up their minds to bear it, and in getting them to be so reconciled, dear Sister Monica did her part nobly'.[51]

Sister Bonaventure soon settled into her new role in South Australia and was at Kensington to welcome Mary MacKillop when she arrived for a short visit between 8 September and 11 October 1899. After her re-election she was so busy that by July it seemed 'years instead of months since the General Chapter'. Busy or not, she was determined to be in Adelaide in time for the retreat in September but could not stay for long because 'business in connection with the Boys' Orphanage necessitate[d] an early return to Sydney'.[52]

As it happened, Mary spent almost her entire visit at Kensington. All the Sisters came in for the retreat and she saw each one individually. As she interviewed local community leaders she made detailed notes about their communities and the conditions under which they were working, and included comments regarding the Sisters' way of living in community and especially their relationships with each other. In most instances she was able to note that, 'Sisters are happy and united'. Occasionally, however, she had cause to make more negative statements such as: 'Sister X is troublesome and does very little', or 'All right except for Sister Y who is in the habit of writing and receiving letters without permission'. Further on it was: 'Sister [the Little Sister] says Sr Z is bold and disobedient, will do what she is told not to do, and gives impertinence to the Little Sister.'[53]

She recorded carefully the number of children in each school, the amount of school money they were paying, the number of music pupils attending each music centre and the Sisters' income from that source. Her annoyance was obvious when she found that the music Sister at Gawler was giving a twenty-year-old man

---

51. MM to her brother, Donald, 16 January 1899.
52. MM to the Sisters from Glen Innes, 25 July 1899. The boys' orphanage to which she referred was at Kincumber on the NSW Central Coast.
53. See Appendix Thirteen for a transcript of Mary's notes.

music lessons at seven pm. Her comment was the terse: 'This must be discontinued.'

In spite of her remarks of three years earlier, Mary seems to have compromised somewhat regarding the Sisters having 'convent' or select, (or were they secondary?), schools beside their parochial ones. The select school at Glenelg had closed at the time of her visit in 1896, but she now found what she called 'convent schools' at Kensington, Brompton, North Adelaide and Mitcham.

One clue confirming that these were fee-paying schools is that in each case there was a significant difference between the fees the Sisters collected on the different sites. Thus, at Brompton they received £3.10 a week (or at least £14 a month) from their 105 convent school pupils, but no more than one pound a month from the 130 children in the parochial school: that is, the convent schoolchildren paid, on average, about thirty-two pence a month while the others paid less than two. The situations in North Adelaide and Mitcham were similar but Mary did not record the same level of information about the school on the convent grounds at Kensington, which closed several months after her visit.

One may ask at this stage whether, in fact, Mary was beginning to see that the teaching of more advanced subjects had become a necessity by the late 1890s. The children who had attended the Sisters' primary schools in the 1860s and 1870s were now parents themselves and were bringing their children along for the Sisters' schools. These people were aware of the advantages they had gained through education and now wanted their children to have even more opportunities than they themselves had enjoyed.

In her comments, Mary also observed that the Sisters were teaching more than a hundred music pupils across their various sites, and that between them, the music Sisters were bringing in a steady income of at least £105 each quarter for the support of the novitiate and the sick Sisters resident at Kensington. The 1896 ruling that novices should not go out to the schools seems to have been allowed to lapse because there were not enough school Sisters to meet the demand for their services. Hence, there was one novice on the staff of the Kensington School while four were working at Russell Street.

On the whole, when Mary left Adelaide on 11 October 1899, she showed her pleasure at what the Sisters were doing even as she continued to challenge them regarding their obligations and responsibilities as members of the Congregation. She ruled that, since they had all met in Adelaide in September, they were to remain in their 'quiet little country convents' for Christmas. She was sure, so she said, that they would be able to 'find enjoyment and nice light occupations' and informed them that, while they could enjoy 'occasional pleasant drives' it would also be good for them to visit 'the homes of [their] pupils and find happiness in making others happy'. In particular, while they could enjoy extra recreation on the great feasts, they were to keep the Rule with regard to their daily prayers and other spiritual duties.[54]

It is highly likely that these Sisters found creative ways of enjoying themselves and preparing for the coming school year over the weeks of the Christmas holidays. One wonders how they might have celebrated the turn of the century—or even if they were aware of the significance of this event. They certainly did not have the means of communication available to their Sisters of a hundred years later when they welcomed a new century and a new millennium. One also wonders whether they were aware of a significant change in the government of Australia—that its six colonies were about to join in a federation and to become the Commonwealth of Australia on 1 January 1901.

There is no evidence to show whether the Sisters had voted at elections for the South Australian Parliament since 1894 when the state government passed an Act enabling all South Australian women to vote. The first surviving reference to the Sisters' right to vote at state and/or federal elections appears in Mary's circular letter of 16 July 1903. During 1902 the new Federal Parliament announced that all citizens had a right to vote and that there was to be a federal election on 16 December 1903. Therefore, Mary and her council decided to encourage all Sisters to assume their responsibilities as Australian citizens by voting at that election, even though, at the time, voting was not compulsory.[55] She wrote:

---

54. MM to the South Australian Sisters, 21 November 1899. Emphasis Mary's.
55. Universal suffrage for federal elections became law in 1902, but was not compulsory until 1915. In South Australia, women gained the right to vote in 1894. Voting at state elections did not become compulsory until 1942.

> It is a duty on us to vote, and for this reason all must have their names on the Electoral Rolls where they are placed. See to this at once. Get advice from some leading man in whom you have confidence, or from the priest, but keep your voting secret.
>
> Find out who are the members proposed for election and vote for those who are considered most friendly to the Church and Religion. Every so-called Catholic (sic) is not the best man.[56]

There are no records indicating the number of Sisters in South Australia or, indeed, across the entire Federation, who enrolled and voted at the 1903 election.

By the time of this election, the new Refuge at Fullarton was fully functional, and still benefitting from the generosity of Joanna Barr Smith and her husband Robert. Besides this, since 1901 Sister Bonaventure had overseen the opening or closure of several Josephite convents and schools. As already mentioned, the Kensington convent school closed in 1900. At the end of 1901 the Sisters withdrew from Gawler in response to O'Reily's request for assistance in finding for the Good Samaritan Sisters a suitable convent and school not too far from Adelaide: one where they could stay when travelling from their Mother House in Sydney to Port Pirie and back. With Mary's blessing, Sister Bonaventure offered him the well-established Gawler convent, school, and music centre.[57] For her part, she now had an extra five Sisters to deploy elsewhere.

These were soon placed for, in late 1904, she needed three Sisters for Caltowie following the retirement of the lay teacher who had managed the school since the Sisters' departure eight years earlier. In that same year, the Dominicans replaced the Josephites at Glenelg, thus freeing four more Sisters for ministry elsewhere.

By the turn of the century the young, energetic Josephites of the 1870s and 1880s were approaching old age and some were suffering from debilitating, age-related health conditions. Fourteen had died during the 1880s and a further eighteen by the end of the 1890s.[58] Kensington, their Provincial house and the most conveniently situated

---

56. MM to the Sisters, 16 July 1903.
57. SC, 3 January 1902, 915.
58. Register of the Sisters, ASSJ, Kensington, SA.

of their city convents, was overcrowded with up to forty-eight Sisters in residence.[59] It was imperative that this place be extended.

Besides this, there was not enough room for everyone at retreat time when all the members of the Province descended upon Kensington for a week or so each year. The situation was such that some needed to sleep in tents. All seem to have accepted this situation without grumbling, however, for in October 1900 Mary informed Cardinal Moran that the Sisters in Adelaide 'made a very happy Retreat and returned to their various missions in excellent dispositions'.[60]

Following her re-election Mary sent to O'Reily an annual donation of £100 towards the liquidation of the Josephite debt, as requested by him on his arrival in 1895.[61] Thanks to that, and the Sisters' hard work, the debt decreased to such a level that by 1900 both she and the Archbishop could consider extending the Kensington convent. When she informed the Sisters of their plans she warned them that they would have to make some 'heavy sacrifices' if the new building was to be under way during 1902.[62] Nothing further happened during that year, however, for on 11 May, Mary suffered a severe stroke while at Rotorua in New Zealand, where she was having treatment for her arthritis. She was laid up in New Zealand for some months.

Eventually, with O'Reily's approval and under Sister Bonaventure's leadership, work began in earnest during 1903. A timely donation of approximately £3000 from Mrs Marion Scanlon (nee Tyson) of Bendigo, Victoria, paid for much of the preliminary work. (In 1898 Mrs Scanlon's daughter, Sister Hyacinth, joined the Josephites in Adelaide and subsequently spent her entire life in South Australia.)[63] Thanks to her mother's generosity, foundations for an L-shaped structure comprising a main building facing Portrush Road and a kitchen/dining room wing behind it were laid in 1903. Because further

---

59. *Australian Catholic Directory*, annual listings for Adelaide Archdiocese, 1895–1901.
60. MM to Cardinal Moran, 27 October 1900.
61. MM to Sr Calasanctius Howley, 17 March 1901.
62. MM to the SA Sisters, 22 December 1901.
63. Register of the Sisters, Kensington, entry no. 406.

funds were unavailable, however, work stopped after the completion of the single storey kitchen wing.

When Mary wrote as follows to the Adelaide Sisters in November 1903, it seems that she was unaware of such delays:

> You will, I am sure, see the wisdom of delaying the Retreat until Easter, for it would never do to go into a damp house, even if the new building would be so far advanced as to admit of being used.
>
> Do all you cheerfully can to assist Sr Bonaventure's views and plans. Submit to a little disappointment and self-denial at Xmas. At Easter you will have your reward, and I think I can promise to enjoy it with you. Pray that I may be with you then.[64]

Even though the new building was incomplete, Mary was in Adelaide for Easter 1904 and stayed on for the Sisters' retreat. The *Southern Cross* reported that, on Saturday, 19 March, the Feast of St Joseph, they were 'exceptionally joyful' because 'their dear Mother General' was there for a visit and that this day also 'marked the completion of a part of the new building so urgently needed'. The reporter went on to say that, acting on the advice of the Archbishop, the Sisters had erected 'only the absolutely necessary parts—a refectory, dormitory, kitchen and scullery'. Despite their limitations, at the time these additions proved a real blessing for the Sisters in the local community.[65]

Mary was far from well, but did not let her health prevent her from visiting as many convents and meeting with as many Sisters as her strength allowed. One outcome of her stroke was that her right arm was paralysed and hence, she was unable to continue her lifelong practice of writing numerous long and detailed letters. While in Adelaide she penned one of the few short letters that have survived from this era. In it she described some of her doings thus:

> I won't attempt to write much. Have just returned from a nice drive and the day is very hot, but am daily gaining strength. Yesterday I visited Thebarton and Hindmarsh convents and

---

64. MM to the SA Sisters, from Girls' Orphanage, 11 November 1903.
65. *SC*, 25 March 1904, p. 189.

the Providence, staying about an hour in the two former and for lunch at the latter, and seeing each Sister, and came home as fresh as when I came out.

Today I return to Kensington for the duties of Holy Week, and on Monday the Retreat commences.[66]

Work on the Kensington extensions was in abeyance until 1905 when, thanks to a substantial donation from Mrs Joanna Barr Smith, it began again. Mary was re-elected Mother General at the General Chapter in March of that year. Sister Calasanctius Howley was elected to the General Council and soon afterwards Mary appointed her to the role of procuratrix (financial manager) for the whole Congregation. Next, Mary appointed Sister Victor Lane as Provincial of South Australia[67] and Sister Andrea Howley (Calasanctius' sister) as first Provincial of the newly established Province of Victoria, a position that she held until the Chapter of 1916.[68]

Soon after her re-election Mary, who was as interested as ever in the comfort of the older Sisters, made what was to be her final trip to Adelaide. Her reason for doing so was to see at firsthand how the work on the new convent building was progressing. When she arrived she was seriously ill, however, and spent most of her time in South Australia at the Fullarton Refuge under the care of Sister Annette Henschke.[69] Despite her illness, she inspected the

---

66. MM to a Sydney Sister, 23 March 1904, quoted in part. That year Easter fell on 3 April.
67. Sr Victor (Ellen Lane) was born in Ipswich, Queensland in June 1858. She joined the Josephites in Brisbane in 1879, came to Adelaide for her novitiate, and was professed there on 8 September 1881. She moved to New South Wales soon afterwards and worked there until appointed to Adelaide in 1905. She was provincial until 1922, and then was in charge of the Refuge until 1930. She then returned to New South Wales where she died on 14 September 1932
68. Following these elections, Srs Calasanctius and Andrea had to leave South Australia, the one for Sydney and the other for Melbourne. See also Jill Barnard, *From Humble Beginnings: The Story of the Sisters of St Joseph of the Sacred Heart, Victoria, 1890-2009* (Richmond, Victoria: Utber and Patullo Publishing, 2009), 198.
69. Sr La Merci Mahoney, writing to the Sisters on 14 September 1905, commented that MM was very sick with an ulcer on her leg. On 3 November 1905, she noted that MM was back in Sydney and that the ulcer was not healed. Sr Annette accompanied her on this long and tiresome journey.

building and was able to reassure the Sisters that it was going ahead as planned, thanks to the continued generosity of the Barr Smiths, and that by the following year they would have 'a proper place in which to make the Retreat'.[70]

Mary was unable to stay in Adelaide for the laying of its foundation stone on 12 November.[71] On the following Friday the *Southern Cross* newspaper gave a detailed report of proceedings, placing particular emphasis on how the Archbishop waxed eloquent regarding the necessity for this building and the benefits the Sisters would gain from it, and also how he pleaded with those present to contribute generously towards its cost.[72] Over succeeding months the work reached a successful conclusion under the supervision of Walter Bagot from the newly formed architectural company of Woods, Bagot.[73]

Several weeks before Mary reached Adelaide, a community of Loreto Sisters arrived there to establish a convent school. Some years earlier, she met the leader of this community's first Australian foundation, Mother Gonzaga Barry and talked with her about the benefits that would follow if she were to make a foundation in South Australia. In particular, she said:

> You must go at once. There is work for you to do in Adelaide that no one else will do. For some time you will have many and great difficulties but eventually you will succeed, and your house there will yet be the most important of all your foundations in Australia.[74]

In later years, Mother Gonzaga often said that she considered Mother Mary to be a saint and that it was on the strength of Mary's words that she made an Adelaide foundation.

---

70. MM to the SA Sisters, 7 August 1905.
71. Sr La Merci Mahoney to O'Reily, 20 October 1905.
72. *SC*, 17 November 1905.
73. Dean W Berry, 'Bagot, Walter Hervey (1880–1963)', *ADB*, (Canberra, National Centre of Biography, Australian National University, 1979) http:// adb.anu.edu.au/biography/bagot-walter-hervey-5092/text8501
74. Mother Francis Tobin, IBVM: *Mother Gonzaga Barry, Her Life and Letters*, vol 4, 397–398.

The Loreto Sisters arrived there on 25 January 1905. Members of the different religious Congregations of women with houses in Adelaide made them welcome. The Sisters of Mercy offered them accommodation while they waited for the final touches to be made to their house in Sydenham Road, Norwood. In the meantime Sisters from several other Adelaide communities worked together to make the place habitable. Finally, when the Sisters moved in, two Blue Sisters (members of the Little Company of Mary) from North Adelaide arrived with a beautifully cooked dinner and a set of altar cruets for the first Mass in the house.

That same afternoon Sister Annette Henschke and a companion called to welcome the Sisters and offered to do all their laundry work without payment for the next twelve months. The newcomers did not accept this offer completely but for many months the Josephites washed their altar linen at the Fullarton laundry for free.

Soon after her arrival in Adelaide in the following March, Mary herself arranged to be driven by phaeton to the Loreto Convent in Sydenham Road to welcome her friend, Mother Gonzaga and her community. Unfortunately for her, by the time she reached the convent, Mother Gonzaga had gone into the city on business.[75] They were never to meet again in this life.

The new wing at Kensington was ready for occupation by the end of May 1906. The day of its official blessing and opening, 22 June 1906, was just one day short of thirty-nine years since the arrival of Mary MacKillop and Rose Cunningham in Adelaide. The rain held off on this damp mid-winter day as about 4,000 people gathered at the southern end of the structure to hear the Archbishop deliver his appeal. The place was decorated with flags and hangings loaned for the occasion by the managers of the four leading drapery businesses in the city, namely, John Creswell, James J Foale, John Martin, and James Marshall.[76]

---

75. Mother Ursula Lyons, IBVM, 'Foundation of Adelaide', MS, Loreto Archives, Marryatville, SA, 020/01/07 & 020/01/08. A phaeton was a light four-wheeled carriage with or without a top. In 1907 the Loreto community moved from Sydenham Road to a house at the western end of The Parade, Norwood and, in December 1920, to a much larger property on what is now (2014) Portrush Road, Marryatville.
76. JJ Foale was grandfather of the author.

Mary, who was not well enough to attend this important event, sent former South Australians, Sisters Calasanctius Howley and Casimir Meskill as her representatives.[77] They, along with a number of Sisters from suburban convents, joined the local community in observing the ceremony from various vantage points in the building and grounds (seemingly out of sight of the gathered crowd).[78] All told, the building cost upwards of £10,000, most of which was realised on or before opening day.[79] One can only imagine how the Sisters felt as they moved into this new building, with plenty of room for everyone at retreat time.

The new convent was not the only major building purchased, refurbished, or built from scratch during this decade, thanks to O'Reily's energy, enthusiasm and financial skills. Another was the Providence. Ever since its foundation, this institution had occupied rented premises. Consequently, the Sisters had needed to move house at least eight times. They always remained within the city and always struggled for survival. In 1905, however, an important change occurred when, with the assistance of the Catholic Church Endowment Society, they purchased Santo's House, a fine property at No. 32, West Terrace, Adelaide, for £1,500.[80] As it happened, this place, which comprised a main building with several detached cottages at the rear, was the Providence for the next forty-five years. For the first time in their history, the Sisters enjoyed the security of ownership and the knowledge that any money they raised could be used for purposes other than the payment of rent.[81]

While these changes were taking place, the Josephites resumed their work with orphan children. They grieved the loss of the orphans when forced to leave the Goodwood Orphanage in 1890. Then, in 1903, they were delighted when O'Reily set up a sanatorium or rest home for 'ladies and children requiring rest and sea air in

---

77. Sr La Merci Mahoney to the Sisters, 2 July 1906.
78. As a general rule, religious Sisters of that era did not take part in public events such as the one described above.
79. O'Reily, John, *New Convent of the Sisters of St Joseph, Kensington* (Adelaide: Southern Cross Printing & Publishing Co, 1906).
80. The CCES is an incorporated body that manages Church finances and property In the Archdiocese of Adelaide.
81. Marie T Foale, *Providence* (Cowandilla, South Australia: Flora McDonald Lodge, 1993), provides a more detailed history of this institution.

quiet and congenial surroundings' and invited them to manage it. Initially, the new home was located in an eight-roomed house in Kalgoorlie Street, Largs Bay, which, according to the Archbishop, was 'the quietest and freshest of Adelaide's watering places'.[82]

Because of the nature of the clientele he expected to take advantage of his new institution, O'Reily expected it to be self-supporting and eventually, to be able to pay for any additional buildings or alterations that might be needed. The sanatorium proved so popular, especially with parents of delicate children, that before long the Sisters were forced to turn away prospective clients. Consequently, the Archbishop paid £2,050 for a large two storey building on the corner of Harrold Street and the Esplanade at Largs Bay and the sanatorium moved there.

While it continued for some time as a haven for women who needed a break from the pressures of home and family management, the Sisters gave high priority to the care of orphaned and homeless children. Before long, and much to the Sisters' joy, the place evolved into an orphanage. As Mary MacKillop, put it: 'For the orphans whose loss we felt so deeply to come to us again is a real pleasure.'[83]

St Joseph's Orphanage, Largs Bay, began with the blessing of Catholic Church authorities. It was more financially secure than St Vincent de Paul's ever was when under Josephite management, and it flourished from the time of its establishment. The Sisters appointed there carried on in the tradition of order, cleanliness and personal care that characterised their previous orphanage work, and applications for admission continued apace. Between 1906 and 1910 they sheltered 152 children, with a maximum of sixty in residence at any given time.[84]

Another sign of Archbishop O'Reily's business acumen was the number of new or enlarged school and convent buildings erected during his time in South Australia. On 23 February 1902, he officiated at the opening of a new brick school in Cannon Street, Port Adelaide, an area with a large Catholic population. Its four classrooms could accommodate at least 300 children. The Sisters, who had returned to

---

82. *SC,* 22 May 1903, 317.
83. MM to O'Reily, 26 June 1906.
84. John O'Reily, *The Catholic Charities in South Australia,* Adelaide, 1911.

the Port in 1877, were living in a large church owned house on the corner of nearby Quebec and Church Streets.[85]

Teaching was not the only activity undertaken by the Port Adelaide Sisters. They also opened their home to homeless children and young girls, some of whom remained with them until old enough to fend for themselves. The Sisters' plan was to educate and train these young people so that they might be 'able to support themselves in callings suitable to their respective capacities'.[86]

These Sisters also established the Guild of St Anthony, a group of lay people through whose assistance they were 'instrumental in the distribution of food and clothing to the poor and needy' who were very numerous in their area.[87] After the sanatorium was established at Largs Bay, the Guild also operated from there. Its members pledged to make regular donations towards the purchase of St Anthony's Bread (that is, food for the poor), or to donate provisions for distribution. The Sisters' role was to dispense food, clothing and, at times, money to those in dire need, and they cared for all, 'without distinction of class or creed'.[88] No one ever counted the number of people assisted through the Guild. In fact, an early Largs Bay account book, which was commenced in 1906, contains a regular monthly entry: 'Outdoor relief, no record kept'.[89]

Over time, and as the St Vincent de Paul Society gained a surer footing in the diocese, the Guild of St Anthony ceased to function. Thanks to their work with the Guild, however, the Sisters developed a well-established tradition of providing food or other necessities for any needy people who came to their convents. Calls on their generosity were particularly heavy during times of depression and unemployment—as was the case during the 1890s and was to be again in the 1930s, when many men took to the roads in search of work. With time, the Sisters came to refer to these men as *St Josephs* and, in most instances, treated them with the respect they would have shown to the original St Joseph if he knocked on their door.

---

85. *SC*, 28 February 1902, 137.
86. *SC*, 29 November 1901.
87. The Sisters named this guild after Saint Anthony of Padua, a thirteenth-century Franciscan friar, noted for his devotion to the poor. *SC*, 28 February 1902, 137.
88. *SC*, 29 November 1901, 837.
89. Largs Bay Account Books, 1903-1910; *SC*, 26 October 1900, 28 February 1902, 3 & 17 December 1909.

It was common in depressed times to hear a Sister announce the arrival of a *St Joseph*. At once, anyone who was free hurried to help in the preparation of sandwiches, the heating of leftover food from the previous night, or the making of a flask of hot tea for their visitor. At Port Augusta, Brompton/Hindmarsh, Port Adelaide, Kensington, and other places where the demand was often high, the Sisters bought extra provisions and prepared food parcels in the mornings before leaving for their day's work. At times the demand was so high that the Sisters gave their own dinners to their hungry visitors. Like their Sisters at Port Adelaide or Largs Bay in earlier times, none of these Sisters recorded the number of *St Josephs* who called on them.[90]

Meanwhile, in 1904 the Adelaide parish had a new church/school erected on the site of the existing cottage school in Pirie Street, where the average daily attendance was 170 children.[91] The Pirie Street and Russell Street Sisters now lived at Kensington and travelled to the city each day, most likely by the horse trams that connected the city with The Parade at Norwood and Kensington. In that same year, the residents of Georgetown welcomed three Sisters back after an absence of seventeen years. Very soon this school was up and running again with an enrolment of forty-four children.[92]

In the western suburban school of Brompton, enrolments stood at between 250 and 275 for the decade ending in 1906. At the time, the older children attended classes in a recently erected schoolroom on the convent grounds while the younger ones did their lessons across the railway line in St Saviour's Church, on the corner of First Street and West Street, Bowden. (When it opened in 1867 this was the first Josephite school outside the city.) While conditions in the schools were adequate, the Sisters' convent on the corner of Chief Street and Port Road was no longer large enough to accommodate all the Sisters on the staff safely. It was imperative that improvements be made to the convent for the benefit of the Sisters.

---

90. Oral accounts, especially from Port Augusta Sisters, recorded during the 1990s.
91. *SC*, 21 October 1904, 667.
92. *ACD*, 1905, entries for the Port Augusta diocese.

Their parish priest, Father Thomas Lee,[93] who was aware of the problem, discussed plans for the extension of the convent with the Sisters and sought the advice of architects from the firm Woods Bagot, before authorising the addition of an upper floor to the building.[94] The builders raised the walls, added seven new rooms on the upper floor and finished it off with a balcony on both sides and at the front. The overall cost was £800 and, of this, Father Lee contributed £50 of his own money towards the cost of the balconies. All was finished by May 1906 when the Sisters moved into their new facilities.

The Jamestown Sisters were next to benefit from the building boom. Bishop Norton laid the foundation stone for a new convent in the January of 1907 and it was ready for occupation by May. Two years later, he authorised the erection of a similar building in Georgetown and performed its official blessing and opening ceremony in May 1909.[95] Life for the Georgetown Sisters was now more comfortable than it was in the 1870s when they lived in the choir gallery in the church and enjoyed (or endured) outdoor cooking and washing facilities. At the end of 1909 the Sisters withdrew from Macclesfield for reasons that have been lost in the mists of time. They were gone from there for ten years.

Sunday 8 August 1909 was a very significant day for the Congregation—and, in time, for the universal Church. It was the day when Mother Mary MacKillop died. The Sisters, their pupils, and members of the wider community were all affected deeply, and for those who knew her and loved her it was a sad day indeed. Sisters everywhere were aware of her failing health although no one knew when the end might come. Finally, on that Sunday morning, at the convent in North Sydney, she 'gently passed away, so quietly that [they] were hardly aware of it although [they] were watching'.[96]

At the time of Mary's death Father Lee was celebrating Sunday Mass in his parish church at Brompton. Sister Xavier O'Leary, who was present, reported:

---

93. This was the Father Lee who, as noted in Chapter Three, helped Mary leave Adelaide safely when the clergy at West Terrace threatened to have her arrested.
94. *SC*, 4 May 1906 & 24 June 1910, 476.
95. *SC*, 15 May 1908, p. 331, 4 December 1908, 839, 21 May 1909, 335.
96. Sr La Merci to the Sisters, 8 August 1909.

> Father Lee was saying Mass… He stopped at the Consecration and I thought he was sick. He afterwards told me that he saw Mother Mary above the altar.[97]

Wherever they were, the Sisters received numerous messages of sympathy and were comforted by the many memorial Masses celebrated for Mary over succeeding days and weeks. Although her death was expected, they grieved her loss deeply and wondered how the Congregation would fare without her leadership. Until then, and even while she was ill, they felt the security of her presence. For the future they would need to continue without her.

Being practical commonsense women, however, the Sisters continued with their various ministries wherever they were. Most were doing well, but those at St Johns were struggling to deal with the management and education of recalcitrant teenagers who had been through the courts. Eventually, Archbishop O'Reily realised that the difficulties the Sisters were encountering far outweighed the benefits they were bestowing on these girls and announced that St Johns would close at the end of November 1909. The girls in residence moved to the government reformatory at Redruth, near Burra, in the Mid North and St Johns was 'abolished' [sic] as an industrial school. Subsequently, the government organised for most of the buildings to be demolished and gradually the site reverted to the abandoned state it was in before 1897.[98]

Throughout the decade beginning in 1900, the *Southern Cross* gave wide coverage to annual concerts and other fundraising events put on by the various schools. It also reported on the school picnics that lightened the lives of children from schools in more disadvantaged areas. Some were treated to train rides to the National Park at Belair, the most exciting part of this journey being when the train went through the long tunnel at Eden Hills, or to visits to other open spaces where they feasted on a selection of home-made cakes and sweets, and competed in various sporting activities.[99]

---

97. Paul Gardiner SJ, *Mary MacKillop: An Extraordinary Australian* (Sydney: EJ Dwyer, 1993), 480–81.
98. SCC, Reports, 1910; *Register* 30 November 1909; *SA Government Gazette*, 3 February 1910, *SC*, 2 September 1909, 681.
99. *SC*, 6 January 1911, 8, 22 December 1911, 1022.

The paper regularly published school and music examination results for all Catholic schools in the state. This practice gave Josephite convents and schools some publicity and enabled the Sisters to see that their results compared favourably with those obtained by the students of other Catholic schools. Taken overall, these reports indicate that the Josephites' pupils had a success rate comparable with that achieved in institutions run by members of other religious congregations, something that gave the less well-educated Josephites greater confidence in their teaching ability.

They also show that some Sisters were sending their students for the university exams of the day. Thus, in 1909, girls from the Kensington, Beulah Road, Russell Street, Port Adelaide, and Mitcham schools passed the Primary Public Examination. (This exam was usually taken by children who had completed the sixth or highest primary school class before they reached the mandatory school leaving age of thirteen.) During the following year, besides carrying the usual school reports, the paper reported that, among others, the music pupils from St Joseph's, Kadina had excelled in their most recent exams.

Standards in Josephite schools were generally high and, regardless of whether they sent children for the university exams or not, the Sisters offered their pupils a wide range of general subjects, including English, Mathematics, English and Irish History, Geography and Latin. In fact, their curriculum for their senior classes was similar to the one that Mary MacKillop prepared for the fifth or most senior class in her schools in 1867. It read that students at this level should:

> Read and study English and Ancient History; Write Essays;
> Parse and Transpose and know generally School Grammar, Latin and Greek Roots, Descriptive and Political Geography of the Continents and of Australia;
> Have a fair idea of School Geography, Arithmetic as far as Simple Interest;
> Should know and understand all the different Catechisms;
> Plain and Fancy Work;
> Boys— Bookkeeping by Double Entry, First Book of Euclid, and Mensuration.[100]

---

100. Woods published Mary's curriculum in the *Directory and Order of Discipline* (Adelaide, 1870), 84 – 86. ASSJ, Kensington, SA.

The principal difference between 1867 and the beginning of the twentieth century was that universal free education was now available to all children in South Australia. It was imperative, therefore, that the Sisters attain the same standards as trained teachers in the free public schools of the day. This required much hard work on their part but they persevered and generally did well.

The teaching of French was not included in Mary's timetable nor, indeed, in that of the Sisters of the early twentieth century. At the time, it was seen as a language suitable only for cultivated young ladies of the upper classes and of no practical use at all to the young people attending Josephite schools. Mary felt strongly about this issue and, in 1901, ruled against its being taught by the Josephites. Therefore, if parents wished their children to study this language they needed to send them elsewhere. It appears, however, that this limitation had little if any affect on the number of children attending the Sisters' schools.[101]

This account of the South Australian Josephites between 1866 and 1910 concludes with Vicar General, Monsignor Frederick Byrne's version of their early story, as recounted by him at the opening of the Brompton convent extensions in September 1906. Byrne was never a strong supporter of the Josephites, but it appears that over the years he came to realise the value of their contribution to Catholic education in particular. He said:

> They [Mary MacKillop & Rose Cunningham] were invited by the Bishop to Adelaide, in which they founded their order. There was at that time great need of religious teachers, for none had yet come to South Australia. It often happens not only to individuals and communities, but even to nations at the beginning of their career, that over zeal is greater than prudence. The over zeal of the Sisters induced them to open schools in places in which they were not required, and in order to supply those schools with teachers they admitted into the community persons unqualified to teach and without religious training. In consequence, complaints were made, and reaction followed, which nearly endangered the existence of the institution. The Sisters of St Joseph need not be displeased

---

101. *SC,* 9 January 1903, 8, and 8 October 1909, 667 carry but two of the many sets of examination results that appeared during that era.

>at this statement, for many religious orders had similar trials in the beginning of their career... It is human to err. The trials which befell the Sisters of St Joseph were hidden blessings, which all trials are when looked at from a supernatural point of view.[102]

Byrne's judgment of the Sisters' early days in Adelaide was close to the mark and, in his old age, he could see that good had come from their many activities and their many trials along the way. By the end of 1909, those who had survived the hardships and difficulties of those years were almost free of debt and could look forward with hope to a future marked by consolidation and expansion.

In the Adelaide archdiocese, 126 Sisters were distributed among fifteen communities, teaching in sixteen schools and managing three charitable institutions. The newest among their schools was at Alberton which opened at the beginning of the 1909 school year. In the Port Augusta diocese, thirty-two Sisters lived in nine long-established communities, managed nine parish primary schools, and cared for some eighteen weekly boarders shared among the Quorn, Pekina and Caltowie convents.

The number of Sisters was greater than it was in 1893, possibly because there were more elderly Sisters residing at Kensington than before, while the number of branch convents and schools was unchanged. Available statistics indicate that school enrolments fell by almost 500 over the previous sixteen years. This decline could be attributed in large part to the exodus of Catholic families from the North during the droughts and the financial depression of the previous two decades.

None of the Sisters knew what the future might bring. As they moved into an era where their foundress was no longer with them, they did know however, that it was their responsibility to carry on in her spirit and according to the traditions of the Congregation that she and Father Woods had founded more than forty years earlier

---

102. *SC*, 11 May 1906, 303.

St Joseph's Providence, West Terrace, Adelaide, 1909.
L. to R: Sisters Elizabeth Etheridge, Claude Riddell, Adrian Riggs, Modesta Noonan & Hilda McNamara with some of the residents at the Providence.

Sr Annette Henschke, Mary's friend.

Mother Bernard Walsh, Second Mother General.

Srs Catherine Ruine (seated on the left) with Srs Andrea and Calasanctius Howley

Sr Augustine Brady

Sisters with Mary MacKillop at Kensington, 1900.

Back Row: Sisters Carolus Büring, Mida McMahon, Antoinette O'Loughlin, Norbert Maguire, Hyacinth Scanlon, Sebastian Conlon, Ethelburga Job, Felicitas Garvey, Adalbert Brazil.

Third Row: Ephrem Crowley, Marina Canny, Magdalen Smith, Gaetano O'Reilly, Bruno Donnelly, Canisius Kearnan, Teresa Eickhoff, Annette Henschke, Isidore O'Loghlin, Gabriel Gillman-Jones, Maro Caulfield.

Second Row: Berchmans Cox, Bernardine Ledwith, Bonaventure Mahony (Provincial), Mother Mary MacKillop, Monica Phillips, Alban L'Estrange, Carita Lee, Adrian Hegarty.

Front Row: Madeleine Carroll, Wilhelmine Dowd, Conrad Pflaum, Cornelia O'Loughlin, Annie MacKillop (Mary's sister), Marian Coghlan, Theodore Prendergast, Carmel O'Loughlin.

Achbishop John O'Reily, Port Augusta, 1888–1894, Adelaide, 1895–1915.

Sr Bonaventure Mahony. Provincial, Adelaide, 1899–1905.

Part 2
In the Tradition of the Founders

'ANZACs of Catholic Education', Spalding, 1921.

Back row: Srs Blandina Hannigan, Aloysius Fitzgerald, Margaret Mary Smith, Ephrem Crowley, Maria Xavier Kinnear, Loretto O'Neill OR Hanlon, Francis Raphael Dooley.

Centre Row: Srs Name unknown, Madeleine Stanley, Uriel Coles, Norbert Maguire, Magdalen O'Reilly, Marian Coghlan, Victor Lane (Provincial), Claude Riddell, Gonzaga Casey, Wilhelmine Dowd, Eustelle Sexton, Bertrand Perins.

Seated at front: Srs Andrea and Calasanctius Howley

Seated on ground: Srs Bede Mahony, Claver Fitzgerald, Cyprian Finn.

Chapter Five
Mission In Focus—Catholic Education: 1910–1929

As the year 1910 dawned, the Sisters who were still grieving the loss of their Mother Foundress, faced the duty of finding her successor. Three months after Mary's death, the acting Mother General, Sister La Merci Mahony, convoked a General Chapter for this purpose.[1] She was not present when the Chapter Sisters met, for she died of cancer on New Year's Day 1910, aged fifty years.

After La Merci's death, Cardinal Moran appointed fifty-five year old Sister Baptista Molloy as interim leader. In due course, the Sisters chose Baptista to succeed Mary as the Congregation's third Mother General with the title of 'Mother'.[2] Her four councillors were Sisters Calasanctius Howley (who became Assistant General in 1905, and was re-elected to the same role), Casimir Meskill (who moved from Adelaide to New South Wales in the early 1880s), Laurence O'Brien (who went to this Chapter from Caltowie),[3] and Agnes Bartholomew (also formerly of South Australia). At the close of the Chapter, Mother Baptista reappointed Sister Victor Lane to the role of Provincial of South Australia and sent Sister Andrea Howley back to Victoria to begin her second term as Provincial there.

---

1. Sister Delegates were those Sisters elected by the total membership of each province to attend the Chapter on their behalf.
2. Mother Baptista (Mary) Molloy was born in Ireland in 1855, went to Queensland with her family while a small child, joined the Josephites in Brisbane in 1872, was professed in 1874, lived there during the years when Bishop James Quinn was pressuring the Queensland Sisters form a diocesan Congregation, moved to NSW at the time of the Josephite exodus from her home state in 1880 and lived there for the rest of her life.
3. After the Chapter, Sr Laurence transferred to Sydney to take up her new role.

The elections over, the Chapter Sisters deliberated on issues relevant to their time. Of particular importance were their discussions relating to the schools. At the time, the various State Governments were raising the school leaving age, and parents who had benefitted from the Sisters' teaching in the 1870s and 1880s wanted their children to have an even better education than they themselves received. The Chapter decided, therefore, to give all novices an opportunity to learn how to prepare students for the variously named public examinations held in each state; to encourage the Sisters to teach all the subjects offered in state primary schools; and to permit Sister Music Teachers to give violin lessons when requested.

The Chapter also confirmed a practice already well established in some Josephite schools in South Australia: that of sending children for the public exams available at the time. As already noted, in recent years the South Australian Sisters' music pupils were gaining excellent passes in their exams and students from some suburban schools were achieving good marks in the Primary Public Exam.

After the Chapter the Sisters kept up this good work and, in September 1915, the *Southern Cross* reported that seventeen students from the Josephite schools at Burra, Peterborough, Kingswood, Port Adelaide, Pirie Street, and Beulah Road had achieved passes in an array of Primary Public Examination subjects including English, Arithmetic, History, Latin, Algebra and Geography. At Beulah Road, one student gained a pass in French. (What had changed since 1901?) As yet, none had presented themselves for the Junior Public.[4]

It was then customary for South Australian children to sit the Primary Public Exam at the end of the Sixth Class (the equivalent of the Grade Seven of later years). They could then remain at school for an extra year or two to study for the Junior Public and, two or three years later, sit the Senior Public or Matriculation exam. Most of the young people enrolled in Josephite schools left as soon as they reached the legal school leaving age of thirteen years. Hence, only a small proportion of them ever sat the Primary Public Exam, while fewer still stayed on for the Junior Public. In fact, it appears that it was 1918 before any Sisters sent pupils for that exam. There is

---

4. *SC* 24 September 1915

no published evidence to suggest that students from their schools sat the Senior Public exam during the period under review.[5]

Over succeeding years, major changes took place in the field of education. In particular, in 1915, the South Australian Government passed new education laws, which all schools were to implement by 1917. Of particular importance to the Sisters were the raising of the school leaving age to fourteen years and the replacement of the Primary Public with the Qualifying Certificate (QC): 'a certificate qualifying a child for admission to a high school.'[6] This was the first time that legislators considered establishing state high schools and they did so because they now expected most children to complete their primary schooling (Grade Seven) before they turned fourteen.

According to the Act, the government was to establish High Schools offering the more academic subjects and Technical Schools where students studied General Technical Subjects, and Agricultural Science or Domestic Arts. The Act also laid down tighter regulations regarding the keeping of attendance rolls and other school records.

The Sisters faced a serious challenge. Like their state school counterparts, they could see the likelihood of a number of the children in their schools gaining the QC at age twelve and then having to spend one or two more years or part thereof at school. The idea of having Catholic children attend state schools was anathema to most Catholics from Archbishops down. Therefore, the Sisters needed to learn how to keep post primary students gainfully occupied during this enforced extension of their time at school.

They began slowly and gradually introduced subjects in the technical, commercial and domestic science areas because these could be useful to the young people when it came to gaining employment. In the meantime, they continued sending children for the Primary and Junior Public exams. Results for the 1918 school year, as published in the *Southern Cross* in early 1919, indicate that so far, no Josephite Sisters had sent children for the QC. Then, in the following year, four students from St Joseph's, Terowie, and five

---

5. The *Southern Cross* of this era has been the source of this information. See also *SC* 20 December 1918, 1046 and 2 & 10 January 1919, 14.
6. Education Act, Act No. 1223 of 1915. See also http://www.austlii.edu.au/au/legis/sa/num_act/ea1223o1915150/

from Wallaroo passed this exam.[7] At about this time, too, the Sisters in charge of most Josephite schools began including a Grade Eight, definitely a post primary class, in the class listings at prize giving times.[8]

The changeover from the old scheme of things was completed in the 1920s when the University of Adelaide set up a new programme of public examinations, namely Intermediate, Leaving and Leaving Honours, to be set by a Public Examinations Board operating under its auspices. The Sisters adapted to these changes with the help of senior teachers from the State Education Department whom the Provincial engaged to run workshops at weekends and during school holidays.[9] She did this because there was no Catholic Teachers' College in South Australia and almost all the Sisters there had gone through the novitiate at Kensington and so did not have access to the Josephite Training School in Sydney. There was no question of their attending the State Teachers' College in Adelaide!

The first evidence of Sisters' having sent students for the Intermediate appeared in the *Southern Cross* of 29 January 1926. In the previous year, one student from Peterborough gained the Intermediate Certificate with passes in seven subjects while two from St Joseph's, Kingswood passed, the one with five subjects and the other with four. Before long, some Sisters were sending students for the Leaving exam as well.[10]

These, however, were the exception rather than the rule, as most children could scarcely wait to escape from school as soon as they turned fourteen! It was essential, therefore, that the Sisters bring them up to as high a standard as possible in the commercial subjects of Typing, Shorthand, Bookkeeping and Arithmetic so that they could gain good positions as typists, stenographers or bookkeepers. Many did and some employers made it known that they preferred young people from the Sisters' schools. In some instances, most notably at the Mount Carmel School at Alberton, the Sisters also taught Domestic Science.[11]

---

7. *SC* 16 January 1920
8. *SC* 16 January 1920, 49; 23 February 1920, 73; 24 December 1920, 1063.
9. Kensington Convent 'House Diary' 1931, indicates that a Mr Grieg and others were teaching English, Arithmetic and Bookkeeping to the Sisters.
10. *SC* 29 January 1926, 17.
11. Initially, the suburb where this school stands was known as Alberton. Over time

The government announced the QC exam in 1915, but it was the early 1920s before it became compulsory. The first Josephite schools to publish QC results were those at Kingswood, Hamley Bridge, Caltowie and Port Adelaide.[12] During this era, when there was strong anti-Catholic feeling among some sections of the public, the Catholic Church saw it as important to show that Catholic school students did well academically and musically. To prove their prowess, therefore, they made much of the publication of exam results in the *Southern Cross*. Schools desiring such publicity submitted for publication a list of those students who had achieved good grades in Commercial, PEB and music exams.[13]

The Sisters' work in the schools and their efforts to cope with the many changes taking place during these years occurred against a background of community living, the opening and closure of convents and schools and the general rhythm of Josephite life. The story of the era under discussion began with the General Chapter of 1910, the election of Mother Baptista as the Congregation's third Mother General and the return of Sister Victor to Adelaide as Provincial.

Several months after Sister Victor's return, she received good news in an official letter from Archbishop O'Reily, where he informed the Sisters that they were virtually free of debt. The almost £7,000 they had owed in 1895 had dwindled to just over £400. He summarised their accounts thus:[14]

---

suburban boundaries changed and it became Rosewater. At the time of writing (2014) this area was designated as Pennington. SC 5 January 1923, 9; 12 January 1923, 39; 19 January 1923, 17; 9 February 1923, 20.

12. SC 5 January 1923, 9; 12 January 1923, 39; 19 January 1923, 17; 9 February 1923, 20.
13. SC 4 Jan. 1924, 9; 2 January 1925, 7; 8 January 1926, 13 & 16; 28 January 1927, 5, 16 & 17 etc.
14. These amounts are given in pounds, shillings, and pence according to the currency of the time. Twenty shillings equalled one pound while twelve pence equalled one shilling. At the time of the currency conversion in 1966, one pound was said to be equivalent to $2, one shilling or twelve pence equalled 10 cents. Sixpence was equivalent to five cents.

Debt, March, 1895:   £6,974 17 4
Expenditure from March 1895,
   to March, 1910:   £5,956 6 8
Total liability to be met: £12,931 4 0
Total receipts: £12,487 10 7
Debt, March, 1910:   **£443**   13 5

O'Reily continued:

> Kensington was the first permanent Mother House of the Josephite Sisters. It was the cradle of their Institute. Its establishment dates back to 1872. Bought and built with borrowed money, its tale from the beginning has been a tale of struggle with debt. After thirty-eight years, the struggle draws nigh its close. Every little helps, and my cheque for £10, herewith enclosed, may, in giving impetus to the effort for which the occasion would seem to call, be of real, even if of little help. I hope it will so prove of help. To none will it be a cause of greater satisfaction than it will be to me, when the first home of the devoted Sisters of St Joseph, South Australian in origin, but now widespread throughout the length and breadth of our sunlit Austral land, shall have monetary burden to bear no longer, and shall, in gladness of heart, stand financially free.[15]

Once relieved of the constant pressure of fundraising, the Sisters looked forward to meeting their new Mother General when she visited later that year. It is likely that very few of them had met her although some of the older Sisters may have remembered her younger sister, Sister Louis, who came to Adelaide from Queensland for her novitiate training, died there in December 1882, aged twenty-two years and became the first Sister to be buried in the Mitcham cemetery. One can imagine that Mother Baptista would have visited her sister's grave soon after her arrival in Adelaide in early October 1910.[16]

---

15. *SC 2* September 1910, 681. Letter dated, Glen Osmond, 26 August 1910.
16. Sr Louis Molloy, born 22 February 1859, was four years younger than Sr Baptista. She died two months before her twenty-second birthday. Register of the Sisters, Kensington, entries 231 and 141.

The Mother General did not travel alone. Accompanying her were Sisters Francis Xavier Amsinck and Augustine Brady, both of whom left Adelaide during the troubles of the 1880s and had not been back since. These Sisters would have noticed the many improvements made since their departure almost twenty-five years previously, even as they grieved the loss of so many of their Josephite companions of those days. They, too, had good reason to visit the Mitcham Cemetery.

Mother Baptista's stay at Kensington was brief, for after a few days she was off to the North with Sister Victor. They went first to Kadina and Wallaroo, which were then in the Adelaide archdiocese. From there they journeyed on to the Port Augusta diocese to visit the Sisters and schools at Georgetown, Gladstone, Caltowie, Jamestown, Quorn, Port Augusta and Petersburg.

The Pekina Sisters met them at Petersburg, where Bishop Norton and local parish priest, Father JG O'Rourke, gave the visitors a formal reception in the presence of the schoolchildren and their parents. The bishop congratulated Mother Baptista on the 'magnificent work' the Josephites were doing throughout Australia and New Zealand and, in particular, in his diocese. He assured her that:

> their own school at Petersburg was one of the most efficient [and that] he was grateful to her for coming personally, that she might become acquainted with the various circumstances of her convents in the diocese and hoped her visit would be beneficial.[17]

During her return journey to Adelaide, the Mother General called on the Sisters at Kooringa (Burra), also in the Port Augusta Diocese, and at Clare, Sevenhill and Hamley Bridge in the Adelaide archdiocese. Next, she paid a brief visit to each metropolitan convent and school and took particular note of St Joseph's Orphanage, Largs Bay with its beautiful grounds and well-stocked vegetable garden. Then, on Friday 28 October, she and her two companions departed on the Melbourne Express for Sydney via Melbourne. According to the *Southern Cross*

---

17. *SC* 28 October 1910, 841.

> Her visitation made a great impression on the minds of the Sisters and their pupils.[18]

By this time of the year, Sisters and school children everywhere were preparing for their annual exams, concerts, displays and distribution of prizes. While these events gave parents and friends a chance to appreciate the Sisters' work with their children, they were also important as fundraisers. In fact, until the 1960s, the Sisters were dependent on the income from such occasions for their support. In many areas, especially in the country, there was a longstanding tradition whereby the people gave the Sisters produce from their farms and gardens on a regular basis, and stocked the Sisters' pantries at the beginning of each school year. One may ask why they did this.

The answer seems to be that the people loved their Sisters because of what they were doing for their children and for the Catholic community in general. What follows may read like a catalogue of new foundations, new buildings to replace old, and other efforts to make Sisters' lives more comfortable. The reports of the laying of foundation stones and/or blessings and openings of new buildings often contained statements to the effect that every modern convenience had been put in place. (One can only wonder what the mod. cons. of the period 1910–1930 might have been.)

Who paid for these buildings? There was no government funding. The Sisters themselves had no fixed income. They accepted school fees, threepence or sixpence per child per week, but never asked for money from those who could not afford it. The buildings were paid for with the small change donated by the parishioners of the area concerned! Why? Because, as already noted, they loved the Sisters who lived and worked among them in the spirit of their foundress, Mother Mary of the Cross MacKillop! The story of the two decades under review is one of almost continuous change and expansion, with equally continuous financial input from the local people.

To begin—early in 1911, the residents of the railway town of Terowie began preparing for the opening of a Josephite convent and school there. Situated 220 kilometres to the north of Adelaide, Terowie was a supply town for the state's vast northeastern region. In 1880, a broad gauge railway linked it to Adelaide while a narrow gauge line

---

18. *SC* 28 October 1910, 841.

connecting the mines in Broken Hill with the smelters in Port Pirie passed through Petersburg, some twenty kilometres to the north. As the population of these areas increased, it became imperative that there should be a connection between the two lines. Hence, in the late 1880s, the government built a narrow gauge line between Terowie and Petersburg. Subsequently, all passengers from Adelaide to Petersburg or beyond changed trains at Terowie, and workers transferred all goods moving between these same destinations from one train to the other. This work was labour intensive and required strong men living on site. Many of the workers involved were Catholics with young families and were keen to have a Catholic school for their children.

The former Terowie Hospital, a large six-roomed wood and iron structure with lofty walls and a surrounding verandah, became the convent. Two of its rooms were used as classrooms and one became a music room, while the Sisters made their home in the remainder. Space was at a premium, especially when they took in short-term boarders from along the Broken Hill line and further out to prepare them for their First Confession and First Holy Communion.

All was in readiness by September 1911 when Sisters Melita Brophy, Antoinette O'Loughlin and Cletus Whelan arrived in the town. Their Provincial, Sister Victor Lane, accompanied them, saw them settled in their new convent, and was present when they opened school for the first time. Forty-two children came on that day and by the end of the week, there were fifty-nine on the roll. A month later, a reporter from the *Southern Cross* commented that:

> Everything (sic) looks happy, and one would imagine the Sisters had been there for a quarter of a century past, so peaceably and orderly does everything seem to go.[19]

Their parish priest, Father William Doyle of Jamestown, visited fortnightly for Sunday Mass and, as a rule, stayed on to celebrate Mass in the convent on the following morning and to visit the school later that day.

---

19. *SC* 10 November 1911, 899.

Soon after the Sisters left Adelaide for Terowie the Carmelite Fathers of Port Adelaide applied for Sisters for a school in the steadily expanding suburb of Woodville, halfway between Adelaide city and the Port. There was no suitable accommodation available there and therefore, the Fathers arranged for the Sisters to reside at Brompton and travel to Woodville and back each day by train.[20] The provincial appointed Sisters Stanislaus O'Callaghan and Januarius Glanville to this new foundation and, in October 1912, they began work in a new church-school on Beaufort Street, Woodville. It was dedicated to Our Lady of the Sacred Heart. Seventeen children came on opening day, and, by the end of the following year, enrolments had increased to seventy.[21]

In 1912–1913, while the Woodville Sisters were settling into the rhythm of train and school timetables, a movement for change was occurring on the other side of town. This was because:

> The old school church (sic) of Our Lady of Dolours at Mitcham [was] inconveniently situated for the greater part of the population of this district, which [included] the growing localities of Kingswood and Hawthorn.[22]

In 1909, the CCES and the parish priest, Father Francis Kelly CP, purchased a large building block on Cambridge Terrace, Kingswood, and arranged for a church-school to be erected there.[23] At the same time, the Archbishop bought an adjoining block as the site for a Josephite convent.[24] Kelly's long term plan was to build a separate church on the southern end of the property and dedicate the original building to school use only. In 1928, when his dream became a reality, he was no longer in charge of the parish.

---

20. This arrangement persisted until 1929 when the Woodville Sisters moved to Port Adelaide. Regardless of whether they lived at Brompton or Port Adelaide, they needed to be fit enough to undertake the long walks between their residences and the nearest railway stations, and between the Woodville station and the school, and to do so in all weathers.
21. Clarrie Bell, *The Parish of Woodville/Findon* (Woodville Parish, 1987), *passim*.
22. *SC* 21 August 1914, 685.
23. *Official Directory of the Catholic Church in Australia*, 1914. The Kingswood-Mitcham area was then part of the Glen Osmond Parish which was managed by the Passionist Fathers.
24. *SC 19* October 1909, 597. House Chronicle, St Paul's Retreat, Glen Osmond, 1909.

It was February 1914 before work on the new convent began. Six months later it was ready for occupation and the Sisters moved there from their convent beside the Josephite Cemetery on Muggs Hill, Mitcham. Then, after a final Mass in the Mitcham church on Sunday, 23 August, workmen moved all the furniture, fittings and school equipment from there to the church-school, which was set up with 'electric light and all modern conveniences'.[25] Soon afterwards, the CCES sold the Maitland Street property and the new owners demolished the old church. Years later (in 1926) the Sisters arranged for the former Mitcham convent to be demolished and for the stone to be transported to Kensington, where they used it to erect a laundry and a large store room on the convent grounds.

1914 was the year when World War I, allegedly the war to end all wars, broke out in Europe, and young Australian men volunteered for service overseas. The Australian Red Cross invited schoolchildren to knit woollen socks for the diggers at Gallipoli and later on, in the trenches of France and Belgium. Many people had relatives on military service and so it was with pride that pupils in Josephite schools, like their contemporaries from other Catholic and state schools, knitted many pairs of socks. In the following year, the children at the Beulah Road School contributed to the soldiers' welfare by taking up a collection at their 1915 Christmas concert in the Norwood Town Hall and giving the proceeds to the War Effort.[26]

At Terowie, the Sisters arranged the evening programme for a grand bazaar to raise funds for a new presbytery at Jamestown[27] and prepared children to take part a school concert.[28] At Quorn, the local people raised money because:

---

25. *SC* 21 August 1914, 685. See also: David Hilliard, *Catholics in Kingswood: the Catholic Church in the Mitcham district, 1869–1994* (Kingswood Catholic Parish Pastoral Council, 1994). In 2010 the Sisters returned some of this stone to the cemetery site where it was used to create a feature wall at the entrance to the cemetery.
26. *SC* 24 December 1915, 1035.
27. *SC* 27 February 1914, 157.
28. *SC* 27 February 1914, 157; 12 June 1914, 465.

> The convent of St Joseph, which was built in 1890, [had been] found to be insufficient in its accommodation for the good nuns and their work.[29]

They added two spacious rooms, surrounded the building with a verandah and renovated the entire structure. Bishop Norton, who laid the foundation stone for these extensions in September 1914, encouraged those present to donate generously towards this project.

From 1913–1917, Sister Benizi Casey was Sister-in-charge at Quorn. A number of the senior students in her care, including several boarders at the convent, did well with their music and academic studies.[30] When, at the end of 1917, when Benizi moved to Terowie, she suggested to some of the parents that they transfer their daughters to Terowie to board at the convent there. Among the young women who made this move were Susan and Madge Gleeson, who later played significant roles as Josephites under the names of Sisters Oliver and Francis Therese. At the time of writing, (2014), descendants of some of those who knew Sister Benizi in either Quorn or Terowie remembered her name with gratitude.[31]

During 1915, the Josephites, who had been in Port Augusta for more than forty years, moved to a new convent on Flinders Terrace.[32] It had

> a very fine bold appearance, flanking Flinders Terrace just on the brow of the Cathedral Hill. It [made] a nice picture, and [was] absolutely the best building of its kind in the town. The bungalow roofs and gables, with the spacious verandahs on three sides, the triple windows of lead lights in the oratory and music rooms, and their corresponding gable roofs [gave] the structure a noble and commanding aspect. The treatment of the exterior [was] in good taste in the Gothic style. The chimneys [were] quaint. The rooms [were] large and lofty. There [were] nine in all without the bathroom, pantry and

---

29. *SC* 18 September 1914, 769.
30. *SC* 22 December 1916, 1029, Quorn results; 22 September 1918, 240 & 3 January 1919, Terowie results. The names of the Gleeson girls and some other students occur in both lists.
31. Interview, Sr Marie Victory, formerly of Peterborough, October 2013. Marie's mother was a student at Quorn during Sister Benizi's time there.
32. *SC* 21 May 1915.

cellar. A fine cool cellar [was] located under the spacious kitchen, and a special form of ventilation [was] provided to communicate fresh air from the gable roof to the cellar room. A washhouse, wood room and other appointments [had] been added, with all necessary water connections. Provision [had] been made for electric light throughout, whenever it [might] be introduced into the town. The work [was] all in the first class style, meant to be the best and most durable.[33]

The bishop was an architect's apprentice before he became a priest and several features of the new convent bore marks of his touch.[34]

Then, during the September of 1915, the O'Mara family of St Peters donated to the Norwood parish for church purposes their 'magnificent property known as Ellangowan'. It was in a good position on Payneham Road just opposite the St Peters Town Hall and for some years, the O'Maras opened it for use as a Mass Centre on weekends.[35] Two months after news of the O'Mara donation became public, Archbishop Spence laid the foundation stone for a church- school on the property and, in due course, two Josephite Sisters took charge of the school.[36] Its initial enrolment was seventy-one children and numbers gradually increased until they reached 171 in 1931. The Sisters teaching at Ellangowan and Beulah Road travelled to their schools from Kensington in every kind of weather, sometimes on foot, sometimes by horse and buggy or tram, and in later years, by car.

Spence attended the opening of the Ellangowan church-school and, after its conclusion, went with the parish priest, Father Connell SJ, to view the school on Bridge Street, Kensington. According to the *Southern Cross*, he was horrified at what he saw:

---

33. *SC* 17 September 1915, 749.
34. Margaret M Press, *John Henry Norton: Bishop of Railways* (Kent Town: Wakefield Press, 1993), 19–20.
35. *SC* 17 September 1915, 749.
36. Archbishop O'Reily died in July 1915 and was succeeded at once by his former coadjutor, Archbishop Robert William Spence OP, an Irishman who had been a member of the Dominican community at North Adelaide since 1898. See: Schumann, Ruth, 'Spence, Robert William (1860–1934)', *ADB* (National Centre of Biography, Australian National University, 1990), http://adb.anu.edu.au/biography/spence-robert-william-8602/text15023

> The old school was in such a dilapidated condition that he (Spence) feared that a strong gust of wind might sweep it away. It was simply fit for pulling down ... The condition of the building and walls was dangerous to the Sisters and children. He told Father Connell without hesitation that the school must come down and a new one be built.[37]

Almost immediately, the Sisters and children moved to a hall at the Marist Brothers' School on Queen Street, Norwood, and the rebuilding of the Bridge Street School began. The Archbishop laid the foundation stone in October 1916, returned for its blessing and opening in February 1917, and dedicated it to the memory of former long-time parish priest, Father Daniel O'Brien SJ.[38]

In early 1917, the people of Hamley Bridge purchased a new convent which was ready for the Sisters when they returned from their retreat.[39] In that same year, the parents had a separate infant room added to the Josephite school in Kadina where there were 112 children on the roll, and Sister Fergus Brosnahan was community leader.[40]

Sister Fergus remained at Kadina until 1920 and during that time suffered a major illness. It seems that she and Sister de Ricci Cooney fell victim to the dreaded 'Spanish flu' pandemic, which caused such havoc throughout the world during the years 1918 and 1919.[41] Sisters who lived through that period used to tell how Sister Fergus appeared to be more dangerously ill than Sister De Ricci, and how the latter prayed that God would take her rather than her younger superior. (Fergus was thirty-seven years old at the time.) De Ricci died on 15 August 1919 aged fifty-three, while Fergus survived and was engaged in active ministry for many years to come.[42]

---

37. *SC* 20 October 1916.
38. *SC* 19 February 1917.
39. *SC* 19 October 1917, 837.
40. Kadina records, and Register of the Sisters, ASSJ, Kensington.
41. http://en.wikipedia.org/wiki/1918_flu_pandemic. Worldwide, millions died from this flu. In Australia an estimated 12,000 died. Many more were infected but recovered.
42. Sr Angela Gapper rsj (1900–1968) to the author, at Wallaroo, early 1960s. Register of the Sisters, ASSJ, Kensington. Sr Fergus Brosnahan was born in New Zealand on 28 December 1880, made her religious profession on 02 July 1900, and died in Adelaide on 25 January 1957.

By 1918, the Sisters were preparing to make a foundation in a district with which they previously had no connections whatever. That was Renmark, the centre of the Chaffey Irrigation Settlement founded on the River Murray in 1887, and was quite close to the borders between South Australia, Victoria and New South Wales. The town itself was founded in 1904 but it was 1927 before it was connected to Adelaide by rail. Until then, the Sisters (and everyone else) travelled there by rough unsealed roads that ran through dense scrub as it made its way across the sandhills of the Murray Mallee region.

At that time, the boundary between the two South Australian dioceses ran along the river: all towns on its northern bank were in the Diocese of Port Augusta while those on the southern side were in the Archdiocese of Adelaide. Renmark became a parish in its own right in 1914, the year when drought caused the river to run dry.

It did rain again, however, and by the end of 1918, the local Catholics had built a school-hall and purchased a convent—they were ready for the Sisters. In the following year, Sister Pius Frost and two companions arrived to find a schoolroom set up with 'the latest school equipment and the most approved type of desks and blackboards'.[43]

Bishop Norton, who attended the opening of the school-hall, praised parish priest, Father PA Connolly, and his parishioners for what they had achieved. Mr Jack Simon, who gave the vote of thanks to the bishop, remarked that school enrolments stood at 111, with an average attendance of 105, and added that seventy-five per cent of the children were not Catholic. This was a fact that, to his mind, 'showed the fine broad spirit of the people of Renmark'.[44] (It also showed that, without the nonCatholic children this school would not have been viable.)

The year 1919 saw the Sisters' return to Macclesfield, where a lay teacher had managed the school for the previous ten years.

During the 1920s, there was a marked increase in the number of Josephite foundations and new convent and school buildings across the state. The first of these was at Spalding, a small Mid-North

---

43. *SC* 11 April 1919, 284.
44. *Murray Pioneer*, 4 April 1919.

town in the Adelaide archdiocese.[45] (It transferred to the Port Augusta diocese some twenty years later.) In March 1921, the *Southern Cross* informed its readers: 'neither trouble nor expense [had] been spared in making the school and housing accommodation [at Spalding] complete and efficient in every respect.'[46]

There was room enough for sixteen boarders and, at opening time, children from within a sixteen-mile radius of Spalding already filled twelve of these places. The women of the district provided utensils ranging from 'saucepans to sheets and a cedar table, from fowls to firewood and a cow', and everyone boasted that the educational facilities in the new school were 'equal to those possessed by children in the city'.[47] The opening of the new convent on Sunday, 17 April, was a grand affair indeed with an estimated attendance of 700 people. The Sisters, who observed the celebrations from the convent verandah, stood out from the crowd. As one writer put it:

> Not the least striking element in the scene was the group of Sisters of St Joseph, 27 in number, on the convent verandah. Among them was Sister Victor Lane, Superior of the Order in South Australia. Their presence, clad in what the Bishop of Goulburn aptly called "the khaki of the church militant" must have reminded many that these women and their associates are in a very true sense the Anzacs of Catholic Education in the Commonwealth.[48]

Except for Sister Victor and her companion, who were from Adelaide, these Sisters were from surrounding convents. Archbishop Spence noted that, within a thirty-five-mile (fifty-six-kilometre) radius of Spalding there were eight Catholic schools run by the Josephites: Terowie, Jamestown, Caltowie, Gladstone, Georgetown, Clare, Sevenhill and Burra.[49]

Two weeks prior to his trip to Spalding, Spence laid the foundation stone for a Josephite convent on a vacant site on West Street, Hectorville. The old convent, which the Sisters had occupied

---

45. *SC* 29 October 1920, 889.
46. *SC* March 1921, 221.
47. *SC* March 1921, 221.
48. *SC* 29 April 1921, 355.
49. *SC* 29 April 1921, 355.

for thirty of their forty years in the district, was much too small and in such a bad state of repair that the resident Sisters were afraid it would come down around their ears.[50]

Next, the people of Terowie built a new school-hall, the Soldiers' Memorial Hall. This 'solid stone structure, ornate and spacious', was required because the small classrooms in the convent were overcrowded. At about the same time, the residents of Quorn raised funds for either a school hall or a new church, leaving the current church building to become a dedicated school.[51]

Back in the city, during August 1921 builders laid 'the foundations of a concrete building to serve as a temporary school and church' in Everard Avenue, Keswick, near the old Kelvinator factory. (Keswick was then part of the Goodwood parish.)[52] According to local historian, Ted Ridge:

> The church school was a stucco-covered, caneite-lined [cane-ite] building, which offered little resistance to cold or heat but served as a tangible reminder of the sacrifices being made by the Catholics of the district ... The senior grades occupied the southern end, separated from the rest by only a heavy woollen curtain, which was not at all soundproof ... In about 1930, a brick building was erected at the rear of the existing stucco structure.[53]

This new building, which comprised an Infant School and a staff room, was paid for with the 'threepences and sixpences' donated by the local people.[54] Some of these people were upset when, some years later, the parish sold the Everard Street property and used the proceeds to build a new church on South Road at Kurralta Park.

Evidence suggests that it was 1925 before this school opened under the supervision of the Sisters of St Joseph with Sister Hyacinth Scanlan as its first principal. The Sisters resided at Kensington, approximately eight kilometres away, and travelled out to the school

---

50. *SC* 2 April 1920, 267.
51. *SC* 29 July 1921 and 15 September 1922.
52. *SC* 29 July 1921, 606; 11 November 1921, 929.
53. Ted (EH) Ridge, *Fifty Years: From Keswick to Plympton, 1938–1988*, compiled by Father Bill Modystack (Plympton, 1988), 16 & 17. Cane-ite is a pre-primed soft pulp board that is very versatile and easy to work with.
54. *Fifty Years: From Keswick to Plympton.*

each day. They made this time-consuming journey by public transport until January 1928 when the Sisters of St Joseph became the proud owners of a new car, a large black Buick saloon which could safely accommodate eight passengers.[55]

Their driver was Herbie Ireland, a young man who spent his entire working life in the Sisters' employ. His most important duty was to ensure that Sisters reached their destinations on time and arrived back at the convent safely at the end of the school day. On 31 January 1928, he drove this car to school for the very first time. Soon afterwards he drove

> two own motor loads (sic) of old Sisters to Hectorville for the day and returned [with them] at 4 pm and 6.30 pm.

It seems that by this time the Sisters were becoming accustomed to car travel. The Kensington Convent diary for June 1928 carries an entry indicating that a fleet of private motor vehicles (apparently not their own) conveyed sixty Sisters to the Jubilee Oval (on Victoria Drive behind the Adelaide University) for the Eucharistic Congress celebrations at 3 pm on a particular Sunday and brought them home safely.

The earliest references to Sisters of St Joseph having travelled in motor vehicles appeared several years before the arrival of the car at Kensington. Six years earlier, in February 1922, Mother Laurence O'Brien visited the Sisters at Clare, where she had served for some time before her election to the General Council in 1910. When she left, 'Mother Laurence, accompanied by the local community, motored to Riverton to board the Adelaide train' Who owned the car and who drove it? Maybe that will have to remain a mystery![56]

It was the end of the decade before another marvel of modern communication, the telephone, became commonplace in Josephite convents! In fact, it was 1929 before there were phones in the Kensington, Lower North Adelaide, Thebarton, Hindmarsh and Port

---

55. Kensington Convent Diary, January 1928. ASSJ, Kensington. See also Ridge, *Fifty Years*, 16 & 17. Ted remembered Srs Bonaventure Flanagan, Alphonsus Farrell, Winifred Booth and Thomas Connery as having been at Keswick during his schooldays.
56. *SC* 22 February 1922, 161.

Adelaide convents and the three charitable institutions. Five years later, there was one in every Josephite house in South Australia![57]

In 1920, the Jesuit Fathers from Norwood opened a new church-school and Mass Centre dedicated to St Peter Claver, in Warwick Avenue, Dulwich. Initially, they engaged a lay teacher because they were unable to obtain the services of any religious sisters.[58] At the end of the year, this teacher left to marry and, from the beginning of 1921, two Josephites filled her place.[59] Among those who served at Dulwich during the early 1920s were Sisters Gabriel Gillman-Jones, Romanus Lavin and Bernard Joseph Boylan.

Within six years, the Sunday congregation at Dulwich became so large that the parish built a large hall at right angles to the original structure to accommodate everyone. When opening it in March 1925, parish priest, Father Corish SJ, announced that the Sisters of St Joseph were moving on in favour of the Loreto Sisters. Archbishop Spence praised the Josephites for their work at Dulwich and commented on how 'different kinds of education were called for in different places and [how] the Sisters of St Joseph were pleased to make room for others'.[60] The Loreto Sisters established a kindergarten there and used St Peter Claver's as a preparatory school for Loreto College, which by then was at Marryatville.[61]

Balaklava, on the mallee plains of the Lower-North region of South Australia was the location of the next Josephite foundation of the 1920s. A Catholic church opened in this wheat farming district in 1910, and by the 1920s, the people were asking for a Catholic school.[62] To this end, they purchased a large house in Scotland Street and Sisters Francis Clare Hughes, Dominic Walsh and Jarlath Miller moved in during April 1922. These Sisters converted two

---

57. *Official Directory of the Catholic Church in Australia*, which was published annually, 1928–1940.
58. At this time, the Loreto convent was located at the western end of the Norwood Parade. Several years were to elapse before it moved to its present site (2014) at Marryatville.
59. *The Rays of the Crucifix: Links in the Chain, A Brief History of the Dulwich-Burnside Parish, 1869–1994* (Dulwich-Burnside Catholic Parish, 1994), 121.
60. *SC* 24 April 1925, 12.
61. Archbishop Beovich to Sister Thecla Morrissey, 22 December 1944, ASSJ, Kensington.
62. *Adelaide Observer*, 11 June 1910, gives an account of the opening of the church.

of the rooms in the house into classrooms and one into a music room. Dominic taught music while Francis Clare and Jarlath ran the school. In the following year they enclosed the surrounding verandah, thus providing extra accommodation for their boarders and music pupils.

It appears that these Sisters began well. Twelve-year-old Sid Quinlan reported to the *Southern Cross* that there were five boarders at the convent and more than forty children on the school roll. He added that the Sisters had several music pupils, including himself, and were teaching a number of young people Shorthand and Typing. Sid concluded by saying that he liked the Sisters very much, and especially his teacher, Sister Jarlath.[63]

Sadly for him, less than twelve months later, during the September school holidays of 1923, Sisters Dominic and Jarlath left Balaklava, rather unexpectedly, from Sid's viewpoint at least. Legend has it that they 'ran away' from this convent, that is, left without informing Sister Francis Clare, and made their way to Adelaide. Sister Joan Redden replaced Sister Dominic but the identity of Sister Jarlath's replacement is unknown.

When Sisters Dominic and Jarlath arrived in the city unannounced, they were asked whether they wished to continue as Josephites and, by so doing, to go wherever they were sent and endure any ensuing difficulties or privations. This was too much for Jarlath who decided that the Josephite way of life was not for her and returned to her family in Victoria. Dominic, who chose to remain a member of the Congregation, accepted an appointment to her home state of New South Wales, where she served as a music teacher until her death at the Mother House in North Sydney in 1983. Of her, it was said that:

> [She] had strong loyalties to her family, to her Congregation, and to her profession—hundreds of her music students thank[ed] her for the training she gave them. She was compulsively drawn to good music, and to things beautiful.[64]

---

63. SC 17 November 1922, 973: Children's Page: 'Children's letters to Wattle Blossom'.
64. Sr Dominic Walsh was born in Western Australia on 4 August 1901, grew up and was educated at Glen Innes in New South Wales, joined the Josephites in Sydney in 1920, made her religious profession in 6 January 1922, was appointed to South Australia soon afterwards, returned to NSW in 1923 and died at North Sydney

One may ask why these two young (in their early twenties) Sydney-trained Sisters decided that they could no longer remain at Balaklava. Was it the loneliness of this small isolated town or was it that Sister Francis Clare tried to retrain them according to her particular South Australian way of being Josephite?

In 1923, school enrolments at Balaklava stood at about fifty children and the Sisters added bookkeeping to the subjects on offer.[65] Young Sid did well with his music studies and was among the first of the Sisters' pupils to gain a diploma in music. By 1925, the convent/school was overcrowded with sixty children packed into very limited space. They needed a separate school building urgently and the parishioners set to work. Before long, it was ready for occupation and the Sisters put the two former classrooms in the convent to good use: one became a music room and the other the boarders' dining room.

Music education reached a peak at Balaklava between 1932 and 1944 when Sister Therese Gleeson (the Madge Gleeson who went from Quorn to Terowie with Sister Benizi) was the music teacher. While she was there, between forty and fifty adults and children enrolled each year to study piano, violin and theory of music with her.[66]

Back in the Port Augusta Diocese, the elderly and, by now, frail Bishop Norton laid the foundation for a new convent at Gladstone during October 1922. He urged the people to donate generously because the Sisters had lived in poor conditions for thirty years and he believed that they should have a new home with up to date facilities.[67] Included in their new seven-roomed villa-fronted residence were a

---

on 12 August 1983. The so-called retraining of young Sisters who went through their novitiate in Sydney, was a practice engaged in by some Sisters who did their training in South Australia. They could not trust that the Sydney Novitiate had the same high standards as the Adelaide one.

65. *SC* 22 February 1923.
66. Balaklava Centenary Book Committee, *Balaklava: Change and Challenge* (District Council of Balaklava, 1977), 72 & 73.
67. One wonders what the most up-to-date facilities of the period 1910–1930 might have been. Reference is made to them in many reports of regarding new convent and school buildings. Did they include running water, ice chests, and septic tanks? Maybe even electricity and a telephone!

passage, a bathroom, a laundry, a kitchen and an enclosed lobby. The Sisters moved in at the beginning of the 1923 school year.[68]

John Norton died on 22 March 1923, just five months after his visit to Gladstone. The Catholics of Peterborough, his home town, were aware of his interest in education and so they honoured his memory by erecting a new school on Bourke Street. The new Bishop Norton Memorial School was only a short distance from the church, the bishop's house and the convent: a more convenient site for all concerned than their previous building across the railway line.

The locals were keen to begin work on the school immediately after Norton's death but that proved impossible. They had to await the arrival of their new bishop, Andrew Killian, who was from Broken Hill in the neighbouring New South Wales diocese of Wilcannia-Forbes.[69] Killian's episcopal consecration took place in Sydney on 26 February 1924 and he arrived in Peterborough soon afterwards.

When he attended the St Joseph's School concert at the end of that year, he reinforced the people's decision regarding their school and urged them to begin fundraising at once. (It was up and ready for the beginning of the 1926 school year.) Killian also announced that the Sisters would soon have a much larger and more comfortable convent, a promise he fulfilled twelve months later when he vacated the two storey episcopal residence built by his predecessor, and moved into a single level house much closer to the church.[70]

In due course, Killian moved into his new presbytery, the Sisters took possession of his former home which they renamed 'St Joseph's Boys' Preparatory College', and they and the children began work in the new school. Why the new name? At Killian's request, the Sisters set the place up to accommodate twenty young boys from as far away as Quorn and the Flinders Ranges to the north and Olary on the Broken Hill line. His aim was to provide access to secondary schooling in a Catholic setting to the sons of families unable to afford the fares and fees entailed in sending their children to the city. During its first year, twelve boys accepted places in this boarding school.

---

68. *SC* 27 October 1922, 901; 18 May 1923, 15 & 8 June 1923, 6.
69. *SC* 16 November 1923.
70. *SC* 9 January 1925, 2; 11 December 1925, 2; 29 January 1926, 7 & 9.

Generally, the Sisters maintained high standards and boarders and day pupils did well at their studies. In 1929, eighteen youngsters gained their QC certificates, some with very high marks, and one boarder passed seven subjects at Leaving Certificate level.[71] The number of boy boarders varied from year to year, reaching twenty in 1930 and then gradually falling off until, by 1936, the demand for places was so low that Killian's successor, Bishop Norman Gilroy, and the Sisters themselves all decided that it would be better if they catered for girls instead.[72]

During 1923, the parishes concerned built a new school and hall at Quorn and erected a comfortable convent for the Sisters at Clare in the Adelaide archdiocese.[73] The new structure at Clare was a

> fine substantial building in the villa style with a verandah on three sides, six large rooms including a very pretty oratory and almost every convenience that it [was] possible to have in a country town.[74]

At the opening and blessing of this building, Bishop Killian made public his dream of setting up a missionary movement that would reach out to the solitary homesteads and the scattered families dotted across the vast inland of the continent. Killian soon proved that he was no idle dreamer for by the end of the decade he had established the Summer Schools, a movement whereby children from isolated families could come to established centres for a period of intensive religious instruction during school holidays.

The first summer school took place at Peterborough in 1931 and, after that, such schools became annual events. Sisters Wilhelmina Dowd, Mel Moroney and Ita O'Sullivan ran the inaugural school and each year several Sisters went from Adelaide to teach the hundred or so youngsters who came in from the outback. The Sisters' role was to instruct the children and care for the girls who were billeted in the convent. Local Catholic families provided accommodation for

---

71. *SC* 10 January 1930.
72. *Official Directory of the Catholic Church in Australia*, entries for Port Augusta diocese, 1926-1939. *SC* 29 January 1926, 9.
73. *SC* 23 February, 13 & 16 March 1923, 13: Quorn, 18 May 1923, 15.
74. *SC* 5 September 1924, 8.

the boys. Generous parishioners prepared meals for hungry children and did any necessary washing and cleaning.[75]

A new convent and school opened at Pinnaroo in the Southern Mallee Region of eastern South Australia in February 1924, when the first Josephite community, comprising Sisters Maria Joseph Coles, Bernard Joseph Boylan and Madeleine Stanley, arrived there.[76] Their new weatherboard school was approximately thirteen metres long and six metres wide with a porch at the front. It was lined with fibrous plaster and there was a metre high dado (sic) of plyboard around each room.[77] A movable screen divided it into two classrooms, commonly known as the 'big room' and the 'little room'. It was 'commodious and well ventilated', (especially through the floorboards), hot in summer and cold in winter, and overlooked neighbouring farms.[78]

When the Sisters reached the town, the convent, which previously served as a hospital, was not ready, so they spent their first few weeks at Pinnaroo in the home of the local Member of Parliament, a Catholic. It was 'one of the most up-to-date houses in Pinnaroo' and the Sisters, who were 'accustomed to humble dwellings', found it 'too luxurious for them'. One can imagine their relief when they moved into their convent, a four-roomed wood and iron structure, surrounded by a wide colonial verandah, three sides of which were enclosed by 1.3 metre high wall of galvanised iron.[79] Maria Joseph and Bernard managed the school while Madeleine, a gifted artist, taught music and painting in oils.

In February 1924, young Brian Carigg wrote to 'Wattle Blossom' from rural Hamley Bridge that there were 'three nice Sisters' at his Josephite school: Sisters Kevin Hughes, Marian Coghlan and Paula Riggs. Brian liked them very much.[80]

Further up the line, at Wallaroo, the number of Catholic families decreased when the copper mines closed. Since most breadwinners were dependent on the mines or the smelting works for their livelihoods, they left the district in search of work. Consequently,

---

75. *The Catholic Story of Peterborough* (Peterborough, 1976).
76. *SC* 1 February 1924, 5 & 29; 8 February 1924, 18.
77. In this instance, the word 'dado' was used to describe wood panelling.
78. *SC 7 March 1924*. The author was a student there during the late 1930s & early 1940s.
79. *SC* 7 March 1924.
80. *SC* 29 February 1924, 15, Children's Page, letters to 'Wattle Blossom'.

school enrolments declined although there appears to have been no question of closing the school.[81]

Back in the city, eight-year-old Marjorie Clarke of Woodville wrote of her nice school with a large playground. She commented that: 'Our Sister has a very large class to teach' but did not name her.[82]

At Thebarton, in Adelaide's western suburbs, school enrolments doubled from ninety-seven in 1913 to 194 in the mid-1920s. At the same time, the number of Sisters in the local community increased from three to six or seven and their little convent was overcrowded. When the parishioners became aware of their situation, they funded the erection of a large new dormitory and also a laundry, verandah and kitchen, all done in the same style as the original structure. That building had accommodated three Sisters: now there were seven living there, with plenty of room for more.[83]

The Josephites at Thebarton gradually extended the scope of their school to include students preparing for the Intermediate Examination as well as for the usual commercial subjects, but it was 1936 before any of their pupils gained the Intermediate Certificate. Over the years, the number of girls staying on at this school gradually increased, although it was never large. Most excelled in commercial studies and, as a rule, those wishing to take up secretarial work found suitable positions soon after they left school.[84]

In January 1925, the Sisters returned to Mintaro: they had left there during the exodus of the 1880s. The Jesuit Fathers from Sevenhill and the locals welcomed them warmly. Enrolments were always small, rarely reaching the thirty mark, but the people of the district supported them well.[85]

At the same time, four Sisters, under the leadership of Sister Marian Coghlan, made their way to Murray Bridge, one of the principal stopping places on the main railway line between Adelaide and Melbourne. Travellers of that era, whether from local trains or the mighty Melbourne Express, looked forward to obtaining a hot drink and a pie or pasty from the refreshment rooms on the station.

---

81. *SC* 1 February 1924, 5.
82. *SC* 19 September 1924, 3.
83. *SC* 30 May 1924, 7 & 8.
84. *SC 14* February 1936, 14 & 15.
85. *SC* 16 January 1925, 12 & 13; 6 February 1925, 19.

Over the years, members of the Murray Bridge community used to go to the station with tea and sandwiches for any Josephite Sisters travelling to or from the eastern states by the Melbourne Express.[86]

The school opened with an enrolment of 103 children and Sister Marian soon had a full complement of music pupils. At year's end thirteen of the Sisters' pupils gained the QC Certificate, four passed exams conducted by Stott's Business College and twenty, including Eileen Gee (the future Sister Colette), sat for music exams at beginners' levels. Among the successful QC students was Roma Lake who also joined the Josephites later on: she was known as Sister Jerome.

These two women both became successful music teachers.[87]

The Josephites made a foundation in Port Lincoln in 1874, but left there during the unsettled times of the 1880s. Forty years later, in March 1926, seven Sisters, under the leadership of Sister Fergus Brosnahan, took charge of a new school, and a convent with accommodation for thirty boarders from the more distant parts of Eyre Peninsula. The arrangement was that, in due course, these 'cultured ladies' (the Sisters) would prepare their students for the Intermediate, Leaving and Leaving Honours examinations.[88]

At the foundation stone ceremony of the new convent/boarding school, Archbishop Spence announced that the State Director of Education approved this school as one where holders of government bursaries could take out their scholarships while preparing for PEB Exams.[89] Things began slowly. In its first year, there were fifty-four children in the primary school with nine boarders and four day pupils in secondary classes. Over the next decade, numbers increased until, by 1937, there were eighty-three primary students, with ten boarders and twenty-one day scholars doing secondary studies.[90]

While at Port Lincoln, Sister Fergus designed a badge for the students' uniforms. It proved popular and before long, the Josephite

---

86. *Garland of St Joseph*, 1 April 1925, 171; SC 30 January 1925, 13.
87. SC 6 January 1926, 15.
88. SC 2 April 1926, 19.
89. SC 28 August 1925, 22.
90. *Official Directory of the Catholic Church in Australia*, 1927–1938.

Sisters in South Australia claimed it for all their schools. With a few local modifications, this badge was still in use in 2014.[91]

In the newly developing eastern suburbs of Adelaide, people were also asking for Josephite schools. There was one at Magill in the Norwood parish for a short time between 1871 and the end of 1873. For the ensuing fifty-four years, the small Catholic community in that area had 'been content with Mass once a month in the Magill Institute'.[92] By the 1920s the western portion of the suburb, now known as Tranmere, was well populated and the Catholic community had purchased a building block on the corner of Magill Road and Birkinshaw Avenue, Tranmere, as a possible site for a church-school.

They were ready to build by the end of 1926 and work went ahead quickly. The Archbishop, who opened it in April 1927, was loud in his praise of the Josephites, especially those who had accepted the Jesuit Fathers' invitation to staff the new school.[93] These Sisters went out each day from Kensington, usually travelling by tram up the Parade past Glynburn Road and then walking across open paddocks to their destination. Many of her past pupils remembered Sister Wilhelmina Dowd, the first principal of this school, with affection.[94]

The year 1927 was noted for new buildings. In May, additions to the Ellangowan School were opened. In June, the Archbishop laid the foundation stone for a new school building at Beulah Road. In August, the Burra convent was extended; additions and repairs were made to St James' Church and the convent at Macclesfield; a new school was erected at Port Augusta and, by December, the Pekina Sisters were able to spread out into newly built extensions to their convent.[95]

In September 1928, work began on St Margaret Mary's Church-School on Torrens Road, Kilkenny (now Croydon), which was largely a farming district at the time. Work progressed well and the school was ready for Sisters Jude Grady, Gerard Majella Hefron and Thomasine Willis to begin teaching there in 1929.

---

91. ASSJ, Kensington, SA. See Appendix Fifteen for further details.
92. *SC* 10 December 1926, 13.
93. *SC* 14 April 1927, 9.
94. Oral history, Tranmere parish, 1990.
95. *SC* 13 May 1927, 11; 10 June, 11; 24 June 16; 8 July, 5; 29 July, 5; 5 August, 4; 12 August, 21; 2 September, 9; 30 September, 18; 21 October, 7; 11 November, 18; 16 December, 13.

At about the same time, the Sisters and pupils of the Brompton school community moved to Hindmarsh. They packed up and transported everything from their Chief Street and First Street school sites and their Port Road convent to premises on Grange Road at Hindmarsh, approximately 1.5 kilometres away. The new convent, on the corner of Albemarle Street and Grange Road, which was formerly a private hospital and was set up to accommodate at least ten Sisters. (This meant that there was room for the Sisters soon to be appointed to the Croydon school.) Next door to the convent, the parish erected a fine three roomed brick school with the most up to date facilities. How the children enjoyed their new, safe playing area! It was very different from the open ground of the median strip along the Port Road, which they used to access by crossing the busy main road between the city and Port Adelaide.[96]

While many changes and developments were taking place in the school scene, other events were also affecting the Sisters' lives. Of great significance for the whole Congregation was the fact that, during 1914, the health of the much-loved Sister Monica Phillips failed and she died on 15 April at the age of eighty years. As they laid her to rest, the Sisters, especially the older members of the community, would have recalled her calm presence during the time of Mary's excommunication in 1871 and her trip to Rome two years later.

They would also have remembered with particular gratitude how she steered them through the dark days of the 1880s and recalled how, after their Mother General and the Mother House moved to Sydney, she watched over their wellbeing as their provincial, a position she held from 1889 to 1899. The younger Sisters would have known her as their Mistress of Novices during the following eleven years and all would have recalled how she lived quietly at Kensington during her declining years, always ready to give wise advice to those who came to her.[97]

---

96. Sr Margaret Donnelly, who was a student at this school at the time of the changeover, used to relate stories of the playground on the Port Road median strip and to comment on how the children felt much safer at Hindmarsh.
97. *Garland of St Joseph* (St Joseph's Convent, North Sydney, 1914).

Even as they grieved Sister Monica's passing, the Sisters rejoiced as they prepared to celebrate the Golden Jubilee of the 1866 foundation of the Congregation at Penola. Sister Calasanctius Howley and several other former South Australians then residing at the Mother House in North Sydney would have been present at the first Mass in the new Mother Mary MacKillop Memorial Chapel on 8 December 1913. They would also have been there when Archbishop Michael Kelly blessed and opened it six weeks later.

Ten days later, on 28 January, these same Sisters would have been present when Mary MacKillop's remains were transferred from the Gore Hill Cemetery in North Sydney to the chapel, where they were reinterred in a vault in front of Our Lady's altar. Among those present were Mary's brother, Father Donald MacKillop SJ from Adelaide, many other Josephite Sisters and numerous representatives of other Religious Orders of men and women. Mary's long-time friend, Joanna Barr Smith, who was still living in Adelaide and was unable to attend, paid for the marble slab that covered Mary's new tomb.[98]

Mother Baptista kept all the Sisters well informed of plans for the events described above and it can be assumed that their thoughts were with their Sydney Sisters on these occasions.[99] As far as possible, they also joined in the celebrations marking the Golden Jubilee of the Congregation in March 1916. They welcomed the publication of the Congregation's first attempt at making MacKillop's life story known, namely the *Life and Letters of Mother Mary of the Cross (MacKillop)* by A Sister of St Joseph. This volume appeared on most Josephite convent bookshelves during that year.[100]

Archbishop O'Reily died in July 1915 and with his passing the Sisters lost a good friend and benefactor. He bequeathed to them a section of his privately owned land at Glen Osmond 'for the use and benefit at all times of the institution known as the Fullarton

---

98. *Advertiser*, 24 October 1919, 9, 'Death of Mrs. Barr Smith'. In this article, reference is made to Joanna's lifelong friendship with Mary MacKillop. Her grave is in the Mitcham General Cemetery, not far from the Josephite Cemetery that she and her husband sold so cheaply to Mary MacKillop in 1880.
99. SC 13 February 1914, 120; Mother Baptista to the Sisters, 5 July 1914 & 1 August 1915.
100. The printed copy states that this work was written by A Sister of St Joseph, (unnamed), published by the Sisters of St Joseph and printed at the Boys' Industrial Home, Westmead, Sydney, March 1916. In Josephite circles, it is claimed that the author was Sister Chanel O'Loughlin of Sydney.

Refuge'—a gesture consistent with the generosity he showed during his years in the archdiocese. The Sisters took possession of this property in September 1915, sold it in September 1918 and, as directed in O'Reily's will, put the proceeds towards the running of the Refuge.[101]

During 1916, the Sisters held their eighth General Chapter and this time Mother Baptista Molloy and her team of councillors from 1910 were all reelected to the same positions of leadership in the Congregation that they had held since 1910. Mother Baptista visited Adelaide during the following year, organising her visit to coincide with the arrival of the Sisters from the branch convents as they came in for their annual retreat during the September school holidays.[102]

Sister Calasanctius Howley, Mother Baptista's assistant, lived in Sydney while she was a member of the General Council. It seems that her sister, Sister Andrea, whose term as Provincial of Victoria expired after the 1916 Chapter, stayed at the Mother House for a time. Both were homesick and longed to return to South Australia, as can be gauged from the following, written on 24 September 1917, that is, at the time of Mother Baptista's Adelaide visit:

> My dear Mother Baptista, Glad to hear of yr. (sic) safe arrival in SA. Wish I were there to stay—please make up yr. mind like a good Mother to let us both (S Andrea and myself) go over there soon for the little remainder of our lives. We promise to be of good behavior—'as far as human frailty will enable us'—that's somewhere in our books I think that quotation.[103]

Neither she nor anyone else could have guessed then that, just over twelve months later, they would be grieving for Mother Baptista. After

---

101. According to O'Reily's will: 'such allotment or the proceeds of the sale thereof [were to] be for the use and benefit at all times of the institution known as the Fullarton Refuge as managed and carried on by the Sisters of St. Joseph.' ACA, HDMS Series ref 0028-0001; Land Titles Office: Hundred of Adelaide, Allotment 19, Section 270, Certificate of Title, Volume 181, folio 95. See: https://www.sa.gov.au/topics/housing-property-and-land/land-services-industry/land-services-group-contacts for further details.
102. SC 5 October 1917, 797.
103. Sr Calasanctius Howley to Mother Baptista Molloy, 27 September 1917.

visiting Adelaide she went to Western Australia where she became very ill.[104] During her return journey, she became so unwell that she had to leave the train in Melbourne where she died on 28 October 1918, aged 63 years. The Sisters transported Mother Baptista's remains to Sydney where they held a Solemn Requiem in the Mother Mary MacKillop Memorial Chapel, for the erection of which she was responsible and in which they laid her to rest.

Following Mother Baptista's death, the Sisters held another General Chapter to elect her replacement. This time, Sister Laurence O'Brien became Mother General. Sister Calasanctius was not reelected to the Council and so she and Andrea returned to South Australia soon afterwards. They made their home at Kensington. Andrea, who lived for another twelve years, died on 22 June 1932 aged eighty-eight years, while her younger sister, Calasanctius, died on 13 December 1933, aged eighty-five. Both were Josephites for more than sixty years and both were buried in the Catholic Cemetery near St Aloysius Church in Sevenhill.[105]

Mother Laurence did not appoint any new provincials in 1918 because those already holding that office had served only two years of their six-year terms. By early 1923, however, these had expired and she replaced them all. Victorian-born Sister Claude Riddell, who spent her entire religious life in South Australia, succeeded Sister Victor Lane, who had been provincial since 1905.[106] Subsequently, Victor moved to the Refuge where she replaced the ailing Sister Annette Henschke as Sister in charge. She returned to Sydney in June 1930 and died there on 14 September 1932, aged seventy-four years.

It was pleasing to note that, in December 1919, the *Southern Cross* carried an article congratulating the Quinlan family of Clare on a special occasion. Their family member, Bridget, or Sister Hyacinth, who was living in Tasmania, was about to celebrate the golden jubilee of her religious profession. The reporter wrote:

---

104. *Garland of St Joseph*, December 1918, 458. Article taken from the *Freeman's Journal*. The nature of her illness was not specified.
105. Sr Calasanctius Howley to Mother Baptista Molloy, 27 September 1917.
106. Register of the Sisters, ASSJ, Kensington. According to Josephite tradition, the Howley sisters were buried at Sevenhill in fulfilment of a promise made to their parents at the time of their entry into the Congregation.

> What a lifetime! What memories it must bring back, and what joys too! The Quinlans have every reason to be proud of their sister, who has laboured so zealously in the cause of religion not only in their native land, South Australia, but also in Bathurst, Wanganui New Zealand and now in Tasmania, where she has been for 27 years.[107]

Sister Hyacinth's sister, Sister Michael, died in Adelaide in 1915.[108] It is likely that many of the younger Sisters in the South Australia of 1919 knew little of Hyacinth's story and nothing of the circumstances surrounding her decision to become a Diocesan Josephite in 1876.

After this, reports of Sisters' golden jubilee celebrations appeared intermittently in the *Southern Cross*. Thus, during 1920 two well-known South Australian Josephites, Mother Laurence O'Brien and Sister Mechtilde Woods celebrated their jubilees. Such occasions were a sign that the Congregation now had 'wise elders' of its own: it was no longer a 'society without grandparents'.

The Sisters received confirmation of their maturity in 1920 when Pope Benedict XV (1854–1922) gave definitive approval to the Constitutions of the Congregation of the Sisters of St Joseph of the Sacred Heart in Australia.[109] Historians claim that the Australian nation came of age during the fierce battles of the 'Great War', 1914–1918. It can be said that the Josephites came of age as a Congregation of Pontifical Right in the immediate post war period. The time was ripe for them to consider the possible canonisation of their foundress.

This work began even before the Josephite General Chapter of 1925 when Mother Laurence O'Brien was elected Mother General for a second term. She informed the Chapter that already she had authorised the printing and circulation of a holy card carrying a prayer for Mary's canonisation. She also announced that moves were afoot to secure that portion of the Penola property on which Mary MacKillop's stable school stood. This purchase was finalised on 23 December 1925.

It is also worthy of note that the St Joseph's Church that Father Woods erected in Penola in 1860 had become unsafe and that, by

---

107. *SC* 12 December 1919, 1003.
108. Sr Michael Quinlan died at Kensington on 5 September 1915, aged sixty-six years.
109. *SC* 9 June 1920, 553.

1924, the local parish had replaced it with a new church building, also St Joseph's, on the same site.[110]

At the 1925 Chapter, the Sisters looked into the possible benefits of obtaining a house in Ireland for a juniorate—a place where young girls and women interested in becoming Josephites could spend some time and, if necessary, complete their schooling, before embarking for Australia.[111] This new phase in the preparation of young Irish women interested in becoming Sisters began with the purchase of a property at Newmarket in County Cork during 1926.[112] Then, in mid-1927, four Josephites, including Sisters Benizi Casey and Mel Moroney from Adelaide, left Australia for Ireland. Their mission was to set up and manage a juniorate at Newmarket.[113]

At about the same time, Sisters in South Australia decided that they too should take steps in the same direction. For many years, the Kingswood Sisters provided boarding places for country girls whose parents could not afford the fees at other Catholic girls' boarding schools in Adelaide. They now decided to encourage any girls, who might be considering the possibility of becoming Josephites, to complete their secondary studies at Kingswood. They publicised their plans with the following advertisement in the *Southern Cross* of 11 February 1927:

> Sisters of St Joseph's Juniorate. The attention of aspirants to the Sisterhood of St Joseph is directed towards the Juniorate at Kingswood where they may enter upon a course of study prior to their entering. For particulars, apply: local Superior or Superior Kensington.[114]

Two of the young girls who answered this advertisement (both were seventeen at the time) and went to Kingswood, Mary O'Brien of

---

110. *SC* 22 August 1924, 13.
111. Minutes of General Chapters, 1875–1931, 2007, 38–42.
112. *SC* 18 February 1927, 9 & 25 February, 7.
113. Mother Laurence to the Sisters, 5 February and 14 May 1927. She named the four as being Sisters Benizi Casey and Mel Moroney from Adelaide, Giovanni Vaughan from Victoria and Magdalen Moriarty from New South Wales. On her return to Australia in 1929, Magdalen became Assistant Mistress of Novices and remained in that position alongside Sister Kevin Hughes until 1936.
114. *SC* 11 February 1927, 14.

Murray Bridge (the future Sister Kevin) and Cecilia Hansberry from the Mid-North (the future Sister Bernardine) gained their Leaving Certificates that year. Both passed in English Literature, History, Maths I, Maths II and Arithmetic, while Cecilia also gained passes in French, Geography and Music. They were the first South Australian Juniors to join the Josephites. Sister Kevin entered in mid-1927, several months before she completed her studies, while Sister Bernardine took that step in March 1928. Kevin spent most of her active life teaching secondary students while Bernardine was a successful music teacher.[115]

Early in 1926, Mother Laurence made two important appointments regarding the future training of prospective Josephites: she appointed new Mistresses of Novices for the Adelaide and Sydney novitiates. For Adelaide, she chose Sister Andrina Clarke to replace Sister Dolores Duffy, while she called Sister Kevin Hughes from her school ministry in Spalding to take on the role of Assistant Mistress of Novices in Sydney. In so doing, she relieved Sister Casimir Meskill of the greater part of the burden of a position that she had held since 1910. Following Sister Casimir's death in 1936, Sister Kevin took her place as Mistress of Novices. Over the years, Sisters who were novices during her time there always spoke highly of her. Sister Nora Kerin of Adelaide once described her as the 'holiest Josephite woman' she had ever met.[116]

One sign of Josephite maturity was that their former pupils (or 'old scholars' as they were called) were forming Old Scholars' associations across the state. The first such appeared in 1915 when former pupils from the Beulah Road School established the Beulah Road Old Scholars' Association. Almost at once, its members set up a scholarship fund to enable children from poor families to remain at school. It was worth eight guineas, a sum large enough to pay for 'one year's tuition in music, in addition to the ordinary school course, including books'.[117]

---

115. SC 3 February 1928, 18; Register of the Sisters, ASSJ, Kensington.
116. Conversations with Srs Nora Kerin and Joan Barry, at Kensington, February 2014. Josephite Web page, Obituary of Sr Andrina Clarke. As stated above, Sister Kevin was at Hamley Bridge in 1924.
117. A guinea was worth one pound and one shilling. SC 8 December 1916, 1420; 20 December 1918, 1046.

During April 1920, members of the Kensington-Norwood Old Scholars' Association, based at Kensington, gathered for their second reunion. At about the same time:

> A number of former pupils of St Joseph's Convent, Stanley Street, [North Adelaide] met for the purpose of forming an O.S.A. (sic) and, in spite of the inclement weather, it was very gratifying to the Sisters to see the large number of girls that were present.[118]

Over subsequent months and years, numerous references to Old Scholars' groups connected with both country and city schools appeared in the Southern Cross. On many different occasions, the members of these groups engaged in fundraising events for the support of 'their' Sisters.

Mary MacKillop's younger brother and soulmate died on 2 February 1925 at his home, the Jesuit house at Norwood. He was seventy-two years old. The Sisters remembered him for his work among the Aboriginal people at Daly River in the Northern Territory, where he was based for several years during the 1890s. After the collapse of the Mission, Donald moved to Adelaide where he continued his work of preaching and giving retreats until ill health forced his retirement. He was buried in the Jesuit plot at Adelaide's West Terrace Cemetery.

Four years later, on 14 January 1929, Annie MacKillop, the last of Mary's immediate family, died in Melbourne, aged eighty years. Annie, the longest-lived of this family, was a strong friend and support to Mary throughout the years, and was present with her big sister when she died in 1909.

In September 1925, the Sisters laid Sister Editha Flanagan to rest in the Mitcham Cemetery. Sister Editha had been in charge of St Joseph's orphanage, Largs Bay for many years and, while there, was largely responsible for the foundation of the Guild of St Anthony and the distribution of St Anthony's Bread. Her trust in Divine Providence was well known and she often reported how she received a particularly generous donation when she most needed

---

118. *SC* 29 October 1920, 889.

it. This donation, which enabled her to clear a large debt owing on the orphanage, was a gift of £3,000 ($6,000) from a Mr Thomas Martin.

Editha's story was that Mr Martin arrived at the orphanage unannounced and offered to assist the Sisters in caring for their garden. She accepted his offer but soon realised that he was weak, ill, and unable to work. She obtained a wheelchair for him, cared for him and arranged for some of the children to wheel him about the premises when required. After six months of kind treatment, Mr Martin presented her with the money. Subsequently she informed him that he was welcome to stay as long as he wished. When he died in October 1914, she had him buried in a corner of the orphanage property.[119]

On a lighter note comes a report of Sister Adalbert Brazil's feast day celebrations at St Mary's School, Lower North Adelaide. She had been there for twenty-two years, and past and present school pupils wanted to show their appreciation for her good work among them. Music teacher, Sister Cyril Coleman, helped the young ones prepare and perform a little concert in her honour.[120] At its conclusion, the youngest child in the school, Mary Littledyke, presented Sister Adalbert with 'a bouquet of beautiful pink and white flowers'. Nancy Sullivan came in with a silver tray on which were 'a fountain pen with ink, a box of choice chocolates and other gifts', and little Billy Chellew gave her 'a silver umbrella on behalf of two past pupils, Masters Rick and Vin Mullins'. That evening about forty of Sister's older friends and past scholars gave her a surprise party. The other Sisters in the community 'were necessarily in the plot and gave valuable help'.[121]

A pleasant interlude during 1925 was the arrival in Outer Harbour, on their way to the Sydney novitiate, of a group of fifty young Irish girls and women whose parents had entrusted them to the care of Father Carroll. This Irish priest had worked in Australia for many

---

119. SC 2 October 1925, 21, 'Death of a Pioneer Sister of St Joseph'. Mr Martin's headstone is no longer visible on the Largs Bay property where the orphanage stood and so it is impossible to find out when he went there or how long he stayed. We do know, however, that he died at the orphanage on 3 October 1914, aged eighty-nine years. (SAGHS, On Line Data base.) No family details appear on this entry.
120. Sr Cyril (Thelma Lucy) Coleman was born on 7 November 1902 at Carlton, Vic. She joined the Congregation in Adelaide in June 1921, was professed on 20 August 1923 and left the Congregation on 26 March 1941.
121. SC 1 May 1925, 18: 'Feast Day of a Sister of St Joseph'.

years and occasionally he returned to Ireland to visit his family and friends. When about to embark for home in mid-1909 he called on Mary MacKillop at North Sydney and she asked him to bring back some good Irish girls to join the Congregation. Carroll took her so seriously that every time he went to Ireland, he canvassed for volunteers to join the Australian Josephites and returned with several willing candidates. His 1925 trip was his last and his most successful. (After this, all prospective postulants from Ireland spent some time at Newmarket before embarking for Australia).

When the travellers arrived at Outer Harbour, members of the Adelaide Catholic Club arranged for 'two motor buses to convey them to the city'. According to the *Southern Cross:*

> Mr E. M. Minogue generously placed his motor car at the disposal of Sister Claude of the Kensington convent, and in the company of Mr H.J. Savage, he conveyed the Sisters to the Outer Harbour. Sister Claude met and welcomed the postulants.
>
> The girls, becomingly garbed in black, were soon ready and anxious to gain a glimpse of Adelaide. Punctually at nine o'clock, the two luxurious motor buses (Pearl Sedans) owned by Mr S. J. Kent of Prospect, left the Outer Harbour. Calls were made at the Largs Bay Orphanage and Fullarton Refuge, and after a run around the outer suburbs, the girls were taken to the Kensington convent. They were entertained by the Sisters until the afternoon and were then taken back by motors to the 'Orana'.[122]

They had a great day. Some weeks later, several of them, including the future Sisters Ita, Zita and Barbara Buckley, returned to Adelaide. The intention was that they should do their novitiate training at Kensington and subsequently, join the South Australian Province. All three served long and faithfully in South Australia.

Over the years, the number of Sisters in the Kensington community increased gradually to about sixty-five. Among them were senior Sisters in frail health and the staffs of the schools at Keswick, Russell and Pirie Streets in the city, Bridge Street at Kensington, Beulah Road at Norwood, and Ellangowan House at St

---

122. *SC* 24 December 1925, 7.

Peters. There was no proper infirmary where sick and frail aged Sisters could be cared for. Therefore Sister Claude encouraged the community to raise money to help pay for significant extensions to the convent, including an infirmary. She launched a public appeal in August 1925, on the occasion of their first fete, which they held in the 'plantation' section of their property.[123]

Work began in early 1926 with the demolition of the eight-roomed house adjoining the chapel, the building that was on the property when the Josephites moved there in 1872. Archbishop Spence, who was there for the foundation stone ceremony in July, returned for the blessing and opening in March 1927. At the time, part of the ground floor of the new southern wing was allocated for administration purposes. The remainder housed a number of elderly Sisters, and there was a large infirmary at its eastern end. Upstairs were several large dormitories and, according to a reporter from the *Southern Cross*

> Another improvement . . . was the extension of the Novitiate accommodation as, owing to the increased number of candidates, space was limited, and it might be mentioned that this was the first Novitiate of the Order, and many young South Australian girls [and others] have passed through it and devoted their talents and their lives to the cause of Catholic education throughout the Commonwealth and New Zealand.[124]

At some time during 1927 Father Moreno, OSB, a well-known exponent of sacred music, arrived from the Benedictine monastery at New Norcia in Western Australia to introduce the Sisters to his new hymns and motets.[125]

The year 1928 began quietly with one noteworthy event, the annual St Patrick's Day procession through the city. As was the case for many years, each Catholic school in the Adelaide metropolitan area

---

123. *SC* 14 August 1925, 12, 4 September, 15. 'The plantation' was a stand of trees in the triangular section at the northern end of the Kensington property where the Mary MacKillop Care Tappeiner Court Nursing Home still stood in 2014. There was an outdoor stage in the northernmost corner of this area.
124. *SC* 29 February 1927, 7.
125. Kensington Convent Diary, entries for 1927.

prepared a float on an Irish theme and the most outstanding received prizes at the end of the day. One outcome was the development of a friendly rivalry between schools run by members of different Religious Orders. Over time, skilled artist and music teacher, Sister Loreto O'Neill, and the children from local Josephite schools produced numerous outstanding floats. The last of these processions took place in 1934.[126]

In September 1928, Australia hosted the International Eucharistic Congress in Sydney and many South Australian Catholics undertook the journey to Sydney. For the South Australian Josephites, however, that journey ended in tragedy. Local Provincial (Sister Claude Riddell) and seventy-six year old Sister Teresa Eickhoff set off from Adelaide on the Melbourne Express looking forward to all that was to transpire over the coming weeks. Little did they dream that one of them would never reach her destination!

The trains in which these Sisters travelled comprised 'dog box' carriages with exit doors on either side, and a rest room with its entrance very close to one of these doors. It appears that at about 4 am while the night train from Melbourne to Sydney was travelling slowly through or near the railway station at Harden in southwest New South Wales, Sister Teresa caught hold of the carriage door handle as she was on her way to the rest room. It flew open and she fell onto the track.

The several published accounts of this accident vary in detail. Some say that she fell near Harden; others claim that the accident occurred at the railway station. All agree that she was badly injured but survived the fall and went by ambulance to the nearby Harden-Murrumburra District Hospital, where the doctors and nurses amputated her badly broken leg and made her as comfortable as possible. Sisters from Sydney hurried to be with her and to support Sister Claude. Teresa remained in the hospital until her death on 19 September 1928. The Sisters had her body taken to the Mother House at North Sydney where, after a Requiem Mass in the Mount Street Chapel, her funeral took place in the Josephite section of the Gore Hill Cemetery.[127]

---

126. *SC* 23 March 1928, 5.
127. *SC* 28 September 1928, 13. *The Register*, Adelaide, 3 September 1928, 8; *The Murrurundi Times and Liverpool Plains Gazette*, 7 September 1928, 1; *The Catholic Press*, NSW, 6 September 1928, 6; *The Gundagai Times*, 4 September 1928, 'Nun's Fearful Accident'; *The Gundagai Independent*, 24 September 1928,

During the whole of the period under discussion, the Sisters at St Joseph's Providence on West Terrace in the city carried on with their ministry of caring for their aged and infirm residents and providing meals and other assistance to the homeless and unemployed men of the West End. They saw at firsthand the difficulties faced by the destitute poor of their neighbourhood, especially the returned soldiers trying to come to terms with their experiences on the battlefront. With the passage of time and the gradual slowing down of the economy, ever-increasing numbers of needy people came to the Providence in search of food and clothing. As one writer commented:

> Few poor people passed the building without going in to see whether they could get anything, and very few indeed went away without getting a meal or something else.[128]

The Sister who had been responsible for assisting the 'down and out' men of the city since about the year 1900 was Hilda McNamara who worked tirelessly for them for at least thirty long years and became a legend among them.[129] She fed them, clothed them, sobered them up, listened to their stories, and at times sheltered them from the police. In return, these men had a lasting respect for her. They knew that she expected certain standards of behaviour, especially in the matter of language, and that she never gave away money.

For many she was their only friend. The story is told (on good authority of course) that one of Sister Hilda's protégés, when about to embark for overseas service during World War I, farewelled her thus: 'Goodbye, Sister 'ilda. (sic) If I don't come back, I hopes I sees you somewhere, in 'eaven or 'ell or somewhere.'[130]

---

1. Oral history, Josephite Sisters and the author's family. Sister Teresa was greatly missed by the Adelaide Sisters and by her many friends and former students, especially from among the Catholic German families in Adelaide.
128. SC 3 May 1929 & 21 March 1930.
129. Sister Hilda (Bridget Teresa McNamara) was born in SA on 21 December 1852. She joined the Josephites in 1870, made her profession in 1872, and was one of the first Sisters to go to Port Lincoln in 1874. She continued as a teacher in several other schools until she was appointed to the Providence in about the year 1900. According to her obituary, she spent thirty years teaching in the schools and thirty at the Providence. She retired to Kensington at about the time she turned eighty and died there on 10 July 1939 aged eighty-nine years.
130. Sister Callista Neagle, 'Notes on foundations' ASSJ, Adelaide.

There is no way of estimating the extent or value of the work done by Sister Hilda and the other Providence Sisters. Like their Sisters in the Port Adelaide/Largs Bay area, they did not record the numbers who came, or the kind or amount of aid they dispensed.

The provision of outdoor relief for the homeless ones did not impinge Sisters' care for their residents. In 1924, when thirty women were crowded into a house built to accommodate twenty, they set out to extend the building. The contract price was £2000. Lack of funding delayed their project but by 1929, they could wait no longer. They went ahead, confident that God would provide what they needed.

They were not disappointed, for a timely gift of £500 from the estate of Daniel Kennelly, late of Port Pirie, enabled them to make a start.[131] To raise the rest, they once again called on the providence of God for aid. When Archbishop Spence laid the foundation stone of the extensions, he launched the first public appeal for funding that the Sisters had made since the Providence opened its doors in 1868. By the end of the afternoon, they had £1,150 in hand, including the Kennelly legacy, and felt confident that God would soon provide the balance of their requirements.

The additions comprised two rooms and a balcony along the West Terrace frontage and a new and larger chapel in the western section of the building. Besides this, the spaces between the old buildings,

> which had no covered communication with each other, [were] filled up by corridors and dormitories that more than doubled the provision for inmates.[132]

According to the *Southern Cross*, when the renovations were completed, the original house had been

> transformed into a roomy and imposing edifice comprising a fine chapel, a dining hall, dormitory, sitting room and

---

131. Will of Daniel Kennelly, died 13 December 1926, Supreme Court of South Australia, Will no 46622.
132. *SC* 3 May 1929 & 21 March 1930.

infirmary, and many rooms not only for the aged poor, but also for young girls.[133]

There was now plenty of room for at least forty mostly elderly women, with a sprinkling of young women and girls in need of protection. They also provided country people with short-term accommodation whenever they needed to be in the city for medical treatment and had nowhere else to stay.

The total cost of the extensions was in excess of £5000, a far greater amount than the Sisters or their friends expected. Thanks to the generosity of their many benefactors, this debt was reduced to less than £1800 by March 1932. Despite their efforts to raise the balance owing, and especially because of the Great Depression that had caused havoc in the world since the end of 1929, they had paid off only another £200 by 1938. Then, in 1940, an anonymous donor left them a legacy of £1590, which enabled them to pay off all that they owed and to consider a further upgrading of their facilities. As was the case since this institution opened its doors in 1868, they trusted in the Providence of God and were not disappointed.

Taken overall, Josephite developments between January 1910 and the end of 1929 were quite remarkable. At the time of the 1910 General Chapter, there were 157 Sisters in South Australia: 125 in the Adelaide and thirty-two in the Port Augusta dioceses. They were living in twenty-four separate communities, teaching some 2,000 children in twenty-four schools and caring for 111 adults and 104 children in three charitable institutions. By 1929, there were 229 Sisters, 183 of whom were in the Adelaide archdiocese and forty-six in Port Augusta. They lived in thirty-three communities, were teaching almost 3,000 children in forty-four schools, and were caring for ninety adults and 150 children in their three charitable institutions.

All this was achieved despite the tragic disruption of the Great War. In May 1920, Pope Benedict XV issued an encyclical letter on peace and reconciliation (*Pacem Dei munus pulcherrimum*), urging Catholics to 'promote all those works of Christian benevolence which bring aid to the needy, comfort to the afflicted and protection to the weak.' He also wrote: 'It would be difficult to exaggerate the

---

133. SC 3 May 1929 & 21 March 1930.

effect of many-sided Christian beneficence in softening the heart and thus facilitating the return of tranquility to the nations.' It seems that the Josephites were already doing those things in their own way in the poorest and the most isolated parts of South Australia.

For them, as for most South Australians, the future looked promising indeed, as the world appeared to be riding on the crest of the wave. Few foresaw the Wall Street Crash of October 1929 or the hardships that would follow, especially the unprecedented levels of worldwide unemployment experienced everywhere during the 1930s. However, because they were living according to the Spirit of their Founders, the Josephites were ready for that challenge when it came.

Sr Victor Lane
Provincial 1905–1922

Mother Laurence O'Brien,
Fourth Mother General of the Congregation

Sr Claude Riddell, Provincial,
1923–1929;
1931–1937

Sr Hyacinth Quinlan, Tasmania.
Golden Jubilee 1919

Sr Adrian Riggs who helped make Altar Breads, 1940s

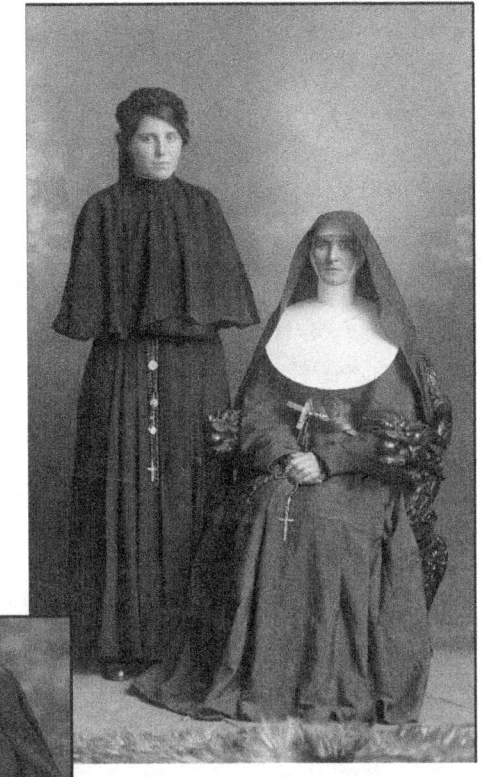

Sr Canisius Kearnan, (Seated), and Mel Moroney (Postulant), 1917.

Srs Francis Clare and Kevin Hughes. Kevin was Mistress of Novices in Sydney, 1927–1943

Sr Teresa Eickhoff, who fell from the train at Harden, NSW, 1928

Some of the students at St Mary's School, Beulah Road, Norwood, 1914

Balaklava Convent, during the 1920s.

The original Kadina Convent, 1910

Chapter Six
Depression and War: 1930–1947

The prosperity that Australia enjoyed during the 1920s was in stark contrast with the hardship and want that many of its citizens suffered during the 1930s. Numerous breadwinners were out of work with little prospect of finding jobs in the foreseeable future. For much of this decade, unemployment in Australia ran at twenty-five per cent. The government set up an unemployment benefits scheme to provide needy people with food but a high proportion of its beneficiaries were required to do compulsory work on roads or in other public utilities in order to qualify for food vouchers.

A severe drought in 1929 brought about a marked reduction in the production of wool and wheat, Australia's main export commodities at that time. Prices fell. Public works were abandoned. Factories closed. Wages and pensions were reduced. Dole queues grew in length, and help was given only to those who could prove their need. Many poverty-stricken families had to leave or were ejected from their homes. In the cities, great numbers of working men, and sometimes their wives and children, were sleeping rough. Some preferred to leave the cities and go *'on the track'* or *'jump the rattler'* to the country in search of work or handouts. While most of these *'swagmen'*. as they were designated, travelled alone, some were accompanied by their wives. Times were tough and the future looked bleak.[1]

Small wonder that neither the Church nor the Josephites were able to initiate many new works during these years. Instead, as the

---

1. J Robertson, '1930–1939', in *A New History of Australia,* edited by Frank Crowley (Melbourne: Heinemann, 1974), 415–419. 'The rattler' was a colloquial term for the goods trains of the day.

Depression deepened, many of the Sisters, most notably those at the Providence in the city, ministered to its victims, especially unemployed men who needed food and/or shelter. A writer for the *Southern Cross* estimated that almost every day during early 1930, at great self-sacrifice to themselves, the Providence Sisters provided meals for at least sixty unemployed men, while possibly having bread and dripping themselves.[2]

In the schools, the Sisters were accustomed to working with poor families, but few had witnessed destitution such as this. Hence, they made every effort to provide needy children with food, shoes, and warm clothes. At the Russell Street School in the city, volunteers assisted the Sisters with the preparation of midday meals comprising vegetables donated by Central Market stallholders and meat from a local butcher named Mr O'Leary. Bert Edwards, a former pupil made good, supported the school throughout his life.[3] In 1931, when the Depression was at its height, he was imprisoned for five years, (allegedly for having committed sodomy in the parklands). Because he did not wish to abandon the Russell Street community, he asked his friend and colleague, Mr John Owen Critchley MP Member for Burra Burra, to look after the Sisters at Russell Street, and by implication, their pupils, while he was incarcerated.[4]

---

2. *SC* 21 March 1930.
3. Albert Augustine (Bert) Edwards, 1888–1963, was one of Adelaide City's most colourful characters—a City of Adelaide man. He attended St Joseph's, Russell Street and worked in many different occupations. During the Great Depression, he did much to help Adelaide's destitute poor. He served on the Adelaide City Council and in the SA State Parliament and in 1931, after he fought bitterly for the welfare of the destitute poor of West Adelaide, he was charged with sodomy and condemned to five years in Yatala Prison. He was released in 1933 and, over time, as his business enterprises prospered, he made large donations to different charities operating in the city. He continued assisting the Providence even after it moved to suburban Cowandilla and opened his home to needy country people requiring medical treatment in the city. Each week he collected surplus food from city shops and markets and distributed it among the charities he supported. His estate of £46,000 was divided between the Sisters of St Joseph and the Adelaide City Council to give happiness, education, and opportunity for advancement in life to children from orphanages or public or private institutions for delinquent children. For further details see: Suzanne Edgar, 'Edwards, Albert Augustine (1888–1963)', *ADB* (National Centre of Biography, Australian National University, 1981), http://adb.anu.edu.au/biography/edwards-albert-augustine-6092/text10437.
4. Robert Fitzsimons, Family history, 28 February 2015. John Critchley was his grandfather.

The Russell Street Sisters continued providing meals throughout the 1930s. Then, during the war years, 1939–1945, they ran a pre-school nursery and kindergarten for children from the age of two, to assist mothers who were at work in munitions factories while their husbands were away on active service. The Sisters liked to remember that Mary MacKillop had a special place in her heart for the poor of this area and visited there whenever she was in Adelaide.[5]

No jobs were available and the Sisters did not demand school fees from destitute families. Therefore, a large number of young people stayed on at school until beyond the mandatory leaving age. The examination results published in the *Southern Cross* indicate that these students made the best of their situation, for post-primary students from Josephite schools were passing exams in commercial and/or general subjects, often with high honours.[6]

The Josephites were managing most of the schools in the hardest hit areas, such as the western and northwestern suburbs of Adelaide.[7] As the suffering of families became more serious, the Sisters gladly accepted help from members of the Society of St Vincent de Paul who organised soup kitchens in parish schools throughout the Adelaide metropolitan area. People who were struggling themselves gave what little they could towards this cause. Times were hard in the country too, and the Sisters based there did everything they could to alleviate the local people's misery. In fact, wherever they were or whatever their ministry, they assisted people in trouble or need.

It was for this reason that they responded positively when, in 1930, Archbishop Spence invited them to take charge of delinquent girls once more. Since the closure of St Johns in 1909 and the transfer of the girls from there to the State Reformatory at Redruth, near Burra in the Mid-North, they had been doing what little they could for the spiritual welfare of the Catholic detainees. Back in 1919, Sister Annette Henschke from the Fullarton Refuge had asked the archbishop for permission to apply to the state government to transfer to the Refuge any Catholic girls detained in Redruth. She explained how she had regretted the closure of St Johns, and how she had always believed

---

5. *SC* 10 December 1965, 3.
6. *SC* 7 February 1930, 8–10, gives the results for 1929. Examination results appeared in each subsequent year until the outbreak of war in 1939.
7. *SC* 5 June 1931, 7.

that there was trouble in that institution because the girls did not have enough to do. She assured the archbishop that there was plenty of work at the Refuge and that they would be well instructed in their religious duties.[8]

Spence considered the matter carefully before deciding that such a move was inadvisable. A small seed had been sown, however, and ten years later it came to fruition with the opening of Genazzano, a Catholic Girls' Reformatory in the Adelaide suburb of Parkside. In 1924, the diocese bought a twelve-roomed house in Young Street, Parkside, adjacent to St Raphael's Church, as a residence for the parish priest. The current priest owned a house nearby, however, and was renting out the church-owned property, little realising how useful it would be in the future.[9]

The girls' reformatory at Redruth closed in 1922 and its inmates were placed in the Salvation Army Girls' Home at Barton House, Enfield. By 1930, there were ten Catholics among them and the question of how best to give them suitable religious training was raised once more. Finally, in July 1930, the chairman of the Children's Welfare and Public Relief Board recommended that they should be moved to a separate 'Reformatory School for Girls of the Roman Catholic Faith'. He urged the Chief Secretary to proclaim such a school under the Maintenance Act of 1926 and to make suitable arrangements for its management.[10] Spence welcomed this decision and made the Parkside house available for this purpose.

He agreed to take the girls on condition that the government contributed towards their support and paid half the cost of renovating the house. He insisted that the Catholic Church retain the right to change the management of the institution at any time and, if necessary, to move it to another location. The Children's Welfare Board accepted his conditions and agreed to pay £1 a week for the support of each girl. As soon as the required agreements were signed, the Church undertook the necessary renovations and invited the Sisters of St Joseph to manage the new reformatory.

---

8. Sr Annette Henschke to Spence, 27 October 1919.
9. Correspondence, Parkside Parish file, ACA.
10. T Price Weir, chairman, Children's Welfare and Public Relief Board, to the Chief Secretary, July 1930.

Three Sisters, under the leadership of Sister Francis Clare Hughes, took charge of the place.[11] They named it 'Genazzano', after a village near Rome in Italy, where people venerate a miraculous picture honouring Mary, the Mother of God, under the title of Our Lady of Good Counsel. They did not record why they chose this name. Facilities at Parkside were limited and the property was too small to allow for the enlargement of existing buildings. Hence, the Church always saw it as a temporary site and looked forward to the day when it could acquire a purpose built institution. The idea of utilising part of the grounds at the Fullarton Refuge received some consideration but the Great Depression was at its height and neither the Church nor the government could afford a new building.[12]

Consequently, the reformatory remained at Parkside until 1943, by which time Adelaide had a new Archbishop, Matthew Beovich. He saw the difficulties facing the Parkside Sisters and, after having found that they were prepared to relinquish the charge of the reformatory, he invited the Sisters of the Good Shepherd to Adelaide to carry on this work. A small group of these Sisters arrived in August 1941 and bought a property known as The Pines, on Marion Road in the Adelaide suburb of Plympton.[13] They renovated the main building to suit their purposes and built a laundry in the grounds. The place was ready for occupation by the end of 1942 and the girls from Genazzano moved there on 15 January 1943.

These girls, like those at St Johns before them, were hard to manage and worked out ingenious ways of breaking the rules and running away. The Sisters in charge found the situation less stressful, however, because at Parkside they had much easier access to help in an emergency. In addition, the number of young people in residence averaged out at between five and six, whereas at St Johns, it was never fewer than fourteen. Even so, the Sisters were glad to hand them over to the Good Shepherd Sisters. In a sense, the Josephites had been waiting for the Good Shepherds since 1867, when they became responsible for the management of the Catholic Women's

---

11. Archbishop's secretary to Weir, 29 July 1930; Monsignor M. Hourigan VG to chairman, 20 August 1930.
12. Spence to Weir, 20 April 1931.
13. By the twenty-first century 'The Pines' had become part of the Southern Cross Aged Care Facility on Marion Road, Plympton.

Refuge in Adelaide. Mary MacKillop herself once explained that the Sisters became involved in charitable works only 'when there were no other religious in the place to whose vocation more particularly such duties pertained'.[14]

While Sister Francis Clare and her community were settling into working with the young women at Genazzano, people in country areas, many of whom were in distress themselves, observed what the Sisters were doing for those in dire need. Therefore these people held functions where they raised money or collected goods for the Sisters, who, as might have been expected, then shared them among the neediest families in their areas. There are many examples of such actions. Thus, at Terowie several Catholic women, who had observed at firsthand how the Sisters helped the workers' families, cooked up a special afternoon tea to raise funds.[15] The Quorn people ran a series of entertainments for the benefit of their local Josephite community.[16]

The parish priest at Port Augusta went ahead with the painting of the convent, 'one of the finest buildings in the town', because it was showing signs of deterioration and, in so doing, he gave several local men a few weeks' work.[17] At Spalding the people raised almost £40 at a ball held in aid of the Sisters and the school.[18] The Catholics of Kadina celebrated the fifteenth centenary of the introduction of the Catholic faith into Ireland by St Patrick with a Communion Breakfast. At the end of the day they donated £10 to the Sisters, to be shared between the Kadina and Wallaroo convents.[19]

A bridge party held in aid of the Kensington convent raised £93, while events at various country towns, including Pekina in the Mid-North and Karoonda in the Murray Bridge parish, also provided much-needed funds. At Jamestown the Old Scholars' Association Ball raised £50 and the Terowie Old Scholars handed £37 to their Sisters after their second annual ball.[20] The Old Scholars held a reunion at Kensington in January 1932, and a few weeks later they conducted a carnival in that part of the convent grounds commonly known as

---

14. MM, 'Observations on the Rule', in *Resource Material*, Issue 3 (Sydney, 1980), 39.
15. *SC* 28 August 1931, 5.
16. *SC* 8 January 1932, 15.
17. *SC* 6 May 1932, 7.
18. *SC* 20 May 1932, 10.
19. *SC* 10 June 1932, 6.
20. *SC* 19 August 1932, 6 & 15; 23 September 1932, 6; 7 October 1932, 8.

'The Plantation'. Their aim was to provide 'a few invalid comforts' for the senior Sisters and to help towards the upkeep of the convent.[21]

One of the comforts made possible by such fundraising was the installation of a fireplace in 'Bethany', the wood-and-iron all-purpose building that Mary MacKillop authorised in 1881. At that time she wrote: 'It is very nice and will prove a great comfort'. In June 1931, the Kensington diarist noted: 'Fire installed in Bethany. A good spot for old and infirm Sisters and also warm for recreation.'[22] It was, in fact, a 'great comfort' to everyone in the community because, even as late as 1931, there was no heating in either the main convent building or the chapel.

Wherever they were, the Sisters enjoyed (or perhaps, endured) the same living conditions as the people among whom they lived and worked. In winter, the only warming in many of their convents came from the wood stove in the kitchen and, maybe, from a fire burning in a fireplace in their community room—and then only when they could afford, or were given, the wood for the fire.

That first Kensington carnival or fete was so successful that its organisers decided to make it an annual event. They constantly urged those who were interested to be generous because it was common knowledge that the Sisters were receiving much less in school fees than was the case in the 1920s. They also knew that there were seventy Sisters residing at Kensington and that, among these, were several young novices and a significant number of retired senior Sisters, the oldest of whom were in their eighties.

Archbishop Killian, who opened the 1935 fete, had transferred to Adelaide from Port Augusta as coadjutor to the ageing and increasingly frail Archbishop Spence in July 1933. Spence, who died in November 1934, was respected by Catholics and non-Catholics alike. People remembered him well for his 'urbanity, common sense, business acumen, tact, and scholarship', he was an outstanding speaker, and was consistent in his support of the Josephites and their works during his time in the diocese.[23]

---

21. SC 13 January 1931, 15.
22. Kensington Convent Diary, 19 June 1931.
23. Ruth Schumann, 'Spence, Robert William (1860–1934)', *ADB*, *(Canberra: Australian* National University, National Centre of Biography, 1990. http://adb.anu.edu.au/biography/spence-robert-william-8602/text15023

After Spence's death, Killian became Archbishop of Adelaide. A 'bush bishop' who cut his pastoral teeth at Bourke in far western New South Wales, Killian had driven hundreds of miles to visit every Catholic family in the outback areas of the Port Augusta diocese. Then, in 1934, this man who was possessed of 'a kind heart', brought his great energy and organising skills to Adelaide.[24]

He paid his first official visit to the Kensington convent in December 1933, while he was still co-adjutor to Spence. The Sisters in the community and students from local Josephite schools welcomed him warmly.[25] During his address from the stage at the northern end of The Plantation, he observed that it would not be out of place,

> seeing the beautiful grounds and [the] magnificent forest under which [they were] all gathered, to recall the foresight and the love of Nature of the great Archbishop, Dr O'Reily, who, with his own hands, had planted [the] trees, whose shade [they now enjoyed]. After all, it [was] a nice tribute to his memory to recall that fact [on that evening].[26]

Fundraising for the Sisters continued throughout the state. In the North the people of Tarcowie held a fete which raised £70. Socials at Yatina, Hornsdale and Pekina and a collection at Appila-Yarrowie raised the £60 guaranteed each year to the Sisters at Pekina.[27] During the first half of 1933, a strong committee of women from Peterborough and surrounding parishes conducted an extensive appeal to raise funds to support the Sisters and their works.

Such activities on the Sisters' behalf gives rise to the question: Why did the people work so hard for them when they, themselves, were also smarting from the effects of the Depression? The answer, it seems, must be that these people, like the members of previous generations of parents and friends, knew and loved the Sisters and genuinely appreciated what they were doing for their children and the wider community. They knew that often the Sisters ate sparingly

---

24. R.J Egar, 'Killian, Andrew (1872–1939)', *ADB* (Canberra: Australian National University, National Centre of Biography, 1983),http://adb.anu.edu.au/biography/killian-andrew- 6955/text12079.
25. *SC* 8 December 1933, 7.
26. *SC* 1 March 1935, 7.
27. *SC* 29 November 1935, 15.

in order to provide meals for the children, and collected second-hand clothes and shoes for those who had none. 'A Catholic Parent' wrote:

> [The Sisters'] work is being carried on against great odds and extreme disabilities . . . In normal years, the school fees represent a fairly stable income, but owing to the bad years, there has been such a drastic falling off here [in Adelaide and suburbs] that the situation is critical.[28]

This writer concluded by urging Catholics to 'do something big for the Sisters of St Joseph'—that was, in this instance, to support the upcoming annual fete at Kensington.[29]

Those enduring the effects of the Depression were scarcely aware that in March 1931 there were changes among the leadership of the Congregation. At the General Chapter of that year, Mother Cyril Elkis from New Zealand replaced seventy-eight-year-old Mother Laurence O'Brien, whose term as Superior General had expired. The Chapter Sisters chose former South Australian, Sister Casimir Meskill (who had been serving in that position since 1910) and Sisters Columbkille Browne, Madeleine Tier and Eulalia Connolly (all of New South Wales) to be members of the General Council. Casimir was both Councillor and Mistress of Novices from 1910 until 1926, when Mother Laurence relieved her of the latter task. She died in office in 1936, aged eighty-five years. At the conclusion of this Chapter, Mother Cyril reappointed Sister Claude Riddell as Provincial of South Australia for a second term of six years.[30]

The Chapter Sisters decided that, given the changes taking place in the various state education systems, Sisters in Josephite schools might teach students studying for examinations up to and including the Leaving Certificate. By so doing, they confirmed the practice of preparing students for this exam that had been current in South Australia since 1924. Another Chapter decision was that girls attending the Juniorate should be kept separate from other children and have their own special teachers.[31]

---

28. 'An Appeal for the Sisters of St Joseph by "A Catholic Parent"', SC 15 February 1935, 7.
29. 'An Appeal for the Sisters of St Joseph'.
30. Minutes of General Chapters, 1875–1931 (North Sydney: Sisters of St Joseph, 2007). Mother Cyril (1871–1956) was sixty years old at the time of her election.
31. *Minutes of General Chapters, 1875–1931* (North Sydney: Sisters of St Joseph,

Mother Laurence, the last of the founding Sisters who joined the Congregation between 1867 and 1871, returned to South Australia in the following August and remained there until her death on 24 August 1945, aged ninety-one years.[32] She was a Sister of St Joseph for seventy-six years, during thirty-five of which she was a teacher in South Australian schools. In addition, she had served in Queensland for six years, was a General Councillor in Sydney for eight, and was Mother General for twelve.

In the meantime, the Diocese of Port Augusta waited almost two years for Killian's successor, Norman Thomas Gilroy (1896–1977) to take up his appointment. The new bishop arrived in April 1935 but his stay was short, for he moved to Sydney as coadjutor to Archbishop Michael Kelly in August 1937. Because Gilroy spent so little time in the diocese, his stay was somewhat uneventful, although he did make a concerted effort to visit its most distant parts and meet its people. As far as the Josephites were concerned, he was not there long enough to make any significant changes beyond the blessing and opening of one new convent and school.[33]

As for the people of both dioceses, they continued to give their threepences and sixpences in support of the Sisters because they appreciated their work for anyone in difficult circumstances. Archbishop Spence helped to provide work for the men by putting money into new building projects. Thus, in July 1932 he blessed and laid foundation stones for two new school buildings. The first was at Woodville where, until that point in time, the existing building served as a church at weekends and did service as a school during the week.

The second, on the Bay Road (Anzac Highway) at Plympton in the Glenelg parish, was a new venture in an area only recently opened up for housing. This church-school building was dedicated to St John the Baptist. Two Sisters from Kensington arrived to take charge at the beginning of the 1935 school year with an initial enrolment of twenty-three children. In 1938 the districts of Plympton and

---

2007).
32. Mother Cyril to the Sisters, 7 August 1931.
33. John Luttrel, 'Bishop Gilroy and the Diocese of Port Augusta', *Australasian Catholic Record*, 80/2 (April 2003): 189–200.

Keswick combined to form a new parish.[34] In September of that year, Archbishop Killian did the honours at the laying of the foundation stone for a new church in Everard Street at Keswick.[35]

The end of 1935 saw the closure of the Josephite school in Pirie Street, Adelaide. Changes in the distribution of the population of the city had caused a significant reduction in enrolments, which fell from 150 in the 1890s to less forty in 1935.[36]

Another church-school that the Josephites accepted at this time was at St Monica's on Main Northeast Road, Walkerville, in the parish of Lower North Adelaide. Thirty-two children enrolled on opening day in January 1932 and numbers gradually increased until they reached 100 in 1941, the year when Walkerville became a separate parish. The Sisters on the staff travelled out there each day from Kensington in the Buick driven by Mr Ireland.

By this time he was making two trips out and back from Kensington each day: one to Russell Street in the city, Keswick and Plympton, the other to Beulah Road, Ellangowan and Walkerville. Either of these journeys could begin first, while Mr Ireland's second group of passengers awaited his return. In the afternoons he made another two trips to bring them all home again.[37]

During the 1930s, the Thebarton parish comprised all the suburbs from there to West Beach. The first parish priest of Thebarton, Father John Healy, who was there during the years 1883–1921, established a Temperance Society known as the Guild of St John the Baptist, and his successor, Father Frank Smyth, (who was parish priest from 1921–1955,) supported it.

Every member of the parish, including every young schoolchild, was pressed to become a member of this society. The priests encouraged members of the Guild to practice thrift and refrain from alcohol. Unsurprisingly, not all parishioners responded as the good Fathers desired! Even so, the Guild and the attitudes it advocated became influential and, as a consequence, it was a

---

34. *Official Directory of the Catholic Church in Australia* (1895, 1905, 1915, 1925, 1935).
35. *SC* 1 July, 7 & 8 July 1932, 6 (Woodville); 29 July, 7, 5 August 1932, 7; I February 1935, 4 (Plympton).
36. *SC* 9 September 1938, 7.
37. While he was in the Sisters' employ, they always referred to or about him in public as "Mr Ireland"

general belief that before World War II more members of the Thebarton parish owned their homes than did their counterparts in any other parish in the Adelaide metropolitan area.[38]

From the mid-1920s onwards, school enrolments at both the boys' and the girls' schools at Thebarton were in the region of 200.[39] Then, as the Catholic population increased in the newly subdivided Richmond end of the parish, the people of that area built a new church-school, and that despite the adversities of the Depression. It was on Brooker Terrace, Richmond, and was dedicated to St Aloysius Gonzaga. Monsignor Michael Hourigan performed the foundation stone ceremony on 10 December 1932.[40]

In the meantime, Father Smyth approached Josephite provincial, Sister Claude, for Sisters to staff his new school and she responded by appointing Sisters Januarius Glanville and Thomas Connery to Richmond. Several weeks later, and before a large crowd of parishioners, Archbishop Spence blessed and opened their new church-school which, he emphasised, was for the people of North Richmond. He strongly discouraged parents whose children were enrolled in other Catholic schools in the parish from moving them to this one.[41]

There was no convent at Richmond but these two Sisters had a fine home at 22 Cowandilla Road (Sir Donald Bradman Drive), Cowandilla, which was within walking distance of their workplace. This large property came to the Sisters of St Joseph by way of a legacy from John Byrne, a successful farmer from Warooka on Yorke Peninsula. He bought the place when he retired to Adelaide in 1911

---

38. *SC* 13 November 1908, 782–83.
39. The boys' school referred to here was the St John the Baptist School in George Street, Thebarton. Until 1942 it was managed by members of the Congregation of the Brothers of St John the Baptist, a small Religious Order of men founded by Father John Healy in 1895 to care for delinquent teenagers and also for homeless men, especially those recently released from gaol. They also had charge of the St John the Baptist Boys' Catholic Primary School at Thebarton. Its members left the boys' home in the early 1940s and transferred the school to the Marist Brothers in 1943. The Congregation ceased to exist during the 1950s. These Brothers did much good work in the Thebarton parish, especially at the school on George Street. Many of their former pupils held them in high regard.
40. *SC* 16 December 1932, 13.
41. *SC* 10 March 1933, 15.

and enjoyed it from then until his death on 29 December 1931, aged eighty-one years.[42]

One can imagine the Sisters' surprise when, in early 1932, they received a lawyer's letter notifying them of Byrne's bequest. He had left the Josephites his ten-roomed, two storey house, and the large block of land on which it stood, on one condition: that they run either a school or a charitable institution there.[43] This bequest could not have come at a better time as it enabled the Sisters to move the Juniorate girls from Kingswood, where they attended the parish school and mixed with the day students, to a place where they lived and worked apart from other children, as recommended by the General Chapter of 1931.[44]

When Sisters Januarius and Thomas moved into Byrne's former home they undertook the role of caretakers of the property while carrying out their duties at the Richmond School. One of their responsibilities was to lock the gate at the main Cowandilla Road entrance each day, a task which they fulfilled faithfully even though the block lacked a back fence.[45] These Sisters continued in their caretaker role until the place was ready for the Juniorate girls from Kingswood.

Turning the house into a boarding school to accommodate up to twenty-five young girls and a community of Sisters required major alterations. Nevertheless, all was in order in time for the beginning of the 1934 school year. One well-wisher wrote:

> Quite by accident I had the pleasure of inspecting the Mount St Joseph's Juniorate at 22 Cowandilla Road, Cowandilla, which is nearing completion. In conversation with the Mother Provincial, I was amazed at the courage and vigour of the Sisters of St Joseph, who, relying solely on the Providence of God and the support of their friends, have ventured out in

---

42. Re Mr Byrne's home, the West Torrens Historical Society notes: This stately home was built in 1883 by a Mr Klaur who, it is said, used to invite his friends to play German 'Oompah' music on the balcony on the roof. At the time of writing (2014), Byrne's property is used by Mary MacKillop Care Flora McDonald Lodge home for the elderly.
43. *SC* 12 February 1932, 7.
44. *SC* 16 March 1934, 7.
45. This story is one of the legends handed down by word of mouth by those who were close to the two Sisters concerned.

these perilous times to extend their activities. But the call is an urgent one.[46]

The opening of the new Juniorate attracted quite a deal of attention among the Catholic community and a quiet excitement continued to build until its official blessing and opening on Pentecost Sunday, 20 May 1934.[47] Eighteen girls enrolled that year and it soon became evident that the house could not accommodate both living and teaching spaces. Therefore, the Sisters commissioned the construction of a school building adjacent to the house. This building comprised a large study hall, a smaller classroom and an entrance porch, and there was a verandah on its northern end. It was ready for use in 1936 when there were twenty-four boarders in residence.[48]

By that time, Sisters and students were basking in the reflected glory generated by the fact that one of the senior girls, Mary Philomena Rodeghiero, had gained the Tennyson Medal for English at the 1935 Leaving exams.[49] Much credit was due to her teacher, Sister Monica Connolly, formerly of Western Australia, whose ability to coach her students in English studies was remarkable. By 1940, two more Juniorate girls, Mary Bernadette Dundon and Teresa Donnellan, had each gained a Tennyson medal.[50] Monica taught English, Latin, French, and History at all levels while Sister Stanislaus Doheny, likewise from Western Australia, was, as exam results indicate, a successful Mathematics and Commercial teacher.

---

46. *SC* 6 October 1933, 15.
47. *SC* 16 March 1934, 7; 20 April 1934, 7; 4 May 1934, 7.
48. *SC* 9 February 1936, 6.
49. *SC* January 1936, 14. *Port Lincoln Times*, 17 January 1936, 6. In 1900 Lord Hallam Tennyson, Governor of South Australia (1899–1902) & son of the poet Alfred Lord Tennyson presented £100 to the University of Adelaide to provide medals as awards for English Literature at the public examinations. The gift provided for the award of a gold medal for Leaving Honours standard and silver medals for Leaving and Intermediate standard examinations. These awards have continued into the twenty-first century when, each year, the University awards a Tennyson Medal to the most successful candidate for English Studies at Matriculation level.
50. Mary Dundon joined the Josephites in 1941 and took the name of 'Sister Jude. For many years, she was a highly respected secondary schoolteacher. She died on 20 July 2012 aged 90 years. Neither Mary Rodeghiero nor Teresa Donnellan became Josephites after they left school.

Sisters Monica and Stanislaus continued their work at the Juniorate until the late 1940s. Then, in 1948 incumbent superior general of the Congregation, Mother Leone Ryan, who was visiting Adelaide at the time, was so impressed with their skill that she invited them to transfer to Sydney to continue their work of teaching in that city.

In spite of the Depression, which was showing some small signs of lifting by the middle of the decade, Catholics did manage a few building projects in different parts of the state. In some instances, parish priests borrowed money from the archdiocese to provide work for unemployed parishioners. Thus, in June 1934, the vicar general, Monsignor Hourigan, who was invited to open a new kindergarten beside the existing Keswick School, commented that:

> When the project of the new building was first discussed, the Catholic people of Keswick took it up with characteristic enthusiasm. It was found that the undertaking would cost something like £500 but the large sum and the bad times did not dampen the ardour of the people.[51]

The parish of Murray Bridge was in the limelight when, in August 1934, Archbishop Killian visited, ready for a busy day. He began at 8 a.m. with a Mass and Confirmation at Tailem Bend, some twenty kilometres away. Then, at 2 pm he was back in Murray Bridge for the Confirmation of seventy-five children and adults in their church. At this ceremony he complimented the young people on their general knowledge of Christian doctrine, saying that much of it was due to the Sisters of St Joseph, who had been there for almost ten years:

> The sight of so many children well versed in the truths of the Faith and so well conducted argued much for the splendid education they had received from the Sisters.

Finally, at 3.30 pm, he participated in the opening ceremony for a new school building adjacent to the convent. It cost £1,124, and more than half its cost was already paid off, thanks to the small donations of the local people and an anonymous gift of £500.[52]

---

51. *SC* 1 June 1934, 12.
52. *SC* 31 August 1934, 4.

In spite of the Depression, this was the era the Sisters were being introduced gradually to two new marvels of modern technology: the wireless (radio) and moving pictures (films/movies). On 29 October 1930, the wireless was 'put on' at Kensington so that the Sisters could hear a concert of Irish music. In June 1935, five Sisters from Kensington went to the Largs Bay Orphanage to view the film *Ben Hur*.[53] Presumably, it was considered to be suitable for Sisters because of its (fictional) biblical association. At about the same time, old scholars and other friends gathered at Kensington to celebrate Sister Claude's feast day. On behalf of those present, their president, Mrs E. M. Gurry, presented Sister and her community with a wireless set.[54]

By the mid-1930s, the motor car was a fixture at Kensington. Besides transporting Sisters to and from their schools, it often ferried them to particular events. Thus, in December 1935, most members of the community attended a function in the Australia Hall in the city. Sadly, according to the Kensington community diarist, 'on one trip there [the] car was collided with'.[55] The writer did not record any details regarding damage or injuries, which suggests that they were minimal. One thing is certain, however: the driver was not one of the Sisters! At the time even those few who were able to drive before they joined the Congregation were not permitted to hold current drivers' licences. It was to be another twenty years before that could happen!

During 1936, South Australians celebrated the centenary of white settlement in their state. When the SA State Government invited the archbishop to organise a religious event as the Catholic contribution to the festivities, he put on the first-ever 'All Australian Catholic Education Congress', which took place in Adelaide from 8–15 November 1936. He announced the Congress in December 1935, involved as many people as possible in its organisation and planning and, by way of the *Southern Cross* newspaper, kept everyone up-to-date with plans and developments.

Early in centenary year, he invited representatives from locally based religious orders and their old scholars' associations to a

---

53. Kensington Convent Diary, 29 October 1930, 8 June 1935.
54. *SC* 14 June 1935, 13.
55. Kensington Convent Diary, 12 December 1935.

meeting that was organising fundraising functions 'to help defray the heavy expenses of the Congress'.[56] What followed was a busy time of celebrations and preparations for the big event. Of particular interest to the Sisters were the thousand-voice choir comprising children from local Catholic schools, a children's Mass, a special Mass for members of religious congregations, and a great procession of all Catholics on its closing day, Sunday, 15 November.

As the Congress drew near, bishops and priests from many parts of Australia and New Zealand, as well as from overseas, descended upon Adelaide. These men regarded the Congress as a demonstration of Catholic solidarity that gave the locals, who comprised less than 12 per cent of the population of South Australia, a sense of pride in their shared faith.[57] The route of the Sunday procession was through the city from Victoria Square to the University Oval (approximately two kilometres away) and involved hundreds of Children of Mary, members of the Holy Name Society, and boys and men from every parish in South Australia.[58] On the sidelines, an estimated crowd of some 60,000 onlookers, including many women and children, were there to see this demonstration of Catholic faith.[59] It was a wet day but neither the marchers nor the spectators seemed to mind being out in the rain.

At the time it was considered inappropriate for the Josephites or, indeed, for the members of any women's Religious Congregations to take their places in public events such as processions. During the course of Congress Week a number of the more senior members of these congregations took part in a conference of sisters of teaching orders in St Cecilia's Hall, Wakefield Street. Sisters were also present

---

56. *SC* 14 February 1936, 11.
57. 1933 census data from *SAPP,* 1934.
58. The confraternity of the Children of Mary was a religious body which aimed at fostering in its members an ardent devotion and love towards the Blessed Virgin Mary. Its membership comprised young single women and girls and its aim was to assist its members to be good Catholics. The Holy Name Society, founded in Adelaide in 1921, was a sodality of Catholic men who promised to honour the Name of God at all times and to become involved in good works in their local areas. Both societies thrived in Australia during the first half of the twentieth century.
59. Attendances on these occasions were often exaggerated but the press estimated some 60,000 in all. It was said to have been the biggest religious turnout in Adelaide until the Billy Graham Crusade of 1959.

with those of their students who were among the 5,000 children taking part in the children's Mass at the Wayville Showground. As already mentioned, some Sisters were involved with the training of the children for the thousand-voice choir but, according to prevailing custom, they were well out of sight behind the stage when the children performed.

Even as South Australia celebrated, civil war broke out in Spain, and Europe was moving inexorably towards World War II. There were Australians fighting on both sides in the Spanish conflict, which raged from 1936 until 1939. The fear of communism was palpable in this country and especially so among Catholics. Many of them supported the views of the right-wing conservative Spanish leader, General Francisco Franco (1892–1970) who was seen as a strong opponent of Communism. This conflict ended in early 1939, and several months later (on 3 September) Britain declared war on Germany and World War II began. For most people, however, Europe was very far away from South Australia and so, for the time being at least, life went on much as usual.

To return to the year 1936, it was an important one for the Josephites for reasons other than the Education Congress or the centenary of white settlement. Of particular significance to them was their return to Penola, the cradle of the Congregation, after an absence of fifty-six years. The local people were delighted to have the Sisters back. They had never forgotten Father Woods and what he did for them while in the district or that it was in their town that he and Mary MacKillop founded the Congregation all those years ago,

When Sisters David Dowd, Angela Gapper and Richard (Patricia) White arrived there in January 1936, several parishioners welcomed them and took them to their new home near the church. Four weeks later Archbishop Killian blessed their convent and laid the foundation stone of their school.[60] These buildings were adjacent to the church and schoolhouse that Father Woods erected during his time in the district. About fifty children arrived on opening day and numbers remained steady for the next decade. The Sisters taught the children

---

60. SC 31 January 1936, 11; 28 February 1936, 14 & 17. The school was renamed 'Mary MacKillop Memorial School' in 1986.

in the church during 1936 and moved into their new up-to-date school at the beginning of the following year.[61]

During 1936 the Sisters also made a new foundation in Berri on the River Murray, another outpost of the Port Augusta diocese. In late January, Bishop Gilroy officially welcomed the Sisters to this town.[62] He met with the Sisters who were posted there: Joan Redden (the music teacher), Irene Roche (who taught the junior grades), Regis (Gwen) Ballinger (who was in charge of grades four to six), and Teresita Cormack (who was responsible for the QC. class and any post-primary students who enrolled). As was the case in many other parishes of this era, the local church doubled as a school, a situation that persisted until the erection of a new school building sixteen years later.[63]

The fireplace in Bethany was not the only improvement made at Kensington during this period. Back in 1928, the chapel underwent a major change, thanks to the generosity of Sister Flavia Sheedy's family, who donated an elaborate marble altar to replace the wooden one that had been there since 1876. Then, seven years later, thanks to a substantial gift from Sister Ligouri Sinn's parents, the Sisters had the whole sanctuary refurbished. New marble altar rails gave it a fine finish and in February 1936, Bishop Thomas Fox of Broken Hill consecrated the altar.

During 1938, the Sisters replaced the dark wooden church-style pews in the chapel with new seating and painted and upgraded its exterior.[64] (Two of those old pews graced the back verandah of the Kensington convent until after the year 2000.) They cut back the upstairs dormitory, which used to cover at least two-thirds of the body of the chapel, leaving only a section large enough for a choir gallery; closed off a connection between the dormitory and the main convent building; changed the square-top windows at second floor level and the tops of the lower windows from a square to a curved design; built a new front porch which became the main

---

61. *SC* 19 March 1937, 4.
62. *SC* 7 February 1936, 15.
63. Michael Johnson, editor, *Our Lady of the River Catholic Church, Berri* (Berri, 2013), 36.
64. *SC* 26 February 1936, 4. Three of Bishop Fox's aunts were Josephites, namely Sisters Cecilia, Mida and Josephine McMahon,

entrance and closed off the doorway at the foot of the choir stairs and created a new entrance into the choir gallery.

While these changes were in progress, the Sisters chose their delegates for the Congregation's twelfth General Chapter, which took place in Sydney in March 1937. In her report to the Chapter on the state of the South Australian province, Sister Claude informed the delegates that, at the time of her speaking, there were 242 professed Sisters, four novices and ten postulants living in thirty-six communities: twelve in the Port Augusta Diocese, and twenty-four in the Archdiocese of Adelaide. All told, the Sisters were teaching 504 music pupils and 3,395 children in forty-four schools. They were caring for the thirty-nine young girl boarders who were spread among various convents across the state and were managing three charitable institutions and the Reformatory at Parkside.

The Sisters re-elected Mother Cyril as Mother General for a second term and she, in turn, appointed Sister de Lellis McDonald (1874-1950) as provincial of South Australia. The Chapter Sisters made only a few major decisions at this Chapter but, rather, did what they could to ensure that the Congregation would carry on into the future in the spirit of Mary MacKillop. (This became more difficult after the promulgation in 1917 of the Revised Code of Canon (Church) Law with its emphases on the letter rather than the spirit of the law.)[65]

At more practical level, the Chapter Sisters decided that in hot weather the Sisters might wear habits made from a lighter material than the kind they were using at the time, and that they could replace their white starched guimps with ones which resembled them exactly but were made from a white celluloid material that cleaned easily and did not require starching or ironing.[66] This Chapter appears to have been one of maintenance, held at a time when all were suffering from the effects of long years of poverty and hardship, endured among the people they served.

---

65. For further details re the Code of Canon Law see:
http://www.attorneygeneral.jus.gov.on.ca/inquiries/cornwall/en/hearings/exhibits/Frank_Morrisey/pdf/26_1917_Canon.pdf
66. Minutes of the General Chapter of 1937. A guimp was a wide, stiffly starched cloth or bib covering the neck and shoulders, and worn as part of the habit by certain Orders of nuns. http://www.thefreedictionary.com/guimp

While the Chapter was in session, the Mount Carmel Girls' School community at Alberton (Rosewater-Pennington) celebrated the opening of a large school, built to accommodate up to 400 students.[67] It comprised five classrooms, two cloak rooms, a domestic science room (appropriately furnished), commercial classrooms, and a music room and was a great improvement on the church- school where the Sisters had taught since their return to Alberton in 1909.[68] At opening time there were 220 children on the roll and numbers remained steady until the arrival of large numbers of children from the Pennington Migrant Hostel in the early 1950s.

Until the end of 1941, the Sisters staffing this school lived at Port Adelaide and travelled to and from the school by train each day. The Carmelite Fathers, who had charge of the parish, noted the hardship that this daily travel entailed and arranged for the erection of a large convent on Russell Street, Rosewater, on a site next door to the school. This building was large enough to house the fourteen Sisters then teaching in the Alberton and Woodville parish schools. As school enrolments increased, however, so did the size of the community. By the end of the decade, seventeen Sisters were residing there and conditions were less than ideal.[69]

The year 1939 began with one of the worst bushfire seasons experienced in southern Australia since white settlement. At Macclesfield in the Adelaide Hills, the Sisters residing there provided the firefighters with food and drink. Then, according to the *Southern Cross*, while the men were enjoying their refreshments,

> the fire contacted with the convent property and the Sisters with their guests succeeded in putting it out, but not before the woodshed had been completely destroyed.[70]

The fire rekindled during succeeding days and did enormous damage throughout the Adelaide Hills and beyond. Fortunately for

---

67. During the period under review, the suburbs of Rosewater and Pennington were part of Alberton.
68. *SC* 26 November 1937, 9.
69. Sisters from schools in other parishes had all moved out by 1954, leaving only the Alberton/Rosewater staff in residence.
70. *SC* 13 January 1939.

the Catholic community of Macclesfield, however, their convent remained intact and its occupants safe.

For most other Josephites, that year began quietly as they carried on with their teaching and charitable works. In some places the opening of the school year was delayed because of a diphtheria epidemic. Once that subsided, however, it was work as usual.

Six months after the fires, South Australia's Catholics were shocked to learn that Archbishop Killian had died suddenly in Melbourne. His successor, Australian born Matthew Beovich of Melbourne, was consecrated a bishop in Adelaide in April 1940. Before coming to South Australia, he was Director of Catholic Education in the Archdiocese of Melbourne and was heavily involved in the planning for and running of the Catholic Education Congress of 1936.

Beovich came from a state where several institutions provided teacher training for both Religious and lay teachers in Catholic schools and was dismayed to find that there was no Catholic Teachers' College in Adelaide. Almost immediately, therefore, he took steps to ensure that all religious sisters engaged in teaching should have access to appropriate teacher training. To achieve this end he set up a Diocesan Registration Board, which met for the first time at St Mary's Training College, Cabra, on 4 December 1940.[71]

The Dominican Sisters and the Sisters of Mercy already had small internal training schools attached to their novitiates at Cabra and Angas Street respectively. On the other hand, the Loreto Sisters and all religious brothers based in Adelaide sent any new members of their Congregations to train in New South Wales or Victoria.[72] The South Australian Josephites were faced with a dilemma and turned to their Mother General for assistance in resolving it. After due deliberation, she and her Council decided to close the Adelaide novitiate and have all prospective Josephites undertake both their novitiate and their teacher training in Sydney. It was a sad day for the Kensington Sisters when they learnt that, after sixty-nine years of operation, their novitiate was about to close.

---

71. 'Cabra' was the name chosen by the Dominican Sisters for their convent and school on Cross Road, Cumberland Park. They came to Adelaide from Cabra in Dublin in 1868.
72. *SC* 6 December 1940, 7, 'Diocesan Registration of Teachers'.

Most of those already teaching in South Australia had done on-the-job training and, while some saw the possible benefits of sending the young Sisters to Sydney, others could not understand why such a major change was necessary. All felt that they were well trained in the spirit of Mary MacKillop in their Adelaide novitiate. Some could not forget Mary's seeming abandonment of them in 1883 or their feeling of loss when the Mother House moved to Sydney, and South Australia became another province alongside New Zealand and the rest of the provinces.

For them, this was another serious loss, the pain of which was not alleviated by the knowledge that Mary MacKillop herself established the Congregation's training school in Sydney during her final years. Their sorrow was lessened somewhat when they discovered that their much-loved mistress of novices, Sister Andrina Clark, was to stay on in South Australia as sister-in-charge of the postulants, and most of them either knew or knew of the highly respected Sister Kevin Hughes, who, as already noted, went from Adelaide to Sydney as mistress of novices in 1926.[73]

The last religious profession ceremony held in the Kensington chapel took place on 9 January 1941. The Sisters who made their vows on that day were Stephen (Dorothy) McMahon, Joseph (Nancy) Ifould, John Bosco (Margaret) Donnelly, and Celine (Mary) Gallagher.[74] For the young postulants of 1940, a trip to Sydney just before Christmas, in spite of the wartime restrictions then in place, was something that most of them neither dreamed of nor expected at the time of their entry into the Congregation twelve months earlier. The first South Australians to go to the Sydney novitiate were Sisters Luigi (Joan) Bunfield, Fabian (Monica) Coonan, Leo (Belle) Connolly, and Bernard (Elizabeth) Brown.

By the time these trainee Sisters were preparing for their move to the Sydney novitiate, the whole world was at war. Australian troops were fighting the Germans in the North African campaign of 1940–1941. Hitler and his armies appeared set to take control

---

73. Mother Laurence to the Sisters, 5 February 1926, announced that she had appointed Sister Andrina to this role in place of Sister Dolores Duffy, who had held it throughout the early 1920s.
74. SC 17 January 1941, p. 4. Sister Celine left the Congregation prior to her final profession.

of Europe when, to the horror of all Australians in particular, in December 1941 word came that the Japanese had bombed the United States naval base at Pearl Harbour in Hawaii. War now raged in both Europe and the Pacific, and Australia itself was vulnerable. Numerous young men and women volunteered for armed service and most went overseas to fight in either Europe or the Pacific. In towns and cities around the Australian coastline streetlights were extinguished, while tracer spotlights scanned the night sky.

Even though South Australia was the farthest state from the war fronts, all schools were instructed to dig slit trenches to shelter the children in case of an air raid. During 1942 the government introduced daylight saving, and supplied everyone with a ration book so that all could have equal access to supplies of tea, sugar, butter, meat and clothing. It also had the machinery in many factories redesigned to enable the production of ammunition for the fighting forces and made it clear to primary producers that their contribution to the war effort was to produce as much food as possible. For many Sisters and their families, this was a time a great sadness and anxiety, as they worried over loved ones who were away on the war fronts, or grieved for those who lost their lives or were imprisoned in Japanese prisoner of war camps.

Even as the Josephites encouraged the schoolchildren to contribute towards the war effort, change was afoot at the Largs Bay Orphanage. Since its inception in 1906, the Sisters had cared for boys and girls from three years old to school leaving age.[75] But not any longer! Soon after his consecration, Archbishop Beovich rationalised the management of the children's homes and orphanages in the diocese.

There were fewer than ten delinquent boys in the St John the Baptist Boys' Reformatory at Brooklyn Park, and so he asked the Brothers of St John the Baptist to change their focus. He had them return these boys to state care and take charge of the older boys from the Largs Bay and Goodwood orphanages, both of which cared for boys and girls.[76] Consequently, in January 1941, some

---

75. Unless their mothers took them when they left the Fullarton Refuge, the Sisters cared for any children born there until they were three years of age, after which they moved on to the Largs Bay Orphanage.
76. The St Vincent de Paul's Orphanage, Goodwood, run by the Sisters of Mercy since 1890.

fifteen boys aged twelve or over moved from Largs Bay to Brooklyn Park, all the girls from Largs Bay went to Goodwood and all primary school-aged boys from Goodwood transferred to Largs Bay. Despite these changes, the number of children at Largs Bay remained more or less constant, as did the number of Sisters ministering there.

The Sisters' involvement in the running of Summer Schools for the Religious Instruction of Children from Isolated Areas where there was no easy access to Catholic schooling had been increasing since their inception in 1931. Each year a number of Sisters devoted at least two weeks of the annual Christmas holiday break to this work. Initially, such schools were held at Peterborough and Port Lincoln where the girls were accommodated in the convent boarding schools and the boys were billeted out with local families. Before long priests in other outback parishes asked for similar schools. The first of these was at Streaky Bay on the Far West Coast of South Australia where a school took place in January 1940. Four Sisters from Kensington instructed the seventy-four children who came in that year. According to the *Southern Cross:*

> All arrangements for the school [were] planned and efficiently carried out in detail by the parish priest, Father Cullinan, and the Catholics of Streaky Bay and district. Cooking, caring for the children and waiting on them [was] attended to by a very zealous and efficient band of women and girls, who spare[d] no pains to make all happy and interested.[77]

On this occasion, the thirty-six boys in attendance were housed at the presbytery, while Father Cullinan found accommodation elsewhere. The thirty-eight girls were billeted in Miss Feltus' 'spacious house', which she leased to the Church for the duration. The State Education Department gave the Catholics the use of the state school buildings for their religious instruction lessons. The Sisters managed the classes and prepared the children for the reception of the different Sacraments, according to their ages. At its end, families rejoiced as nineteen of their youngsters received their First Holy Communion. In the following year the Sisters conducted a similar school at Minnipa on Central Eyre Peninsula.[78]

---

77. *SC* 19 January 1940, 11.
78. *SC* 9 May 1941, 11.

In that same year, four Sisters left Adelaide to make a new foundation at Tailem Bend, a road and railway junction on the eastern bank of the Murray River, 100 kilometres southeast of Adelaide and twenty from Murray Bridge. Their new home, which was flush with the street, was once a butcher's shop and dwelling! The glass shopfront had been removed and the shop area was now the music room. The school, which was also a building that had seen better days, was about 100 metres along the street, past the pretty little St Columba's Church. The local people, mostly railway workers with a sprinkling of dairy farmers from across the river, were generous in their continuing support of both convent and school.[79]

In the May of 1941 the Catholics of Clare celebrated the blessing and opening of major additions to their school. Sisters had been teaching in this district since January 1869, when they lived in a few rooms at the back of the church and, as in so many places elsewhere, taught the children in the church. Now, when Sister Benedetta Murphy was the sister-in-charge, they could enjoy up-to-date facilities in a place which Archbishop Beovich described as 'a centre of culture and learning'.[80]

At about the same time, extensions were added to the Kingswood School and the Jesuits at Norwood set about moving St Joseph's School from Bridge Street, Kensington to a more central location. To this end they purchased a house and land between St Ignatius Church and the main road (Portrush Road). Work on a new school building began in early 1941, but progress was slow because of the war. They called it St Joseph's Memorial School to remind its users of the long history of the Jesuits and, in particular, that it was 400 years since Pope Paul III gave his approval to the Society of Jesus. They also wished to honour the memory of the Jesuit priests and brothers who had ministered in the Norwood parish since its establishment in 1869.[81]

Parishioners were proud that theirs was 'a real school with separate rooms' and, as such, was very different from the Bridge Street premises and most of the schools in neighbouring parishes. One of its special features was a kindergarten room set up for pre-

---

79. *SC* 21 February 1941, 13.
80. *SC* 30 May 1941, 7.
81. *SC* 30 January 1942.

school children. (This was necessary in this time of war, when many mothers were at work helping with the war effort.) The school had a tiled roof—something very new in 1941! Each room was painted a different colour and there were special niches in its walls for statues of saints.

The Sisters and children moved in at the beginning of the 1942 school year and over the next twelve months, volunteers levelled the playground, installed a basketball court, and built a shelter shed. In order to protect the children from the winter rain if it so happened that an air raid occurred at such times, they placed a roof over the mandatory slit trench that was meant to protect them from harm at such times.[82]

Under the leadership of Sister David Dowd, the school enrolled students from Kindergarten to Intermediate (Year Ten). Most of the senior pupils studied commercial subjects with a view to future employment as typists and/or stenographers. Two years later, all post-primary students and their teachers moved to the former Marist Brothers' school on Queen Street, Norwood, and diagonally across an oval from the Memorial School. The Sisters made this move because, at the end of the previous year and after forty years in the Norwood parish, the Marist Brothers vacated their school, which was on the site once occupied by St Joseph's Refuge.[83]

Archbishop Beovich, who was not one to let opportunities pass, saw the Brothers' move as providing a way of bringing together all the secondary students from surrounding Josephite schools. Therefore, he arranged for the refurbishment of the Queen Street premises, which were ready for opening in February 1944 as St Joseph's Higher Primary School. With Sister David as its founding principal, the school's initial enrolment was eighty-three girls, most of whom came from the Josephite schools at Keswick, Plympton, Hectorville, Beulah Road, Ellangowan, Tranmere and Russell Street.

During the 1930s and 1940s the Old Scholars' movement went from strength to strength. A large central group met regularly at the

---

82. Hilary Raimondo, 'The Opening of the New Memorial School' (unpublished Ms 1992).
83. The Marist Brothers left Norwood to take charge of the St John the Baptist Boys' School at Thebarton which had only recently been vacated by the Brothers of St John the Baptist.

Kensington convent while smaller groups of former students were attached to particular suburban or country schools. In October 1940, all came together to hold their inaugural annual Communion Breakfast at the Kensington convent. The following year, 300 former students packed St Joseph's Chapel and then enjoyed the Sisters' hospitality in their refectory, which was suitably decorated for the occasion. Among those present was an elderly woman who was a pupil at the St Francis Xavier's Hall School in 1867 when Mary MacKillop was the class teacher.[84]

In 1943 Archbishop Beovich celebrated Mass for the 400 Old Scholars who packed the Kensington Chapel. Mass over, 'in a flower decked marquee, a very dainty and appetising breakfast was served by the Sisters'. On this occasion the Josephite Mother General, Mother Cyril Elkis and Sister Thecla Morrissey from Victoria were present and moved easily among the visitors.[85] By the following year, the number attending the Communion Breakfast was so large that the chapel could not accommodate them and they held their celebrations in St Ignatius' Church, Norwood.[86]

It seems that Mother Cyril was in Adelaide to install Sister Thecla as provincial in place of Sister De Lellis McDonald who had served in that role for the previous six years. Sister De Lellis, who was ill for most of her time in South Australia, returned to Victoria soon after this event.

Beovich was instrumental in establishing the St Francis Xavier Minor Seminary at Stradbroke Park in the eastern suburbs of Adelaide in 1942. Initially, diocesan priests staffed this institution, where young men and boys began their training for the Catholic priesthood. The Archbishop knew that young men needed plenty of good food and that such an institution could not function without capable housekeepers and cooks. Therefore, he asked Sister De Lellis if she could provide Sisters for this work. The outcome was that Sisters Maria John Lummer, Fabian (Monica) Coonan and Mildred Joseph Nejaim undertook the ministry of housekeeping and providing the students and staff with nourishing meals. Even

---

84. *SC* 19 October 1941, 11.
85. *SC* 8 October 1943, 7.
86. *SC* 20 October 1944, 7. Accounts of these Communion Breakfasts appeared annually for the next several years.

though these Sisters went there gladly (conscious of Mary MacKillop's great respect for the priesthood), they were, in fact, little more than domestic servants in this large establishment.

At the end of 1944 the Sisters withdrew from Pekina where they had served since 1878. For many years there were more than seventy children enrolled at the school. With the passage of time, however, droughts and bad seasons forced so many young people and families to move away, that by the 1940s only ten children were attending the school. It was with great sadness, therefore, that Sister Agneta Case and her two companions packed up and left this little township for the last time.[87]

As the war ground on and families grieved the loss of loved ones, who had died in combat or in prisoner of war camps, children in Josephite schools emulated their predecessors of the 1914–1918 war by donating small sums of money towards the patriotic effort.[88] People were greatly relieved when, on 4 May 1945, hostilities in Europe came to an end. They rejoiced even more when, on 15 August, Japan surrendered and peace was declared in the Pacific, but only after two atomic bombs fell on the Japanese cities of Nagasaki and Hiroshima, inflicting horrific injuries and damage.

When news of the war's end reached Adelaide there was much noisy celebration. It was fortuitous that on this day the Catholic Church celebrated the feast of Our Lady's Assumption into heaven and children attending Catholic schools enjoyed a holiday. It was impossible for the girls boarding at St Joseph's Juniorate at Cowandilla to go home for the day, and so their teachers decided to take them to Waterfall Gully for a picnic. They set out by tram, loaded with picnic baskets and other necessities, eager to make the most of their break from study. To reach their destination they had to change trams in the city. Quite unaware that the war was over, they were caught up in the celebrations. Like everyone else, they were delighted at the news and made the best of their enforced involvement in the excitement as they made their way to the Waterfall Gully tram stop.[89]

---

87. Entries for the Diocese of Port Augusta, Australasian Catholic Directory (1942, 1943, 1944, 1945).
88. *SC* 3 November 1945, 9.
89. The author was one of the girls who picnicked on that memorable day.

Wartime restrictions on travel prevented the Josephites from holding their scheduled General Chapter in March 1943.[90] They met, instead, in March 1945, when Mother Josephine Cahill became the Congregation's sixth Mother General. South Australian provincial, Sister Thecla Morrissey, reported to the Chapter that, in her province there had been small increases in the number of Sisters, convents and schools in the past eight years. In fact, there were now 252 Sisters living in thirty-eight convents, managing forty-seven schools with 3,572 pupils. There was also the Juniorate, while the Sisters still managed their three charitable institutions, and three of them were keeping house for the priests and students at the seminary.[91]

Just twelve months later, on 23 March 1946, fifty-eight-year-old Mother Josephine died from a long illness contracted soon after her election. Her passing meant that the Sisters had to call another Chapter to elect her successor. When, on 19 March 1947, they gathered for their fourteenth General Chapter, they elected Mother Leone Ryan of Sydney as the Congregation's seventh Superior General. On this occasion the delegates decided that trainee Sisters should spend two years in the novitiate instead of one as had previously been the case. The young women who joined the Congregation in 1946 were the first to benefit from this extended time in training.[92]

Sister Michael Xavier Denham, who replaced Sister Thecla as Provincial of South Australia, took up her duties in March 1947. When she arrived she found a state that was on the cusp of change as it prepared for the arrival of child migrants from Britain and displaced persons from Europe. Before long she had learnt about the South Australian summer schools, and in particular, that over the previous summer holidays the Sisters had added Renmark to their list; that this was the first ever summer school held in the Upper Murray region of SA, and that among the children present were twenty-six from the newly-formed parish of Waikerie.[93]

---

90. Mother Cyril to the Sisters, 28 October 1942, wrote that the Apostolic Delegate had 'decreed' that the Sisters were to postpone their Chapter until hostilities had quietened down.
91. Minutes of the 13th General Chapter of the Sisters of St Joseph, 19–23 March 1945.
92. Minutes of 14th General Chapter, 19–22 March 1947.
93. *SC* 21 February 1947.

During her first year in Adelaide, Sister Michael Xavier oversaw the upgrading of the Sisters' living quarters at Kensington. She also organised for the vacant spaces under the staircases at the front of the main building to be converted into music rooms, and had two small sets of steps installed on the front verandah so that music pupils could access these rooms easily. Two years later, she authorised the erection of a new infirmary building close to the existing convent infirmary. The Sisters named it 'Tenison' and it comprised eight single bedrooms and a sunroom. The frail elderly Sisters residing there considered that they were living in luxury as few, if any of them, had ever slept in a private room before this.

At about the same time, Sister Michael Xavier authorised the replacement of 'Bethany', the all-purpose room built by Mary MacKillop in 1881, with a larger recreation and lunchroom, to which were attached a storeroom and a workmen's lunchroom. A gas heater superseded the fireplace of the older 'Bethany', while ceiling fans provided cooling in the summer.[94]

By this time, the war was over and people were settling down again. The two preceding decades had been a time when they dealt with a severe financial Depression and a war that was more destructive than any that had raged before. Small wonder that, overall, it was an era of maintenance rather than of active growth. Josephite numbers had increased minimally, thanks to a steady flow of young women into their ranks and the longevity of the senior Sisters. The Juniorate was flourishing but not everyone was happy that the novitiate had moved to Sydney.

During this time, Sisters withdrew from the Pirie Street School and the Pekina convent and school, returned to Penola after an absence of almost fifty years, opened schools at Walkerville, Richmond and Plympton, and made new foundations at Berri and Tailem Bend. Besides this, they had charge of the domestic arrangements at the seminary and had handed over the care of the delinquent girls from Genazzano to the Good Shepherd Sisters. The Largs Bay Orphanage was now home to young boys aged between three and twelve years.

The 1930s and 1940s were decades when the Sisters strove to hold on to the spirit of Mary MacKillop in a world that was very different from the one which she inhabited. Mary's understanding

---

94. Provincial's Report, General Chapter, North Sydney, 1953.

of Josephite Religious Life had developed as she exercised her ministry in the schools and charitable institutions of her time and, in particular, as she lived in community with the Sisters. By virtue of the fact that she was co-founder of the Congregation she exercised leadership for most of her life. Many of the women who joined her were called to leadership at different times during their lives.

Mary looked upon the governance of the Congregation as service to the community, despite the fact that the Roman Constitutions of 1874 contained the terms 'superior' (higher, over, above) and 'subject' (subordinate) when describing the roles of community leaders and community members. 'Superiors' were directed to ensure the exact observance of the Constitutions and to 'correct defects' among their 'subjects'. Only 'superiors' could have 'a press or anything similar with lock and key' and could 'examine all that [was] left to each Sister for her use, and take away what [they] consider[ed] superfluous'.[95]

By way of contrast, Julian Woods' 'Rules of the Institute of St Joseph' of 1867, specified that the leader of the community was to be known as the 'Little Sister'. Mary defined this Sister's role thus:

> The Superior of each house is called 'Little Sister', and, as her name implies, should so govern as to show that she considers herself the loving servant of all.[96]

In their efforts to protect the members of the Congregation from the dangers of the modern world of their time, the members of the General Chapters of 1937, 1945 and 1947 (and through into the 1950s) promulgated numerous minute regulations regarding how the Sisters should conduct themselves in public and in private. More than anything else, they wanted to be like their foundress, but they were hamstrung by the legalistic approach that developed in religious circles after the publication of the Code of Canon Law in 1917. It, and the subsequent revision of the Josephite Constitutions according to its regulations, tended to draw Sisters' attention away from the spirit of the law and more towards its letter. Consequently, in some

---

95. *Constitutions of the Sisters of St Joseph of the Sacred Heart in Australia*, given at Rome, 21st April 1874, translated into English and printed in Adelaide, 1875, 13. In this context, the word 'press' denotes a cupboard or wardrobe with shelves.
96. Mary MacKillop, *Rules for the General Guidance of the Sisters of St Joseph of the Sacred Heart*, (Sydney: JG O'Connor, 1883), 22.

instances there developed among them a leaning towards legalism which encouraged those in leadership to be exacting and inflexible in their dealings with individual Sisters.[97]

Another twenty years were to pass before the Vatican Council II called for responses to many challenges. It urged Religious Sisters to go beyond external performance, and to read, study and reflect on documents produced by their founders, Mary MacKillop and Julian Woods, and thus to get to the heart of what drove these two people to found the Congregation.

As the Sisters of 1947 looked forward to the coming decade and beyond, they could never have guessed that they were on the verge of changes far beyond anything that they or their Josephite ancestors had ever encountered. Yet, as their story unfolded, it became evident that they faced this unknown future with courage and enthusiasm, and achieved goals undreamed of by those Sisters of earlier times. In this new age they were called upon to minister in places that did not exist prior to World War II, to take up ministries no one had even imagined heretofore, and to move out among the people in new and different ways.

---

97. Margaret McKenna, *With Grateful Hearts! Mary MacKillop and the Sisters of St Joseph in Queensland, 1870-1970* (North Sydney: Sisters of St Joseph of the Sacred Heart, 2009), 310-312.

Sr Andrina Clarke. Mistress of Novices, Adelaide, 1926–1940

Srs Carmella Graney and Thomas Connery, ca. 1920

Sr Mildred Joseph Nejaim who spent all her life providing meals for Sisters and boarders, on her profession day, 12 August 1920

Srs Marie Rose and Stanislaus Doheny

Srs Cecily, Therese and Oliver Gleeson at the beach, 1940s

Postulants, Kensington, 1934
*In 1934, six young women joined the Josephites. They were,
L. to R. Srs Richard (Patricia) White, Regis (Gwen) Ballinger, John Vianney Boyle,
Yvonne Heffernan, Julian Dooley and Marietta Bolitho*

Srs Lucy Crowley, Sebastian Lee and Mildred Joseph Nejaim. 1950s. Note that these Sisters are wearing the soft brown guimps introduced in 1953

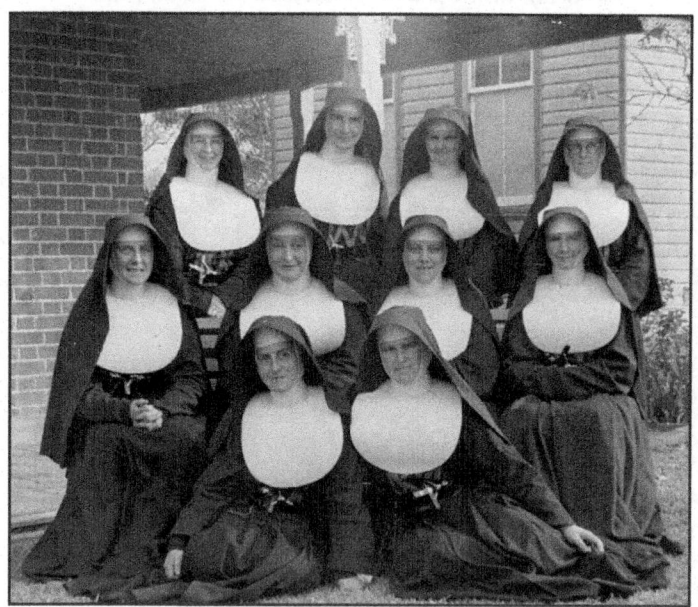

Sisters gathered at Wentworth, between 1950–1952

Back Row: Srs Margaret Mary O'Donnell (Berri), Josephine Keary (Wentworth), Cassian Browne (Renmark), Berenice Conroy (Renmark).

Middle Row: Patricia O'Brien (Wentworth), Mother Leone Ryan (Superior General, Sydney), Jerome Lake (Renmark), Pauline Conroy (Berri).

Front Row: Mercedes Schocher (Renmark), Antonia Hale (Berri).

Sisters in the Hindmarsh Community, 1945.
Back Row: Srs *Patrice Burns, Benedict Hansberry, Verona Quinn, Lucy Crowley, Paulinus Magee, Cyprian Finn*
Front Row: *Josephine McMahon, Paula Paton, Flavia Sheedy, Alvera Fanning.*

Sr Maureen Joseph Meaney on her profession day, 19 December 1932

Sr Vincent McInerney, 1898-1921, on her profession day, 23 January 1919

St Joseph's Juniorate, Cowandilla, 1936.

Chapter Seven
New Challenges—New Ministries: 1947–1967

Changed social and economic conditions during the immediate post war years were the catalyst for many of the developments that occurred in South Australia during that era. At war's end servicemen and women returned home and the subsequent baby boom made a significant difference to the population of the state. The influx of displaced people from Central and Eastern Europe, who came under the Federal Government's Post War Refugee Programme, also gave it a substantial boost. Intergovernmental agreements enabled many Western and Southern Europeans to make the long voyage to South Australia in search of better living conditions and employment opportunities.

A high proportion of the displaced people or 'New Australians', as they were called, came from Poland, the Baltic region, the Ukraine, Hungary and Germany and were Catholic.[1] The same was also true of the Dutch, Italian and Croatian people who arrived at about the same time. Many of the newcomers had large families of young children and most did not speak English on arrival. By 1960, some 40,000 of the new arrivals, approximately half of whom were from Italy, had boosted the number of Catholics in the state. Most settled in the new suburbs that were springing up across the Adelaide metropolitan area. Existing Catholic schools could not accommodate all the Catholic children seeking enrolment.[2]

Archbishop Beovich, who was concerned for the spiritual welfare of all his people, aimed at having a church within walking

---

1. These people were dislodged from their homes during the War and many were used as forced labour by the Germans.
2. Josephine Laffin, *Matthew Beovich: A Biography* (Kent Town: Wakefield Press, 2008), 206.

distance of every Catholic home in the metropolitan area and enough Catholic Church schools to cater for every Catholic child in the diocese. Initially he moved slowly, but by 1960, he had created at least twenty new parishes and authorised the erection of many church and school buildings across the Adelaide metropolitan area.[3] The consequent changes had a profound impact on the Catholic School System and its teachers, including the Sisters of St Joseph, regarding class sizes, the number of schools to be staffed and the introduction of lay teachers into the schools.[4]

Beovich made his first move regarding the creation of new parishes in 1944, when he subdivided the existing Tranmere-Hectorville parish in the eastern suburbs.[5] Large numbers of Italian and other Catholic migrants now lived in the area and the situation was such that one priest could not manage it on his own. One positive aspect of this situation was that the Sisters of St Joseph were managing a school in each of these parishes.

The Hectorville Sisters had lived near their school ever since they took charge of it in 1870. On the other hand, those working at Tranmere travelled out there from Kensington until 1947. During that year, the people of the parish, who had long been aware that it took the Sisters at least forty minutes to get from their convent to the school, set about remedying this situation. They purchased a small house beside the church in Birkinshaw Avenue and set it up for the Sisters. Soon afterwards school principal, Sister Francis Clare Kenny and her three Josephite companions moved in. What a change that was! Instead of having to make a forty-minute journey each way,

---

3. *The Official Directory of the Catholic Church in Australia* (Sydney, 2012–2013).
4. Until the 1950s, only Josephite Sisters taught in Josephite schools in South Australia. Following the influx of migrant children and the baby boom, classes became so large that it was impossible for Sisters to manage them. In some instances, a Sister had a class of 120 children and it was imperative that they be relieved of this impossible burden.
5. Until 1934 the Norwood parish comprised the area between Greenhill, Fullarton and Main Northeast Roads and the Hills Face, with churches on Queen Street and Beulah Road, Norwood, and also at Hectorville, St Peters, Dulwich, and Tranmere. In 1934 the parish was divided into four, namely Dulwich/Burnside, Norwood, St Peters/Beulah Road, and Hectorville/Tranmere. Father Patrick Tangney became parish priest of the last- named and resided at Hectorville. At the time fifty-four children were enrolled at the Hectorville School, and 57 at Tranmere. (Australasian Catholic Directory, 1933 & 1935.)

the Sisters now had only a very short walk from their home to their workplace.

In 1948, four years after the subdivision described above, the Archbishop excised a sizeable area from the Port Adelaide parish to create the parish of Woodville. He appointed Father William Russell, the former Archdiocesan Inspector of Catholic Schools, to be its founding parish priest.[6] At the time, the Woodville Sisters resided at Alberton. They travelled to work by train and, at each end of their journey, they had to walk long distances between the railway stations and their destinations. Within three years of taking charge, Russell had provided them with a convent just a few doors from their school in Beaufort Street, Woodville.[7]

St Joseph's Higher Primary School at Norwood flourished under Sister David Dowd's leadership but further change was in the air. In 1949, the Jesuits announced that they intended using the Queen Street buildings (which were their property) to set up St Ignatius' Jesuit College.[8] Therefore, it became a matter of urgency that the vacant school building in Bridge Street, Kensington be renovated and made ready for the Sisters and students by the beginning of the 1950 school year.

During that same year, two more groups relocated: the Sisters and students from St Joseph's Juniorate on Cowandilla Road at Cowandilla, and the Sisters and residents from the overcrowded Providence on West Terrace, Adelaide.[9] At the time, the Providence Sisters were having to turn away eligible applicants for residential places, and the property was too small and too hemmed in to allow

---

6. The position of Inspector of Catholic Schools lapsed after Woods left Adelaide in 1872. Like his predecessor, Bishop Sheil, Beovich had an interest in education and was determined that there should be a uniformly high standard of teaching in all Catholic schools in the diocese, especially in the area of Religious Instruction. Therefore, early in his episcopate he appointed Father Russell as Inspector of Schools. The recently-ordained future Archbishop of Adelaide, Father JW Gleeson, replaced Russell when the latter moved to Woodville
7. SC, 16 November 1951, 11.
8. This change was possible because the Jesuit Fathers owned the Norwood property.
9. The address of the Juniorate was 22 Cowandilla Road, Cowandilla. At some point between 1950 and 1980 this thoroughfare became known as 'Burbridge Road' and, on 1 January 2001, it was renamed 'Sir Donald Bradman Drive' after the famous cricketer of that name.

for further expansion. It was imperative that they find a larger and more convenient place.[10]

With the assistance of the Archbishop the Sisters purchased a well-established fifty-two acre property at Aldgate. (This place was formerly owned by the Hawkers, a well-known South Australian pastoral family.) Despite its temperate climate and beautiful outlook, it was unsuitable for elderly people because it was not on level ground. The Sisters decided, therefore, to move the Juniorate there and to adapt the former Juniorate buildings at Cowandilla to accommodate the women from the Providence. As this property was all on the level, and had the advantages of being on the Adelaide Plains and close to the city and its people, it was ideal for its new purpose.

The Juniorate Sisters and girls vacated the Cowandilla premises in the May of 1950 to allow for the remodelling of some sections of the existing buildings, and the erection of an accommodation block comprising twenty-seven single rooms and associated facilities near the former schoolroom. They set up a prefabricated cottage from West Terrace as a storage space and workroom for maintenance staff. Finally, all was ready and, in early 1951, the Providence Sisters undertook the daunting task of transferring themselves and their sixty charges to Cowandilla.

Beovich blessed and opened the newly refurbished St Joseph's Providence on 17 June 1951.[11] Soon afterwards the Sisters sold the building on West Terrace to the South Australian Government and by so doing, severed the Providence Sisters' eighty-one year association with the city of Adelaide.[12]

Bert Edwards and others who used to donate food and household items for the benefit of the residents at West Terrace, maintained their generous giving at Cowandilla. On Saturday afternoons the

---

10. *SC* 22 February 1951, 12.
11. *SC* 22 June 1951, 2.
12. *SC* 29 June 1951, 7; S.A. Department of Lands: Land Title 373/244; Transfer No. 42328. The proceeds from the sale of this property were used to pay for the renovations at Cowandilla, which cost £7,000. Marie T Foale, *Providence* (1993), p. 19. At the time of writing, (2014) the site of the West Terrace Providence is occupied by a company known as Adelaide Motors, which sells BMW and other luxury cars. A plaque adjacent to the footpath reminds passersby that it was the site of St Joseph's Providence from 1905 until 1951.

Sisters responsible for the kitchen would wait there for Bert's arrival and they were rarely disappointed. As a rule, he came with trays or bags of bread, bread rolls, buns, cake and vegetables donated at the end of trading by stallholders in the Adelaide Central Market.[13] The Sisters put them to good use for, like their predecessors of the late nineteenth century, this later generation of Sisters was also expert at 'converting provisions which in most houses (were) thrown away, into very useful articles of diet'.[14]

For the Juniorate girls who had moved to Aldgate, it was an exciting time. In addition to doing their normal class work, they explored their new home, became involved in picking fruit from the trees on the property, milking the cows and helping in the garden. They were present when Archbishop Beovich, accompanied by Bishop Thomas McCabe of Port Augusta, officially opened the place on Sunday, 4 March 1951.[15] During 1952 they watched as a new chapel, replete with sacristy and priest's room, was erected beside the main house, and were there for its blessing and opening in February 1953.[16]

As already noted, since the time of their foundation, the Sisters had depended on charity for their survival and had a long-established tradition of begging for their support and accepting donations of food or money, no matter how small. They continued this practice into the 1960s, even though eligible Sisters had been in receipt of the aged pension since 1910. For many years this pension stood at £1 a week, an amount that scarcely paid its recipients' living costs and did not benefit the Sisters' schools or charitable institutions.[17]

---

13. On several occasions during the late 1950s, the author was in the kitchen with the Sister cook of the time, Sister Elizabeth Schultz, when Bert came in with his load of goods.
14. *SCCH*, 2 February 1869, 277. *SC* 3 August 1963, 3.
15. *SC* 23 February 1951, 12 & 9 March 1951, 12. Thomas McCabe (1902–1983), formerly of Lismore in New South Wales, was in charge of the Port Augusta diocese from 1938 until 1952. On 15 November 1951, he was appointed bishop of the new diocese of Wollongong in New South Wales and moved there in early 1952.
16. *SC* 20 February 1953, 3.
17. According to the Department of Social Security, 'History of Pensions and other benefits in Australia' (2009), in 1909 the Commonwealth Government granted the pension to sixty-year-old women who had been resident in the country for at least twenty years. In 1960 the residential qualification changed from twenty

St Joseph's Orphanage, Largs Bay, received significant support from the SA Jockey Club and the patrons of a number of city and suburban hotels, including Bert Edwards' Newmarket Hotel (on the corner of North Terrace and West Terrace, Adelaide) and the Alberton Hotel (on Port Road, Alberton). The hoteliers concerned placed collection tins for the orphans on their front bars so that patrons could fill them with loose change, and Sisters from the orphanage collected the money from these tins. Because they were not self-conscious at having to walk into a crowded bar in their religious habits, they were usually treated with respect by those present.[18]

Prior to World War II, fetes and school concerts were fruitful sources of finance for the Sisters' support. Then, during the immediate post war era, fundraising took a new turn. The government of the day placed greater emphasis on physical education in schools, and so the Sisters opted to make Sports Days their major fundraising events for the year. Since these were held in the cooler months, teachers and children found their preparation less stressful than practising for and presenting school concerts at year's end.

From 1950 onwards, the *Southern Cross* published detailed accounts of Sports Days at Josephite schools in places as widely separated as Quorn, Macclesfield, Hamley Bridge, Georgetown, Balaklava, and the orphanage at Largs Bay.[19] In 1952, for example, it reported that those present 'thoroughly enjoyed the splendidly varied and picturesque programme, presented and executed so impressively by the Largs Bay children'. Each year, Sisters residing at Kensington supported each other by attending at least two Sports Days other than their own.

During the late 1940s and early 1950s, the Archbishop authorised the erection of numerous churches, schools and church-schools in the newly developing suburbs to the north, northwest and west of the city of Adelaide, and created new parishes in many of these regions. Among the new suburbs where the South Australian Housing Trust erected a large number of dwellings were Flinders Park, Seaton,

---

to ten years. http://www.abs.gov.au/ausstats/abs@.nsf/94713ad445ff1425ca2568 2000192af2/8e72c4526a94aaedca2569de00296978!OpenDocument,
18. Interview with Sr Monica Coonan (d 2004), June 1999.
19. *SC* 9 May 1952, 2; 30 May 1952, 2; 12 June 1952, 15; 2 September 1952, 15; 22 May 1953, 2.

Royal Park, Ferryden Park, Woodville Gardens, Mansfield Park and Ottoway.[20] The rent was reasonable and most were close to the factories where recent migrants found employment. Before long there were Josephite schools in each of these suburbs.

One of the first parish priests to have church and school buildings erected was Father Cuthbert Hoy MSC of the Hindmarsh-Flinders Park area, who oversaw the construction of a church-school on Captain Cook Avenue, Flinders Park.[21] Sisters John Evangelist Johnson and Enda Kelly took charge of this school when it opened during 1950 with an enrolment of forty-two children. These Sisters lived in the Josephite convent on Grange Road, Hindmarsh, and, like many of their peers in other areas, travelled to and from school each day by public transport and on foot.

The population of the Flinders Park area increased rapidly. As a consequence, the initial enrolment at the school had more than doubled by the end of 1951, and the school building had to be extended.[22] The influx of children did not stop, however, and by 1960 the church-school was overcrowded again. This meant another building project for Father Hoy, who ensured that this next lot of classrooms was ready for occupation by 1961, the year when Sisters Perpetua Hayes, Columba McNamara and Luke (Maureen) Colbert joined the staff. They came not a moment too soon for, while enrolments for that year stood at 127, they increased to 178 in 1962. Because there were no extra Sisters available, they engaged a lay teacher, one of the first of the many lay people to gain positions in Josephite schools over ensuing years.

During 1955, the Josephites took charge of the Gleneagles School on Grange Road at Seaton, which was an outpost of the Woodville Parish.[23] When Father Russell and his assistant, Father William Collins, arrived at Woodville in June 1948, there was one small

---

20. The SA Housing Trust was a government body, established in 1937, to assist with urban planning and the provision of cheap housing in industrial areas.
21. Father Hoy was a member of the Missionaries of the Sacred Heart, more commonly known as the 'Sacred Heart Fathers', whose parish of Hindmarsh included Flinders Park.
22. *SC* 13 March 1952, 7
23. The Woodville parish comprised the whole area between Woodville North, Grange Road, the Port River and the coastal sand dunes near what was later developed as the West Lakes area and the AAMI Sports Stadium.

church in Beaufort Street, Woodville, and another of similar dimensions in Botting Street, Albert Park. At the time, most of the working people living in the more distant suburbs of Royal Park, Findon or Seaton did not have cars and so found it difficult to attend Mass at either of these churches. Therefore, Russell provided them with easily accessible Mass centres, which doubled as schools during the week. The Dominican Sisters from North Adelaide accepted his invitation to take charge of the Findon School while the Josephites undertook the management of schools at Royal Park and Gleneagles.

When he approached the Provincial (Sister Vincent Ferrer Dolan) regarding the Gleneagles school, Russell made an unusual request: he asked for just *one* Sister! At that time the idea of a Sister working alone was unheard of. Therefore, Sister Agatha (Melita) Howley, who was in charge of this school, had a non-teaching Sister companion, seventy-eight year old Sister Flavia Sheedy, who came out of retirement at Kensington to fill this role. Agatha and Flavia lived in the convent on Beaufort Street, Woodville, and travelled from there to Gleneagles each day.

Most of the fifty-five children present on opening day were of Italian background: their parents tended the market gardens of the area. Over succeeding years enrolments increased and it became more than one Sister could manage on her own. Therefore, Agatha and Flavia, who spent just three years at Gleneagles, moved away and two Dominican Sisters from Findon took their places. Agatha moved on to the newly established motor mission in the Barossa Valley, while Flavia returned to Kensington, where her health gradually deteriorated. She died there on 20 July 1960, aged eighty-three years.[24]

The Royal Park School, which opened in 1957, was in a Housing Trust area bordered by swamps and sandhills. (During the 1970s, this area opened up for settlement and became the suburb and the shopping cum sporting complex of West Lakes and Football Park). Most of the children attending this school were of Polish background with only limited English when they enrolled.

During the previous year a community of Polish-speaking Sisters of the Resurrection came from the United States to set up

---

24. ASSJ, Register of the Sisters.

St Stanislaus House, Royal Park, as a home for needy primary school aged children, including orphans, children from broken homes and children whose mothers were ill or away at work. They all attended St Stanislaus Catholic School along with the day pupils from the area. The Josephites taught there until the end of 1964 by which time the Resurrection Sisters were qualified to teach in South Australian schools.[25]

Ottoway, in the Port Adelaide-Alberton parish, was another suburb where most of the people were of Polish background. The Josephites opened a school in the local church in 1954 with an enrolment of eighty-eight children. The Sisters concerned resided in the Port Adelaide convent, which had reopened only recently after refurbishments, which required its closure and the relocation of the Sisters to Largs Bay for several years. In that same year, two Sisters took charge of the Corpus Christi church-school at Woodville Gardens, an outpost of the Croydon Park parish. Their initial enrolment was 104 children (also mostly from non-English speaking backgrounds).[26]

While the members of the Woodville, Croydon Park and Port Adelaide parishes were providing schools for newcomers, Sisters in several long established areas were facing difficulties of a different kind. They were working in buildings that, during and immediately after the War, easily accommodated all the children in attendance. Then, almost overnight, migrants with little English moved away from the Pennington and Woodside Migrant Hostels and into the suburbs.

School numbers rose dramatically and, in some instances, Sisters faced classes of up to 120 students in rooms built for half that number. The situation was especially difficult in junior grades, where many of the little ones had little knowledge of English. Besides this, the Sisters, like their counterparts in both the state and the Catholic systems, had no training in the teaching of English as a second language.

Sometimes there were not enough desks to go round, but, with characteristic Josephite resourcefulness, the Sisters improvised. At Croydon Park in 1953, for example, some of the children in the

---

25. *SC* 17 July 1964, 11.
26. *SC* 24 February 1954, 2.

infant class sat on boxes with their knees inside the upended fruit cases that were their 'desks' for days, even weeks, while awaiting the arrival of new furniture![27] Parents did not complain back then. They so appreciated being able to have their children in a school!

In some parts of the country renovations and new school buildings were also the order of the day. At Gladstone, Bishop McCabe officiated at the blessing and opening of a much-needed school building in February 1952. The local people had replaced the old church, which had doubled as a school for many years, with a weatherboard, two-roomed purpose-built structure, which was

> a delight to the eye and promised those conveniences so necessary to and so richly deserved by the Sisters [who were about to] teach in it.[28]

Soon after this, McCabe became the first bishop of the new diocese of Wollongong in New South Wales. His successor, Bryan Gallagher from Geraldton in Western Australia, found Peterborough too isolated for his purposes and moved himself and the administrative centre of the diocese to the more centrally located industrial and port city of Port Pirie. He renamed his area of responsibility the diocese of Port Pirie.

The year 1953 was noteworthy for several reasons. Firstly, and of lesser importance, was the move of the Croydon Sisters from their residence at Alberton to their new convent at 286 Torrens Road, Croydon. Parish priest, Father Tom Daly, secured a new home for himself and his assistant, Father Robert Aitken, at some distance from the church and school. Then, on 25 March the Sisters took possession of the priests' former dwelling. Somehow, the new convent was not quite as ready as Daly expected. There were five Sisters and only three beds in the house! Consequently, the two youngest members of the community returned to Alberton that evening. Their problem was solved next day.

Like their peers at Woodville and Tranmere, these Sisters were grateful for the extra time now available to them for their work. Their new home was a standard 1920s type four-roomed house with

---

27. The author was the infant teacher at Croydon in 1953. This image is etched vividly in her memory.
28. *SC* 22 February 1952, 9 &19.

the kitchen, bathroom and laundry in an enclosed lean to at the back. It was so small that there was not room for more Sisters. Therefore Daly, who was in the process of setting up a new school at Woodville Gardens in the following year, added to it a large dormitory with associated facilities in order to accommodate all the Sisters working in his parish.

While the Croydon Sisters were moving house, a number of other Sisters were in Sydney taking part in the Congregation's fifteenth General Chapter. They re-elected Mother Leone Ryan as Superior General and Sister Vincent Ferrer Dolan became Provincial of South Australia. Retiring South Australian Provincial, Sister Michael Xavier Denham, reported that in the Province there were 245 Sisters residing in thirty-eight convents, teaching in forty-nine schools and managing three charitable institutions.[29] Thirty-nine Sisters from the Kensington community were teaching in ten nearby suburban parish schools, namely, St Joseph's Higher Primary on Bridge Street, Kensington, and the primary schools at Beulah Road and William Street, Norwood, St Peters (Ellangowan), Hectorville, Walkerville, Dulwich, Keswick, Plympton, and Russell Street.

One Chapter decision which aroused some general interest was that, on the Feast of the Sacred Heart in June 1953, Sisters could cease wearing the stiff white celluloid guimps introduced in 1937, and replace them with soft brown ones with white over collars.[30] This modification of the Sisters' dress, although seemingly minor, was significant because it indicated that Sisters' dress codes could be subject to change. Although few realised it at the time, this alteration came as a result of a directive from Pope Pius XII at a gathering of religious superiors in Rome during September 1952. On that occasion he said:

> The Religious Habit ought always express your consecration to Christ; that is what everyone expects and desires. Apart from that, let the habit be suitable and answer to the requirements of hygiene. Here we must express our satisfaction that during the course of the year we noticed

---

29. Minutes of the 1953 General Chapter, March 1953.
30. See Chapter Six, fn. 61 for a definition of 'guimp'.

> [that] one or two Congregations have drawn practical conclusions in this point. In a general manner, in those things that are not essential, adapt yourselves [to circumstances] as much as reason and well-ordered charity suggest to you.[31]

Of major concern to the members of the 1953 Chapter was a fear that the spirit of the world was infiltrating the convent, thanks, as they saw it, to the insidious influence of the expanding mass media of the time. As a consequence, Sisters were becoming 'worldly', and paying less attention to their spiritual lives. The Sisters attending this General Chapter were women of a time when popular Catholic piety was strongly influenced by the Cold War, and Catholic teaching was that family prayer, or in their case, community prayer, would lead to peace in the home and peace in the world.[32] As a consequence, the Chapter decided that the Sisters must be protected from anything that might prevent or discourage them from being faithful to their religious vows and must make every effort to become women of prayer. To attain this end, the Chapter promulgated detailed regulations regarding the Sisters' lifestyle. Most Sisters, who were also women of their time and were determined to do their part in bringing peace to the world, accepted the Chapter rulings.

In 1953, however, it was difficult for some Sisters to follow the new regulations in detail because of the increasing pressures of work, especially in schools where they faced large classes. There were too few Sisters and most parishes could not afford to employ lay staff. They were obligated to accept every Catholic child who sought enrolment to ensure that Catholic families observed the seventh commandment

---

31. Address of Pope Pius XII to the Superiors General of Religious Orders and Institutes of Women, Castel Gandolfo, 15 September 1952. ASSJ, North Sydney.
32. David Hilliard, 'Religion in Australia in 1950s', *Journal of Religious History*, 16/2 (1988): 224-225. 'The Cold War' was the name given to the relationship that developed primarily between the USA and the USSR after World War II. It dominated international news bulletins until the fall of the Berlin Wall in 1989, and for many, the growth in weapons of mass destruction was the most worrying issue. It was a clash of very different beliefs and ideology—capitalism versus communism—each held with almost religious conviction, which formed the basis of an international power struggle with both sides vying for dominance. *"What was the Cold War?" HistoryLearningSite.co.uk. 2014.*

of the Church 'To send Catholic children to Catholic Schools'.[33] They could do little to solve the problem of big class numbers beyond encouraging/inviting more young women to join the Congregation. To do this more effectively, Mother Leone missioned several sisters to travel across the country canvassing for new members.

The Australian bishops of the 1950s were aware of the problems of the shortage of religious sisters and the overcrowding of Catholic schools. Therefore, when they met a few weeks after the closure of the Chapter, they decided that:

> the Sisters of St Joseph be invited to undertake— where the Mother General considers it possible—the religious instruction of Catholics living in country and isolated areas distant from Catholic schools.[34]

It fell to the Archbishop of Adelaide to convey news of this decision to Mother Leone in the hope that she would see that their proposal was in line with the Sisters' apostolic work. He wrote:

> In that regard, if and when the Sisters of St Joseph adopt this extension of their existing work, I would hope that you would give favourable consideration to my own plea, namely, that when you have the personnel you would allow me two Sisters who, centred at Aldgate, would move among the many isolated pockets of Catholic parents and children in

---

33. Josephine Laffin, *Matthew Beovich*, 86-92. Catholics were obligated to observe these commandments under pain of sin. It seems that the seventh one was added after the 1937 Plenary Synod of the Bishops of Australia (4-7 December 1937), most likely in response to the teaching of Pope Pius XI in his encyclical *Divini Illius Magistri* on Christian Education, 31 December 1929. These commandments were:
    1. To hear Mass on Sundays and holy days of obligation.
    2. To fast and abstain on the days appointed.
    3. To confess our sins at least once a year.
    4. To receive the Eucharist during Easter time.
    5. To contribute to the support of our pastors and the upkeep of Catholic schools and charitable institutions.
    6. To observe the laws of the Church concerning marriage.
    7. To send Catholic children to Catholic schools.
34. Beovich to Mother Leone, 25 September 1953. ASSJ, North Sydney.

the Adelaide Hills. For my part, I would provide a suitable motor car for transport and the necessary remuneration.[35]

Mother Leone annotated her copy: 'Consultors agreed to proposal. Will commence in His Grace's Archdiocese. If possible, two Sisters in 1955.' It is easy to understand why the archbishop approached the Josephites and why Mother Leone and her consultors responded so readily: since their foundation, the Sisters provided religious instruction to children without access to Catholic schools. There are many records indicating that they went to parochial outstations to prepare children for the reception of the Sacraments. In this instance, neither the bishops nor the Josephite General Council realised that, over time, the Motor Missions would contribute to the shortage of school Sisters: this ministry required young, energetic women who were skilled teachers.

This new work was in addition to the summer schools, which were a fixture in many country parishes and which school Sisters ran during the school holidays. Those at Port Lincoln, Ceduna, Streaky Bay, and Minnipa on Eyre Peninsula and Peterborough were well established, while several new ones were inaugurated during the 1950s. The first of these was at Yorketown, where they became an annual event until the Sisters opened a boarding and day school there in 1957.

From 1954 on, the Sisters ran annual summer schools at Waikerie and Strathalbyn, and indicated that they were open to accepting invitations to any town where one was warranted. The thirtieth Peterborough Summer School took place in 1960, but the momentum did not stop there.[36] During the following decade, there were summer or vacation schools in at least fourteen different localities across the state.[37] Archdiocesan centres were at Croydon and Hectorville in the metropolitan area, and at Bordertown, Kingston, Maitland, Tailem Bend/Karoonda, Meningie and Kangaroo Island

---

35. Beovich to Mother Leone, 25 September 1953.
36. *Witness* (Catholic paper for the Port Pirie diocese, published monthly from 1955), March 1960.
37. With time it became clear that January was not the best month to have children concentrate on the serious work of Religious Instruction. In many instances, therefore, schools were held during the May and/or September school holidays. Hence the change of name from 'Summer' to 'Vacation' Schools.

in the country. Further north, in the Port Pirie diocese, they took place at Waikerie, Port Lincoln, Cummins, Streaky Bay, Ceduna, Hawker, Peterborough, and Snowtown, with an occasional one taking place at Lock or Cleve on Eyre Peninsula, and Georgetown in the Mid-North. Each year, the sixty or so Sisters involved in this work contacted more than 1,000 children and their families.[38]

The vacation schools were important in providing religious instruction to children without access to Catholic schools, but they could not reach everybody. Hence, Beovich's plan to have travelling Sisters teach Religious Instruction (RI) to these children more often than once a year. Besides the regular clientele of the vacation schools, he was anxious that the children of Catholic migrant families, who were settled in areas where there was no Catholic school, also receive religious instruction.

This was a good time to act for in 1940 the South Australian Government had legislated that representatives of the major Christian denominations might conduct RI lessons in state schools for half an hour each week.[39]

Beovich's first area of interest was the thickly settled central Adelaide Hills and the country between there and the River Murray. In this region there was a smaller proportion of Catholic residents than in any other part of South Australia. There were no Catholic schools and a large number of Catholic families were residing in the Woodside Army Camp. Hence, the archbishop's decision to have the Sisters begin a motor mission in that region in 1955, if possible.

There was no one available that year, but Sister Vincent Ferrer was able to release two Sisters for this new work in 1956: Sisters Patrice Burns and Rose Byrne. Rose, who was an experienced teacher, was possessed of one very necessary qualification for this venture. She could drive a car, having gained her driver's licence before becoming a Josephite some twenty years earlier! Patrice, a mature-aged woman, was highly respected for her teaching ability and her practical kindness to families in need. She and Rose moved

---

38. Motor Mission Report, 2, ca. 1964.
39. From 1940 until 1974, South Australian State Government legislation allowed representatives of the different religious denominations in the state to give religious instruction in state schools for half an hour a week.

to Aldgate in early 1956 and began their work by visiting the eighteen state schools in the region.[40]

Besides negotiating times for school visits with head teachers, these Sisters met with clergy from other religious denominations to coordinate visiting times. As a rule, they found these people agreeable when it came to arranging a timetable that suited everyone. The Sisters had few problems in dealing with the local people, but some of the roads they had to negotiate were another matter. Most were narrow, winding and sometimes slippery but, by dint of Rose's skill in handling a car, they fulfilled their mission without incident and were rarely late for lessons.[41]

The Aldgate mission prospered until 7 August 1963 when Sister Patrice died suddenly, aged sixty years, while on a visit to Kensington.[42] Patrice's death was a heavy loss to all concerned and her current companion, Sister Adrian (Pamela) Patterson, was left to carry on until the end of the year. She managed with the assistance of several laywomen who joined her on Tuesdays, Wednesdays and Thursdays, and Sister Martina Farissey who helped out on Fridays and weekends. This mission was in operation for the seventeen years, 1956–1973, that is, until the government abolished RI in state schools in September 1973.[43]

Priests from other parishes observed the Hills mission closely, and soon Sister Vincent Ferrer received requests for Sisters to undertake similar work elsewhere. Thus, in 1958, just two years later, Sisters Agatha Howley and Bernadette Roche went to the Barossa Valley, a place that had only recently acquired a Catholic church building. The Sisters resided in Angaston and followed a similar programme to that developed at Aldgate. Very soon they were at home among the majority Lutheran community and had

---

40. These were in the Birdwood, Blackwood, Mount Barker and Stirling parishes, the most distant from the Sisters' home base at Aldgate being at Mannum on the River Murray.
41. Every week the Sisters visited schools at Woodside, Oakbank, Littlehampton, Wistow, Uraidla, Bridgewater, Lobethal, Lenswood, Basket Range, Houghton, Tungkillo, Palmer, Mannum, Verdun, Hahndorf, Nairne, Belair, and Blackwood.
42. RSJ Web Page, Obituaries of Sisters.
43. Report of the Hills Motor Mission, 1956–1973, ASSJ, Kensington.

gained entry into schools in the Valley itself, as well as in the surrounding farming areas.[44]

Next, Bishop Gallagher applied for two Sisters to operate out of Peterborough and to cover the many small settlements and townships in the parishes of Peterborough, Pekina, Booleroo Centre, Carrieton, Quorn and Port Augusta. He expected that their home base would be at Peterborough, but that, because of the great distances they would be covering, they would spend three nights of each week at Port Augusta. These Sisters travelled almost 800 kilometres a week, mostly on unsealed roads, where dust was a problem in dry weather, and mud and water on (or running across) a road made for hazardous driving after rain.

Two mission Sisters, Patrice Burns (who was on loan from the Hills for the first term) and Edwin (Marie) Taylor took up their appointment in February 1960, when Father Eugene Kenny, diocesan Inspector of Schools, blessed them and their car. They went at once to Port Augusta and during the following week visited the six parish priests and the many schools involved. The 'generous cooperation' of school headmasters and the 'enthusiastic welcome of parish priests and parishioners' made a deep impression on them.[45]

Patrice returned to Aldgate at the end of Term One and Sister Nicholas (Mary) Canny joined Edwin. In November 1961, they reported that they had travelled 73,600 kilometres since February 1960, and had instructed more than 240 children each week. Eighty-three of these had made their First Confession and received their First Holy Communion, while sixty-six were Confirmed. In addition, these Sisters often visited local hospitals and the children's family homes. They had become bogged in soft mud and been rescued by a kindly farmer, and had experienced three punctures. On each occasion, as they struggled to change the offending tyre, a passerby came to their aid.[46]

Hamley Bridge on the northern Adelaide Plains gained its mission in 1962. Then, in 1964, there were four new missions: at Waikerie on the Upper Murray, and in the metropolitan parishes of Adelaide, Hectorville, and Woodville. Finally, in 1966, soon after

---

44. *SC* 18 June 1965.
45. *Witness,* March 1960.
46. Report: 'The Northern Motor Mission', late 1961. ASSJ, Kensington.

low enrolments forced Sisters Julian Dooley and Agneta Case to close the local Catholic school, they set up a mission at Georgetown.[47]

The first Hamley Bridge mission Sisters, Verona Quinn and Mary Robert Aitken, used programmes similar to those developed by other mission Sisters. Initially they were confined to the nine small rural state schools in the parish, as well as the Hamley Bridge High and Primary Schools. By the late 1960s, most of those smaller schools were closed, and they were able to move into the Gawler and Virginia parishes as well.[48]

Sisters Raymond (Joan) Mangan and Denis (Genevieve) Ryan established the Waikerie mission in 1964. The parish gave them a car. The local people made them welcome and were delighted at the way they settled in and found their way around the district from Morgan in the west to Kingston-on-Murray and Loxton in the east, to Wanbi in the south and back to Waikerie on its northern boundary. Each week, these two Sisters travelled more than 800 kilometres, met with over 200 students and visited the children's families, the sick in the hospitals and the elderly in their homes.[49]

These city-bred Josephites found travelling long distances over unsealed roads quite daunting as they operated according to a tight schedule. They generally made their destinations on time but, on rare occasions, were defeated by the treachery of unsealed roads covered in deep sand in summer and slippery mud after the occasional winter rain. Flat tyres were a real hazard and caused long delays when they occurred on lonely country roads.[50]

These Sisters found it impossible to cover the RI curriculum adequately in one short weekly lesson, and so they organised vacation schools as times of intensive preparation for the reception of the Sacraments of Penance, Holy Communion and Confirmation. The first of these schools took place in May 1965, but later the Sisters held them in September because that was when the headmaster of the Waikerie Primary School could give them the use of his

---

47. These Sisters closed the Georgetown school because there were just twenty children on the roll and there was no likelihood of increased enrolments in the immediate future.
48. Report of Mission, ASSJ, Kensington.
49. *SC* 21 August 1964.
50. Verbal reports from Sister Genevieve (Denis) Ryan, 2013.

school for the week. Ecumenical relationships were cordial and sometimes the Sisters attended functions in other churches.

In 1965, they established a branch of the YCS (Young Christian Students Movement) among the senior students at the Waikerie High School. From 1968 onwards, the Waikerie and Barossa Valley missions offered combined holiday camps for secondary students at a campsite on Lake Bonney, near Barmera. The Waikerie mission prospered until late 1971 when the parish priest who welcomed them there moved to another parish. His successor had different ideas regarding how religious education should be offered to the children of his parish. Therefore, he closed the mission and asked the Sisters to leave the area.[51]

The Adelaide city mission, which began in 1964, catered for Catholic children attending metropolitan state schools. Initially, Sisters Verona Quinn and Bernadette Roche, who were based at Hectorville, arranged for the giving of weekly instructions to more than 2,000 children in two secondary, eight primary and two special schools in the Woodville, Hectorville and Campbelltown parishes. They also organised YCS groups in the secondary schools and were gratified when members of these groups joined their peers from Catholic colleges at annual gatherings. These Sisters visited children's family homes and often, where there was a language barrier, found it necessary to use the youngsters as interpreters for their parents.

At each centre, groups of dedicated lay catechists, mostly women, assisted with the work.[52] Once a fortnight they met with the Sisters for assistance with lesson preparation. While their main duty was to help with weekend classes for children preparing for the Sacraments, they were also there each September to assist with the conduct of a vacation school at Hectorville. More than 100 children attended the first of these in 1964, and numbers increased over time.

There were so many students and such heavy demands were placed on the Sisters that, by 1965, it became necessary to divide the city mission into three: the Woodville-Western Suburbs mission with its Sisters living at Woodville, the City-Central mission, which

---

51. ASSJ, Kensington.
52. Catechists were lay people specially trained to give RI lessons.

had its home base at Kingswood, and the Eastern Suburbs mission where the Sisters resided at Hectorville.

Three years later, in 1969, the Provincial, Sister Marie Paul Harford, reported that the Eastern Suburbs mission Sisters were instructing 2,950 children in seventeen schools and the City-Central and Woodville-Western Suburbs missioners were visiting fifteen schools apiece and instructing 2190 young people between them. All told, in that year the nine motor missions were reaching some 7,000 children in 138 schools, and the Sisters concerned were travelling approximately 4,000 kilometres each week.[53]

Even as some South Australian Sisters became motor missioners, others continued their work in the schools and charitable institutions and made several new foundations in different parts of the state. Thus, in January 1954 the people of Barmera welcomed Sisters Ruth Riley and Eleanor Hewish to their town. The local Catholics who were proud of what they had prepared for the Sisters, had been

> very zealous in their efforts to raise the much needed funds for the many essentials associated with any new establishment. Their first social function was a combined welcome for the Sisters and pantry afternoon. This ... was well attended by mothers and their friends, who made the most of this opportunity to view the beautifully appointed convent.[54]

Fifty-seven children enrolled on opening day and the two Sisters soon settled into the rhythm of life in the Riverland.

At the same time, Sisters Dominic (Eileen) McGuire and Paula (Teresa) Cooper were having a very different experience in the timber milling town of Nangwarry, in the pine forests between Penola and Mount Gambier. When the school and convent opened in February 1954, forty-eight of their fifty-seven pupils came from the local state school. Most of the parents were refugees from Europe who went to Nangwarry to obtain work in the forest or at the timber mill. The Sisters had to learn quickly how to teach children who could not understand each other, much less the instructions

---

53. Sister Marie Paul, Province Report, 1969 Special General Chapter. ASSJ.
54. SC 26 March 1954, 2.

being given them. The first languages spoken by most of these 'New Australian' children and their parents included Dutch, Bulgarian, Hungarian, Lithuanian, German, English and Turkish. There were very few children of Anglo-Celtic background at this school.

The Sisters lived in a small, rented Forestry Commission house which, upon their arrival, was furnished with the barest of necessities. In fact, no sooner had they arrived than they had to make a hurried trip to Mount Gambier to purchase basic items for their kitchen and bedrooms. Next day they found that the school lacked essential equipment and furniture. There were no seats or desks or cupboards, no partition separated the two classrooms and there were no toilet facilities for the children. In order to have the school open on time, the local parish priest arranged with the management of the nearby Community Sports Complex for the loan of stools and trestles to serve as makeshift desks, and for the children to have access to the toilets at the complex.

Eventually the new desks arrived. They had been ordered well in advance but were held up somewhere in the South Australian Railways system. These desks were so designed that they could be used as seats for the people attending Sunday Masses. There was no partition in the schoolroom. Sister Dominic's class faced one way and Sister Paula's the other. What a relief it was when, after several weeks of waiting, a partition was installed and the school's own toilet blocks were ready for use. When the siren at the timber mill signalled the workers' lunch time, the children also took their midday break. They all went home for the lunch hour, leaving their teachers free to enjoy their own meal without having to do yard duty![55]

Just over twelve months later, in April 1955, Sisters Regis (Gwen) Ballinger and Julian Dooley travelled in the opposite direction to establish a convent and school in the closed town of Woomera on the gibber plains in the northwest of the state.[56] Woomera could be accessed only by air or by a two to three hour drive from Port Augusta over an unsealed road. (It remained unsealed until well into the 1980s.) Like other residents, the Sisters endured extreme heat

---

55. Sr Teresa Cooper's recollections, Nangwarry File. ASSJ, Kensington.
56. *Witness*, April 1955; *SC* 1 April 1955, 7.

in summer and the red dust that clogged everything for most of the year.

The British and Australian Governments established the Woomera Rocket Range in 1947 to support the so-called Anglo-Australian Joint Project: a 'Cold War' undertaking focused on the development of long range weapons systems, principally to counter the growing intercontinental ballistic missile threat from the former Soviet Union. There was much secrecy in this closed town and all who went there, including the Sisters, required security clearances before they could enter the prohibited area. The heyday of the Range was from 1947 until about 1972, after which the population gradually decreased. At the time of writing (2014) it was little more than a ghost town.

Woomera was home to scientists and army personnel working on weapons testing and research at the Rocket Range and their families. Many were from the United States or the United Kingdom, and few stayed long enough for their children to complete their entire primary education. On the St Joseph's School opening day in 1955, sixty-seven pupils enrolled and numbers gradually increased until they reached a maximum of 130 in 1970. The school doubled as a hall at weekends until 1962 when it moved to a dedicated school building. The Sisters withdrew from Woomera at the end of 1984.

During this time there was also much activity in other parts of the diocese. Thus, in April 1955, Bishop Gallagher visited Spalding for the opening of a new school building comprising a classroom, library and kitchen built by volunteers.[57] Then, in the following January he celebrated the opening of additions to the Josephite school at Renmark.[58]

Soon after his return from Renmark, he invited the Catholic schools in the diocese to participate in a Combined Sports Day at Port Pirie. Subsequently, on 23 August 1956, students from eleven schools met at an oval near St Mark's Cathedral. Among them were representatives from the Josephite schools at Peterborough, Terowie, Jamestown, Caltowie, Gladstone and Georgetown. The youngsters from Peterborough did themselves and their school proud by gaining third place in the competition. In the following

---

57. *Witness*, May 1955.
58. *SC* 11 January 1956.

year, Port Augusta took home the Senior Shield and Quorn carried off the Junior Shield. All involved voted these days a great success, especially for the way they brought together children, teachers and parents from many parts of the diocese.[59]

In January 1957, the bishop was at Port Augusta for the opening of two new classrooms at the Josephite school. While there he expressed his concern at the shortage of Sisters in this era of rapid population growth.

In particular, he stated his belief that the number of children attending St Joseph's at Port Augusta warranted at least seven or eight teaching Sisters instead of the five currently on the staff.[60] (At this point, neither he nor anyone else even considered employing lay teachers.) Enrolments at both Port Augusta and Port Lincoln continued to increase and, by the early 1960s, both schools needed even more new buildings and were augmenting their staffs with lay teachers!

Radium Hill (a small town twenty-three kilometres south of the Barrier Highway on the way to Broken Hill, and about forty kilometres from the New South Wales border) developed because the government considered the nearby uranium deposit worthy of mining. It was established in 1954 and, not anticipating that it would be abandoned seven years later, parish priest and architect, Father Vincent Shiel, built a church dedicated to Our Lady Queen of the World, which he opened in October 1956. During that year and in 1957, he invited two Sisters from Peterborough to conduct vacation schools for the many Catholic children living there. His long term aim was to have the Josephites make a permanent foundation in the town.

Provincial Sister Vincent Ferrer was sympathetic to his cause, and in 1958 she appointed Sisters Uriel McGuire and Mercedes Schocker to this distant mission. When they arrived by plane at the beginning of the 1959 school year almost the entire Catholic population was there to welcome them. The priest's house became their convent while Father Shiel built himself a 'garage-type single room, all purpose presbytery'. Eighty children from many different ethnic

---

59. *Witness*, July & September 1955, September 1957, 4.
60. *SC* 15 February 1957.

backgrounds, that is, most of the Catholic children in the town, enrolled in their school.[61]

This school, a prefabricated timber building consisting of two classrooms, operated for only three years. During that time the Sisters offered the children the 'finer' subjects of sewing and music in addition to the customary school subjects. Then, on 16 December 1961, they closed the school door for the last time and left the town. Soon afterwards, the entire population followed suit. The mine closed. Transportable items from there were moved to other mining sites. Sheil arranged for the convent and school to be transported to Port Pirie where they were reassembled at the Risdon Park Catholic School.[62]

According to the *Witness* of December 1961:

> It [was] isolated; it [was] surrounded by sparsely populated station country. Access roads [threw] up clouds of fine dust all year round. When rain [fell], main roads [became] treacherous and station tracks [were] impassable. The ore worked [was] radioactive. There [were] present as well, the unknown hazards of long periods spent working such ores.[63]

In November 1955, the Catholics of Caltowie, under the leadership of their parish priest, Father James Prendergast, celebrated the golden jubilee of the Sisters' return to their town in 1905, with a special Mass followed by a Communion Breakfast. Among those present were fourteen Josephite Sisters and many past pupils. Few then realised that enrolments in their school were becoming so dangerously low that the Sisters would be leaving Caltowie for good in six years' time. It was a sad day indeed, when the twenty schoolchildren and their parents said a final goodbye to Sisters Tarcisius McNamara and Ronan Meere at the end of 1961.

At Peterborough, celebrations for the diamond jubilee of the Sisters' arrival in 1897 spread across a whole year. They began on 24 February, when a crowd of about 1,100 people gathered 'in lovely sunshine' to witness the blessing and opening of two large classrooms, wide enclosed verandahs and toilet facilities at the

---

61. *Witness*, 1958 & 1959.
62. *Witness*, December 1961.
63. *Witness*, December 1961.

school. These extensions were necessary because school enrolments exceeded 300 children. Bishop Gallagher remarked that 'it was nice to give the Sisters a jubilee present of these comfortable rooms to make their work a little easier'.[64]

A garden party in June was the climax of the year's celebrations. The attendees included thirty-one Josephites, besides numerous old scholars and former teachers, some of whom came from interstate. The high point of this day's festivities was the blessing and installation of a life-sized statue of St Joseph in the convent grounds. After this, the schoolchildren performed 'several entertaining items' for their guests.[65]

Terowie, which was part of the Jamestown parish when the Sisters went there in 1911, joined the Peterborough parish in 1949. During the 1940s and 1950s, which were busy years for the northern railways, the population of this town increased to over 2,000 and a significant proportion of these people were Catholics. They loved their Sisters and celebrated the golden jubilee of their arrival with an anniversary ball in the Institute on Friday, 9 June 1961. On the following day, they held a back to school function followed by a social and on the Sunday, a special Jubilee Mass, followed by a barbeque at the home of one of the parishioners.[66] All events were well attended, even though the people were aware that the future of their town was under a cloud.

In fact, planning for the extension of the broad gauge railway line to Peterborough was underway. By late 1966 it was in use. The busy railway transshipment hub closed. Many families moved away and, as might have been expected, took their children with them. Consequently, school enrolments declined markedly and it fell to the few remaining families to farewell Sisters Leonard Moyse and Gertrude Ryan as they closed the convent and school for the last time and caught the train for Adelaide.

There was also movement in the Archdiocese. To begin, in January 1957, Sisters Dominica Tunbridge, Benedict Hansberry, and Adrian (Pamela) Patterson made a foundation at Yorketown on

---

64. SC 15 March 1957, 2.
65. Peterborough Catholic Centenary Committee, *The Catholic Story of Peterborough* (Peterborough, 1976).
66. Existing records do not give these people's names.

Southern Yorke Peninsula. Their purpose built convent housed up to three Sisters and ten primary school aged girl boarders from outlying districts. Sisters continued teaching at Yorketown until 2001.

By 1960, enrolments at Sevenhill in the Clare Valley were declining and the local convent, which had been the Sisters' home since the 1880s, was inconvenient and lacking in modern facilities. Sisters Verona Quinn and Cecily Gleeson closed the convent at the end of 1960, when Verona moved to Clare from where she managed the Sevenhill School for a further three years. By the end of 1963, when enrolments reached an all-time low of eighteen, she closed it, knowing that these young people would transfer to the Josephite school in Clare for the following year.

During 1959 the Largs Bay Orphanage acquired a purpose built chapel. According to the *Southern Cross:*

> A pleasing addition to the shoreline at Largs Bay came into use when the Archbishop of Adelaide blessed and opened the new chapel at St Joseph's Home for Children. The opening was attended by several hundred visitors.[67]
>
> [In addition], three very modern ablution blocks [had replaced] ancient demolished ones. In short, the remainder of this fine large institution, renovated, repaired and painted, now [looked] out to sea with a quiet, satisfied air of self-respect and graceful complacency.[68]

Prior to this, Sisters and children crowded into one of the convent rooms for Sunday Mass. Space was at a premium in this poorly ventilated space, where it was very uncomfortable during hot weather.

An account of the Largs Bay opening formed but one small part of Sister Vincent Ferrer's report to the Josephite General Chapter of 1959. She also informed the Chapter that there were 265 professed Sisters in the Province, living in forty-five convents and teaching in fifty-four schools. Since 1953, and thanks to the influx of migrant children, school enrolments had doubled to 7,963 pupils. In addition, the Adelaide Hills and Barossa Valley motor missioners were instructing 750 state school children every week.

---

67. *SC* 30 January 1959, 1.
68. Sister Vincent Ferrer Dolan, Province Report, Josephite General Chapter, 1959.

Since her arrival in South Australia in 1953, the Sisters had established four new convents and schools, (three in the Port Pirie diocese and one in the Adelaide archdiocese), while the convents and schools at Quorn and Mintaro were closed because of lack of pupils. (Each had twenty-three attendees at the time of closure.) Besides this, each year the Sisters had conducted at least nine summer or vacation schools during the May, September and Christmas school holidays, with an overall attendance of approximately 500 children. Several Sisters were training the 300 lay catechists engaged in RE in metropolitan state schools. Sisters from the Kensington community were carrying on an important tradition begun by Mary MacKillop and Father Julian Woods, namely, the visitation of the Royal Adelaide Hospital and the prisons.

The Sisters in the Kensington community were enjoying upgraded facilities. St Joseph's High School at Bridge Street, Kensington, previously known at St Joseph's Higher Primary School, now boasted a new science block. The Sisters at the Seminary were enjoying their convent. (The Congregation built and paid for it during 1958.) Sister Vincent Ferrer noted that it was a 'simple, sufficiently roomy, well-appointed place and a decided contrast to the quarters they had patiently endured for years'. What she did not say was that, for the previous sixteen years, these Sisters had resided in a small, poorly set up section of one of the balconies on the Seminary building, while working long hours in the service of the professors and students based there.

Problems regarding the dispersal of smoke from the smoke stack at the Fullarton laundry had been overcome, thanks to the installation of a newly invented smoke arrestor. Fifty-seven mostly elderly women were in residence at the Providence at Cowandilla, and a government subsidy had helped pay for an additional up to date residential wing on that site. Because the number of girls at the Juniorate at Aldgate had increased to twenty-three, the Sisters had erected a new schoolroom and recreation hall for their use.

At the Chapter, Sister Adrian Ryan, formerly of Victoria, became Mother General in place of Mother Leone Ryan who had served in this role for the previous twelve years. Sister Vianney Finnegan from New South Wales became Provincial of South Australia.[69] Among

---

69. Despite their having the same family name, these two Sisters were not related.

important Chapter decisions was one that allowed Sisters working in Home Science schools, kitchens, infirmaries and charitable institutions to wear white habits instead of the heavier, regulation brown ones.

Another even more important change was that Sisters might now recite their regular community prayers (such as the Rosary) in English instead of Latin, and could replace many of their traditional prayers with the Short Breviary or Prayer of the Church (also to be recited in English). In larger communities it had long been a tradition for the Sisters to go in procession from their refectory to the chapel, all the while reciting the psalm *De Profundis* and other set prayers, all in Latin. This was generally referred to as the 'Grace Train' and there were few regrets when it became a casualty of the 1959 Chapter.[70]

Most Sisters readily accepted these changes, which marked a shift towards liturgical and scriptural prayer. In fact, as alterations were made to the liturgy and the teaching of RI in schools, Sisters longed for prayers that were easily understandable and could be prayed with meaning. The dialogue Mass was introduced during the late 1950s and congregational singing was becoming popular.[71] As a consequence, Sisters no longer needed to spend hours tutoring ten-year-old boys in the correct pronunciation of the Latin responses to the Mass prayers. Even before the bishops set out for Vatican II in 1962, priests celebrating Mass began reciting the readings of the day in English.

Sister Vianney Finnegan arrived in Adelaide in April 1959. One of her first public appearances was at the opening of a new building at St Joseph's School, Tranmere in January 1960. This brick structure, which consisted of four classrooms, was built according to the latest educational standards, including 'the use of colour and appropriate insulation'. It replaced the old army hut that had accommodated

---

70. Minutes of the Sixteenth General Chapter of the Sisters of St Joseph, March 1959. Psalm 130 (129 in the Vulgate), generally known as the *De Profundis*, takes its name from the first two words of the psalm in Latin. It is a penitential psalm that is sung or recited as part of Vespers (the Evening Prayer of the Church) and in commemorations of the dead.
71. The term 'Dialogue Mass' was used to describe a Mass where all members of the congregation joined in the responses to the Mass prayers which had previously been said by the young boys who acted as altar servers.

most of the 240 children enrolled at the school each year since the late 1940s. Parish priest, Father Martin Comey, purchased this hut immediately after the war, and subsequently he and several parishioners spent many hours preparing it for parish and school use.[72]

At Jamestown, Sisters and children still occupied the school building erected by Father Aloysius Kreissl SJ in 1885. It was overcrowded and lacked many of the facilities available in modern times. Therefore during 1960, the parish priest had it demolished and replaced it with a building comprising three large, airy classrooms, a separate library, and an enclosed verandah along its full length.

While building work was in progress, Sisters Columba McNamara and Luke (Maureen) Colbert and the children moved to the St James Parish Hall where they managed for several months in less than ideal conditions, all the while looking forward to working in their new school.[73] Sadly for them, it was their successors, Sisters Anselm Brenn von Bronnen and Patrick Fitzpatrick who had that privilege. When the new school opened ninety-nine children enrolled and numbers increased to more than 110 during the following decade.

In May 1962, the Sisters of the Kensington community farewelled eighty-one year old Sister Ethelreda Clark, who met Mary MacKillop when the latter visited Adelaide in 1905. Ethelreda worked as a teacher for most of her active life. Then, in her later years, she became a highly respected prison visitor. Like Mary MacKillop before her, she spent many hours with men condemned to death and their families. Several of her protégés had their sentences reduced for good behaviour and, thanks to her influence, they did well in later life.[74]

In many places, increasing school enrolments and the overcrowding of classrooms put pressure on parishes to extend existing buildings or provide new ones. Such was the case at Thebarton where, in February 1961, the Sisters and their 406 pupils

---

72. SC 29 January 1960, 7.
73. SC 10 June 1960, 4.
74. Sister Ethelreda (Mary Ellen) Clark was born at Ballarat in 1881, joined the Josephites in Adelaide in 1903, was professed at Kensington in 1905 and served in South Australia until her death on 12 May 1962.

moved into a new classroom block facing Kintore Avenue. Enrolments at this school reached the all-time peak of 446 in 1964. All concerned appreciated the new building, but there was a problem.

Traffic controllers noticed that the spire on the nearby Queen of Angels Church provided a landmark for incoming planes on their approach to the Adelaide Airport, which opened in 1955. Consequently, the school was under the flight path and the noise was so bad whenever a plane flew overhead that it was almost impossible for the Sisters and children to hear each other. Teachers dictating shorthand, where accurate timing was paramount, used stopwatches. They paused until the noise ceased and then set their watches again and carried on from where they had stopped.

While the Thebarton Sisters were seeking ways of overcoming noise interference in their school, others were taking charge of one or other of the several new schools opened during the 1960s. The first of these, on Portrush Road, Payneham, opened in 1962. In that year, Sister David (Marie) Marron and a postulant had charge of eighty-three junior primary children, mostly of Italian background. The parents enrolled their children with the understanding that they would be able to complete their primary education at this school.

In the following year, the parish priest of Croydon asked for Sisters for a school at the Mansfield Park end of his parish. Sisters Francis Clare Kenny and Berchmans McMurray began teaching there with an enrolment of fifty-three children. They lived at the Woodville Park convent and travelled to the school in Dudley Street by public transport or by taxi, as the weather dictated.

St Joseph's, Campbelltown, now (2014) known as St Francis of Assisi School, Newton, opened adjacent to the St Francis of Assisi Church in 1965. This was a developing area that was settled mainly by Italian market gardeners, although there were also a number of other young families living in the area. Sister Perpetua Hayes, the founding school principal, was assisted by a young postulant. As was the case at Payneham, the school opened with junior grades only, and gradually built up until it catered for all primary year levels. The initial enrolment was forty children and, as numbers increased, the Sisters engaged lay teachers for some classes.

These openings were counterbalanced by the closure of the Port Adelaide and Russell Street (city) schools in the mid-1960s. Both lost pupils because builders were demolishing the cottages that residents used to call home to make way for industrial developments. For many years, Russell Street had more than 300 pupils but by 1965, numbers had fallen to fifty-six with few prospects for future expansion. At Port Adelaide, enrolments also decreased at a rapid rate with predictions for the future indicating that this trend was unlikely to change.[75]

During August 1962, Archbishop Beovich visited the Hutt Street Meal Centre, run by the Daughters of Charity, to open the Edwards Hall, a facility for homeless people named in honour of Bert Edwards.[76] He spoke of the current shortage of teachers in Catholic schools, and concluded his address by announcing one possible small solution to this problem, namely that:

> The Sisters of St Joseph, who provide teachers in a big proportion of our parochial schools, have made an arrangement with the Daughters of Charity of St Vincent de Paul, whereby the Daughters of Charity will take over the management of the Fullarton Refuge next year. This will ease the teaching position in the schools of the Sisters of St Joseph . . . It will permit the Sisters of St Joseph to consolidate their schools and motor missions.[77]

The fact of the matter was that the Sisters were so overstretched by the demands of their schools and motor missions that they could no longer spare any younger Sisters to replace their sick or ageing peers at the Refuge. These Sisters moved out in November 1963, and the newcomers accepted a work that was rooted in the very foundation of the Congregation. One wonders whether the Sisters of the 1960s were aware that the Refuge was the first charitable institution established by their founders and that it had opened

---

75. ASSJ, Kensington.
76. Hutt Street is in the city of Adelaide.
77. *SC* 10 August 1962. Edwards, who was still alive at the time, may well have been present on this occasion. He died just over twelve months later, on 3 August 1963.

its doors ninety-six years earlier, just four months after Mary MacKillop's arrival in Adelaide.[78]

At the end of 1963, the Sisters withdrew from Berri where the Daughters of Charity had established St Catherine's Home for the Aged two years earlier. Since it was deemed superfluous to have members of two religious orders working in such a small district, the Daughters (not a teaching Order) took charge of the school in addition to St Catherine's.[79] They continued in this role until the end of 1970, when they could no longer staff the school. The Josephites returned in 1971.

Easter Sunday 1963 is remembered well by anyone who was at Mass in the Pinnaroo Catholic Church for, on that day, the nearby wood and iron convent burnt to the ground. While the celebrant was proclaiming his Easter sermon, and much to their horror, some of the ladies in the church were distracted by the sight of clouds of smoke billowing from the convent and raised the alarm. Sister Maura Purcell, who was too ill to attend Mass, was at home. One of the women rushed to her aid and some men carried her from the building before it was totally engulfed in flames. Sister was saved but nothing could stop the inferno. Soon the convent was no more than a pile of ashes and twisted sheets of iron. Sister Maura's two companions, Sisters Genevieve Brace and Anthony Paul (Pauline) Schutze stood by in shock as they tried to comprehend the enormity of what had happened.

Many people, Catholic and non-Catholic alike, sprang to the aid of these now homeless women. The parish priest offered them his presbytery for the time being, and the manager of Ryan's Hotel in the Main Street gave him the use of one of his guest rooms for as long as it would take to rebuild the convent. The Eudunda Farmers' General Store opened up to allow the ladies to collect basic items of clothing and food for the three Sisters. Late that night two Josephites arrived from Adelaide with new habits and other necessities for them.

Almost at once, the Catholic community began collecting money for another convent, even though they had not fully paid off the new school building on its eastern flank. They were mightily relieved

---

78. *SC* 8 November 1963, 1.
79. ASSJ, Kensington.

to find that this structure was undamaged. Plans for its blessing and opening in early May 1963 went ahead. All were delighted when Bishop James Gleeson of Adelaide attended the event and praised them for their generosity and resilience at such a trying time.[80]

He was at Pinnaroo again on the last Sunday of August, this time to bless and open the Sisters' new home, a simple house with four small bedrooms, built on the site of the old convent. As already noted, the Sisters lost everything in the fire. Thanks to the generosity of the people and the shopkeepers of the town, and also several city department stores, the new convent was furnished in record time. On opening day, Rev GH Cooling, on behalf of the congregation of All Saints' Anglican Church, presented his Catholic counterpart with a new ciborium for the convent.[81] After the fire, he chided his priest friend for having put on the most spectacular Paschal fire in the district![82]

Meanwhile, Bishop Gleeson also took part in the blessing and opening of extensions to St Joseph's Convent, Hindmarsh, where the Sisters' accommodation was overcrowded. He encouraged the people to make generous donations towards the cost because the Sisters who lived there were teaching more than 700 of their children in the Hindmarsh and Flinders Park Schools.[83]

Archbishop Beovich was unavailable for this function because he, along with most of his fellow bishops from around the world, was attending the second session of Vatican II, which began in Rome during the previous year. As it happened, the archbishop attended all four sessions of the Council while Archbishop Gleeson, who remained at home for the first three, was present for only the final session. (By then he was Coadjutor Archbishop.) He had much to do in Beovich's absence and so called upon Monsignor Redden

---

80. *SC* 19 April 1963, 1, and 3 May 1963, 3. Auxiliary Bishop James Gleeson was born in 1920 at Balaklava in the Lower North region of South Australia. He was ordained a priest in 1945, became auxiliary to Beovich in 1957, Coadjutor Archbishop with right of succession in 1964, and Archbishop of Adelaide in May 1971 when his predecessor retired. Gleeson retired because of ill health in 1985 and died on 21 March 2000, aged seventy-nine years.
81. *SC* 6 September 1963, 1.
82. *SC* 6 September 1963, 1.
83. *SC* 6 September 1963, 16.

of Mount Gambier to officiate at the foundation stone ceremony for school extensions and a new two storey convent at Murray Bridge.[84]

St Joseph's High School at Bridge Street, Kensington, had been overcrowded for some years. Then, in 1962, the Sisters gained possession of a row of cottages on Phillips Street, facing the back fence of the convent property. On this land, they erected a two storey school building which was ready for occupation during the second term of 1963. It was an exciting time for Sisters and students as they transferred there from Bridge Street. Mother Adrian Ryan, Sister Vianney Finnegan and the High School principal, Sister Oliver Gleeson, were present at its opening. Several years later, the Sisters and the school community renamed it 'Mary MacKillop College'.[85]

During the post war years, Sisters in charge of secondary classes found it increasingly difficult to keep up to date with changing curriculum requirements, especially when it came to the teaching of Science. When Julian Woods and Mary MacKillop founded the Congregation in 1866, a high proportion of the population was illiterate and all that parents asked was that their children learn basic literacy skills.

With Mary's help, the Sisters of that era kept one lesson ahead of their pupils until they mastered the curriculum and could carry on without her supervision. With each succeeding generation, however, parental expectations became greater and many of the Sisters of those generations succeeded, as their Josephite predecessors had done, by keeping one lesson ahead of their students. The situation improved when the novitiate moved to Sydney in 1941, for after that most young Josephites did their teacher training in North Sydney. By the 1960s, however, even that was not enough.

The reason for this change was that by now, many workingmen's children were finishing high school, and the government was requiring that all teachers of senior secondary classes be suitably qualified, in other words, that they have appropriate tertiary degrees. The Sisters' only alternative was to undertake such studies. Therefore, in 1963, six Josephites enrolled at Adelaide University to study a variety of subjects related to their teaching. All studied part time,

---

84. *SC* 9 September 1964, 2.
85. *SC* 24 May 1963, 8.

balancing university work with lesson preparation and other school activities.

While these Sisters were nervous when they first entered the lecture halls at the University in their brown Josephite habits, their coming scarcely caused a ripple on the campus. Sisters from other religious congregations had been attending Adelaide University since the early 1930s and had a reputation for being committed students. These Josephites had a similar attitude towards study and did well. Professor LF Neal, the head of the University's Department of Education, commended their attitude towards study, and remarked on the consistent number of religious Sisters and Brothers who participated in refresher courses for teachers.[86]

Science teaching was not the only area of concern for teachers during the late 1950s and early 1960s. Major changes were occurring in the areas of Religious Instruction, curriculum and methodology. The better to deal with these changes, teachers of religion from all religious congregations in South Australia invited all involved in Catholic schools to attend a series of workshops and lecture programmes given by eminent overseas and local theologians and teachers. Among these were Jesuit educator, Johannes Hofinger, and Scripture scholar, Alexander Jones who stressed the importance of educators using a Christocentric or kerygmatic approach to the teaching of religion, always emphasising the loving Christ of the Gospels rather than the dry dogma of the catechism.[87]

One outcome of these lecture programmes was that Josephite Sisters came into contact with members of other religious orders, in some instances, for the first time. Some found this a traumatic experience for, during their novitiate training they learnt that:

---

86. *SC* 15 May 1964, 10.
87. Mary R Clark, *Loreto in Australia* (Sydney: UNSW Press, Sydney), 198. Johannes Hofinger SJ (1905–1984) was a Roman Catholic religious educator. He was born in Austria on March 21, 1905. Between 1953 and 1970, he had a great impact on Catholic liturgy, religious education and missiology in Asia, the Pacific Islands, Europe, the United States, Australia and South America... After a distinguished career as a seminary professor, international conference organiser, lecturer, workshop leader, popular writer and diocesan religious education leader, Hofinger died in New Orleans, USA, on 14 February 1984. *http://www.talbot. edu/ce20/educators/Catholic/johannes_hofinger/*

> [Sisters of St Joseph] must be poor, humble, and consider themselves the least among all religious orders, studying to keep themselves and their lives hidden in God as the life of St. Joseph was. They must give place and preference to the religious of every other Order, and their highest ambition must be to remain unknown and poor.[88]

At gatherings of religion teachers they sat at the back of the hall and were fearful of mixing with women who, in their eyes, were much superior to themselves. Over time the barriers broke down, and the Josephites came to enjoy the challenge of new ideas. Another breaker of barriers, whether real or imaginary, between members of the different religious congregations, was the Christian Education Association (CEA). This society of teachers from all Catholic schools and colleges in the Adelaide archdiocese came into being during 1964.

Initially, teachers met to compare notes, prepare lessons together, and so on. As the Association became more firmly established, it invited notable theologians, psychologists and teachers from interstate and overseas to address the group. Visiting speakers included, among others, Passionist priests Barnabas Ahern (from the United States), Augustine Fitzsimons, and Jerome Crowe, Jesuits William Dalton and Kevin Penry, Redemptorist Kevin O'Shea, and Christian Brother Gerald Faulkner.

Sister Mary Cronin, an experienced teacher, commented on the excitement that was in the air during this era. She said:

> An energetic Archbishop Gleeson placed his trust in us and we responded by showing that we had confidence in him (by becoming involved in the activities mentioned above).[89]

The need for such input became even more necessary after the publication of key documents from Vatican II. Of particular interest to teachers in Catholic schools and members of Religious Orders were the Constitution on the Sacred Liturgy (*Sacrosanctum Concilium*), published in 1963, the Decree on the Appropriate

---

88. Woods, *Rules for the Institute,* Adelaide, 1867, 1, article 1.
89. Interview with Sister Mary Cronin at Kensington, May 2014 (exact date not recorded).

Renewal of Religious Life (*Perfectae Caritatis*), and the Pastoral Constitution on the Church in the Modern World (*Gaudium et Spes*), both of which appeared in 1965.

Over time, some Josephite Sisters held key positions in the CEA, which continued operating until 1979, when, after much thought and prayer, its members closed it down because by then the services it offered were being duplicated elsewhere. As the Sisters gained in self-confidence, some became involved in the Diocesan Life Campaign established by Archbishop Beovich after his return from the Council in 1965. Others were active members of Christian Life Movement (CLM) groups in their local parishes.

The schools were not the only areas where change occurred. Back at Kensington, Sister Vianney noticed that most of the senior Sisters living there occupied share rooms with little privacy. As soon as practicable, therefore, she arranged for the erection (at the northern end of the property) of a building where the oldest and frailest Sisters could spend their final years. An immediate result of her decision was the clearing of the plantation of the trees that had stood there for the past seventy years.

The long-term benefit of this seemingly drastic action was that the Sisters had a modern, two storey building with twenty-four single rooms, a sizeable kitchen and dining room, and a chapel with a spectacular wall of stained glass windows.[90] It was completed by the end of 1965 but was not used for its main purpose until 1972. The Sisters named it 'Tappeiner Court' to honour the memory of Father Joseph Tappeiner SJ, who did so much to support Mary MacKillop and the Sisters during the Congregation's foundation years.[91]

Sister Vianney's term of office expired at the time of the 1965 General Chapter. Since she knew and understood the as yet unfinished Tappeiner Court building project, however, she was given an extension of time in South Australia and so was back in Adelaide until January 1966. Her task completed, she left by plane at the end of that month, accompanied by ten young postulants who were on their way to Sydney to begin their training as Josephites.[92] Sister Vianney's replacement was Sister Marie Paul Harford, who arrived

---

90. See Chapter Five, fn. 105, for details of the plantation.
91. SA Province Report, 1965 General Chapter.
92. *SC*, 4 February 1966, 3.

in time to be caught up in the arrangements for the forthcoming Josephite centenary celebrations.

Mother Adrian Ryan was elected Mother General for a second term during the Chapter, and at its conclusion she chose South Australian Sister Martin (Lorna) Bourke to be Provincial of Western Australia. The Chapter Sisters approved some minor changes to the Sisters religious habit, their daily timetable and times for community prayers. They also released detailed guidelines regarding the watching of television as the TV was becoming a regular feature in convents. A very important decision was that Irish Sisters be given an opportunity to visit their homeland. (When these Sisters came to Australia to join the Josephites, they did so with the understanding that they would never go home again.) Almost at once, Mother Adrian offered a trip to her homeland to every Irish Sister who had spent forty or more years in Australia. The first contingent from South Australia went home during 1968.

When Sister Marie Paul arrived in Adelaide she found, hidden within the Kensington convent complex, a little publicised Josephite work with a wide impact on the Church in South Australia and the Northern Territory. It was the making and distribution of communion wafers, or 'altar breads', as the Sisters called them. Sisters had been doing this work for local parishes continuously since their move to Kensington in 1872 and had always managed to keep supply ahead of demand.

During the 1960s, when the Church ruled that people needed to fast for only one hour before receiving Communion, the number of communicants increased significantly and so did the demand for altar breads. Consequently, Sisters Cecilia Joseph Maloney, Maria Goretti (Anne) Fitzgerald and Laura La Franki worked full time at this highly specialised task in a dedicated section of the convent. They used custom made machinery to bake layers of wafer thin unleavened bread, cut them to the required shapes and sizes, and have them packed and posted in time to reach their destinations for weekend Masses. They made 1.5 million communion wafers during 1956. In 1964 they supplied 2.6 million, that is approximately 50,000 a week, to 125 parishes across South Australia and the Northern Territory.[93]

During 1970, Sister Anne Fitzgerald explained something of the history of altar bread making at Kensington when she wrote:

---

93. *SC* 14 May 1965, 10, and 16 December 1967, 12.

> In Mother Mary's time the breads were baked between long handled plates, something like waffle irons, which were held over an open fire . . . in a lean-to shed in the back yard of the convent. Later, gas cookers were used until two electric bakers came into use [in about 1950]. Bigger electric bakers were imported from America . . . and Holland . . . together with corresponding electric cutters [during succeeding years].[94]

With time, further changes occurred and by 1994, the Sisters were unable to continue making and/or distributing altar breads. One reason for their closing down was that they found it impossible to have their costly equipment either repaired or replaced. Another was the lack of Sisters able to do this heavy physical work.

During the 1960s, the Congregation undertook a ministry that was close to Mary MacKillop's heart. It sent Sisters to open mission schools in the remote Kimberley region of Western Australia, where the majority of the students were Aboriginal. The first to go there were Sisters Maureen Joseph Meaney of Adelaide and Feargal (Margaret) Lambert of New South Wales who opened a mission school at Wyndham on the far northwest coast in 1963. Four years later Feargal returned to Sydney, two other Sisters from the eastern states went to Wyndham, and Maureen moved forty kilometres south to Kununurra on the Ord River, where Sister Angela Morrison, also from Adelaide, joined her.[95] Maureen served on the mission for six years, returning to Adelaide at the end of 1969, while Angela remained at Kununurra until 1978.

In South Australia, Aboriginal Reserves had been under the control of different religious denominations since the arrival of white settlers in 1836. None of these was Catholic, and it was generally understood that members of the denominations concerned had exclusive access to the reserves. Through contact with Aboriginal families who did not live at the Davenport Aboriginal Reserve near Port Augusta, the motor mission Sisters found that they could visit the people residing there. Therefore, by mid-1968, Sister Antoinette Williams, who was herself of Aboriginal descent, was calling there

---

94. Sister Anne Fitzgerald (Sister Maria Goretti), 'I make Altar Breads! Aren't I Lucky?' in *The Garland of St Joseph*, May 1970, 109.
95. *SC,* 20 January 1967, 3.

on a regular basis. Over time, and thanks to the Sisters' influence, some of the Davenport families sent their children to the Josephite school in the town.[96] This seemingly small incursion into the field of Aboriginal affairs was but the beginning of more serious Josephite involvement during the 1970s and beyond.

The centenary of the Congregation's foundation fell on 19 March 1966. The Sisters, their pupils, and the wider Church marked this occasion with a variety of activities in both city and country. In early March they took part in a special Centenary Mass in the Cathedral. Almost every Sister resident in South Australia was there, along with as many friends and supporters as the building could accommodate.

A week later, children from metropolitan and nearby country schools came together on the Norwood Oval to form tableaux representing the history of the Congregation. Some of the children, dressed in variously coloured hoods and capes, formed maps of Australia, New Zealand and Ireland. Others moved out from points representing Penola and Adelaide to spots indicating the location of the many interstate and overseas places where the Sisters had ministered since 1866. Colourful floats processed around the oval. Each showed an aspect of Mary MacKillop's, Father Woods' or the Congregation's story, beginning with the first Josephite school at Penola and the first Josephite convent in Adelaide, and continuing up to and including the Sisters' educational, social and missionary works of 1966. Approximately 10,000 people attended this spectacular event.[97]

Where distance precluded people from attending the Adelaide celebrations, they held their own nearer to home. Thus, Bishop Gallagher invited Sisters and representatives of school communities in his diocese to a special Mass and celebration at Peterborough during the following October.[98] Penola received special attention as the birthplace of the Congregation and its Catholic community collected enough money to pay for a new convent for the Sisters! At Pinnaroo the people organised a garden party to which they invited

---

96. *SC* 5 July 1968, 10. Mary Cresp, *God's 'Good Time', Sisters of St Joseph in Ministry with Australian Aboriginal and Torres Strait Islander Peoples* (Hindmarsh, SA: ATF Press, 2013), 24-32.
97. *SC* 25 March 1965.
98. *SC* 4 November 1966, 6.

any Sisters who had lived in the local Josephite community or who had entered from the parish.[99] In early November, Channel Ten's news editor, Mr A Anderson presented to the Sisters a colour film of the Norwood Oval celebrations.[100] (Colour film was still very new and so this was a special gift indeed.)

As the centenary year drew to a close, Sisters Charlotte Dowd and Gabrielle Buckley organised for the transfer of the secondary students from the Mount Carmel parish school on Pennington Terrace, Rosewater (formerly Alberton) to new premises on Newcastle Street, just a few minutes' walk away. When the Marist Brothers, who had run a boys' school in the area since the 1890s, closed it and moved out at the end of 1966, they offered their school buildings and monastery to the Josephites. The outcome was that the Mount Carmel Girls' Secondary School, later known as Mt Carmel College, opened in February 1967, and the Brothers' former house became a Josephite convent.[101]

By 1968 the motor missions were in a flourishing condition. Sisters teaching secondary students, whether in Catholic or state schools, encouraged these young people to join the Young Christian Students' Movement (YCS) and became involved in the running of summer schools for them. On 17 February 1967, motor mission Sisters from several different religious congregations met with Coadjutor Archbishop James Gleeson, a strong supporter of this work, for mutual encouragement and exchange of ideas. The Archbishop was at pains to remind them that the motor missions, which now involved religious Sisters and Brothers in every Australian state, had begun in South Australia a short eleven years earlier.[102]

During the 1960s, major improvements were made to the Jamestown, Georgetown, Hindmarsh and Tranmere convent

---

99. *SC* 25 February 1966, 1; 11 March 1966, 2 & 3; 25 November 1966, 10. The Sisters who entered from the Pinnaroo parish were the Byrne sisters, Rose and Raphael (Elizabeth), and Peter Claver (Marie Therese) Foale.
100. *SC* 18 November 1966, 9.
101. ASSJ, Kensington, Newcastle Street file. By this time that part of the Alberton district where the Catholic school was located had been renamed Rosewater.
102. *SC*, 24 February 1967, 1. Seemingly, Gleeson was unaware of or had forgotten the Missionary Sisters of Service, who were founded by Father John Wallis of Burnie, Tasmania, in the mid-1940s and who travelled widely in the backblocks of Tasmania and on the mainland. The difference between the two was that their main focus was more on the family, while the Josephites concentrated more on the schools.

buildings, while eight parishes built or bought new convents for their Sisters. Besides Murray Bridge, Pinnaroo and Penola, which have already been mentioned, the others were at Hectorville, Kadina, Renmark, Macclesfield and Croydon.

Of particular interest was Macclesfield, where Sisters Gertrude Hayman and Monica Phillips made a Josephite foundation in May 1868. With the passage of time, the interior walls of the convent, which had been the Sisters' home since Monica's and Gertrude's time, were so badly affected by salt damp that the place was deemed uninhabitable. In 1967, therefore, the old building was demolished and replaced with a dwelling similar to the new Pinnaroo convent.[103]

In the September of that same year, the Croydon Sisters received the keys to a substantial two storey convent on Eldon Street at Croydon Park. This building, with its twelve single bedrooms, large chapel and more than adequate living space, was a great improvement on their former convent on Torrens Road.[104]

The Sisters in residence in each of the buildings mentioned above now enjoyed individual bedrooms instead of the customary dormitory accommodation of the past. This change, which was a sign of the times, seems to have been the result of discussions between the Provincial and the parish priests concerned. Another unexpected change occurred in 1968 when the Jamestown people offered electric blankets to their Sisters. The Provincial agreed to the Sisters' having them only because she did not wish to appear ungrateful to the generous donors. Within a few years there were electric blankets on the beds in most convents!

While parish priests and provincials were poring over building plans, Brother Damian CP, was devising ways to bring together food service personnel from religious houses for their mutual benefit. In September 1967 he invited the members of this important but often unrecognised group of religious men and women to his home at the Passionist Monastery, Glen Osmond, where he laid before them his plan to establish a Christian Food Research Centre. Sister Marcella Myers of Kensington represented the Josephite cooks.[105]

On the school front, some Josephite secondary schools had so few students that they could not afford to build up-to-date science

---

103. *SC* 30 June 1967, 6.
104. *SC* 15 September 1967, 3.
105. *SC,* 15 September 1967, 12.

laboratories or libraries. Therefore, by the end of the 1960s, the Sisters ceased teaching secondary classes at Kadina, Murray Bridge, Penola and Renmark. Instead, at all except Murray Bridge, they took RI classes and ran YCS groups in the local state high schools. Another change was that the administrators of the Croydon and Plympton parishes, in each of which there were two parish schools, rationalised their situations by having the upper primary children attend one campus and the junior children the other.

At St Joseph's Providence, Cowandilla, the Sisters had always trusted that God would provide for their needs, even as they undertook constant fundraising activities to help support the place. These Sisters felt great relief when the Commonwealth Government made funding available to non-government organisations such as theirs, for the improvement of their facilities. The first government grants enabled the erection of extra accommodation during the mid-1950s. Several years later, further government funding made possible the building of MacKillop Court, a block of nineteen independent living units for elderly women who were able to care for themselves.

It appeared that registration would be beneficial for the wellbeing of the Home and so, in August 1961, the Sisters applied to the West Torrens Board of Health for official approval to use the Cowandilla premises as a Rest Home for the Aged. (Cowandilla is in the West Torrens Council Area.) The Board approved their application on condition that the Sisters make certain alterations to the buildings and observe the provisions of the Health Act and the Local Government Act in relation to maintenance. In January 1962, the Commonwealth Department of Health acknowledged their licence. From then on the Home was open for inspection by a Commonwealth Medical Officer, and the Sister in charge had to be a fully qualified registered nurse.[106] The first such nurse to fill this role was Sister Maria Goretti Greenslade, who served there from 1962 until 1966.

The number of people seeking admission to the Providence increased over the years, and by 1967 the Sisters were considering further expansion. They put their plans on hold, however, because just then the State Government announced its decision to implement

---

106. Health Act Amendment Act, 1947: Act No. 48 of 1947, South Australian Statutes, 1947, Bray Library, North Terrace, Adelaide.

the so-called MATS Plan (the result of a Metropolitan Adelaide Transport Study authorised in 1964 by the State Premier of the day, Sir Thomas Playford). This plan recommended the building of a new north-south freeway through the western suburbs, and in the process, the swallowing up of hundreds of properties including the Providence.[107]

In these uncertain times the Sisters found it difficult to maintain standards of care. They were unable to obtain sufficient staff, and their residential accommodation was deemed to be substandard. The government indicated that the closure of the place was imminent, that is, unless they made some important changes. At that point, Sister Peter Julian (Brenda) Keary, a skilled nurse, arrived to take charge of the nursing care and Sister Paul Bates became the administrator of the home. That the institution survived this crisis was due in large measure to Brenda's nursing and people skills, Paul's administrative ability, the support of Dr Alan Green from the Department of Health, and last but not least, the fact that the government shelved the MATS Plan in 1970.[108]

In summary, much happened in South Australia between 1947 and 1968. During the 1950s and early 1960s, the Sisters accepted responsibility for a number of newly opened convents, schools and motor missions in metropolitan and country areas. They withdrew from the Fullarton Refuge because of their inability to continue staffing it and closed eight schools because of declining enrolments. (The last of these was at Dulwich which closed in 1968.) St Joseph's Orphanage at Largs Bay underwent significant alterations and once again became home to small girls as well as boys. At Cowandilla, the Providence Sisters were caring for fifty-three elderly women, and were hoping and praying for survival in a seemingly hostile environment. Mary MacKillop College, Kensington had five new classrooms, with new science laboratories and a library at the planning stage.

---

107. *SC* 10 November 1967 and 5 January 1968.
108. Sr Brenda Keary, interview and written report, March 2014. Brenda served at Cowandilla for the ten years, 1968–1977, while Sr Paul was administrator there during 1970 and 1971. See Marie T Foale, *Providence: 125 Years of Aged Care, 1868–1993*, passim. (Sisters of St Joseph Aged Care Services, 1993), for a full account of the history of the Providence.

There were 258 professed Sisters living in forty convents between Port Augusta in the north and Nangwarry in the south, Port Lincoln in the west and Renmark in the east. In their schools, the Sisters were educating 5,800 primary aged children and more than 900 secondary students with the assistance of sixty-nine lay teachers. Nine motor missions were reaching almost 9,000 children. Twenty-two music teachers were giving lessons to almost 1,000 young people in Josephite music centres across the state.

There were no lay teachers in the schools when Sister Vincent Ferrer gave her report to the General Chapter of 1959. Since then, the number of Sisters had fallen by seven; they were living in five fewer convents and teaching 1,311 fewer pupils. What turned out to be a progressive and irreversible decline in the membership of the South Australian province had begun, although at this point it was almost imperceptible. All that happened during the years 1948–1967 was against a background of ever-increasing change. Then, as the sixties neared their end, the challenge to Religious Sisters to adapt and renew their lives became louder and more imperative.

In January 1965 (some months before the release of *Perfectae Caritatis* (the Vatican Council's Decree on the Adaptation and Renewal of Religious Life) the Apostolic Delegate, Archbishop D Enrici, invited the leaders of all religious communities of women in Australia to attend a special congress in Perth where he challenged them to adapt to modern life. He stressed the importance of any upcoming Council documents relating to religious life and challenged them to ask what their founders would be likely to do in the current circumstances, what changes would guarantee peace within religious communities, and what needed to be done to attract more vocations. He warned the leaders to make sure that any adaptations they made were in line with the special aims and spirit of their particular congregations.[109]

Enrici forewarned Congregational leaders to be ready for inevitable and irreversible change. When *Perfectae Caritatis* became public in October 1965, it challenged all members of religious congregations

> to return to the sources of the whole of Christian life, and the primitive inspiration of the institutes, and to adapt to the changed conditions of the time.[110]

---

109. *SC* 22 January 1965, 1.
110. Austin Flannery, OP, editor *Vatican Council II: The Conciliar and Post Conciliar Documents* (1975), 612, #2.

That was one mighty task, and in the year 1967 it was just beginning. The implementation of the Council decrees relating to religious life lay in the future. Few of the current members of the Congregation could have imagined what the execution of those decrees might mean for them.

Sr Ethelreda Clark, the Prisoners' Friend, 1954

Sr Zita Buckley packing Altar Breads at Kensington, 1980s

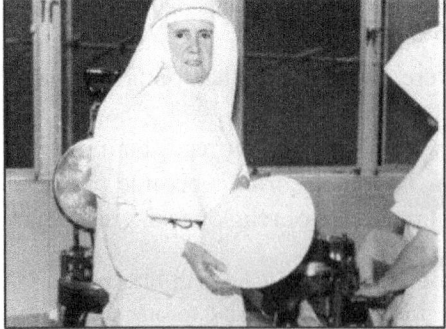

Sr Cecilia Joseph Maloney in the Altar Bread room at the Kensington convent. She is holding a large round communion wafer that is ready to be cut into ten large hosts for use at Mass. Partly hidden is Sr Anne Fitzgerald

Sr Patrice Burns, the first Motor Missioner, with Sr Dorothy McMahon before 1953

Sr Jude Dundon on her graduation day, late 1960s

Sr Margaret Atkins on her profession day in 1958

Sr Flavia Sheedy, Sr Melita's companion at Gleneagles (Seaton)

The McNamara sisters at Aldgate, late 1950s.
Standing: *Srs Tarcisius and Francis*
Seated: *Sr Raymond, their sister who belonged to the Our Lady of the Sacred Heart Congregation, and Sr Columba.*

Sisters outside St Peter Claver's School, Dulwich, 1955.
Standing: *Srs Peter Claver (Marie Foale), Andrina Connolly.*
Seated: *Srs Miriam McLaughlin, Imelda McLean, Benedetta Murphy*

Sr Joan (Raymond) Mangan teaching out of the car boot at the Wanbi State School, 1960s.

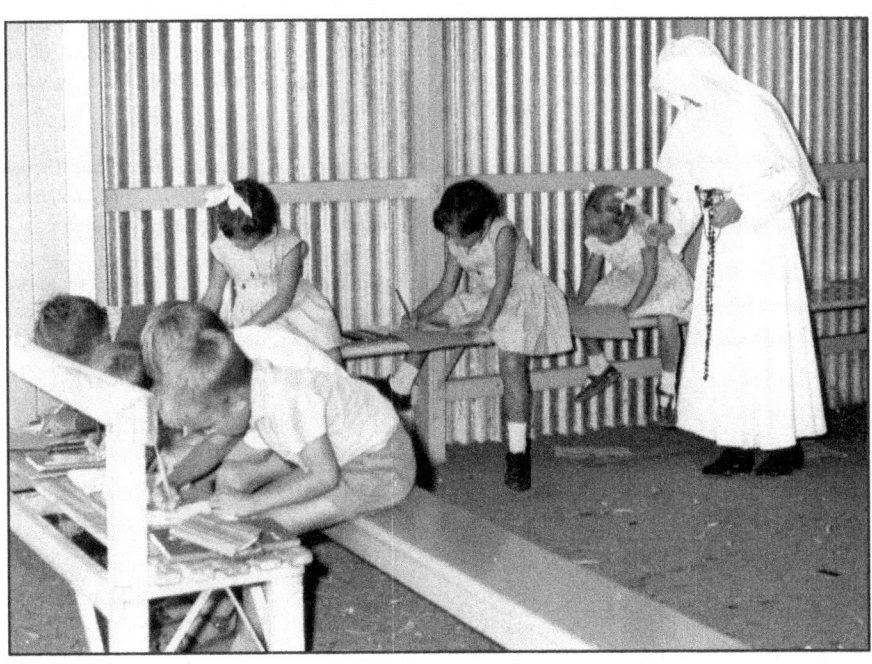

Sr Genevieve (Denis) Ryan teaching RI in the children's shelter shed at the Wanbi State School.

Diamond Jubilee of the arrival of the Sisters of St Joseph in Peterborough, 16 June 1957.
Back row: Srs Maurice Roche, Carmelita Thompson, Lucille (Teresa) McNamara, Marie Therese (Joan) Barry, Anthony (Patricia) O'Dea, Tressa (Nora) Kerin, Joan Dundon, Sylvanus Enright, Desmond Cormack [partly hidden].

Middle Row: Srs Luigi (Joan) Bunfield, Edwin (Marie) Taylor, Pauline Conroy, Julie Therese Quinn, Bernardine Hansberry, Vincent Barry, Rita Brosnahan, David Dowd, Gertrude Dickinson, Mildred Joseph Nejaim, Gregory (Geraldine) Stringer, Angela Mary Tonkin

Front Row: Srs Paschal Maher, Lucy Healy, Paula Patton, Loretto Hanlon, Irene Roche, Vincent Ferrer Dolan (Provincial), Oliver Gleeson, Columba McNamara, Martina Farissey, Sebastian Lee.

Part 3
Return to the Charism of the Founders

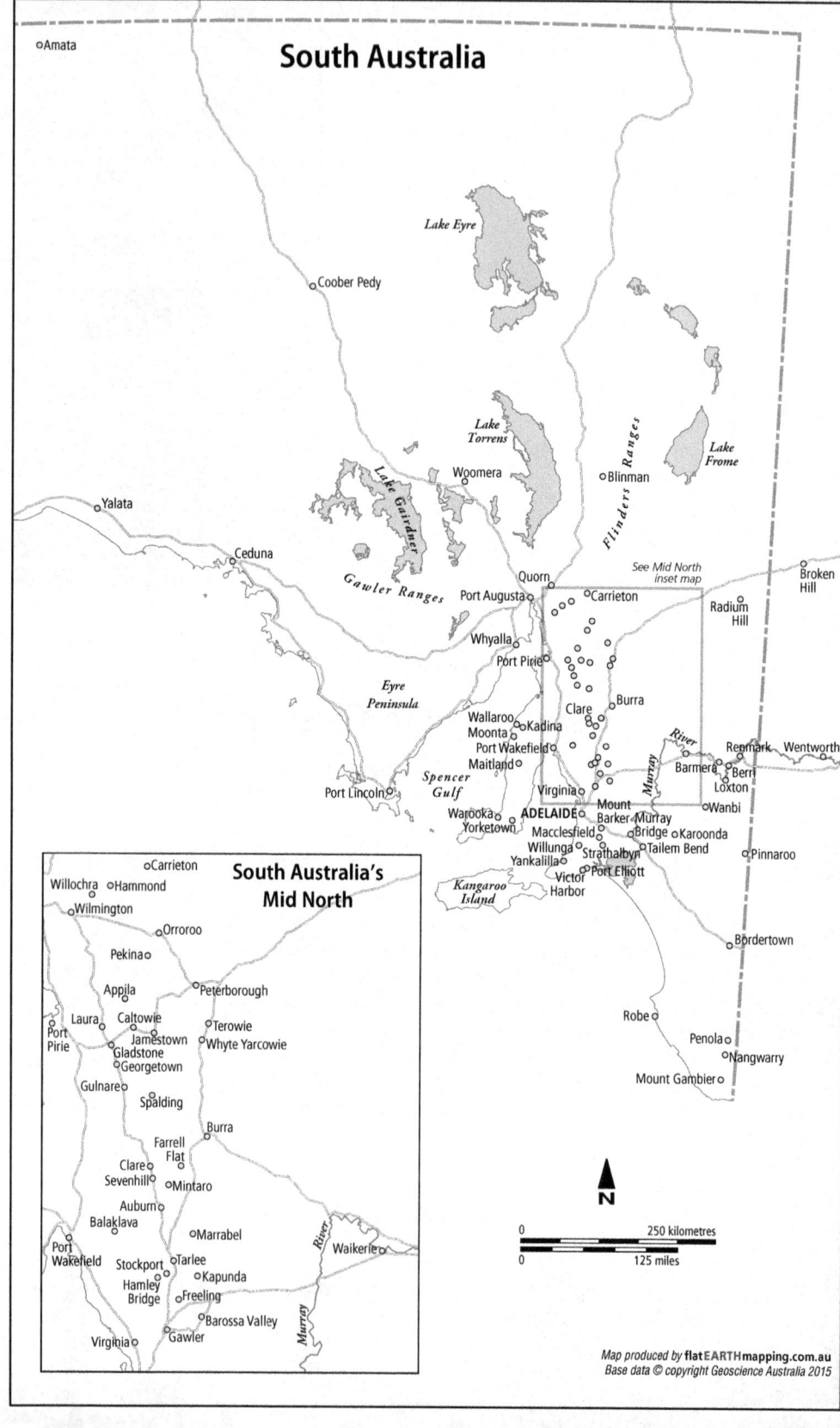

Chapter Eight
Adaption and Renewal: 1968–2010

'Adapt', 'renew', 'update', 'change', 'charism', 'spirit of the founders', 'signs of the times', 'delegation', 'subsidiarity', 'accountability'! These are some of the buzzwords being tossed around in Catholic religious orders and congregations in the watershed years immediately after Vatican II.

All the Council documents were published by the end of 1966. Of particular interest to Religious were the Decree on the Adaptation and Renewal of the Religious Life, *Perfectae Caritatis* (October 1965), and Pope Paul VI's Apostolic Letter, *Ecclesiae Sanctae* (August 1966),[1] with its norms for the implementation of the decree.[2] These documents challenged religious Sisters and Brothers to return to the Gospel and to the spirit and aims of their founders, and to commence a period of adaptation and renewal according to the conditions of their time. As a beginning, all religious congregations across the world were to hold Special General Chapters within three years of the promulgation of *Perfectae Caritatis*.

For the Josephites, this meant revisiting the life stories of their founders and the founding Sisters of the late nineteenth century and, like them, reflecting on what it meant to be a Sister of St Joseph. Those founding women discerned how to be Sisters in the

---

1. *Perfectae Caritatis (Of Perfect Charity)*, promulgated on 28 October 1965, was one of the most influential documents to come out of the Council. See *The Documents of Vatican II*, edited by Walter M Abbott, SJ (London: Geoffrey Chapman, 1966), 466-82.
2. A widely used translation of Paul VI's instructions appeared in 1975 as 'Norms for Implementing the Decree for the Up-to-date Renewal of Religious Life', in Austin Flannery, OP, editor, *Vatican Council II: The Conciliar and Post Conciliar Documents* (Leominster: Fowler Wright, 1975), 625 *et seq.*

Australian colonies and New Zealand. All, including Mary MacKillop herself, relied on the spiritual guidance of Father Woods and, after his departure, benefitted from that of other wise priests, especially Father Joseph Tappeiner SJ. They were women of their times, aware of the toughness of colonial living, the lack of educational opportunities for the poor and the dearth of priests to minister to people in isolated settlements. Those nineteenth-century Australian Sisters faced many crises as they formed a Religious Congregation that has thrived in their country and beyond.[3] While overseas in 1873, Mary MacKillop told of life in the colonies, prefacing her remarks with the comment:

> It is an Australian who writes this, one brought up in the midst of many of the evils she tries to describe.[4]

After Mary's death the Sisters used her 'Rules for the General Guidance of the Sisters' in conjunction with the Constitutions and, as far as possible, lived according to her spirit, as defined in those rules and the lived traditions of the Congregation.

As already noted, the promulgation of the newly edited Code of Canon Law by the Church in 1917 and the subsequent revision of the Josephite Constitutions caused some Sisters to develop a tendency towards legalism while some of those in leadership became exacting and inflexible in their dealings with individual Sisters. The call of Vatican II was to go back beyond the Code to the Congregation's founding stories and rediscover its founding spirit.

The world of the 1970s was a very different place from the one that those first Josephites inhabited. Two world wars, a major financial depression, and the gradual development of a cosmopolitan Australia all contributed to major changes in its inhabitants' way of life. The world was becoming a global village and new ways

---

3. These women were Australian either by birth or by choice. Approximately one-third of the founding Sisters were born in Australia, one-third came to Australia with their families while still very young, and one-third migrated as young adults. See also Marie T Foale, *The Josephite Story*, 37 and Appendix Four.
4. Mary MacKillop, 'Necessity for the Institute', August 1873, in *Resource Material from the Archives of the Sisters of St Joseph of the Sacred Heart*, Issue No. 3 (January 1980), 51.

of transport and communication, the motor car, the aeroplane, the telephone, the wireless, television, moving pictures and more were bringing it into people's homes and into convents in ways undreamed of during Mary MacKillop's lifetime.

Television arrived in Australia in time for the Melbourne Olympic Games of 1956. It proved so popular that by the early 1970s, there was a television set in almost every home and every convent. As each new gadget was invented, it had its day until an even more sophisticated item replaced it. Over time, electric typewriters, word processors, computers, CD players, mobile phones and other electronic gadgets became commonplace in the wider community and among the Sisters.

Many families had cars, and the number of motor vehicles garaged at convents and of Sisters with driver's licences increased throughout the 1970s.[5] Aeroplanes replaced trains and ocean liners as people's preferred method of travel, and with time, the Sisters of this era became as comfortable in airports as their predecessors were in railway stations.

During the immediate post Vatican II era, numerous theologians, scholars and musicians published their works on a type of tape that could be played on a reel-to-reel tape recorder. To enable Sisters to hear the content of these tapes (which replaced the reading aloud of texts from spiritual books that was a regular part of their morning routine), most Josephite communities in South Australia acquired these recorders. Within a decade portable cassette recorders superseded the reel-to-reel ones and each Sister was free to have one for her own use. Before long Sisters were recording talks by visiting speakers for future reference. At about this time, the *Southern Cross* reported that:

> Tape recorders were well to the fore [and in Josephite hands] when the Christian Education Association members listened to (a lecture) at Loreto College.[6]

---

5. Colour TV reached Australia in about 1975 and today (2014) few can remember life without it.
6. SC 14 July 1972, 6, features a photograph showing two Josephite Sisters with cassette recorders on their knees.

By the 1970s too, the transistor radio was commonplace both outside and within the convent. Shopping for the necessities of life became easier for everyone because the supermarket, which first appeared in Australia in the early 1960s, was rapidly replacing the corner store in suburbs and towns across the country.

The 1960s were a decade of social upheaval. The 'baby boomers', that is, the children born between 1945 and 1964, were growing up and, as they did so, they challenged the values of their parents' generation.

Feminism, (movements and ideologies aimed at defining, establishing, and defending equal political, economic, educational and social rights for women) became strong during this era. For the first time ever, married women could join the public service and before long they were demanding equal rights and equal pay.

There was a strong call for racial equality and a new consideration for the environment. In 1962, Indigenous Australians gained full voting rights at national elections. Five years later 'white Australians' voted that this country's First Peoples be counted on the census, that is, that they be recognised as citizens of their own land, something that had not happened since white settlement in 1788!

As already noted, two world wars, the financial depression of the 1930s, and the influx of non-Anglo-Celtic immigrants into the country all played important parts in shaping the society of the 1960s and beyond. When the Congregation celebrated the centenary of its foundation, Australia was a very different place from the one its founding Sisters knew.[7] In short, this was a new world calling for a renewed Church and a renewal of religious life.

In the past, the Josephite way of life was predictable. Sisters knew their places in the community, the Church and the wider world, and acted accordingly. They celebrated the Church as the Rock of Ages, solid, strong, invulnerable. They knew that, in every part of the western world and wherever western influence was strong, Mass was celebrated in Latin. They were also aware that, no matter where in the world they might find themselves, they would be at home in a Catholic Church and would understand what was happening,

---

7. The longest lived of the founding Sisters, Mother Laurence O'Brien, who was born in 1853, died in Adelaide on 24 August 1945.

even if the people gathered in that place spoke a language other than English.

Then came Vatican II. The language of the Mass and other major liturgical functions changed from the age-old Latin to the vernacular, which, in Australia, was English. Entire church congregations could take an active part in the liturgy, especially through the answering of the responses once reserved for altar servers. As time passed, young girls were taking their turn as altar servers. Congregational singing was encouraged as never before, and a plethora of new hymns with English words appeared.

Church furniture was rearranged so that altars were near the front of the sanctuary and the priest celebrant faced the people. Where possible, the seating was positioned in a semi-circular pattern around the altar. By the early 1970s, lay people, including Sisters, were taking their places as Extraordinary Ministers of the Eucharist at Masses in their local parishes.[8] Similarly, members of the laity were being invited to be readers and commentators at Sunday liturgies and Sisters needed to ensure that they knew when it was their turn to fill these roles.

The Communion procession was introduced and from then on almost everyone received Holy Communion while standing. As a consequence, altar rails became redundant and were removed from many churches. These changes touched the Josephites in a particular way in 1972 when they enlarged the sanctuary of the Kensington convent chapel. This operation entailed the removal of the marble altar rails and the bringing forward of the lower part of the main altar, also of marble, so that the celebrant could face the congregation.[9]

In some rural areas a 'Liturgy of the Word with Communion' replaced the traditional Josephite practice whereby the members of a local community prayed an extra Rosary together on days when they were unable to attend Mass. Bishop Gallagher initiated the new

---

8. An Extraordinary Minister of the Eucharist is a non-ordained person (and this includes women as well as men) who assists the priest with the distribution of Holy Communion when needed, especially in places where there is a large congregation at weekend Masses.
9. This altar was the one donated by Sister Flavia Sheedy's family in 1928. Sister Ligouri Sinn's parents had paid for the marble altar rails at some time during the 1930s.

liturgy during 1969 when he sent to each Religious community in his diocese a copy of the service for such days, along with detailed directives as to its conduct.

The Sisters' ministries and way of being together in community also changed greatly. Ever since the foundation years, most members of the Congregation had come from lower middle or working class families. Mary MacKillop believed that the best way for these Sisters to live in harmony with the few who had enjoyed greater opportunities in their youth was for the latter to

> have nothing to do with instrumental music ... [to] make a sacrifice of any taste, and strive to forget any knowledge they may have got, upon entering the Institute.[10]

That may have worked during the late nineteenth century but, by the 1960s, school attendance was compulsory and the children of working class parents had much the same opportunities as their wealthier peers in the field of secondary education.[11] In order to meet the needs of this time, the teaching of senior secondary students became an important Josephite ministry. Rather than forget any knowledge gained in their earlier years, it was imperative that Sisters improve their knowledge and update their qualifications for the sake of those to whom they were ministering. Therefore, as already noted, some of them enrolled at universities or other tertiary institutions.

At centenary time in 1966, it may have seemed that the Congregation had come of age and could settle into a comfortable old age where every Sister enjoyed a lasting sense of security. But that was not to be! Unlike the founding Sisters who had no wise elders to turn to for advice along the way, the younger members of this era did have older women to mentor them. However, many younger Josephites were restless and longed for change, while some of their elders, especially those who had joined the Congregation before 1940, were fearful. Their secure world seemed to be falling apart: for them it was a hard time indeed. In fact, for some Sisters of

---

10. Mary MacKillop, 'Necessity for the Institute', 60
11. South Australian Education Act, No. 507 of 1891: 'An Act to further amend the Education Act, 1875'.

each age group, it was too hard and they turned their backs on convent life altogether.

During the turmoil of the 1870s, thirty-eight (approximately one-third of the first 127 Sisters to wear the Josephite habit), left the Institute.[12] During the 1970s (after almost 100 years of apparent stability when few Sisters left the Congregation), at least nineteen (about 8½ per cent) of the 225 Sisters then in South Australia did just that. Their reasons for going were many and varied. It appears that for some, the tensions surrounding changes in Church and convent proved too great to bear. Others moved out because change was not happening quickly enough. Others yet again withdrew for personal reasons. For all, those who left the Congregation and those who stayed, the post-Vatican II era was a time of serious soul-searching. Some were excited at future prospects, while for others it was a time of grieving for the loss of what had been.

Vatican II challenged members of religious congregations to adapt, renew and update their lives. Josephite leaders obeyed the Council's instructions with courage tinged with fear. Most Sisters in senior leadership positions in the late 1960s and early 1970s had made their religious profession in the years between the promulgation of the revised Code of Canon Law in 1917 and World War II. For them, Josephite religious life had always been ordered and predictable.

They knew, however, that they must act even though they could not anticipate the outcome. With great courage, therefore, they set about organising a Special General Chapter according to the Council's prescriptions, one of which was that every member of the Congregation be involved in the process. To achieve this end, the Mother General, Mother Adrian Ryan, sent each Sister a questionnaire covering many aspects of Josephite life and mission, called Provincial Chapters to meet in each Province during the latter half of 1968, and announced that a Special General Chapter would take place in 1969. These Chapters were to be followed by the regular six-yearly Provincial Chapter of 1970 and the General Chapter of 1971, as specified by the Josephite Constitutions.

In 1968, the South Australian Sisters elected thirty-five of their number to attend the Provincial Chapter and, while it was in session, to choose delegates and draw up proposals for

---

12. Marie T Foale, *The Josephite Story*, 39.

consideration at the upcoming General Chapter.[13] Before drafting their proposals, all present studied information gleaned from the questionnaires or submitted by individual Sisters or groups, and revised their knowledge of the lives and works of the founders. Their main sources of information about the founders were the few extant biographies of Mary MacKillop and Julian Woods and the vast corpus of unpublished letters and other documents that they left behind.[14]

The 1969 Chapter ruled that Sisters might experiment in their way of living and praying together in community, and that the Josephite Constitutions should be updated and rewritten. Sisters Denis Earle, Campion Roach and Mary Reardon accepted the task of preparing a draft Constitution for presentation at the 1971 Chapter. On that occasion, the Sisters decided that it be circulated across the Congregation, so that every Sister could be involved in this important work. In Adelaide, the Provincial, Sister Joan Luff, distributed a copy to each Sister and encouraged her to study its content either alone or with a group.

The change in the Sisters' religious dress (which might be viewed as a symbol of what the 1969 Chapter was hoping to achieve) was of particular interest to the general public. From 15 August 1969, every Sister was free to wear a simpler, softer veil, and a lighter habit made of less material (prior to this she needed twelve yards, or approximately 10.8 metres of material to make one habit). She could replace her stiff leather belt with a soft cloth one, wear a smaller rosary on her belt, and exchange her large wooden crucifix for a small metal one on a brown cord worn around her neck. Many, especially from among the younger Sisters, could scarcely wait for changeover day while a minority watched and waited for general reactions before making a move.[15]

---

13. SC 12 September 1969, 5
14. The only books available at this time were: Mary MacKillop, 'Life of Rev. JET Woods', 1903. This was in manuscript form until 1983. A Sister of St Joseph, *Life and Letters of Mother Mary of the Cross (McKillop)* (Sydney, 1916). George O'Neill, SJ, *Life of Mother Mary of the Cross (McKillop)* (Sydney, 1931). George O'Neill, SJ, *Life of Rev. Julian Edmund Tenison Woods* (Sydney, 1929). Osmund Thorpe, CP, *Mary McKillop*, (London, 1957).
15. SC 12 September 1969, 5.

At subsequent Chapters the Sisters discussed their dress code, their daily timetables and so on. With time, however, they came to place greater emphasis on their need to be women of prayer, and to be actively involved in structuring their lives in community for mission. In 1977 they decided that they should wear a simple religious dress and veil, with a crucifix and/or religious emblem, in colours ranging from brown to fawn to white, that is, in any shade of brown that was available. At the 1983 Chapter they ruled that the wearing of the veil be optional, and by the 1989-1990 Chapter, the Sisters' dress code was almost a non-issue. On that occasion the Chapter ruled that:

> In keeping with the Gospel way of life, our dress as Sisters of St Joseph is simple in style. Our distinguishing symbols are the plain silver ring, our emblem and/or our crucifix. The wearing of the veil and rosary beads is optional.[16]

Some found the change of dress difficult indeed. It appeared to them that, by abandoning the garb that Mary MacKillop and so many others wore with pride, they were abandoning all that she and the founding Sisters stood for. It seemed to these Sisters that the lived traditions of the Congregation were under threat. As early as 1969, Mother Adrian, who was aware of a developing conflict situation, saw fit to remind everyone that they needed 'great patience, tolerance and respect for another's point of view' during this time of change.[17]

The Chapter Sisters of 1969 also looked at other areas where change seemed necessary. They recognised the need for school supervisors to support teaching Sisters and assist them in the areas of curriculum and discipline. In South Australia, Sister Maurice Roche became the supervisor of Josephite primary schools and Sister Teresita Cormack undertook a similar role in the secondary schools. Both these women visited the schools regularly and organised practical seminars on specific subject areas, as requested

---

16. Final Report, Twenty-Second General Chapter of the Sisters of St Joseph, Baulkham Hills, 1989-1990, 19. The emblem is a special brooch that only professed Sisters of St Joseph may wear.
17. Mother Adrian to the Sisters, 23 May 1969, as cited in Margaret McKenna, *With Grateful Hearts!* 310.

by the teaching Sisters. The Director of Catholic Education, Mr John McDonald, noted Sister Maurice's good work and offered her a consultative position at the Catholic Education Office in Adelaide, where she worked until her retirement in 1981.

The advisability of having Sisters teach school and music concurrently also came up for consideration. For many years, some Sisters living in country communities of two or three gave music lessons before and after school and on Saturday mornings and taught in the school during the day. While some enjoyed the challenge of this situation, others found it a heavy burden and so the Chapter decided that, where possible, it should be discontinued.

At the 1971 General Chapter fifty-seven year old Sister Denis Earle became the ninth Mother General of the Congregation. Immediately after its closure, she appointed Sister Concepta (Joan) Luff from Western Australia to be Provincial of South Australia, and chose Sister Mechtilde (Mary) Byrne from the Largs Bay Orphanage to fill a similar role in a Sydney Province. Sister Martin (Lorna) Bourke (formerly of SA), who had been Provincial of the Western Australian Province since 1965, was elected to the membership of the General Council in Sydney, a position which she held until 1983.

Among other things, the 1971 Chapter gave Sisters the option of reverting to their baptismal names. Many accepted this offer with alacrity, while others moved more slowly. Occasionally a change of name caused some confusion, especially when, for example, Sister Peter closed the classroom door on Friday afternoon, and returned on Monday morning as 'Sister Mary'. It soon became evident that there was a plethora of Sisters Mary and Sisters Margaret, to name but a few, and so began the previously unknown practice of using Sisters' family names at all times.

Prior to this, Sisters' family names were a well-kept secret, even within the community. Mary MacKillop forbade Sisters from discussing family affairs in an attempt to ensure equality and lack of distinction between all members of Josephite communities, regardless of their level of education or social class, or the financial status of their families. In fact, she included the following maxims in her 'Rules for the General Guidance of the Sisters':

> Conversations of a worldly nature, such topics as politics, marriages, family affairs, positions in life, superiority of birth or education, nationality, etc. are strictly forbidden.
>
> It is also strictly forbidden to speak of what any Sister may or may not have brought into the Institute.
>
> Those who may have received a more polite [refined] education than ordinary, or who may have moved in higher worldly positions, must always remember that they have left these things outside the doors of St Joseph's Convent . . . [and] must imitate [the example of Jesus] and become the least among their Sisters.[18]

These were difficult and challenging times. At Mother Denis' Requiem in June 1991, Sister Mary Reardon commented that:

> It was a time of great pain for Mother Denis and for many of the Sisters as well. The struggle to be true to the call of the Church, as discerned by individuals and groups in their minds and hearts, created tension and deep hurt, a hurt that reflected the differing visions of what it meant to renew and to adapt in fidelity to the Spirit of the Congregation.[19]

During the 1970s communal prayer was still the norm and Sisters put much effort into finding meaningful ways of reciting the Hours of the Divine Office and praying their daily Rosary. They were free, however, to arrange their daily timetables around their specific ministries: something that was a great relief to school principals who were often late home because of after-hours staff or school board meetings, parent-teacher conferences and so on.

It was much the same for those working in the fields of adult education, the religious instruction to schoolchildren or the training lay catechists. Until the early 1970s the motor mission Sisters had a clearly defined way of managing their work in the state schools.

---

18. Mary MacKillop, 'Rules for the General Guidance of the Sisters of St Joseph', 1883, 10, articles 4, 5 & 6. These articles were reprinted verbatim in the 'Customs & Practices of the Sisters of St Joseph', 12, par. 5, 6 & 7. This updated version of Mary's 'Rules' was a companion volume to the Constitutions, and was printed in the early 1950s.
19. Mother Denis Earle, Obituary, ASSJ. The information regarding these Chapters is drawn from the Chapter reports released at their conclusion. They contain details of the findings but not of the discussions that preceded them.

Then, in 1973 the South Australian State Government reversed its policy of allowing RE teachers access to state schools during school hours. Consequently, Sisters involved in this work became parish pastoral associates or parish workers.

Their new role was to assist parish priests by playing a part in the organisation of parish liturgies, visiting families, the sick and the elderly, training and supporting lay catechists, and, with their assistance, taking part in or supervising RE classes after school hours or at weekends. Circumstances varied from parish to parish, but in many instances the Sisters also met with parents, held family days, offered parishioners opportunities for times of prayer and renewal, and became involved in RE camps and vacation schools.

As a rule, two Sisters worked together on each motor mission. With the change, it became common for just one Sister to be employed in a parish. Thus, for example, one Sister, who resided at Penola, managed the South East Mission, which was established in 1973 and comprised the parishes of Bordertown, Kingston, Millicent, Mount Gambier, Naracoorte and Penola.

With time, and given that from the late 1980s lay people could qualify for the position of parish worker through study at the Adelaide College of Divinity, and that there were fewer Josephites to fill these positions, Sisters withdrew from many of the parishes where they had been serving. They left Hamley Bridge in 1974, Georgetown in 1978, the Barossa Valley in 1982, Hectorville in 1986, Murray Bridge and Woodville in 1987 and Hindmarsh and Croydon in the late 1990s. In fact, by 2010 only five remained: those operating out of Wilmington in the Far North, Clare in the Mid-North, Salisbury/Elizabeth in the metropolitan area, Tailem Bend on the Lower Murray, and Bordertown in the Lower South East.

The motor missioners were not the only ones to experience change throughout this era for in some areas decreasing school enrolments were forcing convent and school closures. The Sisters withdrew from Balaklava in December 1969, after forty-eight years of Josephite presence. Burra, where they had ministered for 101 years, closed at the end of the 1970 school year. A year later came the closures of the schools at Beulah Road, Norwood, which had been a Josephite stronghold since 1872, and at Macclesfield in the Adelaide Hills where, except for several years early in the twentieth century, there had been a Josephite presence since 1868. These moves (all of which were made with regret), enabled Sisters to take up new ministries in other areas, and, in particular, made it possible for the South Australian Province to accept responsibility for the Catholic school at Wentworth in 1970.[20]

When Sisters Regis (Gwen) Ballinger and Constance Conroy closed the school at Macclesfield and moved away, the two Sisters in charge of the Macclesfield, Strathalbyn and Mount Barker motor mission moved in. They used the convent as their home base until the mission closed in 1989, and there was a Josephite presence in Macclesfield until 2010.

At the end of 1973, approximately 250 parishioners and former students farewelled Sisters Florence Chigwidden and Berenice Conroy from Spalding.[21] At about the same time, Sisters Francis Clare Kenny and Mel Moroney left Lower North Adelaide where the Josephites had been teaching since 1869. These two Sisters moved away because enrolments had been declining for many years and because, in particular, a high proportion of the children attending the school came from suburbs outside the parish.[22]

There were some bright spots along the way, such as when, in April 1973, Archbishop Gleeson opened a new wing comprising a science laboratory and library at MacKillop College, Kensington. A significant percentage of the funding for this building came from the Commonwealth Government, which by then was committed to offering direct assistance to education in the government and the non-government sectors alike.[23]

Two months later, the Sisters at Woodville moved into their new Mother Mary of the Cross Convent on Beaufort Street, Woodville Park. This well-appointed structure, which could accommodate up to eight Sisters, was conveniently located between the parish church and the school.[24]

---

20. Wentworth lies near the junction of the Darling and Murray Rivers in New South Wales and is more than 800 kilometres southwest of Sydney.
21. *SC 28* December 1973, 5.
22. *SC 14* December 1973, 7.
23. *SC 13* April 1973, 1.
24. *SC 8* June 1973, 5.

Closure and amalgamation occurred in 1975 when the Josephite school at Kadina closed and the children from there began taking a daily bus journey to St Joseph's at Wallaroo, which they renamed Kalori.[25] The Wallaroo Sisters lived in a new convent at Kadina (the old one had been demolished), to allow for the demolition of the seventy year old Wallaroo convent and its replacement with classrooms. At the time of St Mary MacKillop's canonisation in 2010, staff and students of this school renamed it the 'St Mary MacKillop School' and claimed that theirs was the first school in South Australia to bear this title. The Sisters withdrew from Kalori in 2002 and at about the same time a senior Sister took up residence in a unit attached to the diocesan-owned Star of the Sea Aged Care Home in Wallaroo.

As the above information indicates, by the mid-1970s the days of expansion, of the 'new openings' that were so numerous during the 1950s and 60s, were ending. An important reason for this was the Congregation's declining membership, which was due to natural attrition and the lack of new recruits. The number of professed Sisters in the state reached an all-time high of 265 in 1959. After that, it gradually fell off. It had fallen to 258 in 1965, 237 in 1977, 211 in 1983, 186 in 1989, 162 in 1995, 146 in 2001, 126 in 2007, and 105 by late 2010.

At first, this loss of membership was barely perceptible but gradually its effects became evident. Thus, during the latter half of the 1970s the Congregation relinquished the principalships of the St Francis of Assisi School at Newton and St Joseph's at Kurralta Park (formerly Keswick) in order to fill new positions in other schools. The Sister from Kurralta Park became the founding principal of St David's School at Tea Tree Gully, a rapidly growing outer suburb to the northeast of Adelaide. At the end of 1977 the Sisters withdrew from the Gawler-Hamley Bridge motor mission and closed the Tailem Bend convent.[26]

During the following year things appeared to look up somewhat. New school buildings on the Payneham and Croydon school

---

25. Kalori is an Aboriginal word meaning message stick.
26. SC 6 January 1978, 2. The Sister Principal of the Tailem Bend School, Sister Agnes Walsh, moved to nearby Murray Bridge and travelled out there each day. A lay principal replaced her in 1981.

campuses came into use, the school and parish communities at Renmark, Croydon and Nangwarry celebrated significant milestones in the development of their schools.[27]

That reprieve was short-lived, however, for during the years between 1977 and 1983 inclusive the Sisters closed the Gladstone convent and withdrew from Siena College, Findon, and the schools at Flinders Park, Gladstone, Newton, Payneham, St Peters, Tailem Bend and Walkerville. At about the same time, they ceased offering individual music lessons at Cowandilla, Tranmere, Renmark, Rosewater, Port Augusta and MacKillop College, Kensington. They left the Woodville Gardens School and Woomera convent and school in 1984. The school at Pinnaroo closed in 1985, and the Sisters withdrew from the schools at Tranmere in 1985, at Barmera, Kensington (Bridge Street) and Kingswood in 1986, at Jamestown in 1988 and at Rosewater in 1989.[28]

That was not the end, however, for by 2010 Sisters had moved away from a further twenty schools and, in some cases, associated convents as well. These included schools at Berri, Nangwarry and Thebarton in 1996, the Dulwich Special School and Ottoway in 1997, Hindmarsh, Murray Bridge, Tea Tree Gully and the convent at the former Seminary (Rostrevor) in 1998, and the Renmark convent and school in 1999. In the following year they withdrew from the Croydon convent and school, Gladstone (a Sister returned there briefly in 1994) and the Plympton School.

In 2001 they left Aberfoyle Park and Yorketown, followed by Clare and Wallaroo in 2002, Hectorville and St Anne's Special School, Marion in 2004, Richmond in 2006, Woodville in 2007 and Peterborough in 2010. This decade also saw the closure of convents at Aldgate, Kadina, Macclesfield, Pinnaroo, Port Lincoln, Rosewater, Thebarton, Woodville and Yorketown.[29] As a consequence of these moves, by 2010 most of the 105 Sisters in the province were living and ministering in or near the Adelaide metropolitan area.

---

27. SC, 8 June 1978, 2 & 20 July 1978, 4, Croydon & Payneham buildings; 31 May 1979, 15, Nangwarry; 7 August, 4 & 23 October 1979, 3, Renmark; 22 February, 2 & 1 March 1979, p. 9, Croydon & Woodville Gardens.
28. The term 'close' means that the school ceased to exist as such. 'Left' or 'withdrew' imply that the school continued to operate under lay leadership.
29. See Appendix One for further details regarding Josephite foundations in SA.

Behind all these changes there was still much activity. During the late 1960s Sisters began moving into the more public diocesan arena. Thus, when Archbishop Beovich established the Diocesan Pastoral Council he invited Josephite provincial, Sister Marie Paul Harford, to represent the Religious Sisters of the archdiocese. Subsequently, other Josephites filled different roles on the Council. Then, when the Catholic Education Office (CEO) and Beovich established the South Australian Commission for Catholic Schools, (SACCS), Sister Raymond (Kathleen) Burford, Principal of Mary MacKillop College, Kensington, became one of its founding members.

Sister Patricia Flinn was a founding member of the staff of the Confraternity of Christian Doctrine (CCD) Office when it opened in February 1971. (It was run by a team which included a religious Sister, a diocesan Priest, a religious Brother and a laywoman.) Their mandate was to co-ordinate the work of the motor missions and parish CCD groups in providing religious education for children attending state schools.[30] Over subsequent years Josephites were well represented in the CCD office, which evolved into the Centre for Continuing Religious Education (CCRE) in the late 1970s, and some ten years later became known as the Catholic Adult Education Service (CAES).[31]

Siena College, Findon, the first Regional Catholic Girls' Secondary College in Australia to be managed by a Catholic Education Office (CEO) instead of a particular Religious Congregation, opened in 1971. It came into existence because during the late 1960s the CEO, local parish priests and leaders of the Congregations concerned (Sisters of Mercy, Dominicans and Josephites) realised that the small 'secondary tops' on the many parish primary schools in Adelaide's western suburbs were no longer viable and amalgamated them into one 'new unusual school' for girls. They called it 'Siena College' after St Catherine of Siena, set it up in the suburb of Findon, and enrolled only those students who resided in a clearly defined geographic area.[32]

Siena was, in fact, a different kind of school and its establishment caused a ripple in Catholic educational circles across the nation

---

30. *SC* 9 January 1973, 1.
31. *SC* 17 December 1971, 7.
32. *SC* 26 February 1971, 3.

because it was staffed by Sisters from its feeder schools: Findon and Semaphore (Dominican), Henley Beach (Mercy) and Hindmarsh and Woodville (Josephite). Girls from St Joseph's, Thebarton enrolled there from 1972–1974 inclusive, after which they had access to a co-educational secondary school in their own parish. The first Sisters to teach at Siena were Kevin (Eileen) Taylor rsj, Patricia Davis OP, Mary Densley rsm and Mary Vincent rsm. The founding Principal of the college was Sister Mary Martin (Mary) Cahill OP. Sister Kevin (Eileen) remained at Siena for four years, and there was a Josephite Sister on the college staff until 1983.

Initially Siena enrolled students from Years Eight to Eleven and girls interested in Year Twelve studies neded to go elsewhere. One option open to them was to finish their schooling at St Michael's College, Henley Beach, an all-boys school managed by the De La Salle Brothers.[33] If girls who enrolled there were to succeed in this all-male environment, they needed support. Therefore, after consultation with the CEO, the Brothers requested that a Josephite Sister join St Michael's staff. Sister Catherine Clark, who went there in 1972, was the first to fill this role and a Josephite served at St Michael's from then until 1985.[34]

A similar situation existed at St Paul's College, Gilles Plains, a boys' school run by the Christian Brothers. Initially, like Siena, Josephite-run Mount Carmel College, Rosewater, did not offer tuition at Year Twelve level. When, in 1977, the Sisters did enrol Year Twelve students, the class was too small to be workable. The Brothers at St Paul's were in a similar predicament regarding their senior boys and so, after negotiations between the two schools, the Brothers offered places at St Paul's to girls from Rosewater. Mount Carmel College purchased a small bus and Sister Margaret Lamb took up her appointment as bus driver cum teacher at St Paul's. She drove the girls from Mount Carmel to Gilles Plains each morning, performed her teaching duties and, at the end of the day, returned

---

33. St Michael's College is a boys' secondary school that has been run by the De La Salle Brothers since its inception in the 1950s. In 1972 the Brothers successfully undertook limited co-education at senior secondary level.
34. For a fuller discussion of the establishment and development of Siena College, see Marie T Foale & Denis Toohey, *In Joyful Hope: The Story of Siena College, 1971-2001* (Norwood, SA: Peacock Publications, 2004).

herself and her passengers to Rosewater. This situation persisted for several years.

Prior to the early 1970s, the Marist Brothers at Thebarton were educating boys from Year Three to Year Twelve while the Josephites taught junior primary boys along with girls at all levels. By this time, the population of the Thebarton area was in decline and there were fewer children of schoolgoing age. Therefore, in 1974, those responsible decided that the Brothers' School in George Street should become a co-educational secondary school and that all primary aged boys and girls should attend St Joseph's in Kintore Avenue. They renamed the whole complex 'Kilmara College', with a senior and a junior campus. The Brothers maintained their presence at George Street, one Josephite Sister joined the staff of the secondary school and another continued as principal of the primary school.[35]

As the exodus of people from Thebarton continued, school enrolments decreased. Consequently, Kilmara Senior School closed in 1991; the local state school ceased operations at the end of 1992 and Kilmara Junior School struggled on with falling numbers until the end of 1996. In January 1997 it combined with St Joseph's, Richmond, to become the Tenison Woods Catholic School. The forty or so students from Kilmara moved there amid hopes that the work of Catholic education begun at Thebarton nearly 140 years earlier would continue in the same spirit at their new school, where there was a Josephite Sister on the staff.

Sisters Geraldine Stringer and Meg Goodfellow remained in their 111-year-old Thebarton convent and maintained their involvement in the parish for as long as Geraldine was employed there as a parish worker. These Sisters liked to remember that Mary MacKillop stayed in the oldest part of their convent when she visited the school in 1897 and, as was her custom, she spoke to each child and shared some lollies among them. The Josephites' direct association with the Thebarton parish ceased in early 2004 when the two Sisters moved out. Soon afterwards, Geraldine joined the Josephite Mission in Peru.

From the early 1960s all Catholic schools were benefitting from the limited financial support being given them by State and Federal Governments. As a first step, the Commonwealth financed the

---

35. The word 'Kilmara' is a combination of the names MacKillop and Marist.

erection and setting up of libraries and science laboratories in secondary schools. Then in 1969, the State Government made a grant of $10 per annum for each primary aged child attending a Catholic school. This money was administered by the parish priest with the advice of the school principal and a school board comprising parents and other laymen and women from the local area.

Over time government funding increased to more realistic levels. Consequently, schools had fixed incomes and could afford to employ lay teachers and reduce class sizes. In particular, the Sisters could concentrate on their teaching without having to organise and run fundraising events such as school concerts, sports days or fetes. Moreover, they could take study leave, confident that the schools would not be disadvantaged by their absence. The 1970s were a good time for undertaking tertiary study because the Commonwealth Government, under Prime Minister Gough Whitlam, abolished tuition fees at Australian universities.[36] Hence, for each Sister student, the Congregation needed to pay only Student Union fees and incidental costs relating to the subjects that she was studying.

Given these circumstances, the provincial of the time, Sister Joan Luff, arranged for eight Sisters to enrol for full-time study each year. Some attended university or TAFE colleges while others went to interstate institutions where they undertook a range of courses including theology, scripture, catechesis and missiology. Those given such opportunities took them seriously indeed and, by 1976, ten had completed university degrees and several more were in the process of doing so. By this time, too, three Sisters had been overseas to undertake advanced courses in Catechetics, Spiritual Direction and Religious Formation. Sister Joan reported to the 1977 General Chapter that:

> The widening of expertise and experience resulting from all these forms of intensive study, besides adding to the Sisters' personal development, [was] having a marked effect on the impact of the Sisters of St Joseph in both their professional and lay fields of activity.[37]

---

36. Gough Whitlam was Prime Minister from 1972 until 1975.
37. Sister Joan Luff, 'Report on the State of the Province', 1977, 9.

While changes were occurring in the field of education, a great deal of activity was taking place at the Providence at Cowandilla. As soon as the State Government shelved its MATS Plan in 1970, the Sisters in charge, Brenda Keary, formerly Peter Aloysius, and Paul Bates, applied to the Commonwealth Government for assistance in upgrading the facility. The grant they received covered almost half the cost of building and furnishing a new wing large enough to house twenty elderly women in need of nursing care and of renovating all other buildings on the property. Finding the remainder required much hard work at the fundraising level.

The opening of extensions and renovations in June 1972 marked the beginning of a new era for the Providence. Mary MacKillop and Father Julian Woods gave this institution its name because it was their intention that it should rely solely on the Providence of God for its support. The Sisters now felt that, since they had a more secure source of income, they could no longer call it 'Providence'. They renamed it 'Flora McDonald Lodge', to perpetuate the memory of Mary MacKillop's mother whose maiden name was Flora McDonald and who was a woman noted for her trust in the Providence of God.[38] Following the change, the Sisters commissioned artist Vik Mednis to execute a mural symbolising Flora's life and the founding of the Sisters of St Joseph by her famous daughter. Initially they mounted it in the foyer of the new nursing wing but later on transferred it to the new chapel where it hung in pride of place for many years.

Over time, and with financial assistance from State and Commonwealth Governments, Sister Brenda (who stayed for ten years) and her successors engaged qualified staff and kept up to date with the maintenance of the place. All involved were delighted with these improvements, but they felt that the home needed one more thing—a chapel large enough to accommodate all residents, Sisters and staff. The existing chapel, a large double room on the ground floor of the convent, was adequate when the Providence first moved to Cowandilla. For some years, however, only a small proportion of the residents had fitted in there comfortably and, as a rule, they held Sunday Masses and special celebrations in the ladies' recreation hall (the large schoolroom of Juniorate days).

---

38. *The Garland of St Joseph,* September 1972, 26.

While governments provided for the material needs of the elderly, they did not extend their bounty to the funding of buildings devoted to their spiritual welfare. The need was great, however, and so the Sisters themselves assumed responsibility for the erection of a chapel. Thanks to the fundraising skill of Sister Maureen Joseph Meaney and the generosity of the residents, friends and benefactors from throughout South Australia and beyond, Flora McDonald Lodge was blessed with a fine, functional chapel in June 1976.

At the time, the government made available some funding for three new hostel rooms and a matron's suite to go behind the chapel, and also for nine additional hostel rooms, the building of which followed closely upon that of the chapel. With the completion of the extra rooms, which they named the 'Luff Wing', there was space for every resident in purpose built accommodation.[39] Subsequently, the two storey building became 'convent only'.[40] At last, it appeared that the complex was complete. But that was not the case.

By the late 1980s further upgrading was required. Once again, the Sisters applied for and received Commonwealth assistance to the tune of $2.2 of the $3.6 million they needed for the erection of a secure nursing wing and hostel accommodation for an additional eighteen elderly people. These new buildings came into operation in 1993.[41] A Josephite administrator managed Flora McDonald Lodge until 2010.

The Sisters' involvement in aged care widened in 1987 when they took charge of St Catherine's Nursing home in Berri. The Daughters of Charity, who had been there since 1961, were no longer able to staff the place. Sisters Margaret Donnelly, Irene Roche and Nancy Hannon were the first Josephites to minister at St Catherine's. Since then the Sisters have carried on in working with the residents of this home in various roles including as nurses, administrators and pastoral care Sisters.[42] During the late 1990s this relatively small, inter-

---

39. The Luff Wing was named after Sister Joan Luff, the SA Provincial at the time when it was constructed.
40. Sister Joan Luff, 'Report on the State of the Province', 1977, 5.
41. Marie T Foale rsj, *Providence*, 26-29.
42. Maryellen Thomas rsj, *Home: The Story of St Catherine's, Berri* (Berri: St Catherine's, 1994), passim. Sr Maryellen was CEO and Director of Care at St Catherine's from 1994-2009 inclusive.

denominational home was recognised nationally and within the State of South Australia for its high level of safe practice.

At St Joseph's Orphanage, Largs Bay, the Sisters carried on quietly until the early 1970s, caring for young boys between the ages of three and twelve years. Then, following legislative changes regarding childcare, it became a short-term home, with thirty-four boys and girls in residence at any one time. The Orphanage School closed and any children of schoolgoing age attended local schools. Further changes occurred in 1975 when the orphanage building was subdivided into four self-contained units with eight children in each. The emphasis was still on short-term care, and any children who required lengthy stays were housed in a separate unit.

Despite alterations in funding arrangements and close cooperation between the Department of Community Welfare, the Archbishop of Adelaide, and the Josephite provincial, further changes in the area childcare forced the closure of the orphanage at the end of 1980. Soon afterwards, the Sisters refurbished the former school and laundry block on the property to become a hostel for retired Sisters while the large main building became a base for the Urban Aboriginal Apostolate.

The Josephite community at Kensington underwent a significant change in its membership in June 1972 when twenty-four of its most senior members relocated to the recently refurbished Tappeiner Court Home for Retired Sisters (the home built by Sister Vianney Finnegan during the previous decade). The day chosen for their move was the feast of St John the Baptist, Saturday 24 June.[43]

The Sisters also selected this day so that an equivalent number of active school Sisters could assist their elders, many of whom had not changed their residence for years. Each one was given an active assistant to help her clear her former room and transport her possessions to her new one. More importantly, the Sister Assistants had to see that their elderly charges arrived there safely and, under their close supervision, unpack and put away their belongings as directed. Most of these Sisters owned little beyond a few changes

---

43. At that time, 24 June was generally regarded as the day in 1867 when Mary MacKillop and Rose Cunningham arrived in Adelaide from Penola. The *Advertiser*, 25 June 1866, however, indicates clearly that the two Sisters reached Port Adelaide on Sunday, 23 June 1867.

of clothing, two religious habits and veils, and their prayer books. Helping them was a privilege indeed.

This move was significant for most of these Sisters, including seventy-six year old Gerard Majella Hefron who became crippled with rheumatoid arthritis early in her religious life.[44] All were delighted, even if, perhaps, somewhat overwhelmed by the enormity of what was happening and especially by the realisation that each one now had a room to herself. Before this day, very few of them had ever enjoyed the luxury of having a room of their own. Sister Maro Caulfield, aged ninety-one, was heard to remark: 'There seems to be a bit of excitement around the place today', while eighty-nine year old Sister Brendan McNamara, commented: 'I think the Lord made a mistake: it should have been a two-hundredfold reward He promised'.[45] All quickly settled in and prepared to make the most of their new home for as long as possible.

Within five years, Tappeiner Court was a registered nursing home for the aged and was employing qualified lay staff to supplement the work being done by the Sisters. With time, as the number of Sisters requiring care at Tappeiner Court became fewer, members of other religious congregations and laymen and women were admitted there.

Forty-eight Sisters remained in the Kensington community after the senior Sisters moved out. In the convent there were vacant rooms and some empty spaces in the dormitories. Therefore, after due consideration, the Sisters arranged for the subdivision of the larger dormitories into single rooms or cubicles. Before long every Sister residing there and, indeed, in most other Josephite convents across the state, had a room of her own. What a change this was,

---

44. The author was a member of the Kensington community at this time and had the privilege of assisting Sister Gerard Majella with the move. While Sister Gerard was so disabled physically that she could not take an active part in the packing and unpacking, she knew exactly what she owned and ensured that her few possessions were put in 'the right place'.
45. *The Garland of St Joseph*, September 1972, 26. Sister Brendan was referring to the Gospel of Matthew, 19:29, where the text reads: 'Anyone who has left, houses, brothers, sisters, father, mother, children or land for the sake of my name will be repaid a hundred times over (a hundredfold) and also inherit eternal life.'

especially for those Sisters who used to sleep in dormitories or along open balconies.[46]

During the period 1968–2004, death took 139 Sisters, most of whom had spent their final years at Tappeiner Court. The majority were older women who had been members of the Congregation for many years and included some who joined it during Mary MacKillop's lifetime. The longest-lived of these was Sister Conrad Pflaum. She was a postulant at Kensington when Mary MacKillop visited there in 1899 and met her again during her 1905 visit. Sister Conrad died at Tappeiner Court on 16 November 1979, aged ninety-nine years, and with her passing that personal link with the foundress was broken forever.

Among the elderly Sisters who died during this period, were three much younger Sisters who lost their lives as a result of separate motor vehicle accidents. Tragedy struck for the first time in May 1971, while the provincial, Sister Marie Paul Harford, and the Chapter delegates were on Chapter in Sydney. On the morning of the final day of the first school term, 6 May 1971, fifty-three year old Sister Antonia Hale, local superior of the Rosewater community, principal of the Mount Carmel Parish Primary School and acting provincial during Sister Marie Paul's absence, died as the result of a collision at a railway crossing not far from her school.

Little more than twelve months later, came the shocking news that, on the evening of 25 August 1972, thirty-one year old Sister Mary (Antonia) Harradine of Jamestown in the Mid-North had met a similar fate at the junction of the road from Crystal Brook and the main Port Pirie to Jamestown Road. Jamestown teenager, Anne Wenham, who was a passenger in Mary's car, also lost her life. Mother Denis travelled to South Australia to attend Mary's and Anne's funerals.

Seventeen years later, on 30 November 1989, sixty-two year old Sister Patricia (Pat, formerly Anthony) O'Dea, Principal of St Joseph's School, Nangwarry, died in a crash near Tarpeena on the Penola–Mt Gambier Road. This accident occurred after sunset, in teeming rain, while she was driving alone towards a nearby

---

46. Woods, *Rules*, Article 2, 'Of the houses' reads: 'The Sisters shall, where it is convenient, all sleep in one dormitory.'

campsite where some of the schoolchildren were staying. The driver of the other vehicle was unhurt.[47]

As already mentioned, the Sisters continued their long tradition of doing pastoral visitation of people at home, in hospital or in gaol into the latter half of the twentieth century and beyond. Among the Sisters engaged in this work were Thomasine Willis, a school Sister, who for many years visited patients in the Royal Adelaide Hospital every Saturday. She rarely missed a week and was there a week or two before her sudden death on 1 December 1981, aged seventy-eight years.

Sister Paul Bates went regularly to the Hillcrest Mental Hospital until ill-health prevented her from doing so. (She died in 1977, aged seventy-seven years.) Sister Desmond Cormack (1917–2002) served in Pastoral Ministry in the Norwood Parish after she retired from school teaching. She visited the hospitals and nursing homes in the area and also went to the Hillcrest Hospital from time to time.

These are but a few of the numerous Sisters who, over the years, gave some of their time to the ministry of visiting the sick in hospital and at home. During the 1980s, some Sisters became fully accredited hospital and prison chaplains. Others undertook Inter-Church Trade and Industry Mission (ITIM) chaplaincies at places such as the Onkaparinga Woollen Mills in the Adelaide Hills, and the city base for the operator-assisted services of Telecom until that service closed down.

Catherine House, a project of the Sisters of Mercy, was established in the city in 1988 to provide short-term accommodation for adult women, who were affected by homelessness for reasons other than domestic violence and were unaccompanied by children. For some years a Josephite worked with the Mercy Sisters in direct care and administration, while other Josephites and Associates offered their services as volunteers. Others yet again gave a hand at the Hutt Street Meal Centre, which was run by the Daughters of Charity and which provided meals and support to the homeless people of Adelaide and surrounds.

At Norwood, Sister Eileen Travers (1927–2013) became involved in a council-operated Isolated Persons Project. For many months during 1988–1989 she walked the streets on a door-knocking mission,

---

47. Sister Patricia O'Dea, Obituary, ASSJ.

in an attempt to locate homeless and deprived or isolated people and encourage them to attend the Norwood Day Centre. She also supported the mentally ill who were living in boarding houses. The chairperson of this project wrote of Sister Eileen that:

> Despite the difficulties the project is experiencing, Sr Eileen Travers has been of great assistance to individuals as well as management through her contact with the client group. She is most caring and passionate in undertaking this difficult task. Her contribution as an outreach worker is highly appreciated. On behalf of the management committee, I'd like to formally acknowledge Sr Eileen Travers' work.[48]

During the 1980s and 1990s, a number of other Sisters with the appropriate qualifications undertook short-term ministries, with the knowledge that when they completed their task or their contract ran out, it was unlikely that another Josephite would replace them. Thus, for example, one Sister joined the staff of the Archdiocesan Marriage Tribunal while two others worked as lecturers at St Francis Xavier's Seminary. Another became archivist for the Archdiocese, a position which she held for twenty years. Yet another was chairperson of the South Australian Education Commission for several years beginning in 1996. Others answered a call to go to the Daly River Mission in the Northern Territory where, for five or so years from 1989, they worked with Aboriginal people and families with alcohol-related problems.

Some Sisters became social workers, counsellors, psychologists or psychotherapists. One worked as an immigration agent assisting refugees arriving in boats in their struggle for permission to stay in Australia. In fact, it is impossible to detail the breadth or depth of different Sisters' involvement in work for the poor and disadvantaged of South Australia and beyond.

During the period under review, change was also afoot in other areas of Josephite involvement. Thus, during the late 1960s the Sisters realised that the family home was the best place for the nurturing of religious vocations. Therefore, in 1971, Sister Joan Barry and her community bade farewell to the last of the Juniorate

---

48. The Chairperson, Isolated Persons Project, Norwood, to Sister Margaret McKenna, 1988 (exact date not recorded.)

girls from Aldgate. The Aldgate property was in a fine location with a large house and chapel, a hall and a schoolroom. Hence, it was an ideal site for the holding of renewal programmes for Sisters, as decided upon at recent Chapters.

With this in mind, they erected 'Winella', a new 'motel-style' building comprising thirty single bedrooms with associated bathroom and kitchen facilities, converted the share rooms on the upper floor of the main house into single rooms, and upgraded the buildings and grounds.[49] By the end of 1973 it was ready for the twenty-eight participants in the first Tertianship, a ten-week renewal programme for Sisters from across the Congregation. At its conclusion, these women voted it a great success and declared their accommodation to have been at least 'five star'. In all, approximately 170 Sisters from every Australian state and New Zealand took part in six Tertianships, the last of which was held in 1978–1979.

During the 1970s and 1980s the Sisters also made Aldgate available for a variety of different gatherings, retreats, prayer days, seminars and courses. Archbishop Gleeson used it for residential meetings between himself and, among others, the major superiors of religious orders. The leaders and clergy of different religious denominations met there and some secondary schoolteachers took students there for day retreats. By the late 1980s, the Sisters were in a position where they could put into practice their 1982 Provincial Chapter decision that 'the Province consider the possibility of establishing a simple prayer house situated in the midst of ordinary suburbia'. They selected Aldgate for this project and, from 1990 onwards, utilised it as a place of prayer, healing and hospitality for the whole South Australian Church.

Sister Pamela Patterson was chosen to plan and direct this venture. Her premature death in 1992 at the age of fifty-seven came as a blow to the work, but the other Sisters directly involved in it carried on. Gradually the demand for the kinds of programmes they offered declined. Their presentations had ceased altogether by 2008 and the Congregation sold the property in March 2009. Josephite involvement in the giving of spiritual direction and the

---

49. *SC* 24 August 1973, 6. The name 'Winella' was chosen because of its association with Mary MacKillop who lived in Winella Cottage at Penola with her two sisters in 1866.

directing of retreats did not stop, however, as a number of qualified Sisters continued this work in other localities around Adelaide.

Over the years, Sisters celebrated significant anniversaries in their lives with the members of their communities. Until 1941 first profession and renewal of vows ceremonies took place at Kensington. Final profession or 'life vow ceremonies', as they were called, were usually held in the Mother House. This meant that, after 1890, when the Mother House moved to Sydney, South Australian Sisters went there for that event. War prevented interstate travel from 1941 until 1945 and any Sisters due for Life Vows during those years made them at Kensington. After the war, however, they resumed the practice of travelling to Sydney for the occasion. It continued until 1977 when the Chapter decided that Sisters could choose the time and place of their final profession.

The first South Australians to take advantage of this decision were Sisters Loreto O'Connor, Brigette Sipa and Theresa Swiggs. On Sunday 22 January 1978, the Kensington chapel was crowded with family, friends and Sisters for this, the first final profession ceremony held there since 1945.[50] Over subsequent years a number of other Sisters celebrated their final profession in South Australia, some in the Kensington chapel, some at St Ignatius Church, Norwood and some in their home parishes. Then, almost thirty-three years later, in December 2010, Sister Gail Leslie had the privilege of making her first profession in the Kensington chapel—the first such profession since 1941. This occasion was very special because just a few weeks previously, on 17 October, Mary MacKillop was canonised a saint of the Catholic Church.

During her later years, Mary MacKillop often acknowledged when individual Sisters were professed for twenty-five years, but insisted that this jubilee should be observed quietly.[51] Since March 1918, when the Sisters celebrated the golden jubilee of Sister Francis Xavier (Blanche) Amsinck's religious profession, they had honoured any members of the community who reached this milestone in a

---

50. *SC* 27 January 1978, 1.
51. MM to Sr Calasanctius Howley, 16 July & 8 August 1894; to Sisters Patricia Campbell and Andrea Howley, 8 August 1894; to Sister Annette Henschke, 9 August 1894. Mother Bernard Walsh to MM, 20 March 1898, to name but a few.

special way.⁵² Ten years later, Sister Francis Xavier and, over time, a number of other Sisters, commemorated their diamond jubilees. The Special General Chapter of 1971 ruled that Sisters professed for twenty-five years should also be honoured for this achievement and that they could invite their families and friends to share in the occasion.

One of the first to take advantage of the new ruling regarding families and friends was Sister Laura La Franki, who made her religious profession in Sydney in January 1924 and spent the following fifty years in Adelaide. For eleven of those years she managed the kitchen at the seminary and, on the occasion of her jubilee, twenty-six priests who had enjoyed her cooking during their seminary years, honoured her by concelebrating her Jubilee Mass in the Kensington chapel. The homilist at this Mass commented that 'the virtues of love, dedication and self-sacrifice were very evident in her life'.⁵³

Laura, who was of Italian background, hailed from Wonthaggi in Victoria. Her first appointment was to the Providence, where she stayed for twenty-four years. Besides preparing meals for the household, she was one of the many Sisters who did duty as sacristans at St Patrick's Church in Grote Street and St Francis Xavier's Cathedral in the centre of the city. This role required a great deal of walking because the Providence Sisters did not own a car and there were no direct bus or tram routes between the Providence and these churches. It was not easy for someone who was on her feet for most of the day but she loved this work. After leaving the Providence, Laura served at the seminary, and subsequently at Kingswood, Kensington, Aldgate and Largs Bay.

Laura was but one of that outstanding but unsung group of Josephites who spent most of their lives working in large kitchens, preparing meals for Sisters, boarders, orphans, inmates or residents in the larger Josephite establishments across the state. Few of their names are remembered in Josephite folklore but the Congregation

---

52. Blanche Amsinck was the second Sister to make her religious profession, which she did on 19 March 1868. Mary MacKillop, who was the first, but did not survive long enough to celebrate her golden jubilee, made hers on 15 August 1867.
53. *SC* 11 January 1974, 5.

owes a great deal to their dedication and hard work. Another group of Sisters, most of whose names have slipped from popular memory, are those who spent almost their entire lives at the Providence or the Orphanage, or worked with the unmarried mothers, former prisoners, and other women who found shelter at the Refuge during difficult phases in their lives.[54]

During the period under review, the Josephite way of being underwent many changes. Until 1956, when motor missions were first established, the annual destination or appointment list drawn up by the provincial of the time named the 'community leader' or 'superior', the 'music teacher', and the school Sisters for each place. Sisters based in the charitable institutions or the seminary lived in communities attached to their workplaces and seldom moved from one to the other while most retired senior Sisters belonged to the Kensington community and rarely moved elsewhere.

Apart from the two or three Sisters making and distributing the altar breads, those who were in charge of the kitchens in the larger houses and those who worked in the other institutions, most able-bodied Sisters other than those on the motor missions, were teaching in schools. This was especially true of the 1950s and 1960s when the schools were bursting at their seams.

By the 1970s the old certainties were gone. When Sister Joan Luff drew up destination lists during her time as provincial (1971–1977), she needed to find parish coordinators, Sisters to fill positions at the CCRE and the CEO and a full time coordinator of renewal and ongoing formation for the Sisters, as well as decide who could be released to do full time study for that year. Thus, for example, in 1977, of the 237 Sisters living in thirty-five communities, thirty-eight were school principals and thirty-three were members of school staffs. Sixteen former motor missioners were parish pastoral associates or parish workers in seven country districts and five city parishes. Several Sisters were on leave to study theology, scripture

---

54. Some of the Sister cooks of the latter half of the twentieth century were Sisters Michelle Ryan, Stephanie Stephens, Elizabeth Schultz, Elaine Liddy, Monica Coonan, Marcella Myers, Jane Owen and Dorothea Reid. Some of the few Refuge Sisters whose names are remembered are Sisters Bernardine Ledwith, Annette Henschke and her niece, Therese Vincent Henschke, Helena Bolger and Finbar Cremin. Sister Finbar kept the Refuge accounts for the best part of fifty years.

and catechesis at interstate institutions. In total, only seventy-one (or less than one-third of the Sisters in the province) were working in the schools.

Sister Joan completed her term as Provincial at the time of the 1977 General Chapter. Her successor was South Australian born Sister Mary Reardon, who had lived and worked in New South Wales for some years. At the same time, Sister Elizabeth Murphy from Western Australia became the Congregation's tenth Mother General and Sister Lorna Bourke was re-elected to the General Council. After the close of the Chapter, Elizabeth invited Sister Teresita Cormack to move to Sydney to become bursar, that is, finance officer, for the Congregation.

Elizabeth Murphy held the reins from 1977 until 1989. Her immediate successor was Sister Mary Cresp of South Australia, the first locally born woman to fill this role. After her came Sisters Giovanni Farquer from Victoria (1995–2001), then Katrina Brill from New Zealand (2001–2007), and finally, Anne Derwin of New South Wales (2008-2013).

When Mary Reardon completed her term of office as Provincial in 1983, her successor was Sister Margaret McKenna, a native of Queensland. In due course, came Sisters Catherine Clark (1989–1995), Josephine Huppatz (1995–2001), Christine Rowan (2001–2007), and Marion Gambin (2008–2013).[55]

At about the time of the 1977 Chapter, some Sisters made known their desire to find more intensive ways of working among the poor in the spirit of Mary MacKillop and Julian Woods. Several felt called to work with urban Aboriginal people. Others saw that the care of people with disabilities was a work dear to the heart of Mary MacKillop, who invited Bessie, a woman with an intellectual disability, to live in the Kensington community.[56] Many were disturbed when they observed the disruption caused to families

---

55. See Appendix 14 for a full listing of provincials and Superiors General from 1866-2014.
56. MM to Sr Ignatius O'Brien, 6 July 1871, wrote, 'Kiss dear Bessie for me, the poor dear creature. I am sorry to think she is suffering'; to Sr Monica Phillips, 26 September 1884: 'The enclosed picture is for Bessie who is, I trust, well and happy. Give her my love and tell her I don't forget her.' There are at least eleven references to Bessie in Mary's letters to Sisters in South Australia.

by extreme poverty and homelessness and set out to do something about it.

Sister Ursula Hoile had long wished to work among the poor in an overseas setting. Finally, after a time of intense prayer and research, the Congregation accepted a mission in Peru. In April 1981, four Sisters, including Ursula, moved to Lima, where she remained until the year 2000. After her return, Sisters Geraldine Stringer and Katrina Van Ruth volunteered to go there at different times and carry on the same work among the poor and disadvantaged people of that country.

Sisters concerned about the plight of Aboriginal people in South Australia, sought ways to support and assist them, and some became directly involved in this work. Thus, in 1979 Sister Michele Madigan moved into a Housing Trust home in the northwestern industrial suburb of Taperoo. While living among poor neighbours, she became involved in political advocacy for the Aboriginal people on several fronts. These included the Pitjantjatjara and Maralinga Land Rights Campaigns and the Aboriginal Community College, which moved into the former St Joseph's Orphanage building at Largs Bay in 1981 despite strong objections from some local people. After a time, Sisters Ann Duyndam and Michele moved to a house in Fletcher Road, Largs Bay. From there they worked directly among the Aboriginal people, leaving their successors at Taperoo to carry on a more general neighbourhood ministry.

Over the years since 1982 in particular, many Sisters have been involved, either directly or indirectly, in projects aimed at improving the situation of Aboriginal people in our society. The Port Augusta Sisters ensured that Aboriginal children and their families were welcomed into the Caritas College community. When the Aboriginal College vacated the Largs Bay building in 1984, the province supported and facilitated the setting up of the Aboriginal venture, Kura Yerlo, ('By the Sea') on that site. After that, several Sisters, including Sisters Michele Madigan and Kenise Neill, lived and worked with Aboriginal people in towns and settlements including Yalata and Ceduna on the Far West Coast of SA, Coober Pedy and the Anangu Pitjantjatjara Yankunytjatjara (APY) Lands in the far north-west of the state, Port Augusta on the Upper Spencer Gulf and Murray Bridge on the Lower Murray River.[57]

For decades, Sister Mary Robert Aitken worked with Aboriginal people in Adelaide's inner city and metropolitan areas, visiting those in hospitals and in the parks, taking her place as a member of the Kura Yerlo Board and being actively involved in the Royal Commissions on Aboriginal Deaths in Custody and the Hindmarsh Island Bridge (on behalf of the Ngarrindjeri People). A number of Josephites, including Sisters Mary Robert, Margaret Kenny, Susan Pollard, Joan Evans and Marie Faulkner, as well as two Carmelite Sisters formed a Reconciliation Circle which continued to meet beyond 2010. By then, there was a Reconciliation Garden in the grounds of the Kensington convent and a plaque acknowledging the Aboriginal people's prior ownership of this land was in place near the convent.

Sister Genevieve Secker felt drawn to engage in caring for adults living with intellectual disabilities. She put her ideas to the 1982 Provincial Chapter where the Sisters decided that:

> The Congregation [of the Sisters of St Joseph] support a house for the disabled (sic), 'Ain Karim,' after the style of those operated by L'Arche, because there [was] no such facility in South Australia and people with intellectual disabilities [were] a vital part of the Church.[58]

Matters moved quickly until, by the end of November 1984, this new ministry had a base in Bristol Avenue, Enfield, and Sister Genevieve was ready to receive her first resident. Over time 'Ain Karim' changed and developed and, by 2010, provided a permanent home for twenty people with an intellectual disability. Its aim: to support "adult men and women with an intellectual disability . . . [and] enable them to live happy and fulfilled lives in a life-giving and welcoming community where people [lived] together in mutual respect and understanding."[59]

---

57. Mary Cresp, *God's 'Good Time'* (Hindmarsh, SA: Atf Press, 2013), passim.
58. Report, SA Provincial Chapter, 1982, 6.
59. Marie T Foale, *Ain Karim, Twenty-five years, 1984–2009* (Enfield, SA: Sisters of St Joseph Ain Karim Ltd., 2009), 35.

The Provincial Chapter of 1982 also recommended that the province set up 'a group to enter into a process of discernment about [the Sisters'] continuing involvement in the childcare apostolate'.[60] The outcome of this group's deliberations was the establishment of St Joseph's Family Care Centre at Mitchell Park, a short-term supported accommodation shelter for homeless families, managed by Sisters Teresa Taggert and Vynette Barnden.

Its Mission was to

> strive to recognise and respect the dignity and self-worth of each person, to support them as individuals and families and to help them discover whatever they required to develop and grow.[61]

The first family moved in on 4 January 1985, and by 1990 the centre had an annual turnover of approximately eighty families and 200 children. St Joseph's was widely recognised as a unique and successful model of working with homeless families with highly complex needs, and assisting them to bring about a turnaround in their life circumstances. That is, those at the Centre worked to ensure that people left it with the confidence and skills to enable them to remain housed, with a high level of family function, rather than continuing the cycle of homelessness and itinerancy.

The centre, which did not have a fixed income, relied on the Providence of God for its support. This came through the generosity of its benefactors and fundraising, along with a gradually increasing level of government funding. In 2010 the government introduced a new tender process for funding and St Joseph's was passed over in favour of another organisation. Consequently, and much to the disappointment of those involved, St Joseph's Family Care Centre ceased its ministry among homeless families.[62]

During the late 1980s, Sister Majella O'Sullivan became a pastoral associate with the Catholic Deaf Community of Adelaide. With time she became well known and respected in this area of work and was often called upon to interpret in sign language for

---

60. Report, SA Provincial Chapter, 1982, 12.
61. Mission Statement, St Joseph's Family Care Centre, Mitchell Park, (part thereof).
62. Sister Teresa Taggert rsj, 'Remembering St Joseph's Family Care Centre, Mitchell Park, SA, 1984-2010', unpublished Ms passim.

deaf people on occasions such as funerals, marriages, baptisms, parent/teacher interviews and school graduation ceremonies. She said:

> My ministry is vast and varied. What I have learnt over the last 25 years [since 1989] is that I cannot do or be without my God. I love the challenges which face me each day, and the reward is knowing that I've tried my best at giving a deaf person access to something I used to take for granted—the message that I can hear[63]

From the earliest days of the Congregation, Mary MacKillop encouraged Sisters who were unable to be actively involved in its works to spend time praying for the active ones. Over the years, it became an established practice for the senior Sisters at Kensington to meet in the chapel each morning after breakfast to pray together the entire fifteen mysteries of the Rosary (that is all of the Joyful, Sorrowful and Glorious Mysteries), for the intentions of the Sisters out on ministry.

Some of these Sisters also helped with household duties, gave music lessons to children from neighbouring schools, or visited people in their homes or the hospitals. For many years, Sister Mechtilde Woods, who was blind for most of her adult life, gave instructions in the Catholic Faith to people referred to her by the local parish priest. She was assisted and then succeeded by others. One of the more notable of these was Sister Gabriel Gillman-Jones who carried on this work until shortly before her death in 1956, aged eighty-seven years.[64]

As the school Sisters arrived home at the end of the day, some Senior Sisters sat on the back verandah to welcome them and hear firsthand accounts of the day's happenings. When Sisters came in from the country for the school holidays, the Kensington Sisters

---

63. Interview with Sister Majella O'Sullivan, 17 August 2014.
64. Sister Mechtilde (Ellen Henrietta Woods) was born in Adelaide on 24 September 1854, joined the Josephites in 1868, aged fourteen years, was professed on her sixteenth birthday in 1869, and died at Kensington in 1928. Sister Gabriel (Rose Henrietta Gillman-Jones) was born in Bunbury, WA, on 4 April 1869. She joined the Josephites at Kensington, SA, on 4 March 1888, was professed on 29 September 1890, and died at Kensington on 18 May 1956, aged eighty-six years.

used to gather in little clusters to hear the latest news from the new arrivals' places of ministry. They made it a real homecoming for the country Sisters![65]

Following the changes made by Vatican II and, more importantly, the Senior Sisters' move to Tappeiner Court, the practice of praying the fifteen mysteries of the Rosary together gradually died out. Even so, many retired Sisters spent much of their day praying for those engaged in active ministry. At the same time, some older, semi-retired Sisters living in suburban or country communities felt a strong desire to become involved in an organised ministry of prayer.

Their wish was fulfilled when, in 1978, the Conference of Major Superiors of Religious Women (South Australia) sponsored a six week live-in programme for Sisters who were either retired or were approaching retirement from active ministry. They invited members of several different Congregations, including two Josephites, Sisters Constance Conroy and Laura La Franki, to join a planning committee. Constance, who was a skilled stenographer, became its secretary and both she and Laura invested much time and energy into preparing for the programme. Finally, on 26 February 1978, thirty-nine Sisters from seven different Religious Congregations arrived at St Joseph's, Aldgate, for the first Tabor experience. When the visitors left six weeks later they took with them 'a special happiness—a togetherness—which still continued for years afterwards'.[66]

The Tabor renewal programme continued for six years. Once it was well established and thanks to the encouragement of its Jesuit chaplain, Father Charles Mayne, a senior priest, the Sisters undertook a new venture: the Tabor Ministry of Prayer. Archbishop Gleeson, who was delighted with the idea, provided them with monthly prayer intentions which they printed in both English and Italian and sent out to the parishes. As Sister Constance put it in a letter seeking a papal blessing:

---

65. The author remembers these practices well and recalls the welcome there at Christmas time. These Sisters were so interested in you yourself and in every little bit of news you could tell them
66. Sister Constance Conroy, 'Tabor Story, 1978–1984', unpublished Ms. 1984, 2. The Sisters named the programme Tabor because it was on Mount Tabor that Jesus was transfigured and the apostles accompanying him had what could be described as a special prayer experience.

> The idea was to spread this prayer throughout the whole archdiocese (a formidable task for old ladies), but GOD MUST WANT IT because already in nearly 2 years, we have 8,000 pray-ers. (Sic)[67]

The response from Rome was not long in coming. In a letter dated 10 May 1983, a Papal Secretary conveyed the Pope's Apostolic Blessing to the group.[68]

Father Mayne commented:

> This is my sixtieth year as a Jesuit and I think I can say that no other apostolate has been as satisfying as being part of the various Tabor Course and group activities.[69]

While she was secretary of the Tabor committee, Sister Constance was engaged in parish ministry in the inner suburban parish of Thebarton. There she visited the homes of people in need, Catholic and non-Catholic alike, especially the sick and the elderly. Gradually she built up an ecumenical network in readiness for the time when she would no longer be able to do this work herself. In January 1984 the Mayor of Thebarton named her 'Citizen of the Year', in recognition of her work among the people of the district.[70]

Much happened during the decades following the Special Chapter of 1969. It was an exciting time but also one of grieving as Sisters farewelled friends who decided that Josephite religious life was not for them, closed convents and schools, and withdrew from ministries that used to define who they were. They did not give up hope, however. Some became involved in new ministries while

---

67. Conroy, 'Tabor Story, 1978–1984', 13, Letter to Pope John Paul II, 16 April 1983.
68. Conroy, 'Tabor Story, 1978–1984', 14; SC 30 June 1983, 1 & 5.
69. Charles Mayne SJ, Chaplain of Tabor, 14 May 1984, quoted in Conroy, 'Tabor Story'. Father Mayne was born in England in 1906, joined the Jesuits in 1924, was ordained in Ireland in 1937, and died in Melbourne in 1990. See John N Molony, 'Mayne, Charles (1906–1990)', ADB (National Centre of Biography, Australian National University, 2012),http://adb.anu.edu.au/biography/mayne-charles-14953/text26142.
70. Sister Constance Conroy was born at Hindmarsh on 9 August 1911, joined the Josephites in March 1938, was professed in 1940, and taught junior grades in a number of country and city schools. She moved to Thebarton in 1978, retired from there in 1988, and died at Flora McDonald Lodge, Cowandilla, on 13 October 1992, aged eighty-one years.

others assisted with the training of lay people to carry on their works in the spirit of Mary MacKillop and Julian Woods.

One way of keeping the founders' spirit alive was to implement the 1977 General Chapter recommendation that Sisters look at different ways whereby people might become associate members of the Congregation. The idea developed gradually and the 'Josephite Associates in Mission' came into being during the late 1980s. By 1990, there were 185 Associates in South Australia and numbers continued to grow over subsequent years. Their Mission Statement read:

> As Josephite Associates, we respond to the call to live the charism of Mary MacKillop in our daily lives in our own unique way. We support one another by friendship, prayer and service to make a difference in our local area and so further the reign of God.[71]

For some, however, that was not enough. By the mid-1990s and in response to calls from women wishing to be even more closely affiliated with the Congregation, the Sisters considered new concepts of membership. Eventually, after years of study, prayer and consultation between Sisters and interested women, several of the latter felt a strong call to live the charism of Mary MacKillop in communion with the Sisters of St Joseph for the sake of mission. These women made a covenant of affiliation with the Congregation, that is, they became 'Covenant Josephites'.[72]

One unintended outcome of the decline in the membership of the Congregation was that some Sisters needed to live alone and over time, this became an accepted practice. The Sisters experimented in different models of community so that by 2010, the year of Mary MacKillop's canonisation, the 105 Sisters in the province had a well-established network of functioning 'communities without walls'.

Mary's canonisation in 2010 was but the climax of the process initiated by Mother Laurence in 1925. This process received a boost in February 1972 when Cardinal-designate James Knox, Archbishop

---

71. Associates' Web Page: http://www.sosj.org.au/being-involved/2col-index.cfm?loadref=54
72. The option of becoming a Covenant Josephite is open to both women and men. For further information see: http://www.sosj.org.au/being-involved/index.cfm?loadref=235

of Melbourne, announced that the Congregation for the Causes of Saints in Rome had recognised Mary's cause for canonisation[73] and that, for the future, she would be known as 'Servant of God, Mary MacKillop'. Knox expressed his conviction that, in due course, she would become Australia's first canonised saint.[74]

His announcement gave impetus to those striving to rediscover the spirit of the founders of the Congregation. During the late 1960s the Perthville Congregation of Sisters of St Joseph, founded from Adelaide in 1872, commissioned one of their number, Sister Margaret Press, to research and write a book on the life and times of Father Julian Woods. This book, 'Julian Tenison Woods: Father Founder', appeared in bookshops and on Josephite library shelves during 1979. It proved to be but the first of the wave of new works about Mary and Julian that appeared during subsequent decades.[75]

At the Kensington convent, the Sisters set up the original novitiate area (the basement or crypt beneath the chapel), as the Mother Mary of the Cross Resource Centre. Sister Callista Neagle was in charge there and, whenever possible, she gathered as much relevant material as possible for the benefit of the Sisters themselves, and for that of researchers and other interested people. She often told how, when she began this work, she kept the history of the Congregation and its founders stored in shoe boxes in her bedroom.[76]

Pilgrimage to sites sacred to the memory of the founders enabled Sisters and their friends to become immersed in their stories. The first group of pilgrims to visit Adelaide comprise fifty senior Sisters from across the Congregation. They arrived in October 1978 and while there, they visited many of the local places once hallowed by the presence of Julian Woods and Mary MacKillop.[77]

---

73. Ian B Waters, 'Knox, James Robert (1914–1983)', *ADB*, (Canberra: National Centre of Biography, Australian National University, 2007), http://adb.anu.edu.au/biography/knox-james-robert-12752/text22999
74. *SC* 9 February 1973, 3.
75. SC 12 January 1968, 9: 'A Black Josephite (she wears blue) visits SA'. Margaret Press rsj, *Julian Tenison Woods: Father Founder* (Sydney: HarperCollins, 1979). St Paul Publications republished this book in 1994 and 2004.
76. At the time Sr Callista Neagle was the teaching principal of the St John the Baptist School at Plympton.
77. *SC* 5 October 1978, 19.

Over time the pilgrimage has become a significant part of the Josephite way of telling the Woods–MacKillop story. Local pilgrimages were first mooted in Adelaide in the late 1980s. Over the next several years, the Sisters arranged a series of day and weekend trips to places associated with Mary and Julian and the early Sisters. They also took busloads of pilgrims to visit Mary MacKillop's tomb in Sydney in 1997, 1999, 2003 and 2009, calling at Penola and Mary's birthplace in Melbourne along the way. Each October from about 1996 onwards, the South Australian Sisters welcomed members of an annual National Pilgrimage with participants from every Australian state, New Zealand and overseas.

Sister Judith Thompson, who came from Queensland in 1987 to assist those running 'Renew' programmes in the Port Pirie diocese, offered invaluable guidance to Sisters planning local pilgrimages. The first pilgrimage, a day trip to Adelaide sites associated with the founders, took place during 1990.

A much-awaited launch of a reprint of Father Osmund Thorpe's Life of Mary MacKillop, which first appeared during 1957, took place in 1981. Then on 9 September 1982, came the publication of Father Bill Modystack's *Mary MacKillop: A Woman before her Time*. This popular version of Mary's story sold well.[78]

On 15 October 1989 all Josephites celebrated the centenary of Julian Woods' death. In Adelaide the most important event on that day was the launch of Marie Foale's book, *The Josephite Story*, in the schoolroom at Franklin Street. Julian was also remembered at a symposium in Penola where Father Roderick O'Brien of Naracoorte was keynote speaker, and in an exhibition on 'Julian the Scientist' in the Ira Raymond Room at the Barr Smith Library of the University of Adelaide. Sister Margaret Press was responsible for the organisation and setting up of that display.

By the mid-1990s all who were sufficiently able-bodied took an active part in the events surrounding the beatification of Mary MacKillop. News from Rome that Pope John Paul II would travel to Sydney to beatify her in January 1995 gave rise to a flurry of activity across the Congregation and especially in South Australia where it all began. Every Sister was invited to Sydney for the

---

78. William Modystack, *Mary MacKillop: A Woman before her Time* (Adelaide: Rigby, 1982).

occasion and those who made the journey were at the Randwick Racecourse to hear the Pope declare Mary MacKillop to be Blessed. Hundreds of Sisters and thousands of their friends and supporters took part in this ceremony.

South Australian celebrations began several weeks earlier with a procession headed by a Pilgrim Cross from Penola and comprising a large number of students from Josephite schools with supervising adults. Some participants carried banners bearing the names of the more than 140 convents and schools where Sisters had lived and worked since 1866. They marched from the west end of Grote Street, the site of Mary Mackillop's first home in Adelaide, to St Francis Xavier's Cathedral, the location of her first school there. After a prayer service in the cathedral, the cross was taken to the Kensington convent chapel and from there it went to Sydney for the beatification ceremony.

The SA celebrations concluded with a special event at Football Park (AAMI Stadium) at West Lakes, where Mary's unique relationship with South Australia was acknowledged, acclaimed and re-enacted. The new Mary MacKillop Exhibition Centre at Kensington opened during 1995 with an exhibition featuring aspects of the early days of the Congregation in Adelaide, Kensington and Norwood. In 2001 this exhibition was replaced by "What Would Have Become of Them?" a display showing the unique ways in which the early Sisters took their motto to heart and reached out to the poor and disadvantaged of their time.

In August 2009 the Sisters commemorated the centenary of Mary MacKillop's death in a number of ways including a moving ritual on the vigil of her anniversary, 8 August 2009. This was but a prelude to the excitement of her canonisation on 17 October 2010.[79] For many months previously, Sisters and their helpers all worked hard to ensure that everything was in readiness for the great day. Sister historians and storytellers were called upon to visit widely separated local areas and corroborate or, at times even refute, stories about how Mary MacKillop visited their town or

---

79. 'Canonisation' means that the holy person is recognised worldwide and venerated as a saint for the Universal Church. The feast-day (usually the anniversary of the person's death) is listed in the universal Church calendar and the liturgy and prayers of that day may be used in every country in the world.

travelled through it on the way to somewhere else. Many of these stories had been handed down from generations past.

At Morphett Vale the people remembered that it was in their little church that Mary was 'recommunicated' with the Church in February 1872.[80] The people of Wallaroo, Moonta and Kadina were proud to recall that Mary knew their towns well, for she visited there on a number of occasions and stayed at Kadina for several weeks during the winter of 1871. At Yankalilla the locals were delighted to acknowledge that their town was chosen for the Josephites' first country foundation. At Peterborough representatives from many different localities in the Mid-North came to hear of 'their' Mary's numerous and wide-ranging visits to that region.

The Mitcham Council erected plaques at significant sites associated with the Josephite presence in their suburb and acknowledged in a special way the friendship between Mary MacKillop and Joanna Barr Smith, whose home was in that area. The owner of a thriving automotive business located on the former site of St Joseph's Providence, West Terrace, Adelaide, commissioned the making and erection of a plaque on the footpath outside his premises, thus reminding passers-by of the contribution the Josephites made to the City of Adelaide by their presence there for so many years. And so the list goes on.

Everywhere there was a sense of excitement as canonisation day drew near and a number of local celebrations took place on the day itself. The largest of these were in Penola and Adelaide. Hundreds of people descended upon the former to join with Emeritus Archbishop Leonard Faulkner in acclaiming Mary on the very spot where, 144 years earlier, she said 'yes' to Father Woods' invitation that she become the first Sister of St Joseph. In Adelaide, the celebrations began at the Mary MacKillop Centre, Kensington, and concluded with a viewing of the canonisation ceremony from Rome.

From early in the morning, there was a buzz of excitement at the Centre as people came together to set up stalls selling food or MacKillop trinkets. Then, as the crowd swelled, those in charge of

---

80. 'Recommunicated' is a term coined by the Year Seven students of Antonio Catholic School at Morphett Vale to describe what happened to Mary when her sentence of excommunication was lifted.

the catering had a busy time. People came in ones and twos and dozens, on foot, by car and by the busload, and those with vehicles were pleased to find that the nearby Mary MacKillop College oval was offering free parking for the day. Adelaide's weather was kind and everyone was able to enjoy the entertainment provided by the MacKillop College choir and band. At last it was time to set out in procession from the Centre to the Mary MacKillop Plaza, that is, the space between St Francis Xavier's Cathedral and Victoria Square in central Adelaide. Several thousand people happily walked along the five-kilometre route, singing MacKillop hymns and songs as they went.

As evening approached the crowds swelled. Many set up folding chairs, laid blankets on the grass, or otherwise made themselves comfortable in front of the television screen on the outer western wall of the cathedral. They listened to music as they waited for the Mass to begin and, in particular, for that special moment in history. Once Rome came on line, everyone strained to spot any of their friends in the crowd. The Josephites were recognised easily because of their distinctive teal scarves. A hush fell as the pope began the Mass and anyone could have heard a pin drop when he began the ritual of canonisation. All felt privileged to have witnessed the moment when that great Australian woman, Mary of the Cross MacKillop, became her native country's first canonised saint.

So ends this account of the Sisters of St Joseph from the birth of the Congregation on 19 March 1866 to the canonisation of its co-founder, Mary MacKillop, on 17 October 2010. Much happened during those 144 years. There were dark times and bright times, times of growth and expansion interspersed with times of decline, times of stability and times of change, and through it all, the members of the Congregation never forgot their call to do what they could to remedy the evils and ills of their society. They were educators still, although few of them operated in classrooms any more. They looked out for the welfare of the poor and disadvantaged in different ways. In short, even though they were older and fewer in numbers, they were still Mary MacKillop women, faithful to her challenge to

> do all the good they [could] and never see an evil without trying how they [might] remedy it, and thus to take a most lively interest in every external work of charity in the gaols,

poor houses, and hospitals, so as to leave nothing untried, no matter how difficult, provided it [might] advance the glory of God, the good of souls, and the prevention of sin in the world. This [was and still is] their mission, for though the Institute [had and still has] its peculiar [particular] duties, yet the religious must do any good that they can, and make their charity all embracing. (Woods, *Rules for the Institute of St Joseph*, 1867, par. 13.)

Archbishop James Gleeson meeting with Mother Denis Earle, and Srs Margaret Foreman and Concepta (Joan) Luff, SA Provincial, early 1970s.

Srs Loreto O'Connor, Brigette Sipa and Theresa Swiggs who made their final profession in the chapel at Kensington in January 1978, seen here with Bishop Philip Kennedy and Archbishop James Gleeson after the ceremony.

Sr Maureen Colbert with Aboriginal children at Kununurra, ca. 1970.

Srs Callista Neagle and Concepta (Joan) Luff) discuss the Mary MacKillop Archives, mid 1970s

Srs Andrina Connolly and Michelle Cresp at Port Linc 1978

Sr Elizabeth Murphy, meeting with SA Provincial, Margaret McKenna and her Council, mid-1980s.
L to R. Srs Elizabeth Murphy (Congregational Leader), Patricia O'Dea, Mary Canny, Catherine Clark, Elizabeth Murphy (SA, member of Provincial Council), Margaret McKenna (Provincial).

Sr Constance Conroy shows the citation she received from the Thebarton Council in 1984

Celebrating Sr Elizabeth Schultz's 90th birthday, 2009.
Elizabeth's sister, Mrs Nell Critchley, Srs Marion Gambin (Provincial) & Elizabeth, at St Catherine's Home, Berri.

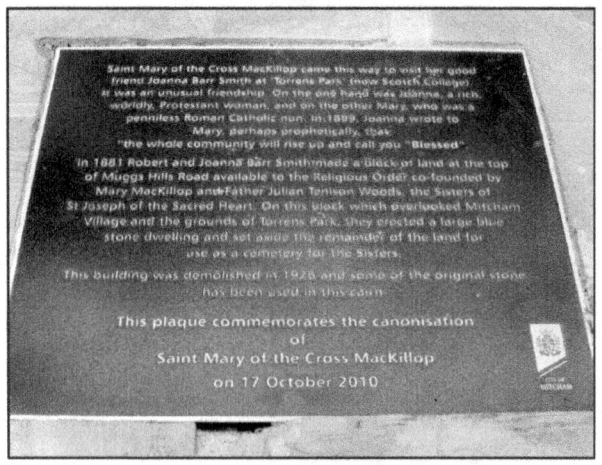

Plaque at Mitcham, commemorating the friendship between Mary MacKillop and Joanna Barr Smith

Appendices

1. Josephite Foundations and Ministries in SA, 1866–2010 — 379
2. Recruits from the South East of SA & Western Victoria, 1866–1870 — 391
3. Number of Women who joined the Congregation and of Josephite Foundations, SA, 1867–1871 — 393
4. Sisters' Daily Timetable, 1866–1960s — 397
5. Sisters' Daily Prayer Schedule, 1866–1960 — 399
6. Schools that remained open during Mary MacKillop's excommunication period, 1871–1872 — 401
7. Schools from which the Sisters withdrew, 1871–1872 — 403
8. Reasons for Mary MacKillop's Excommunication, 1871 — 405
9. Irish Women who accompanied Mary MacKillop to Australia to join the Congregation, 1874–1875 — 411
10. Mary MacKillop's absences from and times at home in SA, 1867–1909. — 417
11. Closures of SA Convents, Schools & Institutions, 1880–1893 — 419
12. Convents, Schools & Institutions in SA, 1895 — 421
13. Mary MacKillop's Report on SA Visitation, 1899. — 423
14. Mary MacKillop re Languages & Select Schools, Sydney, 1901 — 431
15. Congregational, Provincial & Regional Leaders, 1867–2014 — 435
16. South Australian Provincials & Regional Leaders, 1870–2014 — 437
17. Josephite Monogram — 439

Appendices

APPENDIX ONE
South Australian Foundations, 1866–2010

	COUNTRY	SUBURBAN
1866	**PENOLA:** Convent & School: 1866–1871 1875–1885 1936–2010 → R.E.C. Millicent: 1984–1998 South East Motor Mission, (S.E.R.E.C.): 1973–1997	
	MOUNT GAMBIER: 1866–1867	
1867		**ADELAIDE CITY:** St F.X. Cathedral Hall School: 1867–1871 Poor School, Franklin Street: 1869–1871 Convent: Grote Street: 1867 Mother House: Franklin Street: 1868–1871
		BOWDEN / BROMPTON: School only: 1867–1871 1876–1887 Convent & School: 1887–1928 Moved to Hindmarsh: November 1928
	YANKALILLA: 1867–1874	**REFUGE:** City: 1867–1870 Mitcham: 1870–1872 Norwood: 1872–1902 Fullarton: 1902–1963
1868	**KAPUNDA:** 1868–1893	**QUEENSTOWN:** 1868–1871
	WILLUNGA: 1868–1881	**PENINSULA, MEAD ST, ETHELTON:** 1868–1871.
	GAWLER: 1868–1901	**ORPHANAGE:** City: 1868–1872 Mitcham: 1872–1875 Burnside: 1875–1888 Goodwood: 1888–1890

	MACCLESFIELD: School: 1868–1871 1875–1909 1920–1969 Motor Mission: 1970–1989 Residence Only: 1991–2011	**PROVIDENCE:** **CITY:** Various locations: 1868–1905 West Terrace: 1905–1951 COWANDILLA: 1951–2010 → (SEE COWANDILLA FOR FURTHER DETAILS)
		ALBERTON: (RUSSELL STREET, ROSEWATER / PENNINGTON)) School: 1868–1871 1882–1885 1909–1986 Convent: 1941–2006
		PORT ADELAIDE: 1868–1871 1877–1965
1869	**WALLAROO:** School: 1869–2002 Star of the Sea Nursing Home: 1992–2010 →	**NORTH ADELAIDE:** 1869–1871
	KADINA: School: 1869–1974 Residence: 1869–2001	**THEBARTON:** School: 1869–1871 Convent & School: 1883–1996 Pastoral Presence: 1978–1988 Pastoral Associate: 1996–2005
	ST JOHNS, via KAPUNDA: Convent & School: 1869–1876 Reformatory: 1897–1909	**SOLITUDE OF MARY, HOME FOR PENITENT WOMEN:** Various Sites: 1869–1877
	CLARE (FIRST FEW WEEKS AT ARMAGH WHERE SISTERS TAUGHT IN BUTLER'S SHED): School: 1869–2002 Convent: 1869–2010 →	**GLENELG:** 1869–1903.
	ROBE: 1869–1871 1872–1879	**MARION:** Convent & School: 1869–1891 Residence Only: 1985–2003

	MOUNT BARKER: 1869–1871 **Pastoral Worker:** 1974–1995	
	QUEENSLAND: *1869–1880*	
1870	BURRA (KOORINGA): 1870–1970	GLEN OSMOND: 1870–1871.
	MOONTA: 1870–1880.	
	MORPHETT VALE: 1870–1879.	MITCHAM: **Refuge:** 1870–1872 **School:** 1870–1914 **Moved to Kingswood:** 1914
	GREENOCK: 1870–1875	HECTORVILLE: **School:** 1870–2004 **Motor Mission:** 1964–1973 **Resident in parish:** 1870–2010 →
	MARRABEL: 1870–1873.	LOWER NORTH ADELAIDE: 1870–1973
	TARLEE: (GILBERT / NAVAN) 1870–1890 **Note:** There is no real proof of sisters having been at Gilbert or Navan. Several lay teachers are named in the records.	
	RHYNIE: 1870–1876	
1871	BAGOT'S GAP: 1871–1883.	GRAND JUNCTION: (A FEW MONTHS ONLY) **School only:** 1871–1871
	PORT AUGUSTA: School: 1871–2010 → Convent: 1871–2010 → Motor Mission: 1971–1997	MAGILL: 1871–1873
	HOYLETON: 1871–1875	
	AUBURN: 1871–1887	
	UNDALYA: 1871–1881	

1872	**HAMLEY BRIDGE:** Convent & School: 1872–1973 Motor Mission: 1962–1977	**KENSINGTON CONVENT:** Sisters' residence: 1872–2010 → Convent School: 1872–1900 Mother House: 1872–1889 Province Centre: 1889–2010 →
	STOCKPORT: 1872–1881	**NORWOOD: BEULAH ROAD** School only: 1872–1971.
	VIRGINIA: 1872–1886	
	MINTARO: 1872–1889 1925–1957	
	BATHURST: 1872–1876	

1873		**KENSINGTON: BRIDGE STREET:**
		School only:
		  Primary: 1873–1941
		    (Moved to William Street,
		    Norwood: 1942)
		  Secondary: 1951–1962
		  Junior Primary: 1972–1986

	POLISH HILL RIVER: 1873–1877	
	LOWER WAKEFIELD: 1873–1874	

	GEORGETOWN:
	Convent & School:
	  1873–1887
	  1904–1965
	Motor Mission:
	  1966–1980	

	FARRELL FLAT/HANSON: 1873–1889	
	BLINMAN: (Part of one year only) 1873–1873	

1874	**PORT LINCOLN:**
	  1874–1886
	  1926–2009
	  Boarding school:
	    1926–2009	

1875	**MANOORA:** 1876–1892.	**ADELAIDE, PIRIE STREET:** School only: 1875–1935.

1876	**BAKER'S FLAT: (NEAR KAPUNDA)** School only: 1876–1877	
	HEAD STATION: 1876–1879	
1877	**LAURA:** 1877–1887	**ADELAIDE, RUSSELL ST:** School only: 1877–1880 1882–1965.
	APPILA–YARROWIE: 1877–1889	
	CALTOWIE: 1877–1896 1905–1961	
	MINTARO STATION (MERILDEN): 1877–1880	
	YACKAMOORUNDIE, (GULNARE SOUTH): 1877–1883	
	FREELING: 1877–1878	
	SALTIA: 1877–1879	
	MAITLAND: 1877–1889	
1878	**PEKINA:** 1878–1944	
1880	**SEVENHILL:** 1880–1964	
	PORT ELLIOTT: 1880–1884	
	ORROROO: 1880–1882	
	JAMESTOWN: **School:** 1880–1988 **Music:** until 1997 **Pastoral presence:** 1995–2008	
	PORT WAKEFIELD: 1880–1881	
	SYDNEY & ARMIDALE: *1880–1890* →	
1881	**WAROOKA:** 1881–1882	

	WHYTE YARCOWIE: 1881–1891	
1882	WILLOCHRA: 1881–1883	
1883	STRATHALBYN: 1883–1889	
	NEW ZEALAND: *1883 _*	
1887	*WESTERN AUSTRALIA:* *1887–1890 & 1906 →*	
1889	QUORN: 1889–1959	
1890	GLADSTONE: 1890–1979 1994–2000	
1897	PETERBOROUGH: 1897–1997. 1999–2000 2003–2010 → **Boarding school**: 1926–1978 **Motor Mission**: 1960–1970 **(Moved to Port Augusta, 1970)**	
1903		LARGS BAY: Orphanage: 1903–1980
1911	TEROWIE: 1911–1966.	
1912		WOODVILLE PARK **School:** 1912–2007 **Convent:** 1951–2003 **Motor Mission:** 1964–1973
1914		KINGSWOOD: FOUNDED FROM MITCHAM, 1914: **Convent:** Cambridge Tce: 1914–2001 Tutt Avenue: 2001–2010 → **School:** 1914–1986 **City Motor Mission:** 1964–1973
1917		ST PETER'S ELLANGOWAN: **School only:** 1917–1980 **Pastoral Worker:** 1981–1998
1919	RENMARK: 1919–1999	

1921	SPALDING: 1921–1973	
1922	BALAKLAVA: School: 1922–1969 Pastoral presence: 1994–2001	DULWICH: School only: 1921–1925 1945–1968. St Patrick's Special School: 1969–1997
1924	PINNAROO School: 1924–1988 Pastoral presence: 1989–2007	
1925	MURRAY BRIDGE: School: 1925–1998. Pastoral presence: 2002–2010 →	KESWICK: (MOVED TO KURRALTA PARK, 1960) School only: Everard St, Keswick: 1925–1959 South Rd. Kurralta Park: 1960–1977
1927		TRANMERE: School only: 1927–1949 Convent & school: 1949–1985 Convent only: 1985–2007
1928		HINDMARSH: MOVED FROM BROMPTON, 1928) School: 1928–1998 Convent: 1928–2001 Parish worker: 1977–1996
1929		CROYDON PARK: (FORMERLY KILKENNY) School only: 1929–1953 Convent & School: 1953–2000 Pastoral worker: 1973–1997
1930		PARKSIDE: GENAZZANO–GIRLS' REFORMATORY 1930–1944
1932		WALKERVILLE: School only: 1932–1979
1933		RICHMOND: School only: 1933–1986. 1997–2006

		COWANDILLA:
		Convent: 1933–2010
		Juniorate: 1934–1950
		  Moved to Aldgate: 1950
		Providence: 1951–1972
		  Changed name to Flora
		  McDonald Lodge, 1972.
		Flora McDonald Lodge:
		  1972–2010 →

1935		**PLYMPTON: FORMERLY MORNINGTON** School only: 1935–2000

1936	**BERRI:**
	Convent & School:
	  1936–1964
	  1971–1996
	St Catherine's Home:
	  1987–2010 →	

1941	**TAILEM BEND:**
	Convent & school:
	  1941–1981
	Parish Worker:
	  1994–2010 →	

1942		**ROSTREVOR:** **Seminary:** 1942–1998
		NORWOOD: WILLIAM STREET: **Primary School only** **MOVED THERE FROM BRIDGE ST.** 1942 **St Joseph's Memorial School:** 1942–1982

1944		**NORWOOD / KENSINGTON:**
		Secondary School only.
		ST JOSEPH'S HIGHER PRIMARY:
		  Queen St Norwood:
		  1944–1950
		  Bridge St Kensington:
		  1951–1961
		Renamed: ST JOSEPH'S HIGH
		SCHOOL: 1957
		  Phillips St, Kensington:
		  1963–1970.
		Renamed: MARY MACKILLOP
		COLLEGE: 1970
		Mary Mackillop College:
		  1970–2010→

1950		ALDGATE: Juniorate: 1950–1971 Spirituality Centre: 1972–2008
		FLINDERS PARK: School only: 1950–1981
1954	BARMERA: 1954–1986.	WOODVILLE GARDENS: School only: 1954–1984
	NANGWARRY: 1954–1996	OTTOWAY: School only: 1954–1997
1955	WOOMERA: 1955–1984	GLENEAGLES: (NOW SEATON) School only: 1955–1957
1956		ADELAIDE HILLS MOTOR MISSION: Aldgate: 1956–1971. Macclesfield and other places: 1972–1997
1957	YORKETOWN: 1957–2001	ROYAL PARK: School only: 1957–1964
1958	BAROSSA VALLEY : Motor Mission: 1958–1982	
1959	RADIUM HILL: 1959–1961	
1962		PAYNEHAM: School only: 1962–1982
1964	WAIKERIE: Motor Mission: 1964–1971	
1965		CAMPBELLTOWN (NEWTON): School only: 1965–1981.
		MANSFIELD PARK: School only: 1965–2005
1967		ROSEWATER: (NEWCASTLE ST) Mt Carmel College: 1967–1988. 1996–2006
1970	WENTWORTH, NSW: 1970–1979	
1971		FINDON: SIENA COLLEGE: School only: 1971–1983
		SCHOOLS SUPERVISOR / C.E.O. CONSULTANT: 1971–1981

1973		HENLEY BEACH: ST MICHAEL'S COLLEGE: School only: 1972–1988
1977		TEA TREE GULLY: School only: 1977–1998
		GILLES PLAINS: ST PAUL'S COLLEGE: School only: 1974–1983
1979		TAPEROO, YONGALA STREET: Neighbourhood Ministry: 1979–1989
1981	PERU MISSION: 1981–2010 →	LARGS BAY, FLETCHER RD: Aboriginal Ministry: 1981–1991
1982		ABERFOYLE PARK: School & Parish Work only: 1982–2001
1984		AIN KARIM: A HOME FOR ADULTS WITH AN INTELLECTUAL DISABILITY: 1984–2010 →
		MITCHELL PARK: FAMILY CARE CENTRE: 1984–2010
1985		MARION: Convent only: 1985–2003 St Anne's Special School: 1997–2004
1986		APOSTOLATE FOR THE DEAF: 1986–2010 →
1989	DALY RIVER N.T.: Aboriginal Ministry: 1989–1993	
1990	YALATA COMMUNITY: Aboriginal Ministry: 1990–1992	
1992		ELIZABETH NORTH Parish Ministry, 1992–1993
1993	COOBER PEDY: Aboriginal Ministry: 1993–2001 2004–2007	
1994		HALLETT COVE: Parish Ministry: 1994–2010 →

1996		SA CATHOLIC EDUCATION COMMISSION, CHAIRPERSON: 1996–2006
		NATUROPATHY: 1996–2004 →
1997		SALISBURY / ELIZABETH: Parish Ministry: 1997–2010 →
1998	WILMINGTON: Parish Ministry: 1998–2010 →	
1999		ALDGATE: COROMANDEL ROAD: Audio–visual, Visual Printing: 1999–2010 →
2000		JUNGIAN ANALYSIS / PSYCHOTHERAPY: 2000–2010 →
2001	PORT PIRIE DIOCESE: Pastoral Ministry: 2001–2010 → Vicar for Religious: 2009–2010 →	
2002	PORT PIRIE: (INCLUDING WHYALLA & RURAL NORTH) Social Work Ministry: 2002–2010 →	
2002	CEDUNA: Aboriginal Ministry: 2002–2004	
2004	MINISTRY FOR REFUGEES: (MIGRATION/ OFFICER) 2004–2007	PORT AUGUSTA: ENFIELD: 2008–2010 →
2006		FINDON /UNDERDALE: NAZARETH COLLEGE: School only: 2006–2010 →
2007	APY LANDS–AMATA: Aboriginal Ministry: 2007–2010 →	
	SOUTH EAST/ BORDERTOWN: Pastoral Ministry: 2007 →	

NOTE: As of the more recent years leading up to 2010, South Australian Josephites have been engaged in many different ministries. It has not been possible to include every one of these in this chart. One notable omission is the music ministry. It is important to remember that until the early 1980s there was a music teacher in almost every community across the state and that these Sisters played an important role in supporting Kensington and the Novitiate. By 2010 only a very small number of Sisters was involved in music teaching. In 2010 Sisters were residing in a variety of different places but a conscious decision has been made to exclude from this list any dwellings which are not directly associated with a particular ministry

APPENDIX TWO

Recruits From The South East of South Australia and Western Victoria: 1866–1870

NAME	PLACE OF ORIGIN	DATE OF ENTRY
Mary MacKillop (Mary of the Cross)	Portland, Western Victoria	19 March 1866
Rose Cunningham (Rose)	Governess, Western Victoria	June 1867
Blanche Amsinck (Francis Xavier)	Governess, Fitzgerald Station, Harrow, Western Victoria	November 1866
Mary Wright (Clare)	schoolteacher, Bridgewater, via Portland, Western Victoria	July 1867 LEFT, 1881
Julia Fitzgerald (Francis of the Five Wounds)	Sister to owner of Fitzgerald Station, Harrow, Western Victoria	October 1867
Margaret Nolan (Agatha)	Glenmire Station, near Casterton, Western Victoria	March 1868s
Anna Phillips (Monica)	Portland, Western Victoria	May 1868
Grace Walsh (Bernard)	Governess, Western Victoria	May 1868
Jane Britt (Jane Francis)	Penola, South Australia Pupil of Mary MacKillop Entered at 14 years of age	May 1868 LEFT Sept. 1871

Ellen Wright (Gertrude)	Portland, Western Victoria. Sister to Clare	January 1870 LEFT 1881
Ellen Hudson (Celestine)	Mount Gambier, SA. Pupil of Blanche. Entered at 15 years of age.	February 1870 - LEFT Sept. 1871

APPENDIX THREE

Number of Women Who Joined the Congregation & of Josephite Foundations, 1867–1871

YEAR	MONTH	NO. OF ENTRANTS	FOUNDATIONS: Schools & Charitable Institutions	NO. OF CHILDREN in Schools & Institutions
1867	July	5	1	
	August	1		
	September		1	
	October	2	1	
	November	1	1	
	December	1		
		10	4	324

SUMMARY: 31 December, 1867

10 Sisters: 1 professed **Ministries:** 3 schools **Ages:** Mean 25
7 Novices 1 charitable institution Median 23
2 Postulants Range 21-34

1868	January	3	1	
	February	3		
	March	1		
	April	2	1	
	May	8	2	
	June	3	2	
	July	4	1	
	August	6	2	
	September	1		
	October	4		
	November	1		
	December	4		
		40	9	1200

SUMMARY: 31 December, 1868

50 Sisters: 9 professed **Ministries:** 11 schools **Ages:** Mean 21.6
31 Novices 3 charitable institutions Median 20
10 Postulants (The Orphanage was both a Range: 14-34
School & an Institution)

1869	January	3	3	
	February	1	1	
	March	3	3	
	April	3		
	May	2		
	June	6	4	
	July	3		
	August	4		
	September	2	2	
	October	2	1	
	November	3	1	
	December	2 (1 in QLD)	1 (Qld)	
		34	16 (15 in SA)	2,800

SUMMARY: 31 December, 1869

82 Sisters: 36 professed   **Ministries:** 24 schools   **Ages:** Mean   21.0
           35 Novices   4 charitable institutions   Median   20
           11 Postulants   1 community in Qld.   Range   4-39
             2 Novices left the Congregation during this year

1870	January	6	3	
	February	5(2 in Q)		
	March	2		
	April	1	2	
	May	4	1	
	June	4	1	
	July	1	1	
	August	4	2	
	September	3		
	October			
	November	1		
	December			
		31	10	Not available

SUMMARY: 31 December, 1870

111 Sisters: 67 professed   **Ministries:** 32 schools   **Ages:** Mean 23.6
            35 Novices   4 Charitable   Median 22
             9 Postulants   Institutions   Range 14-40
               1 Novice left the Congregation during this year

1871	January	2	2	
	February	2	2	
	March	3		
	April	1		
	May	2	1	
	June	1	2	
	July	1		
	August			
	September			
	October	3		
	November			
	December			
		15	**7**	Not available

SUMMARY: 31 December, 1871

109 Sisters: 75 professed **Ministries:** 20 schools **Ages:** Mean ca. 23
 27 Novices   1 charitable institution   Median ca. 22
 7 Postulants   Range 15-41
 17 Sisters left the Congregation towards the end of this year

APPENDIX FOUR
A: Sisters' Daily Timetable, 1866–1960s

This is a general outline of the daily timetable that the Sisters observed on weekdays until Vatican Council II. Local circumstances sometimes allowed for minor variations, for example, where there was no Mass on a weekday, the Sisters could have an extra half hour of sleep, or where the Sisters in charge of charitable institutions made changes to fit in with their residents' daily programme.

5.00 a.m.	Rise
5.25 a.m.	Morning prayer in the chapel
5.30 a.m.	Morning meditation
6.00 a.m.	Angelus, two litanies or other shorter prayers.
6.10 a.m.	Morning Mass at Kensington convent. In other places where Mass was at 7.00 a.m. the Sisters did household chores between 6.10 a.m. and Mass time.
7.00 a.m.	At Kensington–breakfast At branch houses–Mass
7.45 a.m.	At Kensington–spiritual reading for 15 minutes Elsewhere–breakfast followed by 15 minutes of spiritual reading.
8.00 a.m.	Music teachers often taught their first lesson at 8 a.m. School Sisters set out for their places of work and those engaged in other ministries began their daily duties.
8.30 a.m.	School, music teaching, other duties
5.00 p.m.	Rosary, Litany of Our Lady, Act of Reparation.
5.30 p.m.	Sisters attended to schoolwork, preparation of the evening meal etc.
6.00 p.m.	Six o'clock prayers–Angelus, the Litany of the Saints and some shorter prayers.
6.10 p.m.	Evening meal
7.00 p.m.	Evening Meditation
7.30 p.m.	Evening Recreation
8.30 p.m.	Night prayers
9.00 p.m.	Sisters retired for the night
10.00 p.m.	Lights out.

APPENDIX FIVE
Sisters' Daily Prayer Schedule, 1866–1960s

Each day the Sisters spent approximately three hours engaged in reciting certain set vocal prayers, meditating or reflecting in silence on a passage from the Gospels and taking part in the celebration of Mass.

They always recited the more common prayers, that is, the Our Father, the Hail Mary, the Salve Regina (Hail Queen of Heaven), the Angelus, the Litany of the Saints and some Psalms in Latin. Other shorter prayers, including the ordinary morning and night prayers and most litanies, were said in English.

The first changes occurred after 1959 when some parts of the Prayer of the Church, recited in English, replaced most of the shorter prayers and litanies. What follows is a general outline of the daily prayers recited by the Sisters before 1960.

5.25	Morning prayers – short prayers in English
5.30	Morning Meditation – silent prayer
6.00	The Angelus – in Latin, followed by litanies in English
12.00	At weekends: Angelus in Latin, followed by the Dolour Rosary, in Latin. (The Dolour Rosary was divided into seven sections with one Our Father and seven Hail Marys in each. During each decade those reciting this Rosary reflected on the Seven Sorrows of Mary, the Mother of Jesus.)
5.00	Five decades of the Rosary, in Latin, followed by the Litany of Our Lady in English and an Act of Reparation, also in English.
6.00	The Litany of the Saints, in Latin, followed by some short prayers in English.
7.00	Evening meditation – silent prayer.
8.30	Night prayers – Examination of conscience followed by some short prayers in English.

Grace before and after the midday and evening meals was recited in Latin and, in larger communities such as Kensington, was usually followed by a procession to the chapel during which the Sisters recited the De Profundis (Psalm 130), also in Latin. (This was a penitential psalm that was said or sung in many churches and monasteries as part of evening prayer and in commemorations of the dead).

APPENDIX SIX
Districts where Sisters Remained while Mary Mackillop was under Sentence of Excommunication, 1871–1872

DISTRICT	SCHOOLS	PRIEST/S IN CHARGE
Gawler	Gawler	Christopher Reynolds
Kadina	Kadina Wallaroo Moonta	William Kennedy
Kapunda	Kapunda St Johns Greenock Bagot's Gap.	Charles H. Horan OFM
Marrabel	Marrabel Tarlee (including Gilbert & Navan)	Charles Van Der Heyden
Morphett Vale	Morphett Vale Marion	Peter Hughes
Norwood	Hectorville Magill	Joseph Tappeiner SJ John Hinteroecker SJ
Sevenhill	Clare Burra Hoyleton Auburn Rhynie	John E. Pallhuber SJ Joseph Polk SJ Aloysius Kreissl SJ Matthias Hager SJ Anton Strele SJ Leon Rogalski SJ
Willunga	Willunga Yankalilla	James Quinlan

NOTE: All the priests listed here, with the exception of Father Horan, supported Mary MacKillop and the sisters during this difficult time. It appears that Father Horan kept sisters in his parish with a view to his setting them up under his control as a diocesan or even a parochial sisterhood. He did not succeed in this quest.

APPENDIX SEVEN
Schools that Closed while Mary Mackillop was Under Sentence of Excommunication, 1871–1872

DISTRICT	PRIESTS IN CHARGE	CONVENTS & SCHOOLS
ADELAIDE	Timothy Murphy Bernard Nevin Michael Kennedy Robert Cleary	Poor School, Franklin St St Francis Xavier's Hall School Thebarton Glenelg/Mitcham
NORTH ADELAIDE	James A Nowlan until April 1872, then Theodore Bongaerts	North Adelaide Irishtown Grand Junction Bowden
PORT ADELAIDE	T. Bongaerts until November 1871 M. O'Connor after January 1872	Port Adelaide Le Fevre Peninsula Queenstown
MOUNT BARKER	James Maher	Mount Barker Macclesfield
PENOLA	M O'Connor until January 1872, then Charles Van der Heyden	Penola Robe
PORT AUGUSTA	Modestus Henderson O.F.M. Cap.	Port Augusta

Note:
With the exception of the Dutch priests, Father Theodore Bongaerts, who was dismissed unceremoniously from his mission at Port Adelaide in November 1871, and Father Charles Van der Heyden, who was appointed to Penola in 1872, the priests named above all followed Father Horan's lead and urged the bishop to bring the allegedly unruly colonial Josephites under control, even if his action should result in their disappearance from South Australia.

APPENDIX EIGHT
The Reasons Behind Mary MacKillop's Excommunication[1]

Bishop Lawrence Bonaventure Sheil, Adelaide's third bishop, excommunicated Mary MacKillop from the Church on 22 September 1871, less than three years after he gave his formal approval to the Congregation of the Sisters of St Joseph founded by her and Father Julian Woods.

His reasons for so doing were many and complex and may be summarised as follows:

1. **Some Adelaide priests mistrusted Father Woods, the co-founder of the Congregation with Mary MacKillop, because:**
   - he had upset some of them by his seemingly high-handed manner when acting in his role as Director of Catholic Education.
   - they looked upon him as an impractical idealist and dreamer
   - they believed him to be unqualified for the work of founding a Religious Congregation because he lacked previous experience in the training of female Religious
   - they were afraid that scandal might result from his alleged failures as director of the young Sisters. Their concern was exacerbated when several Sisters claimed that they were the recipients of visions and other manifestations of God's favour

---

[1] Excommunication is a form of censure for alleged serious offences against Church law, by which a member of the Catholic Church is excluded from the congregation of believers and from the rites of the church, is barred from receiving the Sacraments and from burial in consecrated ground. The offender may be received back into the Church after confessing his or her sin and doing penance for it.

and, as a consequence, appeared to believe that they had a licence to behave inappropriately.

In addition, it was well known that:
- one priest (Father Charles Horan), had vowed to bring down Father Woods by destroying the Sisters of St Joseph. He was angry with Woods because the latter had been instrumental in having Horan's good friend, Father Patrick Keating, dismissed from the diocese for alleged indecent behaviour with some children at St Joseph's School, Kapunda.

In early August 1871, the group of priests in question pressured Bishop Sheil to send Woods away from Adelaide in order to:
- lessen his influence over the Sisters
- enable them to enforce changes to the Josephite rule of life.

They were convinced that the Congregation could not survive without such changes.

2. **This Congregation was radically different from the Irish Religious Orders already known to these priests because**:
    - It drew the greater part of its membership from among the working classes
    - Some Sisters were barely literate when they joined it
    - A significant proportion of them was colonial born
    - All were of equal status regardless of their educational or social backgrounds
    - They worked among the poorest sections of society
    - They relied solely on school fees and alms for their support
    - Where necessary they begged for assistance from local businesses, food stalls and so on.
    - They lived in rented or Church-owned accommodation instead of in houses that they owned
    - They moved about openly in public and visited very poor homes, gaols and hospitals in every town where they had schools.

3. **The governance of the Congregation** differed from that of most Irish and European Religious Orders in that it was a centralised form of organisation. That is, there was one general superior who was responsible for all major decisions regarding the running of the Congregation as a whole, even when there were foundations in more than one diocese.

Most contemporary Irish Orders were under the control of the local bishop of any diocese where they had made foundations.

In some Irish parishes the parish priest had a say regarding the management of Religious communities with schools or charitable institutions in his area.

4. Besides all this, **in Ireland, few if any dioceses had Directors of Catholic Education,** and it is likely that, if there were such, they would not have had the sweeping powers that Bishop Sheil bestowed upon Father Woods before he went overseas in 1867.

   Hence, some Irish priests in Adelaide disliked Woods intensely and resented their being prevented from having complete control over their local Josephite convents and schools.

   They felt that the only possible solution to their dilemma was to bring this apparently independent Josephite Congregation into line with the Irish Orders or to close it down altogether.

   In their minds, members of Religious communities should:
   - be divided along class lines into choir Sisters (the ladies) and lay Sisters (the servants)
   - live an enclosed, monastic way of life
   - educate the children of the rich who paid fees so that they could help the poor who came to their convents for assistance
   - never leave their convents or monasteries to visit the poor in their homes, the hospitals or the gaols.

5. **Mary MacKillop,** who understood the Congregation to have Central Government and to have been founded for the education of the children of poor families in isolated places in colonial Australia, made her position clear to the bishop. She informed him that, if he decided to change the Josephite Rule of Life, she would, as a matter of conscience, be obliged to leave the Congregation and look for another place where she could live out her vocation in the way she felt that God was calling her.

6. **Bishop Sheil**, who was very unwell, was most upset when he read Mary's letter. He became extremely angry at what he believed was her impudence and decided to remove her from her position as leader of the Congregation. Matters came to a climax when several

of the priests led him to believe that she had disobeyed his orders. Almost at once he decided to punish her by excommunicating her from the Church. He did not expect any resistance from the Sisters, and so, when they declared their determination to remain faithful to their rule, he dismissed almost half its members from the Congregation and evicted the resident community from their convent in Franklin Street.

AFTER EXCOMMUNICATION and TOWARDS 'RECOMMUNICATION'[2]

The bishop soon realised that he had acted unwisely. In particular he grasped the awful truth that:

- by excommunicating Mary he had set in motion a process for the closing down of at least two thirds of the sixty plus Catholic schools in the colony.
- the strength of the people's support for Mary and the Sisters, as well as for Father Woods, was so great that some went so far as to
  - speak out publicly in their favour
  - vilify him in the local papers
  - complain about him and his supporters to Rome.

For her part, Mary still respected him and was very upset over what appeared in the papers. In fact, she behaved in an exemplary manner and would not allow anyone to speak against the bishop while in her presence.

She kept together most of the Sisters who had been dismissed from the convent and supported and encouraged them as much as possible. She never doubted that God was with them and that all would soon be well again, in whatever way God might will it to be.

During the months after Mary's excommunication, Bishop Sheil's health deteriorated rapidly and by February 1872 he was seriously ill. When he was close to death, he took steps to right some of the wrongs he did during his time in Adelaide.

The best known of these actions was the lifting of the sentence of

---

2. Recommunication is a term coined by the Year Seven students of Antonio Catholic School, Morphett Vale to describe what happened when the bishop removed Mary's sentence of excommunication and restore her rights to full communication with the church.

excommunication from Mary MacKillop. Because he was too ill to do this personally, he delegated Father Peter Hughes of Morphett Vale to remove Mary's sentence in his name and restore her to her former position as head of the Congregation. She was under sentence for five months.

This event occurred in the Catholic Church at Morphett Vale on 22 February 1872. One week later, on 1 March 1872, Laurence Sheil was dead. Mary MacKillop and the Sisters prayed beside his coffin overnight from the time of its arrival in the cathedral until his funeral on the following day. During succeeding months, she and most of the dismissed Sisters resumed the wearing of their religious habits in special ceremonies at St Ignatius Church, Norwood. About fifteen Sisters chose not to return. By June, the Sisters' lives were much more settled. Mary then reappointed Sisters (including those who had continued working during this troubled time) to their schools and charitable institutions .

APPENDIX NINE
Irish Women who Came To Australia With Mary Mackillop In 1874 To Join The Congregation

1. **ALBAN (ELLEN) L'ESTRANGE**
   BORN: 24 October 1839, Westmeath, Ireland, to William L'Estrange & Mary Cole.
   ENTERED RELIGIOUS LIFE: 23 October 1874
   PROFESSED: 28 April 1876
   DIED: Kensington, South Australia, 13 April 1921, aged 81 Years
   BURIED: Mitcham SA
   OTHER INFORMATION:
   Alban became Little Sister at Kensington after 1899 General Chapter.

2. **BERCHMANS (MARY) COX**
   BORN: Dublin, Ireland, 15 August 1848, to Patrick Cox & Henrietta Russell
   ENTERED RELIGIOUS LIFE: 29 October 1874
   PROFESSED: 10 September 1876
   DIED: Kensington, SA, 9 September 1923, aged 75 years
   BURIED: Mitcham, SA
   OTHER INFORMATION: Novice Mistress, Adelaide, 1910-1916. Stationed at Pekina 1883 (Ref. Monica to MM 28 March 1883)
   In Sheila McCreanor ed. *"Mary MacKillop in Challenging Times"*, Mary wrote to the then Archbishop Moran on 6 January 1885 that Sr. Mary Berchmans was *"one of eight surviving postulants I brought out from Ireland, not one of whom cost the Diocese of Adelaide one penny."*

3. **COLUMBA (MARY JANE) WILSON,**
   BORN: Kiltealy, Enniscorthy, Co. Wexford, Ireland, 17 June 1856 to unknown parents.
   ENTERED RELIGIOUS LIFE: 23 October 1874

PROFESSED: 28 April 1876
DIED: 19 August 1883, at Pekina, South Australia, aged 27 years.
BURIED: Pekina, SA Laurentia
OTHER INFORMATION: Sr Monica to Mother Mary, August 1883: *Poor S Walburgh is still lingering and very happy waiting for her release. Sr Columba the same. S. Berchmans (Cox) and S Laurentia (Cosgrove) are with her at Pekina.*

4. **DOMINICA (MARY) HEALY**
   BORN: Dublin, Ireland, date of birth & parents' names unknown
   ENTERED RELIGIOUS LIFE: October 1874,
   RECEIVED THE HABIT WITH OTHER POSTULANTS BUT WAS NOT PROFESSED.
   OTHER INFORMATION: a note in the Register of the Sisters reads: *Dismissed as being of unsound mind, 1876*

5. **GAETANO (SUSAN) O'REILLY**
   BORN: Co Cavan, Ireland, date of birth and parents' names, unknown
   ENTERED RELIGIOUS LIFE: October 1874
   PROFESSED: 28 April 1876
   DIED: 2 February 1888 at Kensington, age unknown
   BURIED: Mitcham, SA
   OTHER INFORMATION: Was stationed at Kapunda in 1883
   (ref. Monica to MM 28 March, 1883)

6. **MARY JOHN (MARY LOUISE) O'GRADY**
   BORN: Dublin, Ireland, date of birth and parents' names, unknown
   ENTERED RELIGIOUS LIFE: 29 October 1874
   RECEIVED THE HABIT WITH OTHER POSTULANTS BUT WAS NOT PROFESSED.
   A note in the Register of the Sisters reads: *Left at end of novitiate, April 1876*

7. **PATRICIA (SABINA) CAMPBELL**
   BORN: Ballinakill, Loughrea, Co. Galway, Ireland on 15 December 1853 to John Campbell & Margaret Darvan (Derwan)
   ENTERED RELIGIOUS LIFE: 19 October 1874

PROFESSED: 28 April 1876
DIED: Leichhardt, NSW, 24 May 1934, aged 80 years
BURIED: Northern Suburbs Cemetery, Sydney
OTHER INFORMATION: Sister of Sister Mary Patrick (1861-1923) At the time of Bishop Reynolds' Episcopal Commission of 1883, Patricia, who was stationed at Georgetown, refused to take the oath of secrecy required by the bishop, and immediately after her interview informed Mary MacKillop of the kinds of questions the sisters were being asked. She gave strong leadership to the sisters during Mary's exile.
Patricia was a member of the General Council from 1899 until 1910. She remained in New South Wales after that and died there in 1934.

8. PIUS (MARGARET) MURPHY
BORN: Co. Wicklow, Ireland on 30 November 1845. Parents' names unknown.
ENTERED RELIGIOUS LIFE: 27 October 1874
PROFESSED: 10 December 1876
DIED: Kensington, 28 November 1882, aged 37 years
BURIED: Mitcham SA

9. RODRIGUEZ (CATHERINE) O'BRIEN
BORN: Dublin, Ireland, 19 April 1858 to John T. O'Brien & Bridget Grimly
ENTERED RELIGIOUS LIFE: 8 (4) December 1874
PROFESSED: 6 January 1877, Kensington
DIED: Kensington, SA, 10 July 1928, aged 70 years
BURIED: Mitcham SA

10. ROSE (FRANCES) KANE
BORN: Dublin, Ireland, date of birth and parents' names unknown
ENTERED RELIGIOUS LIFE: 29 October 1874
DIED: Kensington, on Good Friday, 26 March 1875 **BURIED:** West Terrace Cemetery, Adelaide **OTHER INFORMATION:**
Rose (Frances) Kane died on Good Friday 1875, less than three months after her arrival in Australia and before she or the other members of her group received their habits. It is not known

whether she received her habit and/or made her religious profession on her deathbed, but that is highly likely.

11. SCHOLASTICA (ELLEN) BYRNE
BORN: Co. Wicklow, Ireland, 28 October 1848, names of parents unknown
ENTERED RELIGIOUS LIFE: 27 October 1874
PROFESSED: 28 April 1876
DIED: Kensington, SA, 20 March 1913, aged 64 years.
BURIED: Mitcham SA
OTHER INFORMATION:
Cousin of Sr M Francesca Holland

12. THOMAS (JANE) McGINN
BORN: Co. Cavan, Ireland, 1 November 1845, to Arthur McGinn & Jane Nugent
ENTERED RELIGIOUS LIFE: 31 October 1874
PROFESSED: 28 April 1876
DIED: Kensington, SA, 22 February 1920, aged 74 years
BURIED: Mitcham SA

13. URSULA (MARY) TYNAN
BORN: Athy, Co. Kildare, Ireland, 24 April 1849. Parents' names unknown.
ENTERED RELIGIOUS LIFE: 26 October 1874
PROFESSED: 28 April 1876
DIED: Boulder, Western Australia, 15 October 1905, aged 56 years.
BURIED: Boulder, Western Australia
OTHER INFORMATION: Separated from the Mother House under Bishop Matthew Gibney of Perth, Western Australia. She was leader of his diocesan Josephites until her death in 1905.

Mary MacKillop wrote regarding Ursula's decision to stay in WA: "*It is sad that Sister Ursula proved unfaithful in WA. We can all take a lesson from this, & let obedience & dependence on our superiors ever be our guide – poor child, she will never be happy – pray for her that she may not lose her reason.*" [MM to the Sisters, 1 April, 1890).

See Marie Foale: *The Josephites Go West* for further details re Ursula.

14. WILFRID (MARY) HAYES
BORN: India, 5 April 1858. Parents' names unknown.
ENTERED RELIGIOUS LIFE: 8 September (December), 1874
PROFESSED: 24 May 1877, Kensington.
Wilfrid left the Congregation on 18 August 1883, just before she was due to make her final profession. Nothing further is known of her.

15. POSTULANT NO. 15???? It appears that two other women also travelled with Mary, Their surnames, Backs & Kennedy, appear on the facsimile copy of Mary's ticket from London to Adelaide as published in the hard backed copy of William Modystack, *Mary Mackillop: A Woman before her Time* (Rigby, Adelaide, 1982), but do not appear in the Josephite 'Register of the Sisters'. The names, as they appear in Modystack's book, are Murphy, Campbell, Byrne, O'Brien, Kennedy & Backs, that is, the future Sisters Pius, Patricia, Scholastica and Rodriguez and the two women, Kennedy and Backs, of whom nothing further is known.

APPENDIX TEN
Mary Mackillop's Times Away from South Australia, 1867–1883

Queensland foundation	8 Dec 1869–late April 1871
Overseas	28 March 1873–4 January 1875
Queensland	April–September 1875
Bathurst	15 January – late February 1876
Queensland	March – July 1878
Queensland	Nov 1878–January 1879
Queensland and Sydney	4 April 1879–March 1880
Sydney	February–March 1881
Sydney	Dec 1882–June 1883
Sydney – permanent move	November 1883

TOTAL TIME AWAY: 4 years 2 months.

MARY MACKILLOP'S TIMES IN SOUTH AUSTRALIA AND WHERE SHE WENT EACH TIME SHE LEFT THERE

	WENT TO:
1860 – 1861, Penola Station	Portland
1866 January – 20 June 1867, Penola	Adelaide.
24 June 1867 – 8 December 1869, Adelaide	Queensland
05 April 1871 – 28 April 1873, Adelaide	Rome
04 January 1875 – 27 April 1875, Adelaide	Queensland
09 September 1875 – 10 January 1876, Adelaide	Bathurst
26 February 1876 – 23 March 1878, Adelaide & SA country	Queensland
01 September 1878 - late November 1878, Adelaide	Queensland
17 January 1879 – April 1879, Adelaide	Queensland
27 March 1880 – 1 February 1881, Adelaide	Sydney
01 April 1881 – 26 January 1883, Adelaide	Sydney
21 June 1883 – 17 November 1883, Adelaide	Sydney
20 July 1896 – 07 January 1897, Adelaide & SA country visitation	Victoria

14 January 1897–06 October 1897, as above	Victoria
08 September 1899–11 October 1899, Adelaide	Victoria
10 August 1901–20 August 1901, Adelaide	Victoria
18 September 1901–10 October 1901, Adelaide	Victoria
03 March 1904–07 June 1904, Adelaide	Sydney
07 August 1905–shortly after 12 November 1905 Was sick at Fullarton for much of this time.	Adelaide. Sydney

APPENDIX ELEVEN
Closures of Josephite Schools & Institutions
1880–1893
In what was the Adelaide Archdiocese in 2010

CONVENTS & SCHOOLS	OPENED	CLOSED	REASONS, IF ANY GIVEN
Moonta	1869	1880	Low enrolments
Mintaro Station	1877	1880	" "
Stockport	1872	1881	" "
Undalya	1871	1881	" "
Port Wakefield	1880	1881	" "
Warooka	1881	1882	People could not support the Sisters
Bagot's Gap	1871	1883	None given
Port Elliott	1880	1884	Low enrolments
Alberton	1882	1885	Low enrolments
Penola	1868 1876	1871 1885	Withdrawn by Mary. Sisters went to Sydney
Virginia	1872	1886	" "
Auburn	1871	1887	" "
Maitland	1877	1889	" "
Strathalbyn	1882	1889	" "
Mintaro	1872	1889	" "
Hanson	1873	1889	" "
Tarlee	1870	1890	" "
Marion	1869	1891	None given
Manoora	1876	1892	None given
Kapunda	1868	1893	Left at request from parish priest. Replaced by Dominican Sisters.
CHARITABLE INSTITUTION:			
St Vincent de Paul's Orphanage	1868	1890	Ordered to leave by Archbishop Reynolds

CLOSURES OF JOSEPHITE SCHOOLS 1880–1892
In what was the Diocese of Port Pirie in 2010

CONVENTS & SCHOOLS	OPENED	CLOSED	REASONS, IF ANY GIVEN
Orroroo	1880	1882	Low enrolments
Willochra (Hammond)	1881	1883	Low enrolments
Gulnare	1877	1885	Sisters went to Sydney
Port Lincoln	1874	1886	" "
Georgetown	1873	1887	" "
Laura	1877	1887	" "
Appila	1877	1889	" "
Whyte Yarcowie	1881	1891	Low enrolments

NOTE: In 1887, Mother Bernard chose four Sisters from South Australia to make the first Josephite foundation in Western Australia. Archbishop Reynolds claimed that she closed the Georgetown school to free Sisters for this new venture. (Reynolds to Kirby in Rome, ca. 1888).

TOTAL NUMBER OF CLOSURES OR WITHDRAWALS ACROSS THE ENTIRE COLONY OF SOUTH AUSTRALIA, 1880–1893 = 29

APPENDIX TWELVE
Josephite Convents & Schools, SA, 1895 Archdiocese of Adelaide

Convent	Community Leader	No. of Sisters	Schools from Kensington	No of Children
Kensington	Monica Phillips	33	Pirie Street, Adelaide	148
			Russell Street, Adelaide	242
			Beulah Road, Norwood	170
			Bridge St. Kensington	124
Brompton	Stanislaus O'Callaghan	7		149
Clare	Marianna Wall	3		73
Gawler	Hilda McNamara	5		132
Glenelg	Anastasia Roe	6		44
Hamley Bridge	John Baptist Fitzgerald	2		26
Hectorville	Margaret O'Loghlen	2		53
Kadina	Felix O'Rourck	4		64
Macclesfield	Felicitas Garvey	3		38
Mitcham	Matthew Welsh	4		56
North Adelaide	Benedicta Phelan	4		132
Port Adelaide	Editha Flanagan	9		274
Sevenhill	Maria Skudder	2		42
Thebarton	Cyril Welsh	4		94
Wallaroo	Raphael McKeown	3		52
Refuge	Annette Henschke	7	No. of inmates unavailable	
Providence	Elizabeth Etheridge	4	Ibid.	
TOTAL		17 communities	102 Sisters	18 schools	1913 children

DIOCESE OF PORT AUGUSTA (PORT PIRIE)

Convent	Community Leader	No of Sisters	No of Children
Port Augusta	Calasanctius Howley	5	155
Caltowie	Winifred Hogan	3	54
Gladstone	Berchmans Cox	2	30
Jamestown	Thomas McGee	3	89
Burra	Dominic Clifford	3	50
Pekina	Paulina Hiney	3	78
Quorn	Germaine Scanlan	4	93
TOTALS	**7 Communities**	**23 Sisters**	**549 children**

OVERALL TOTALS:
24 communities   25 schools   125 sisters   2462 students

NOTE: This list has been included because it was the first time ever that the Australasian Catholic Directory published a full listing of Josephite convents and schools in South Australia.

Source: *Australasian Catholic Directory, 1895.*

APPENDIX THIRTEEN
Mary Mackillop's Report of SA Visitation, 1899

CONVENT	LITTLE SISTER	COMMUNITY MEMBERS	SCHOOLS	NO ON ROLL	FEES PAID	MUSIC FEES	GENERAL COMMENTS
Brompton	Stanislaus O'Callaghan (10)	Cyprian Ryan Benedict Ahern Martina Rogers Claude Riddell Modesta Noonan Flavia Sheedy Stanislaus O'Callaghan Julianna O'Brien John Naughton Wilhelmina Dowd (postulant)	Convent Claude Flavia Martina Wilhelmina Parochial Stanislaus Cyprian Julianna Benedict Infants John Kitchen Modesta	105 130	£3.10 a week Not more than 20/- a month	20 @ 21/- a quarter. (Reduction for 2 or more per family)	Sisters happy – can be seen by happy manner. Most are invalids. Sr Stanislaus does not complain.
Thebarton	Marianna Wall (4)	Rose Naughton Inez McCarthy Philippa (maybe Philippa Mahony)	Parochial	79	20/- a week	13 @ 21/- If 2, 35/- a quarter	Happy united community. Rule carefully observed, diary kept, also accounts. There are no debts.
North Adelaide	Andrea Howley (6)	Sylvester Howley Lucy Crowley Etheldreda Mahony Rita Gaffney Conrad Pflaum (postulant)	Parochial Convent	115 34	20/- a week 26/- a week	6 @ 21/- 10 @ reduced fees	No comments
Port Ade- laide	Editha Flanagan (7)	Borgia Fay Matthias King Mel McKenna Aquin Dowd Germaine Scanlon Norbert Maguire	Parochial	264	?	?	Sisters are happy and united. No debt but about £50 due to them. The Sisters make altar breads, mend linen and give the priest breakfast – and all they get is £5 a year. Receive Holy Communion on weekdays before Mass but not on Sundays when Mass is seldom ever before 5 to 9.

St Joseph's Refuge, Fullarton, opened 1902. Note chimney from laundry in background.

Location	Superior	Other Sisters	School type	Students	Fees	Music	Comments
Gawler	Peter Gough (5)	Alphonsus Drislane Patrick Campbell De Lellis Learhinan Francis de Sales Mahony	Parochial	140	31/- a week	?	Sister [the Little Sister] says Sr De Lellis bold, disobedient, will do what she is told not to do, gives impertinence to the Little Sister. Sr Patrick of same opinion as Sr De Lellis. Young man of 20 coming at 7 p.m. for music. This must be discontinued.
Hamley Bridge	Celestine Windmell (3)	Gertrude Gill Dominic Clifford	Parochial	52	9/- a week	9 @ 21/- a quarter	Happy. Little Sister thinks Gertrude much better with good, kind Little Sister as needs encouragement. 6 roomed convent. School taught in church. Individual Sisters must not have money, even with permission as this is ruinous to the spirit of the Rule. Music teachers have no authority independent of Little Sisters.
St Johns	Helena Hartney (4)	Cyril Welsh Jane Francis McDermott Ignatius McCarthy	Girls' Reformatory	12 girls	Nil	Nil	All right except for Ignatius. In habit of writing and receiving letters without showing them to the superior and made presents without asking permission. Her influence on the girls has not been for their good
Kooringa (Burra)	Flora Doherty (4)	Alacoque Smith Melita Brophy Marian Coghlan (postulant)	Parochial	30	4/1½ a week	3 @ 1/6 a week	No comments
Sevenhill	Maria Skudder (2)	Bruno Donnelly	Parochial	?	3/10¾ a week	Nil	Three State children for whom they receive 15/- a week. Happy. Keep rule but not always diary.
Clare	Felicitas Garvey (3)	Adalbert Brazil Bertilla McGrath	Parochial	68	21/- a week	10 @ 21/- a quarter. If 2, 15/- ea.	No complaints. Rule kept. Happy and united. Diary and accounts kept.
Gladstone	Berchmans Cox	One unnamed sister	Parochial	35	7/6 a week	?	No comments
Jamestown	Borromeo Hurley (3)	Bertrand Kerin Kevin Hughes	Parochial	44	7/- a week	2 @ 21/- 2 – 35/- for both together	Happy, united community. Pleasing to their pastor. Debts, 20/-

Petersburg (Peterborough)	Benizi Casey (4)	Anne Joseph Stone Ida Bolger Euphrasia Gilmore	Parochial	127	29/-	4 @ 18/6 4 @ 21/-	Debts, £15. Hope liquidated after concert. Happy in community.
Pekina	Pius Frost (3)	Donatus Kreutzer John Evangelist Agnew	Parochial	50	For 9 months. - £35. Ball £7, Concert £24.	2 @ 25/-	No debts. Have all they want. John Evangelist troublesome & does very little. Diary and accounts kept.
Quorn	Agatha Nolan (4)	Winifred Hogan Helena (not Hartney) De Britto Sweeney	Parochial	86	18/- per week	8 @ 25/- Where 2 in family, 15/-	V happy community. No fault to find. Big debt paid and new piano bought @ £20. Still owing about £7
Port Augusta	M. Joseph Harvey (4)	Ursula Butler Clothilde Roughan Agnes (postulant)	Parochial	80	22/- a week	7 @ 21/- 2 – 35/- (for both together)	Boarders – 1 @ 10/- a week. A happy community. Debts down to £9 (from £46). If Agnes be changed would like a singing Sister, preferably Adalbert from Clare, as 2 singers there.

Location	Superior	Sisters	School Type	Number	Fee		Comments
Wallaroo	M. Anne Byrne OR Stone? (3)	Anastasia Roe Blandina Hannigan	Parochial	79	20/- a week	Nil.	No comments
Kadina	Paulina Hiney (4)	Antonia Wilson Gonzaga Casey Reginald O'Loughlin	Parochial	100	24/- a week	6 @ 21/-	No comments
Macclesfield	Dominic Clifford (2)	Augustine Woods	Parochial	38	8/2 a week	Nil	Debts – none. Recommends change for Blandina for health. Good needle and fancy work required.
Hectorville	Raphael McKeown (2)	Borgia Fay	Parochial	46	10/- a week	Nil	Debts £33.3s
Mitcham	Matthew Welsh (5)	Gabriel Gillman-Jones Fabian Gildea Clare George Maria Anne Hogan	Parochial Convent	63 10	12/- a week	?	Nine boarders paying total of £50.3 a quarter. No debts. Happy united community, no complaints, but admits there has been trouble through Sr Gabriel's hasty ways.
Glenelg	Gertrude Mary Dewe (4)	Anne Byrne or Stone Baptista Long Romuald (not O'Donoghue)	Parochial	70	£10.3.9 a quarter	?	Debts – only monthly bills to butcher, baker, 7/- to grocer, £2 to Donaldson for habit material. Have to pay £2.2 a month rent. Archdeacon gives £25 a year, for which have to make altar breads, provide oil, brooms, wicks for church and do all the washing and ironing. United and happy. Sr Anne doing fairly.
Kensington Schools	Thomas McGinn Placida O'Brien.	Scholastica Byrne Felix O'Rourck A Novice Catherine Ruine Celsus Deering	Parochial Convent	78 30	16/- a week	– –	No comments [Note: The parochial school was in the hall in Bridge Street, Kensington, while the Convent School was on the convent grounds.]
Beulah Road School (Norwood)	Isidore O'Loughlin	Sebastian Conlon Fara Daly Antoinette O'Loughlin Mida McMahon Hyacinth Scanlon Carolus Büring	Parochial	170	48/- a week	–	All but Sister Sebastian are novices.

Pirie Street School (Adelaide)	Ephrem Crowley	Thomasine O'Brien Rodriguez O'Brien A postulant	Parochial	115	25/- a week	—	No comments
Russell Street School	Laurence O'Brien	Hilda McNamara Teresa Eickhoff 4 novices	Parochial	311	68/-	14 [no fees listed	No comments

PLACES NOT MENTIONED IN MARY MACKILLOP'S LIST:

Convent or Institution	No of Sisters	Community Leader	Schools	Institutions	No. of Students	No. of Inmates
Kensington	48	Sr Bonaventure Mahony: (both Provincial and com-munity leader)	Pirie Street, Adelaide Russell Street, Adelaide Beulah Road, Norwood Bridge Street, Kensington Convent, Kensington		115 311 170 78 30	
Refuge	8	Sr Annette Henschke		Refuge		42 adults 21 Children
Providence	6	Sr Elizabeth Etheridge		Providence		10 women

SOURCES: Mary MacKillop, Diary, 1899.

Transcribed at the Archives of the Sisters of St Joseph, North Sydney by Sr Marie T. Foale, 1981

Australasian Catholic Directory, 1900

NOTE: Sisters' family names have been added the better to identify the Sisters mentioned.

APPENDIX FOURTEEN
Mother Mary re Select Schools & the Teaching of Languages

Talk given at Mount Street, North Sydney, 1901

Mother Mary's address to the Sisters:

Sisters, I have something of very great importance to say to you. If this were to be my last chance of speaking to you, if I were dying, I would think this one thing of the greatest importance because it has to do with the holding of the teaching and the spirit of our Institute.

You have heard some of the life of our Father Founder read–you can see from it what was the spirit he wished to have amongst us. He said what I am going to say and he said a great deal more. If he could rise and come to us now his spirit would reproach us. It would be a great evil were I to pass this over without warning you of it.

Never forget that our schools were established to teach poor children–we have not the very poor here like the great cities of old countries–but the poorer classes who will attend primary or parochial schools, these are our care. There are high schools, and intermediate schools, but they are not *ours*.

Now Sisters, there is a great deal of talk about examinations. Ever bear in mind that our schools–parochial schools–must be up to the mark, but we are not to teach accomplishments in these. What is required by the Standard of Proficiency we *must* teach: but Sisters, we are never to teach foreign languages.

But I heard with sorrow that a silly Sister, not far from here, got lessons in French, and then commenced to teach others. It appears she did not know this was forbidden. Many others might do the same–but you all know now you are not allowed. You can never do so. If you are in doubt, you have a Provincial and a Mother General to consult.

You may think a class for Matriculation requires a knowledge of French. I understood it is optional to take French or Latin—then learn Latin. Every Sister could easily have a knowledge of Latin—she might in some cases ask a priest to help her but for this she must always ask permission from the M. General.

In New Zealand a Sister pleaded hard to be allowed to teach the violin, or the school would have to be given up. I said No—give up the school, if you cannot do otherwise. I would not allow the violin to be taught. I allowed her to give a boy some lessons without payment, but it must not be taught as a usual thing. Another case where we opened in New Zealand at Temuka, priests and people urged the Sisters to have a select school. Some ladies there had a select school, but were giving it up. Even some of the Sisters went in for the select schools, or they said we should lose those nice children. 'They will go to Timaru'.

'By all means', I said, 'let them go to Timaru. We won't alter our system of teaching. We have nothing to do with select schools. I would rather they leave when the ladies close the select school. It is like the dog in the manger. We are for poor parochial schools—the Sacred Heart at Timaru is for the higher classes. Are those nuns to be deprived of a living because we want all the children?'

After all most of those children came to us. Again—in Auckland, St Benedict's School some years ago—there was trouble about a service class. To my horror I find French has been taught there, connived at by a weak superior. I must ascertain whether the Provincial has connived at this—if so, she must make public reparation or be deprived of her office: we give her the benefit of the doubt.

I cannot speak too strongly on this point. If it is true that the Little Sister of Bacchus Marsh is teaching French, she will not be Little Sister next year. She may teach Latin, not French. Supposing you cannot send pupils for Matriculation without French—well, give up Matriculation, give up everything rather than break our rule. If anyone tells you I allowed this anywhere, give it a flat denial. I am prepared to give up St Benedict's if it must be done, on principle.

You heard of the early days in Adelaide when Mrs John George Daly desired to send her little son to the Hall School thinking the governor's grandson would give a tone to the school. Father Woods who was spoken to on the subject referred the lady to me. She requested that her son might be permitted to have a seat beside my desk, but I declined to make any distinctions. Her husband, son of the governor, said I was quite right, though his little boy was excluded.

You know many of the first Sisters were able to teach higher schools. The Bishop said: Send them to teach high schools, and let the others go to the Orphanages, but we would not be won over. If we could not be allowed to carry out our rule we would take the alternative his Lordship offered. So we struggled on– and now how could I meet my God if I permitted any deviation. I charge you under the vows, that you will have to answer for any deviation from parochial schools.

Let those pay for languages who want to learn them, but let them go elsewhere. I want you to be very careful of this. Pray that we may keep the rule, love the rule, watch over the rule. Pray much for this during the retreat.

ASSJ, North Sydney, Series 14, box 463, item 11, *Mary MacKillop Retreat Notes and Spiritual Writings. Transcribed by Mary Cresp rsj*

APPENDIX FIFTEEN
Superiors General & Congregational Leaders 1867–2014

Mary MacKillop	1867–1885
	1899–1909
Bernard Walsh	1885–1898
Baptista Molloy	1910–1918
Laurence O'Brien	1918–1931
Cyril Elkis	1931–1945
Josephine Cahill	1945–1946
Leonie Ryan	1947–1959
Adrian Ryan	1959–1971
Denis Earle	1971–1977
Elizabeth Murphy	1977–1989
Mary Cresp	1989–1995
Giovanni Farquer	1995–2001
Katrina Brill	2001–2007
Anne Derwin	2007–2013
Monica Cavanagh	2013–

APPENDIX SIXTEEN
South Australian Provincials & Regional Leaders, 1870–2014

1. Teresa McDonald — Provincial 1870
2. Michael Quinlan:
    Provincial for a short time in 1883.
3. Monica Phillips
    Assistant General. 1884–1888
    Acting Provincial: 1888–1889
    Provincial: 1889–1899
4. Calasanctius Howley
    Provincial, Port Augusta Province, 1889–1896
5. Bonaventure Mahony — 1899–1905
6. Victor Lane — 1906–1922
7. Claude Riddell — 1922–1930
    1931–1937
8. De Lellis McDonald — 1930
    1937–1943
9. Thecla Morrissey — 1943–1947
10. Michael Xavier Denham — 1947–1953
11. Vincent Ferrer Dolan — 1953–1959
12. Vianney Finnegan — 1959–1965
13. Marie Paul Harford — 1966–1971
14. Concepta (Joan) Luff — 1971–1977
15. Mary Reardon — 1977–1983
16. Margaret McKenna — 1983–1989
17. Catherine Clark — 1990–1995
18. Josephine Huppatz — 1996–2002
19. Christine Rowan — 2002–2008
20. Marion Gambin — 2008–2014
21. Margaret Cleary — 2014–

APPENDIX SEVENTEEN
St Joseph's Schools Badge: South Australia

St Joseph's Schools in South Australia have used this badge since the 1920s.

Sr Fergus Brosnahan designed it in about 1926 (the year when the Sisters returned to Port Lincoln after an absence of forty years) for the uniforms of the boarders and day scholars at St Joseph's, Port Lincoln. Soon afterwards the Sisters of St Joseph adopted it for use on a statewide basis and, with a few local modifications, it is still in general use.

The Latin words 'In Omnibus Caritas' translate as "Love in Everything". The **gold** colour represents the Divine and Human love referred to in the motto. **Blue** is symbolic of Mary, the mother of God and spouse of St Joseph who is symbolised by the **brown**. 'Joseph' means 'Growth' and so the lily stands for the integrity of his life and character and for the growth to wholeness, which is nourished in students attending St Joseph's schools.

Sisters and children setting off from the wharf at Port Lincoln for a day's outing on the water. The photo is undated but the dress of the children suggests that it was taken in about 1930. All the girls' hats have the badge on them.

Bibliography

Newspapers & Magazines:
Adelaide Observer, 1910
Adelaide Punch, 1869
Catholic Monthly, 1883–1889
Catholic Record, 1880
Chaplet and Southern Cross, 1871–1872
Garland of St Joseph, 1906–1972
Gundagai Times, 1928
Irish Harp, 1870–1872
Murray Pioneer, 1919
Northern Argus, 1869
Pasquin, 1869
Protestant Advocate, Adelaide, 1872
South Australian Advertiser, 1867
South Australian Register, 1850–1928
South Australian Tablet, 1876–1877
Southern Cross, 1889–1983
Southern Cross and Catholic Herald, 1867–1869
Witness (Diocese of Port Pirie) 1955–1985

Other Primary Sources:
Abbott, Walter M, ed, *The Documents of Vatican II*, Geoffrey Chapman, London 1966
Annual Letters, College of St Aloysius, Sevenhill, 1877–1890, Archives of the Society of Jesus, Melbourne
Australasian Catholic Directory, 1888–1975

Constitutions of the Sisters of St Joseph of the Sacred Heart in Australia, given at Rome, April 21 1874, translated into English and printed in Adelaide, 1875

Evans, Barry, 'Mary MacKillop's Journeys', unpublished Ms, ASSJ, North Sydney, 2010

Flannery, Austin, ed, *Vatican Council II, The Conciliar and Post Conciliar Documents*, Dominican Publications, Dublin, 1975

Geoghegan, Patrick, *Pastoral Letter of Patrick Bonaventure, by Divine Grace and Favour of the Apostolic See, Bishop of Adelaide, to the Clergy and Laity of the Diocese, on the Education of Catholic Children*, Adelaide, 1860

Henschke, Patricia OP, 'Anniversary of Glenelg Catholic Parish', 6 June 2009, unpublished Ms, Glenelg Catholic Parish, Glenelg, SA

Horan, Father Charles, *Funeral Oration on the Right Rev. Dr Sheil OSF*, Advertiser Press, Adelaide, 1872

MacKillop, Mary, *Rules for the General Guidance of the Sisters of St Joseph of the Sacred Heart*, JG O'Connor, Sydney, 1883

Minutes and Reports of General Chapters of the Sisters of St Joseph of the Sacred Heart, 1875–2007, ASSJ, North Sydney

Minutes and Reports of South Australian Provincial Chapters of the Sisters of St Joseph of the Sacred Heart, 1968–2007, ASSJ, Kensington, SA

Neagle, Callista rsj, 'Notes on foundations', ASSJ, Kensington, SA

Nevin, Father Bernard, 'Northern Areas Record Book', 1874–1887, ACA

O'Reily, John, *New Convent of the Sisters of St Joseph, Kensington*. Southern Cross Printing & Publishing Co., Adelaide, 1906

------ *Reports on the Liabilities of the Archdiocese of Adelaide*, Southern Cross Printing & Publishing Co, Adelaide, 1896–1911

------ *Report on the Liabilities of the Diocese of Port Augusta*, Port Augusta, 1890

------ *The Catholic Charities in South Australia*, Southern Cross Printing & Publishing Co, 1911

Public Instruction Act, New South Wales, 1880 http://www.governmentschools.det.nsw.edu.au/story/instruction_act.shtm

Resource Material from the Archives of the Sisters of St Joseph, Issues no. 3, 4 and 5, ASSJ, North Sydney, 1980–1981

Reynolds, CA. *The Institution of the Sisters of St Joseph of the Most Sacred Heart of Jesus in Australia,* Adelaide, 1876
South Australian Government Gazette, 1897
South Australian Lands Titles Office, Registration books, 1875–1930
South Australian Parliamentary Papers, 1883–1960
South Australian Statutes, 1851–1960
The Official Directory of the Catholic Church in Australia, 2012-2013, Sydney, 2012
Woods, Mechtilde, 'History of the Sisters of St Joseph', unpublished Ms. ca. 1918.
Woods, JET. *A Book of Instructions for the Sisters of St Joseph of the Sacred Heart,* Southern Cross Office, Adelaide, 1870
------ *Directory and Order of Discipline of the Sisters of St Joseph of the Sacred Heart,* Southern Cross Office, Adelaide, 1870
------ *Rules of the Institute of St. Joseph for the Catholic Education of Poor Children,* Southern Cross Office, Adelaide, 1868

Secondary Sources:
Balaklava Centenary Book Committee, *Balaklava: Change and Challenge,*
District Council of Balaklava, Balaklava SA, 1977
Barnard, Jill, *From Humble Beginnings: The Story of the Sisters of St Joseph of the Sacred Heart, Victoria, 1890-2009,* Utber & Patello, Richmond, Victoria, 2009
Bell, Clarrie, *The Parish of Woodville/Findon,* Woodville Parish, 1987
Berry, Dean W. 'Bagot, Walter Hervey (1880–1963)', *ADB*, National Centre of Biography, Australian National University, Vol 7, 1979. http://adb.anu.edu.au/biography/bagot-walter-hervey-5092/text8501
Bickerton, Ian J. 'Reynolds, Christopher Augustine (1834–1893)', *ADB*, National Centre of Biography, Australian National University, Vol 6, 1976. http://adb.anu.edu.au/biography/reynolds-christopher-augustine- 4470/text7293
------ 'Sheil, Laurence Bonaventure (1815–1872)', *ADB*, National Centre of Biography, Australian National University, Vol 6, 1976. http://adb.anu.edu.au/biography/sheil-laurence-bonavent ure- 4568/text7497

Bray, J. J. 'Way, Sir Samuel James (1836–1916)', *ADB*, National Centre of Biography, Australian National University, Vol 12, 1990. http://adb.anu.edu.au/biography/way-sir-samuel-james-9014/text15875

Byrne, Monsignor Frederick, *History of the Catholic Church in South Australia*, Adelaide, 1914

Cahill, A. E. 'Moran, Patrick Francis (1830–1911)', *ADB*, National Centre of Biography, Australian National University, Vol. 10, 1986. http://adb.anu.edu.au/biography/moran-patrick-francis-7648/text13375

—————— 'Vaughan, Roger William Bede (1834–1883)', *ADB*, National Centre of Biography, Australian National University, Vol 6, 1976. http://adb.anu.edu.au/biography/vaughan-roger-william-bede-4773/text7941

Clark, Mary Ryllis, *Loreto in Australia*, University of New South Wales Press, Sydney, 2009

Conroy, Constance, 'Tabor Story, 1978-1984,' unpublished Ms. 1984, ASSJ, Kensington, SA

Cresp, Mary, *God's 'Good Time', Sisters of St Joseph in Ministry with Australian Aboriginal and Torres Strait Islander Peoples*, ATF Press, Adelaide, 2013

—————— *In her Footsteps*, Sisters of St Joseph of the Sacred Heart, Western Australia, Perth, 2012

Crowley, Marie, *Women of the Vale: Perthville Josephites, 1872–1972*, Melbourne, Spectrum Publications, 2002

Cunneen, Chris, 'Abbott, Gertrude, 1846-1934', *ADB*, National Centre of Biography, Australian National University, Vol 7, 1979. http://adb.anu.edu.au/biography/abbott-gertrude-4960/text8227

Czernezkyj, W, ed, *Pekina, Century and Beyond*, Pekina History Committee, Pekina, SA, 1974

Dulwich–Burnside Catholic Parish, *The Rays of the Crucifix: Links in the Chain, A Brief History of the Dulwich-Burnside Parish, 1869–1994*, Dulwich, SA, 1994

Edgar, Suzanne, 'Edwards, Albert Augustine (1888–1963)', *ADB*, National Centre of Biography, Australian National University, Vol 8, 1981. http://adb.anu.edu.au/biography/edwards-albert-augustine-6092/text10437

Fenner, Charles 'A Geographical Inquiry into the Growth, Distribution and Movement of Population in South Australia, 1836-1927', in *Transactions of the Royal Society of South Australia*, vol 53, 1929

Fitzgerald, Anne, (Sister Maria Goretti), 'I make Altar Breads! Aren't I Lucky?' in *The Garland of St Joseph*, North Sydney, May 1970

Foale, Marie T, *Ain Karim, Twenty-five years, 1984-2009, Sisters of St Joseph*, Ain Karim, Enfield, SA, 2009

------ *Providence: 125 Years of Aged Care, 1868-1993*, Sisters of St Joseph Aged Care Services, Adelaide, 1993

------ *The Josephite Story, the Sisters of St Joseph, 1866-1895*, Sisters of St Joseph, North Sydney, 1989

------ *The Josephites Go West*, Notre Dame University, Perth, 1995

------ *Think of the Ravens, The Sisters of St Joseph and Social Welfare*, Sisters of St Joseph of the Sacred Heart (SA) Inc. Adelaide, 2001

Foale, Marie T, & Toohey, Denis, *In Joyful Hope: The Story of Siena College, 1971-2001*, Peacock Publications, Norwood, SA, 2004

Fogarty, Ronald, *Catholic Education in Australia, 1806-1950*, 2 volumes, Melbourne University Press, Melbourne, 1959

French, M, 'O'Reily, John (1846-1915)', *ADB*, National Centre of Biography, Australian National University, Vol 11, 1988. http://adb.anu.edu.au/biography/oreily-john-7921/text13781

Gibbs, R.M. *Under the Burning Sun: A History of Colonial South Australia, 1836-1900*, Southern Heritage, Mitcham, SA, 2013

Gardiner, Paul SJ, *Mary MacKillop, An Extraordinary Australian*, E.J. Dwyer, Sydney, 1993

Hartshorne, Heather, *Faith of our Fathers in Semaphore, 1907-2007*, Seaview Press, West Lakes, SA, 2007

Hilliard, David, *Catholics in Kingswood: the Catholic Church in the Mitcham District, 1869-1994*, Kingswood Catholic Parish Pastoral Council, Kingswood, SA, 1994

Laffin, Josephine, *Matthew Beovich, A Biography*, Wakefield Press, Adelaide, SA, 2008

Luttrel, John, 'Bishop Gilroy & the Diocese of Port Augusta', *Australasian Catholic Record*, vol. 80, no. 2, April 2003: pp. 189-200

Johnson, Michael, editor, *Our Lady of the River Catholic Church, Berri*, Catholic Parish, Berri, SA, 2013

Kovesi, Catherine, *Pitch Your Tents on Distant Shores*, Playwright Publishing, Caringbah, NSW, 2006

McCreanor, Sheila, ed., *Mary MacKillop and Flora - Correspondence between Mary MacKillop and her mother, Flora McDonald MacKillop*, Sisters of St Joseph, North Sydney, 2004

------ *Mary MacKillop and a Nest of Crosses, Edited Correspondence with Fr Julian Tenison Woods 1869–1872*, Sisters of St Joseph, North Sydney, 2011

------ *Mary MacKillop and her Early Companions, A Collection of Letters from 1866–1870*, Sisters of St Joseph, North Sydney, 2013

------ *Mary MacKillop in Challenging Times 1883–1899: A Collection of Letters*, Sisters of St Joseph, North Sydney, 2006

------ *Mary MacKillop on Mission to her last Breath, Edited Correspondence about the Foundation of the Sisters of St Joseph in Aotearoa New Zealand 1881–1909*, Sisters of St Joseph, North Sydney, 2009

McKenna, Margaret, *With Grateful Hearts! Mary MacKillop and the Sisters of St Joseph in Queensland, 1870–1970*, Sisters of St Joseph, North Sydney, 2009

MacKillop, Mary, *Julian Tenison Woods: A Life*, Introduced and annotated by Margaret Press, Harper Collins, Melbourne, 1997

Mayes, Reg G, *Pictorial History of Port Augusta*, Adelaide, SA, 1974

Modystack, William, *Mary MacKillop: A Woman before her Time*, Rigby, Adelaide, 1982

------ *Fifty Years: From Keswick to Plympton, 1938–1988*, Plympton Catholic Parish, Plympton, SA, 1988

Molony, JN, 'Mayne, Charles (1906–1990)', in *ADB*, National Centre of Biography, Australian National University, Vol 18, 2012. http://adb.anu.edu.au/biography/mayne-charles-14953/text26142

Murphy, Sister Mary Attracta, 'Annals of Holy Cross Province, 1868–1960', unpublished history of the Dominican Sisters in South Australia, Cabra Convent, Clarence Park, SA, 1948, revised 1960

Northey, Helen, *Living the Truth: The Dominican Sisters in South Australia, 1868–1968*, Holy Cross Congregation of Dominican Sisters (South Australia), 1999

O'Collins, Gerald, 'Glynn, Patrick McMahon (Paddy), 1855–1931', *ADB*, National Centre of Biography, Australian National

University, Vol. 9, 1983. http://adb.anu.edu.au/biography/glynn-patrick-mcmahon-paddy- 6405/text10949

O'Loughlin, Sister Chanel, *Life and Letters of Mother Mary of the Cross (McKillop)*, Sisters of St Joseph, Sydney, 1916

O'Neill, George, *Life of Mother Mary of the Cross (McKillop)*, Pellegrini & Co, Sydney, 1931

------ *Life of the Rev JET Woods, 1832-1889*, Pellegrini & Co, Sydney, 1928

Peterborough Catholic Centenary Committee, *The Catholic Story of Peterborough*, Peterborough Catholic Parish, Peterborough, SA, 1976

Pike, Douglas, 'A Society without Grandparents', in EL French, ed, *Melbourne Studies in Education*, 1957-1958, Melbourne University Press, Melbourne, 1958

Press, Margaret, *Julian Tenison Woods: Father Founder*, St Paul Publications, Sydney, 2004

Raimondo, Hilary, 'The Opening of the New Memorial School', unpublished Ms, St Joseph's Memorial School, Norwood, 1992, ASSJ, Kensington, SA

Richards, Eric, 'Solomon, Emanuel (1800-1873)', *ADB*, National Centre of Biography, Australian National University, Vol 6, 1976. http://adb.anu.edu.au/biography/solomon-emanuel-4623/text7613

Robertson, JR, '1930-1939', in Frank Crowley, ed, *A New History of Australia*, Heinemann, Melbourne, 1974

Schumann, Ruth, 'Spence, Robert William (1860-1934)', *ADB*, National Centre of Biography, Australian National University, Vol 12, 1990. http://adb.anu.edu.au/biography/spence-robert-william-8602/text15023

Sheahan, Patricia, *A History of the Gawler Catholic Parish to 1901*, Catholic Parish of Gawler, Gawler, SA, 1998

Sisters of St Joseph, eds, *Memories of Mary by Those Who Knew Her: Sisters of St Joseph, 1925-1926*, John Garratt Publishing, Mulgrave, Victoria, 2010

Swann, Peter, *Kapunda and the Mary MacKillop Connection*, Making a dif: (sic) Peter Swann, Kapunda, 2010

Taggert, Teresa, 'Remembering St Joseph's Family Care Centre, Mitchell Park, SA, 1984–2010,' unpublished Ms., 2012, ASSJ, Kensington, SA

Thomas, Maryellen, *Home: The Story of St Catherine's, Berri*, St Catherine's Home, Berri, SA, 1994

Thorpe, Osmund, 'Geoghegan, Patrick Bonaventure (1805–1864)', *ADB*, National Centre of Biography, Australian National University, Vol 4, 1972. http://adb.anu.edu.au/biography/geoghegan-patrick-bonavent ure- 3602/text5589

Tobin, Mother Francis, *Mother Gonzaga Barry: Her Life and Letters*, vol 4, n.d., Loreto College Archives, Marryatville, SA

Travers, Peter, 'O'Loghlin, James Vincent (1852–1925)', *ADB*, National Centre of Biography, Australian National University, Vol 11, 1988. http://adb.anu.edu.au/biography/ologhlin-james-vincent-7905/text13747

Van Dissel, Dirk, 'Barr Smith, Robert (1824–1915)', *ADB*, National Centre of Biography, Australian National University, Vol. 6, 1976. http://adb.anu.edu.au/biography/barr-smith-robert-63/text7591

Vermeeren, Jodie, *St Andrew's Catholic Church, Balaklava, 1889–1989*, Balaklava Catholic Parish, Balaklava, SA, 1989

Walsh, Margaret, *Opening the Door to a Saint*, Good Samaritan Sisters, Sydney, 2010

Waters, Ian B., 'Knox, James Robert (1914–1983)', *ADB*, National Centre of Biography, Australian National University, Vol. 17, 2007.http://adb.anu.edu.au/biography/knox-james-robertt-12752/text22999.

Index

A

Aboriginal Ministry: 227, 315, 360, 361, 388, 389, 444.
Ain Karim: 361, 388, 445.
Alberton: 86, 196, 259, 279, 282, 285, 286, 317, 380, 419.
Aldgate: 292, 293, 303, 324, 343, 355, 356, 364, 386, 387, 389.
Altar Breads: 314, 315, 322, 358, 423, 424, 427, 445.
Amsinck, Sr Francis Xavier: 33, 50, 56, 62, 67, 70, 96, 125, 199, 357, 391.

B

Balaklava: 84, 211, 212, 213, 239, 282, 308, 340, 385, 443, 448.
Barmera: 295, 296, 343, 387.
Barossa Valley: 284, 292, 294, 302, 340, 387.
Barr Smith, Joanna & Robert: 71, 92, 107, 113, 149, 159, 172, 175, 176, 221, 370, 376, 448.
Bathurst: 31, 44, 54, 55, 57, 61, 63, 64, 65, 72, 73, 76, 89, 92, 95, 96, 100, 101, 104, 108, 109, 110, 224, 382, 417.
Beatification: 8, 369.
Beovich, Archbp. Matthew: 7, 211, 243, 260, 262, 264, 265, 266, 277, 278, 279, 280, 281, 289, 291, 307, 308, 309, 312, 344, 445.
Berri: 307, 343, 349, 350, 376, 386, 445, 448.
Bethany: 95, 245, 257, 269.
Beulah Road (School): 65, 162, 184, 194, 203, 205, 219, 226, 238, 266, 278, 287, 341.
Blinman: 67, 68, 69, 79, 80, 382.
Bourke, Sr Lorna: 313, 338, 359, 382, 427.
Bowden: 22, 23, 81, 131, 181, 379, 403.
Brisbane: 30, 31, 35, 48, 51, 54, 65, 72, 73, 89, 160, 175, 192.
Brompton: 182, 185, 202, 220, 379, 385, 421, 423.

Brosnahan, Sr Fergus: 206, 218, 326, 439.

Burra: 30, 63, 78, 80, 130, 141, 183, 194, 199, 208, 219, 240, 241, 340, 381, 401, 422, 425.

Byrne, Fr Frederick VG: 79, 85, 93, 94, 108, 131, 147, 156, 185, 186, 444.

Byrne, John, 251.

Byrne, Sr Mechtilde, 338.

Byrne, Sr Rose, 291, 316

Byrne, Sr Scholastica, 120, 148, 414, 427.

C

Caltowie: 77, 78, 130, 150, 166, 160, 172, 186, 193, 197, 199, 208, 298, 300, 383, 422.

Campbell, Sr Patricia: 127, 133, 149, 168, 356, 412.

Canonisation: 8, 224, 342, 366, 367, 369, 370, 371.

Carroll, Sr Angela: 33, 34, 37.

Casey, Sr Benizi: 162, 204, 225, 426.

Centenary (Sisters): 313, 316, 317, 332, 334.

Centenary (State): 254, 255, 256.

Central Government: 103, 121, 122, 146, 149, 407.

Champion, Sr Veronica: 62, 104, 136, 137, 145, 146, 154.

Christian Education Association (CEA): 312, 331.

Clare: 29, 62, 77, 78, 141, 144, 199, 208, 210, 215, 264, 301, 302, 340, 343, 380, 401, 421, 425, 426.

Clarke, Sr Andrina: 148, 226, 272.

Conroy, Sr Constance: 341, 364, 365, 375, 444.

Conroy, Sr Pauline, 274, 326.

Cowandilla: 178, 240, 251, 252, 267, 277, 279, 280, 303, 319, 320, 343, 348, 349, 365, 380, 386.

Cremen, Sr Bridget: 48, 63, 67, 104.

Croydon: 219, 220, 285, 286, 287, 290, 306, 318, 319, 340, 343, 385.

Cunningham, Sr Rose: 16, 33, 56, 177, 188, 350, 391.

Curriculum, School: 18, 24, 144, 184, 294, 310, 311, 337.

D

Debt: 46, 71, 93, 94, 100, 101, 106, 107, 111, 134, 135, 136, 140, 145, 153, 154, 161, 165, 173, 186, 197, 198, 228, 234, 423, 424, 425, 426, 427.

Denham, Sr Michael Xavier: 268, 287, 437.

Depression: 180, 186, 234, 239ff 276, 330, 332.

Dolan, Sr Vincent Ferrer: 284, 287, 302, 338, 437.

Dowd, Sr Wilhelmine: 189, 191, 215, 219, 256, 265, 279, 317, 326, 423.

Dulwich: 211, 278, 287, 320, 324, 343, 385, 444.

E

Earle, Mother Denis: 336, 338, 349, 373, 435.

Education: vii, xi, xii, 2, 3, 4, 6, 7, 17, 18, 20, 21, 23, 25, 26, 36, 40, 42, 45, 52, 78, 80, 95, 100, 101, 138, 144, 159, 170, 183, 185, 193ff, 208, 211, 213, 214, 218, 230, 240, 247, 253, 254m 256, 260, 263, 279, 282, 289, 295, 298, 304, 306, 210, 311, 312, 316, 330, 331, 33, 334, 338, 339, 340, 341, 344, 345, 346, 348, 354, 289, 405, 406, 407, 442, 445, 447.

Edwards, Bert240, 280, 282, 307, 444.

Eickhoff, Sr Teresa: 428.

Elkis, Mother Cyril: 247, 266, 435.

Episcopal Commission, 1872: 54, 61,413.

Etheridge, Sr Elizabeth: 26, 27, 59, 82, 142, 168, 187, 421, 429.

Excommunication: vii, 30, 45, 48, 49, 54, 114, 128, 220, 370, 405, 408, 409.

F

Finnegan, Sr Vianney: 303, 304, 309, 350, 437.

Flanagan, Sr Editha: 81, 210, 227, 421, 423, 424.

Franklin Street: 23, 28, 35, 38, 39, 46, 64, 83, 92, 142, 168, 368, 379, 408.

G

Gawler: 25, 32, 37, 49, 61, 63, 89, 141, 157, 159, 169, 172, 294, 342, 379, 401, 421, 425, 447.

General Chapter: 69, 106, 128, 130,132, 136, 139, 144, 146, 154, 155, 157, 164, 166, 167, 168, 169, 175, 193, 197, 222, 223, 224, 234, 247, 251, 258, 268, 269, 270, 287, 288, 296, 320, 313, 321, 329, 335, 336, 338, 347, 359, 366, 411, 442.

Geoghegan, Bp Patrick: 1, 2, 11, 15, 17, 442.

Georgetown: 67, 77, 78, 81, 98, 126, 127, 130, 133, 151, 181, 182, 199, 208, 282, 291, 293, 298, 317, 340, 382, 413, 420.

Gilroy, Bp Norman: 215, 248, 257, 457.

Gladstone: 129, 130, 160, 161, 199, 208, 213, 214, 286, 298, 343, 384, 422, 425.

Gleeson, Archbp James: 279, 308, 309, 312, 317, 341, 355, 364, 373.

Gleeson, Sr Cecily, 301.

Gleeson, Srs Therese & Oliver: 213, 273, 326.

Guild of St Anthony: 180, 227, 233.

Guild of St John the Baptist, 249, 250.

H

Hale: Sr Antonia: 274, 352.
Hamley Bridge: 61, 63, 141, 197, 199, 206, 216, 282, 293, 294, 340, 342, 382, 421, 425.
Harford, Sr Marie Paul: 296, 313, 344, 352, 437.
Harradine, Sr Mary: 353.
Hayman, Sr Gertrude: 48, 56, 63, 108, 114, 117, 122, 125, 318.
Hectorville: 30, 49, 63, 146, 157, 208, 210, 266, 278, 287, 290, 293, 295, 318, 340, 343, 381, 401, 421, 427.
Henschke, Sr Annette: 125, 126, 142, 153, 160, 116, 165, 166, 168, 175, 177, 187, 189, 223, 242, 356, 358, 421, 429.
Hindmarsh: 174, 181, 210, 220, 275, 283, 309, 317, 340, 343, 345, 361, 365, 379, 385.
Honner, Sr Laurentia: 90, 98, 111.
Horan, Fr Charles OFM: 39, 42, 44, 51, 52, 54, 100, 401, 402, 404, 406, 442.
Howley, Sr Agatha, 284, 292,
Howley, Sr Andrea: 52, 56, 67, 70, 86, 108, 109, 127, 141, 156, 175, 191, 193, 223, 356, 423, 424,
Howley, Sr Calasanctius: 29, 56, 67, 70, 78, 110, 137, 145, 154, 173, 175, 178, 188, 191, 193, 221, 222, 223, 356, 422, 437.

Hughes, Sr Ambrose: 62, 68, 75, 85.
Hughes, Sr Frances Clare: 211, 243.
Hughes, Sr Kevin: 216, 225, 226, 237, 261.

I

Irish Postulants: 67, 76, 127, 229, 411ff.

J

Jamestown: 78, 103, 127, 130, 141, 160, 182, 189, 201, 203, 208, 244, 298, 301, 304, 317, 318, 343, 352, 383, 422.
Jesuits: 5, 49, 67, 77, 79, 80, 84, 91, 264, 279, 312, 365.
Jubilee, Congregational: 221, 224.
Jubilees, Sisters: 20, 224, 236, 356, 357.
Juniorate: 225, 248, 251, 252, 253, 267, 268, 269, 276, 279, 280, 281, 303, 349, 355, 386, 387.

K

Kadina: 29, 44, 62, 86, 92, 108, 184, 199, 206, 239, 244, 318, 319, 342, 343, 370, 380, 401, 421, 427.

Kapunda: 39, 40, 41, 47, 63, 67, 77, 85, 92, 107, 131, 155, 156, 159, 163, 164, 379, 380.

Kensington: viii, xi, 27, 30, 43, 47, 58, 64, 65, 70, 72, 76, 81, 92, 93, 97, 106, 107, 113, 114, 115, 117, 136, 137, 138, 140, 141, 142, 148, 154, 155, 157, 158, 159, 162, 169, 170, 172, 173, 175, 177, 178, 181, 184, 186, 189, 196, 198, 205, 206, 209, 210, 211, 219, 220, 223, 224, 226, 227, 229, 230, 244, 245, 246, 247, 249, 254, 257, 261, 269, 273, 278, 279, 282, 284, 287, 292, 303, 305, 309, 313, 314, 318, 320, 333, 341, 343, 344, 350, 351, 352, 356, 357, 358, 359, 361, 363, 367, 369, 370, 382, 386, 397, 421, 429.

Keswick: 209, 210, 230, 249, 253, 266, 287, 242, 385.

Killian, Bp/Archbp Andrew: 214, 215, 245, 246, 248, 249, 253, 256, 260.

Kingswood: 194, 196, 197, 202, 225, 226, 251, 264, 295, 343, 357, 381, 384.

L

Lane, Sr Victor: 104, 148, 154, 175, 193, 201, 208, 223, 236, 437.

Ledwith, Sr Bernardine: 59, 110, 165, 189, 358.

Lee, Father Thomas: 106, 182, 183.

Lee, Sr Sebastian: 148, 274.

Libel Case: 52, 53.

Luff, Sr Concepta: 338, 373, 374, 437.

M

Macclesfield: 25, 29, 89, 106, 129, 182, 207, 219, 259, 260, 282, 318, 341, 343, 380, 427.

MacKillop, Mary: Ch, 1-4 passim.

Mahony, Sr Bonaventure: 48, 73, 75, 105, 167, 189, 190, 429, 437.

Mahony, Sr Francis de sales: 164, 425.

Mahony, Sr La Merci: 109, 164, 193.

Mary MacKillop College: 310, 341, 344, 371.

McDonald, Sr de Lellis: 258, 266, 437.

McDonald, Sr Teresa: 29, 31, 32, 38, 55, 57, 63, 437.

McMullen, Sr Anne, 41, 63.

McMullen, Sr Josephine: 22, 33, 38, 62, 72, 73, 74, 77, 81, 83, 84, 85, 110, 145, 146.

McNamara, Sr Hilda: 187, 232, 421, 428.

Meskill, Sr Casimir: 29, 48, 63, 168, 178, 193, 226, 247.

Ministry of Prayer (Tabor): 376, 377.
Mitcham: 30, 32, 56, 92, 107, 113, 114, 116, 136, 157, 158, 159, 170, 184, 198, 199, 202, 203, 221, 227, 370, 379, 381, 403, 421, 427.
Mitchell Park: 362, 388.
Moran, Archbp/Cardinal Patrick: 78, 107, 117, 118, 119, 121, 122, 123, 124, 131, 132, 133, 135, 165, 166, 168, 173, 193, 411, 444.
Morrissey, Sr Thecla, 211, 266, 268, 437.
Mother House, SA: 6, 29, 32, 35, 56, 64, 73, 76, 93, 96, 136, 137, 138, 198.
Mother House, Sydney: 118, 132, 134, 145, 172, 221, 222, 261, 356.
Motor Mission: vii, 7, 284, 290, 291, 292, 296, 302, 307, 317, 320, 321, 323, 340, 341, 342, 344, 358, 379, 380, 381, 382, 384, 387.
Mount Barker: 29, 42, 106, 291, 341, 381, 403.
Murray Bridge: 217, 218, 226, 244, 253, 264, 309, 317, 319, 340, 342, 343, 361, 385.
Music Teaching: viii, 80, 137, 138, 139, 144, 164, 169, 170, 172, 184, 197, 201, 204, 212, 213, 216, 218, 226, 228, 230, 257, 258, 259, 264, 269, 299, 321, 334, 338, 371, 383.

N

Nangwarry: 296, 297, 321, 343, 352, 387.
North Adelaide: 29, 30, 81, 108, 131, 158, 162, 164, 170, 177, 205, 227, 228, 249, 284, 341, 380, 381, 403, 424.
Norton, Bishop John: 157, 160, 182, 199, 204, 205, 207, 213, 214.
Norwood: 44, 49, 60, 62, 65, 71, 108, 142, 145, 165, 177, 181, 203, 205, 206, 211, 219, 227, 230, 238, 264, 265, 266, 278, 287, 316, 317, 341, 353, 354, 356, 369, 379, 382, 386, 401, 421, 427, 429.
Novitiate: 19, 22, 47, 51, 76, 92, 104, 107, 109, 111, 125, 140, 155, 158, 167, 170, 175, 196, 198, 213, 226, 229, 230, 260, 261, 262, 268, 269, 310, 311, 367, 412.

O

O'Brien, Sr Ignatius: 29, 47, 160, 168, 193, 210, 223, 224, 236, 247, 332.
O'Brien, Mother Laurence, 34, 37, 41, 42, 54, 55, 73, 360, 428, 435.
O'Dea, Sr Patricia: 326, 375.

O'Meara, Sr Austin: 130, 131.
O'Reily Bp. /Archbp. John: 129, 130, 131, 134, 135, 145, 146, 147, 153, 154, 155, 156, 157, 165, 172, 173, 176, 178, 179, 183, 190, 197, 198, 205, 221, 222, 246.
Old Scholars: 226, 227, 244, 245, 254, 255, 266.
Orphanage, St Joseph's, Largs Bay: 154, 169, 174, 179, 199, 227, 228, 229, 240, 254, 262, 270, 282, 302, 320, 338, 350, 360, 384.
Orphanage, St Vincent de Paul: 25, 26, 45, 90, 135, 146, 147, 178, 263.
Orroroo: 80, 87, 88, 92, 103, 107, 130, 383, 420.

P

Pallhuber, Fr JE SJ: 77, 78, 79, 401.
Parish Pastoral Associates: 340, 353.
Pekina: 79, 80, 130, 141, 144, 153, 160,186, 199, 219, 244, 246, 267, 269, 292, 383, 422, 426.
Penola: 1, 2, 3, 4, 6, 11, 15, 16, 18, 19, 20, 25, 29, 36, 42, 81, 83, 89, 104, 105, 118, 120, 126, 140, 221, 224, 225, 256, 269, 296, 316, 317, 319, 340, 350, 353, 355, 368, 369, 370, 379, 391, 403, 404, 417, 419.

Peterborough: 155, 160, 194, 196, 204, 214, 215, 216, 246, 263, 286, 290, 292, 293, 298, 299, 300, 301, 316, 326, 343, 370, 384.
Petersburg: 155, 157, 160, 162, 163, 199, 201, 426.
Phillips, Sr Monica: 216, 29, 47, 54, 56, 67, 68, 76, 85, 88, 108, 115, 118, 120, 121, 124, 125, 126, 132, 135, 137, 143, 148, 149, 154, 155, 163, 167, 189, 220, 318, 359, 391, 421, 437.
Pilgrimage: 367, 368.
Pinnaroo: 216, 308, 316, 317, 318, 343, 385.
Pirie Street, Adelaide: 81, 83, 157, 162, 181, 194, 230, 249, 269, 421, 428, 429.
Plympton: 209, 243, 249, 266, 269, 287, 319, 343, 367, 386.
Port Adelaide: 25, 29, 43, 52, 81, 143, 181, 184, 194, 197,202, 220, 233, 259, 279, 285, 380, 403, 404, 424.
Port Augusta Sisters: 43, 44, 62, 67, 68, 78, 84, 88, 98, 109, 111, 137, 138, 141, 154, 162, 181, 199, 204, 219, 244, 293, 299, 321, 343, 361
Port Augusta, Diocese of: 90, 129, 130, 133, 134, 146, 147, 153, 157, 160, 186, 199, 207, 208, 213, 246, 248, 257, 258, 281, 422.
Port Lincoln: 67, 68, 126, 218, 232, 263, 290, 321, 420, 439.

Port Pirie: 76, 77, 78, 104, 160, 161, 172, 201, 233, 286, 298, 300, 352, 368, 389, 420, 422.
Prison Ministry (Gaol): 4, 5, 6, 22, 26, 92, 250, 353, 371, 406, 407.
Providence of God, 228, 233, 234, 252, 348, 362.
Providence, the: 5, 26, 27, 30, 33, 45, 82, 83, 90, 141, 142, 146, 157, 161, 168, 169, 175, 178, 187, 232, 233, 240, 279, 280, 303, 319, 320, 349, 357, 358, 370, 380, 386, 421, 429.
Punyer, Sr Immaculata: 90, 123.

Q

Quinlan, Sr Hyacinth: 56, 57, 64, 236.
Quinlan, Sr Michael, 62, 121, 149, 437.
Quinn, Bp James: 30, 100, 193
Quinn, Bp Matthew: 44, 48, 54, 55, 61, 93, 95, 117.
Quorn: 84, 129, 159, 186, 199, 203, 204, 209, 213, 214, 215, 244, 282, 293, 298, 302, 384, 422, 426.

R

Radium Hill: 299, 387.
Reformatory, State: 91, 156, 183, 241, 263
Reformatory, St Johns: 155, 163, 164, 242, 243, 258, 381, 385, 425.
Refuge: 5, 22, 26, 29, 30, 32, 33, 45, 59, 74, 90, 110,111, 125, 141, 142, 146, 147, 154, 156, 165, 172, 175, 222, 223, 229, 242, 243, 244, 262, 265, 307, 320, 358, 379, 381, 421, 429.
Refugees: viii, 177, 296, 354, 389.
Renmark: 19, 207, 269, 274, 298, 318, 319, 321, 343, 384.
Reynolds, Bp/Archbp CA, 50, 51, 52, 54, 55, 61, 64, 65, 66, 68, 71, 72, 74, 79, 80, 81, 93, 94, 95, 98, 100, 101, 102, 203, 104, 105, 107, 108, 110, 111, 112, 115, 117, 118, 119, 120, 121, 122, 123, 125, 127, 128, 131, 133, 134, 135, 137, 140, 141, 142, 146, 147, 154, 155, 156, 401, 413, 419, 420.
Richmond: 250, 251, 269, 343, 346, 385.
Riddell, Sr Claude: 187, 223, 231, 236, 247, 423, 437.
Robe: 62, 83, 84, 103, 104, 380.
Royal Commission, 1883: 5, 91, 155, 361.
Rules of the Institute: 5, 24, 32, 34, 38, 42, 66, 82, 270, 330, 339, 372.
Russell, Archdeacon Patrick: 20, 35, 41, 94, 105, 106, 108, 123, 142, 158, 159.
Russell, Fr William: 279, 283, 284.
Russell Street, 81, 82, 83, 157, 162, 170, 181, 184, 230, 240,

241, 249, 259, 266, 287, 306, 380, 383, 421.
Ryan, Mother Adrian: 303, 309, 313, 335, 435.
Ryan, Mother Leone: 253, 268, 274, 287, 435.

S

Scanlon, Sr Hyacinth: 189, 427.
Schmidt, Sr Leonard: 58, 99, 109, 112, 113.
School Examinations, Public: 194 196, 218.
Seminary: 100, 266, 268, 270, 303, 311, 343, 354, 357, 358, 386.
Settled Areas: 18, 76, 80, 159.
Sevenhill: 5, 43, 44, 49, 67, 77, 78, 84, 103, 199, 208, 217, 223, 301, 302, 383, 401, 421, 425.
Sheil, Bp, Laurence: 3, 16, 17, 30, 42, 44, 45, 46, 49, 51, 54, 60, 66, 131, 279, 300, 405, 406, 407, 408, 409.
Siena College: 343, 344, 345.
Smyth, Fr John: 18, 31, 39, 40.
Smyth, Sr Raymond: 29, 47, 56, 62, 110, 111, 149, 159,
Solomon, Emanuel: 10, 47.
Spalding: 207, 208, 226, 244, 298, 341, 385.
Spence, Archbp R OP: 205, 206, 208, 211, 218, 230, 233, 241, 242, 243, 245, 246, 248, 250.
St Francis Xavier's Cathedral Hall School: 19, 61, 146.
St Ignatius Church: 50, 60, 65, 142, 264, 266, 356, 409.

St Johns, School: 29, 30, 85, 255, 156, 380.
St Johns: Reformatory: 156, 163, 164, 183, 241, 242, 243, 380.
St Peters (Ellangowan): 205, 230, 287, 343.
Strathalbyn: 89, 126, 140, 150, 290, 341, 384, 419.
Summer / Vacation schools: 7, 215, 263, 263, 290, 294, 295, 299, 302, 317, 340.

T

Tailem Bend: 253, 264, 269, 290, 340, 342, 343, 386.
Tappeiner Court: 230, 313, 350, 351, 352, 364.
Tappeiner, Fr Joseph SJ: 38, 51, 49, 50, 55, 64, 65, 66, , 68, 71, 77, 110, 313, 330, 401.
Terowie: 195, 200, 201, 202, 203, 204, 208, 209, 213, 244, 298, 301, 384.
Tertianship: 355.
Thebarton, 29, 157, 174, 210, 217, 249, 250, 265, 305, 306, 343, 345, 346, 365, 380, 403, 421, 423, 424.
Tranmere: 219, 266, 278, 286, 304, 317, 343, 385.

V

Vatican II: 7, 8, 271, 304, 309, 312, 321, 329, 330, 331, 333, 335, 364, 397.

Vaughan, Archbp. Roger: 74, 96, 101, 106, 107, 117, 167, 225.

Visionaries: 33, 34, 35, 36, 38, 55.

W

Waikerie: 269, 290, 293, 294, 295, 387.

Wallaroo: 29, 44, 62, 196, 199, 206, 216, 244, 342, 343, 370, 380, , 401, 421, 427.

Walsh, Mother Bernard: 16, 33, 56, 63, 67, 70, 78, 95, 104, 109, 110, 113, 127, 131, 134, 135, 136, 145, 53, 155, 165, 187, 356, 391, 435.

Warooka: 86, 87, 103, 251, 383, 419.

Willochra: 79, 88, 103, 126, 130, 384, 420

Willunga: 25, 29, 62, 77, 89, 103, 379, 401.

Withdrawals: 95, 147, 159, 160, 420.

Woods, James: 46, 52, 114.

Woods, Julian: Ch, 1, passim, 61, 64, 66, 70, 73, 74, 75, 82, 86, 100, 106, 143, 145, 146, 159, 186, 225, 256, 257, 270, 271, 303, 310, 311, 316, 330, 336, 348, 359, 366, 367, 368, 370, 406.

Woods, Sr Mechtilde: 29, 46, 52, 90, 91, 107, 114, 115, 143, 224, 363.

Woomera: 297, 298, 343, 387.

Wright, Sr Clare: 16, 22, 23, 29, 31, 76, 94, 105, 391.

Wright, Sr Gertrude: 16, 48, 75, 392.

Y

Yankalilla: 22, 23, 24, 62, 77, 370, 379, 401.

Yorketown: 290, 301, 343, 387.

This is an engaging account of the mission, growth, and expansion of the Josephites.

It is the work of an insider whose knowledge and insights are exceptional: the author is a senior member of the Josephites and as a seasoned archivist and historian has had long familiarity with her subject.

It is based on solid research, and makes dextrous use of rare sources in the Josephite archives: personal letters, diaries, the minutes of Congregational chapters and conferences. Often we sense that we hear the voices of the past!

*A valuable contribution to Australian religious and social history, it deserves a wide
readership.*

Dr Robert Fitzsimons
Lecturer in
Church History, St Barnabas'
Theological College, Adelaide

This book throws new light on large areas of the history of the Catholic Church in South Australia and illustrates the central role played by Religious Sisters in the shaping of Australian Catholicism. The Sisters of St Joseph are well known because of their founders and yet largely unknown because their story has never been told. For this task, Sister Marie Foale combines a deep understanding of the ethos and inner spirit of the Josephites with the skills of a trained historian. Never See a Need is a judicious and sensitive account of the works undertaken by the Sisters of St Joseph in South Australia and of the faith and resilience of the Josephites themselves.

Dr David Hilliard OAM
Flinders University

Lightning Source UK Ltd.
Milton Keynes UK
UKOW01f1950220917
309708UK00005B/349/P